PROPHECY &
APOCALYPTICISM
The Postexilic
Social Setting

Stephen L. Cook

FORTRESS PRESS   MINNEAPOLIS

For Catherine Elizabeth
my darling, my beautiful one (Cant. 2:10)

PROPHECY AND APOCALYPTICISM
The Postexilic Social Setting

Cover design: Ann Artz

Library of Congress Cataloging-in-Publication Data

Cook, Stephen L.
    Prophecy and apocalypticism : the postexilic social setting /
Stephen L. Cook.
        p.   cm.
    Includes bibliographical references and indexes.
    ISBN 0-8006-2839-X (alk. paper)
    1. Apocalyptic literature.   2. Prophecy.   3. Millennialism.   4. Bible.   O.T.
Ezekiel XXXVIII–XXXIX — Criticism, interpretation, etc.   5. Bible.   O.T.
Zechariah I–VIII — Criticism, interpretation, etc.   6. Bible.   O.T. Joel —
Criticism, interpretation, etc.   7. Jews — History — 586 B.C.–70 A.D.   I. Title.
BS646.C66   1995
221′.046 — dc20   95-23148
                                                                                      CIP

Manufactured in the U.S.A.   AF 1–2839
99   98   97   96   95   1   2   3   4   5   6   7   8   9   10

Contents

Preface

As the twentieth century draws to a close and a new millennium begins, renewed popular and scholarly interest in the Bible and apocalypticism is inevitable. Unfortunately, clear weaknesses in the current scholarly consensus about the nature and origins of biblical apocalypticism continue to hinder its critical interpretation. Indeed, an especially problematic overarching interpretation of apocalypticism characterizes our current situation. This is the view that apocalyptic eschatology emerged among alienated, peripheral, or disenfranchised groups. This common understanding is associated with a sociological theory that apocalyptic groups stem from deprivation. Despite its current popularity, deprivation theory is contradicted by sociological and anthropological data and cannot account for significant biblical texts.

In this book I attempt to point out the failings of deprivation theory and to provide alternative sociological understandings of the development of Israelite apocalypticism. The methodological and sociological groundwork for this effort is laid in chapter 2. This chapter defines apocalypticism and critiques deprivation theory. Chapter 3 formulates an alternative sociological framework that can account for a wider range of millennial groups than a deprivation model, including power-holding groups. By examining apocalyptic groups that hold power, the study develops understandings needed to interpret biblical apocalyptic texts that appear to come from the center of postexilic Israelite society.

Chapters 4–6 apply this survey of millennial groups in power to a reinvestigation of the proto-apocalyptic literary units in Ezekiel, Zechariah, and Joel. The study investigates the inadequately addressed questions of the origins, sociology, and history of the groups behind these texts. In each case, the proto-apocalyptic genre of the text and its central-priestly idiom and provenance are established. Syntheses of these results indicate that the proto-apocalyptic and hieratic characteristics of all three texts are two dimensions of a single social setting. In other words, in direct contradiction to deprivation theory, Ezekiel 38–39, Zechariah 1–8, and Joel represent biblical proto-apocalyptic literature that originated among priestly groups holding power.

The final chapter summarizes the findings about the central social settings of the proto-apocalyptic sections of Ezekiel 38–39, Zechariah 1–8, and Joel, and explains the broader implications of the investigation.

During my work on the problem of the origins of Israelite apocalypticism, I have received help and support from several individuals whom I would like to acknowledge. First, I am most grateful to my former teacher Robert R. Wilson, Yale University, for his direction and unstinting support. The project has also benefited from the insightful comments and suggestions of Ellen F. Davis and Saul M. Olyan. My thanks are extended as well to John Schneider for his expert advice on writing and style.

On a more personal level, I acknowledge the steadfast love and longstanding support of my mother and father, Dr. and Mrs. William Henry Cook. I could not have asked for better parents. I was inspired, too, by the commitment to learning and the resolve of Dr. Arthur Ray Jacobs, my wife's father, who died unexpectedly while I was still working on this project. Above all, I am indebted to my wife, Catherine Elizabeth Cook, for her strength, compassion, and humor during our graduate years together at Yale. Not only has Catherine assisted me with preparing this monograph, she has helped me keep apocalyptic chaos out of my life and confined to this project. Cathy, "There's a new world somewhere, They call the Promised Land; And I'll be there someday, If you will hold my hand."

Abbreviations

1Q, 2Q, 3Q, etc.	Numbered caves of Qumran, yielding written material
1QH	*Hôdāyôt* (*Thanksgiving Hymns*) from Qumran Cave 1
1QM	*Milḥāmāh* (*War Scroll*)
1QS	*Serek hayyaḥad* (*Rule of the Community* [*Manual of Discipline*])
1QSa	Appendix A (*Rule of the Congregation*) to 1QS
1QSb	Appendix B (*Blessings*) to 1QS
4QMMT	*Miqṣat Maʿaseh Torah* from Qumran Cave 4

AB	Anchor Bible
ANEP	*The Ancient Near East in Pictures.* Ed. James B. Pritchard. 2d ed. Princeton, N.J.: Princeton University Press, 1969.
ANET	*Ancient Near Eastern Texts Relating to the Old Testament.* Ed. James B. Pritchard. 3d ed. Princeton, N.J.: Princeton University Press, 1969.
ATD	Das Alte Testament Deutsch

BA	*Biblical Archaeologist*
BASOR	*Bulletin of the American Schools of Oriental Research*
BHS	*Biblia Hebraica Stuttgartensia.* Ed. K. Elliger and W. Rudoph. Stuttgart: Deutsche Bibelgesellschaft, 1977.
Bib	*Biblica*

BJRL	*Bulletin of the John Rylands University Library of Manchester*
BKAT	Biblischer Kommentar: Altes Testament
BR	*Biblical Research*
BWANT	Beiträge zur Wissenschaft vom Alten und Neuen Testament
BZAW	Beihefte zur ZAW
CAT	Commentaire de l'Ancien Testament
CB	Cambridge Bible for Schools and Colleges
CBC	Cambridge Bible Commentary
CBQ	*Catholic Biblical Quarterly*
CD	Cairo (Genizah text of the) *Damascus* (*Document*)
CTA	*Corpus des tablettes en cunéiformes alphabétiques découvertes à Ras Shamra-Ugarit de 1929 à 1939.* Ed. A. Herdner. Mission de Ras Shamra 10. Paris: Imprimerie Nationale, 1963.
Eng.	English Bible Text
ErIsr	Eretz Israel
FB	Forschung zur Bibel
FOTL	The Forms of the Old Testament Literature
HAR	Hebrew Annual Review
HAT	Handbuch zum Alten Testament
HR	*History of Religions*
HSM	Harvard Semitic Monographs
HSS	Harvard Semitic Studies
HUCA	*Hebrew Union College Annual*
IB	*The Interpreter's Bible.* 12 vols. Ed. G. A. Buttrick, et al. Nashville: Abingdon, 1951–1957.
ICC	International Critical Commentary
IDB	*The Interpreter's Dictionary of the Bible.* 4 vols. Ed. G. A. Buttrick. Nashville: Abingdon, 1962.
IDBSup	*Supplementary* volume to *IDB*
IEJ	*Israel Exploration Journal*
Int	*Interpretation*
JAAR	*Journal of the American Academy of Religion*

JB	Jerusalem Bible
JBL	*Journal of Biblical Literature*
JETS	*Journal of the Evangelical Theological Society*
JJS	*Journal of Jewish Studies*
JNES	*Journal of Near Eastern Studies*
JQR	*Jewish Quarterly Review*
JSOT	*Journal for the Study of the Old Testament*
JSOTSup	Journal for the Study of the Old Testament — Supplement Series
JSS	*Journal of Semitic Studies*
JTS	*Journal of Theological Studies*
KAT	Kommentar zum Alten Testament
KJV	King James Version
KTU	*Die keilalphabetischen Texte aus Ugarit einschliesslich der keilalphabetischen Texte ausserhalb Ugarits.* Ed. M. Dietrich, O. Loretz and J. Sanmartin. Kevelaer: Butzon & Bercker, 1976.
LXX	Septuagint
MT	Masoretic Text
NAB	New American Bible
NASB	New American Standard Bible
NCBC	New Century Bible Commentary
NEB	New English Bible
NICOT	New International Commentary on the Old Testament
NIV	New International Version
NJPS	The new Jewish Publication Society of America translation: *TANAKH*
NRSV	New Revised Standard Version
OBT	Overtures to Biblical Theology
Or	*Orientalia*
OTL	Old Testament Library
OTS	*Oudtestamentische Studiën*
OTWSA	*Die Ou Testamentiese Werkgemeenskap in Suid-Afrika*
RB	*Revue biblique*

RelSRev	*Religious Studies Review*
RGG	*Religion in Geschichte und Gegenwart*
RSV	Revised Standard Version
SB	Stuttgarter Bibelstudien
SBLDS	Society of Biblical Literature Dissertation Series
SBT	Studies in Biblical Theology
SEÅ	*Svensk exegetisk årsbok*
SJT	*Scottish Journal of Theology*
TDNT	*Theological Dictionary of the New Testament.* 10 vols. Ed. G. Kittel and G. Friedrich. Grand Rapids, Mich.: Eerdmans, 1964–1976.
TDOT	*Theological Dictionary of the Old Testament.* Ed. G. J. Botterweck and H. Ringgren. Grand Rapids, Mich.: Eerdmans, 1974–.
TEV	Today's English Version
TSK	*Theologische Studien und Kritiken*
TWAT	*Theologisches Wörterbuch zum Alten Testament.* Ed. G. J. Botterweck and H. Ringgren. Stuttgart: W. Kohlhammer, 1973–.
TZ	*Theologische Zeitschrift*
Vg	Vulgate
VT	*Vetus Testamentum*
VTSup	Vetus Testamentum, Supplements
WBC	Word Biblical Commentary
ZA	*Zeitschrift für Assyriologie*
ZAW	*Zeitschrift für die alttestamentliche Wissenschaft*
ZTK	*Zeitschrift für Theologie und Kirche*

1

Introduction

One of the most fascinating questions raised by the proto-apocalyptic texts of the Hebrew Bible is the nature of the groups and societies that produced them. Who were the authors of these texts, which picture the cataclysmic end of the cosmos and the ushering in of a fabulous new era, and what sorts of communities do they represent? Many readers believe that if the texts' authors really saw the world apocalyptically, they must have been fringe figures, perhaps troubled psychologically. Others find in apocalyptic literature sane warnings for our time of ozone depletion, unchecked population growth, and the spread of nuclear weapons. Still others find in the apocalyptic writers clear insight into the impossibility of genuine community on earth without divine intervention.

Led by Otto Plöger and Paul Hanson, many scholars have reached a consensus about the nature of biblical proto-apocalyptic groups. Their "conventicle approach" assigns proto-apocalyptic texts sociologically to the losers of the political disputes and power struggles that are held to have characterized the restoration community.[1] There are fundamental prob-

1. Otto Plöger's work was first published as *Theokratie und Eschatologie* (Neukirchen: Neukirchener Verlag, 1959). The second edition is available in English as *Theocracy and Eschatology,* trans. S. Rudman (Richmond, Va.: John Knox, 1968). Paul Hanson's major study of the proto-apocalyptic texts is *The Dawn of Apocalyptic* (Philadelphia: Fortress, 1979). A "conventicle approach" sees proto-apocalyptic texts as written within small religious communities that meet secretly for fear of those in authority.

lems with this view, and I propose to argue for a sociological theory that better clarifies the background of the proto-apocalyptic texts.

The wide acceptance of the conventicle approach is understandable. It offers an approach to the Israelite proto-apocalyptic texts that appears to clarify their sources and nature and to answer the form-critical question of the social setting of this literature. The conventicle approach even tallies with sociologists' current explanation of the origin of apocalyptic groups in non-Israelite societies: the causal theory of relative deprivation. Deprivation theory holds that apocalyptic groups arise among people who are marginalized, alienated, or at least feel deprived of what is essential to their well-being.

Significant anomalies, however, are now calling into question the current consensus about a deprivation background for the biblical proto-apocalyptic texts. The Hebrew Bible contains groups of texts that deprivation approaches cannot successfully interpret. I intend to examine these text groups and to assess the broader implications of a different approach to them.

My thesis is that the following proto-apocalyptic texts are *not* products of groups that are alienated, marginalized, or even relatively deprived. Rather, they stem from groups allied with or identical to the priests at the center of restoration society. First, the proto-apocalyptic description of the end-time assault of "Gog of Magog" in Ezekiel 38–39 expresses the same central-priestly motifs and concerns as the rest of the book of Ezekiel. Second, proto-apocalyptic texts in Zechariah 1–8 appear to have been written in support of the Second Temple establishment. Zechariah's visions aim at establishing a postexilic temple-centered community and are infused with central-cultic images and theology. Third, the early apocalyptic descriptions of cosmic upheaval and of the pouring out of the Spirit in the book of Joel also look like literature from the priestly center of postexilic society. The book is replete with central-cultic terms and motifs, and it calls for implementation of central-cult practices.

It is unlikely that the apocalyptic sections in these three text blocks are late intrusions into their pro-priestly contexts. Rather, these proto-apocalyptic texts have been produced by power-holding priestly groups, not marginal and deprived groups. In what follows, I attempt to test and confirm this thesis.

Apocalypticism and Prophecy in Prior Research

Historical-Critical Investigation of Apocalyptic Texts

Although historical-critical investigation since the nineteenth century tried to trace the roots of apocalyptic texts, several tendencies prevented progress in understanding this literature's actual social background.[2] Being unsympathetic with apocalyptic worldviews, scholars looked for extra-Israelite sources, contemporary with the apocalyptic texts of the third or second century B.C.E., to account for apocalypticism's supposed pessimism, determinism, and even schizophrenia as due to foreign influence.

Julius Wellhausen viewed apocalypticism as devoid of theological value, and he had trouble fitting it into his understanding of the evolution of Israelite religion. Because Wellhausen believed the prophets represented the apex of Israel's ethical thinking and were the bridge to the religion of the New Testament, he viewed both Old Testament and New Testament apocalyptic writings as a curiosity at best.[3] Even the prominent work of R. H. Charles (1855–1931), the "grand old man" of apocalyptic literature, did not dissuade most scholars from arguing that the apocalyptic writings were somehow irrational and difficult to relate to their Protestant idea of the mainstream of biblical religion. Although Charles devoted a lifetime of study to apocalypticism, its language remained foreign to him. He could never empathize with the apocalyptic world and consistently viewed it as foreign to Israel's worldview.[4]

The notion that apocalypticism was a foreign import in Israel was also supported in Germany by form critics such as Hermann Gunkel, who

2. Historical-critical investigation of biblical apocalyptic literature began in the nineteenth century. Two of the earliest critical works on this literature were those by Friedrich Lücke and Adolf Hilgenfeld. See Lücke, *Versuch einer vollständigen Einleitung in die Offenbarung Johannis und in die Gesammte apokalyptische Literatur* (Bonn: E. Weber, 1852); and Hilgenfeld, *Die jüdische Apokalyptik in ihrer geschichtlichen Entwicklung* (Jena: F. Mauke, 1857). Lücke argued that apocalyptic writings developed out of prophecy. Hilgenfeld argued that the historical-critical method should be applied to the question of the origin of apocalyptic literature. See the overviews by Paul Hanson, *Visionaries and their Apocalypses* (Philadelphia: Fortress, 1983), 4; and John J. Collins, *The Apocalyptic Imagination: An Introduction to the Jewish Matrix of Christianity* (New York: Crossroad, 1984), 1–5.

3. The modern appreciation of the importance of apocalypticism in New Testament theology was not anticipated by Wellhausen. Wellhausen's disinterest in the apocalyptic writings is clear from the paucity of their treatment in his *Prolegomena to the History of Ancient Israel* (Gloucester, Mass.: Peter Smith, 1973; 1st ed., 1878). See the discussion of Klaus Koch, *The Rediscovery of Apocalyptic* (Naperville, Ill.: Allenson, 1972), 36; and Collins, *Apocalyptic Imagination*, 1.

4. For this assessment of Charles's attitudes, see the discussion of James Barr, "Jewish Apocalyptic in Recent Scholarly Study," *BJRL* 58 (1975): 32. Charles's work did, however, provide the scholarly community with a number of important primary sources for the study of apocalypticism. For example, see R. H. Charles, *The Apocrypha and Pseudepigrapha of the Old Testament* (Oxford: Clarendon, 1913).

sought to relate biblical apocalyptic literature to the ancient Near Eastern mythological texts brought to light in the nineteenth century.[5] In turn, Sigmund Mowinckel, Gunkel's student, accorded much importance to Persian influence in the rise of apocalypticism.[6] In particular, Mowinckel argued that the origin of the dualism in apocalyptic literature could be traced to Persia. This view of Persian religion as the background of apocalyptic literature was popularized for the English-speaking world by H. H. Rowley and D. S. Russell, both of whom connected Persian influence with the rise of apocalypticism in Israel.[7]

More recent scholarship has rightly attacked the understanding that apocalypticism was a foreign transplant into Israel. It has become clear that it was inadequate to explain the apocalyptic writings through recourse to Persian dualism.[8] Focusing on the immediate environment's influence caused misunderstandings about the period of origin of apocalypticism and about the history and sociology of the centuries preceding the full-blown Hellenistic apocalypses.

The focus on a Persian matrix for apocalypticism was a significant factor in the general lack of scholarly attention to the sociology of the groups that produced (proto-)apocalyptic literature in Israelite society. Even as late as the work of Rowley and Russell, the Israelite social background of apocalyptic literature was not properly explored.

5. See Hermann Gunkel, *Schöpfung und Chaos in Urzeit und Endzeit* (Göttingen: Vandenhoeck & Ruprecht, 1895). Another important German contribution was that of Hugo Gressmann, *Der Ursprung der israelitisch-jüdischen Eschatologie* (Göttingen: Vandenhoeck & Ruprecht, 1905).

6. See Sigmund Mowinckel, *He That Cometh* (Nashville: Abingdon, 1954). In addition to tracing apocalypticism to Persian roots, some earlier scholars of the late nineteenth century had seen Persian or Zoroastrian influence on all of Judaism. See David Winston, "The Iranian Component in the Bible, Apocrypha, and Qumran: A Review of the Evidence," *HR* 5 (1966): 185.

7. See H. H. Rowley, *The Relevance of Apocalyptic* (London: Lutterworth, 1944); and D. S. Russell, *The Method and Message of Jewish Apocalyptic*, OTL (Philadelphia: Westminster, 1964); and *Apocalyptic: Ancient and Modern* (Philadelphia: Fortress, 1978). For discussion of Rowley and Russell, see Barr, "Recent Scholarly Study," 10–14; and Ernest W. Nicholson, "Apocalyptic," in *Tradition and Interpretation*, ed. G. W. Anderson (Oxford: Clarendon, 1979), 191–92.

8. Nevertheless, recent study suggests some Persian influence on Second Temple religion, especially an influence of Iranian ethical dualism on the Qumran writings. See Winston, "Iranian Component," 183–216; Shaul Shaked, "Qumran and Iran: Further Considerations," *Israel Oriental Studies* 2 (1972): 433–46; and Richard N. Frye, "Qumran and Iran: The State of Studies," in *Christianity, Judaism and Other Greco-Roman Cults,* Morton Smith *Festschrift,* ed. Jacob Neusner (Leiden: E. J. Brill, 1975), 3:167–73.

Although Rowley was keenly interested in apocalypticism, for the most part his work merely described the literary characteristics of apocalyptic texts. Like other mid-twentieth-century scholars, Rowley did not explicitly use sociology and anthropology in his biblical studies. He confined his topic to Jewish apocalypticism and did not draw on cross-cultural parallels.[9]

Just as it was inadequate to evaluate apocalyptic literature as late or decadent over against so-called mainline biblical traditions, so also it was insufficient to study this literature merely by characterizing its literary distinctiveness and unique ideas and distinguishing it from prophecy. The nonsociological approaches to apocalyptic texts did not fully appreciate the sources and nature of this literature. Indeed, these methods left unanswered half of the form-critical problem, the question of the social setting of the literature.

The last several decades of the twentieth century have seen significant advances in understanding the nature of the groups and societies behind (proto-)apocalyptic texts. The position popularized by Rowley is no longer generally accepted. Rather, modern scholarship, while still allowing for Persian influence, has downplayed the idea of apocalypticism as a Persian import and has been more attentive to the social background of apocalyptic texts.[10] The discovery of the first Dead Sea Scrolls in 1947 was a

9. See the historical summary by Philip R. Davies, who states that Rowley's account is "couched essentially in terms of Jewish history, religion and literature alone" ("The Social World of Apocalyptic Writings," in *The World of Ancient Israel,* ed. R. E. Clements [Cambridge, England: Cambridge University Press, 1989], 255).

10. Several factors have contributed to a modern revival of interest in biblical apocalyptic writings. Klaus Koch has outlined some of these (see his discussion in *Rediscovery*). Koch himself is often given credit as a starting point for the modern interest in biblical apocalyptic writings, even though he is sometimes thought to have raised more problems than he solved. Another factor in the revival of interest in apocalyptic has been the emergence of theologians who emphasize apocalyptic religion. The foundations for this emphasis were already laid in the late nineteenth and early twentieth centuries by scholars who interpreted early Christianity as an apocalyptic movement. (See Johannes Weiss, *Jesus' Proclamation of the Kingdom of God* [Philadelphia: Fortress, 1971; 1st German ed., 1892]; Martin Kähler, *The So-Called Historical Jesus and the Historic, Biblical Christ* [Philadelphia: Fortress, 1988; 1st German ed., 1892]; and Albert Schweitzer, *The Quest of the Historical Jesus* [New York: Macmillan, 1957; 1st German ed., 1906].) Then, in the last half of the twentieth century, some scholars who took the apocalypticism of early Christianity seriously stressed its positive theological contribution to the gospel of Jesus and Paul. See Ernst Käsemann's claim that "apocalyptic was the mother of all Christian theology" ("The Beginnings of Christian Theology," in *New Testament Questions of Today,*

leading development in this connection. After the scrolls began to be translated, scholars realized that the Qumran community was an actual example
of an ancient millennial group.[11] This new evidence for the study of apocalypticism impelled scholars to start focusing on the social background of
this type of religion.

A watershed was reached when scholars began looking to Israelite society, not Persia, for the background and setting of apocalypticism.[12] In
1959, Otto Plöger presented an influential original study of the origins
and development of Old Testament apocalyptic literature.[13] His argument
traced two lines of development in Israelite religion. One of these lines
had no traces of eschatological thinking, while the other was thoroughly
apocalyptic. Plöger associated these two lines of thought with two groups
that opposed the policies of Antiochus Epiphanes. One group, the Hasidim, produced the Daniel apocalypse and represented a dualistic-
eschatological tradition. In contrast, the second group, the Maccabeans,
interpreted events from a noneschatological point of view and saw themselves as involved in a this-worldly revolt against mundane oppressors.

The significance of the Hasidim and the Maccabeans for Plöger was
that they represent two lines of thought that can be traced backward in
time. Plöger traced these lines of development back to two groups within
the postexilic Israelite community. He reconstructed a postexilic "theocratic" group represented by P and the Chronicler. These theocrats, he believed, were interested only in cult and law. Thus, they had a realized eschatology with no tolerance for apocalypticism.[14]

Opposed to this group were the ideological forebears of the Hasidim,

---

trans. W. J. Montague [Philadelphia: Fortress, 1969] 102); and the role that apocalyptic has played in theologians such as Wolfhart Pannenberg and Jürgen Molt-
mann. For discussion of apocalyptic in these theologians, see Koch, *Rediscovery,*
14–15; Barr, "Recent Scholarly Study," 24–26; and Hanson, *Visionaries,* 7.

11. The terms *millennial* and *millenarian* are often used by sociologists and anthropologists to describe groups similar to those that biblical scholars describe as
apocalyptic. For discussion, see Sylvia L. Thrupp, "Millennial Dreams in Action:
A Report on the Conference Discussion," in *Millennial Dreams in Action,* ed. S.
Thrupp (The Hague: Mouton, 1962), 11–12.

12. Stanley B. Frost is usually considered an early representative of this newer
scholarship (see his "Apocalyptic and History," in *The Bible in Modern Scholarship,*
ed. J. P. Hyatt [Nashville: Abingdon, 1965], 99–112).

13. As noted in note 1 above, the work was first published as *Theokratie und
Eschatologie.*

14. A note on terminology is in order at this point. Plöger's work uses the term
theocracy (*Theokratie*) to refer to a rule of the priests at the center of postexilic society. In contrast, Hanson prefers the term *hierocracy* to denote the same priestly

who organized themselves into antiestablishment conventicles (secret groups meeting for religious purposes). Plöger viewed these conventicles as holding on to the prophetic word, and within them the cult officials' opponents kept the prophetic spirit alive. Within these proto-Hasidic groups, which produced Isaiah 24–27, Zechariah 12–14, and Joel, Plöger found the origins of apocalypticism. Plöger thus rejected the notion that apocalypticism was imported from Persia, and instead he established a trajectory leading from Israelite prophecy to apocalypticism.

From one perspective, Plöger's thesis represents an advance. Although earlier scholars, such as Rowley, had argued that a historical situation of distress and persecution was behind Jewish apocalyptic, their arguments lacked sociological precision. In contrast, Plöger went beyond Rowley in specifying an inner-Israelite social matrix as the cause of the distress. Intergroup conflict within Israelite society was, he believed, the essential issue.[15] Plöger's approach has some roots in the nineteenth-century sociological work of Ferdinand Tönnies, who developed a distinction between "community" (*Gemeinschaft*) and "society" (*Gesellschaft*).[16] Whereas earlier scholars spoke in general terms about Jewish distress, Plöger's sociological understanding specified apocalyptic literature as the product of a *Gemeinschaft* alienated from the postexilic priestly establishment.[17]

Relying on the work of Plöger, Paul Hanson has developed similar ideas, combining them with theses developed by Frank Moore Cross.[18]

---

government (*Priesterherrschaft*). Hanson's term may be the more specific one, because in the case of a theocracy (a government where a god is held to be the ruler), the officials implementing the deity's will might not necessarily be priests. In this book, however, both terms will be avoided. As the discussion of Zechariah in chapter 5 below will show, Wellhausen's notion that the priests of Persian-period Yehud ascended to governmental hegemony, ruling the society in the place of civil leaders, is overstated. This does not mean, of course, that no priests shared central power in this period.

15. See Davies, "Social World," 256.

16. For discussion of Tönnies, see Andrew D. H. Mayes, *The Old Testament in Sociological Perspective* (London: Marshall Pickering, 1989), 7–17.

17. Ibid., 14.

18. See Frank Moore Cross's *Canaanite Myth and Hebrew Epic* (Cambridge, Mass.: Harvard University Press, 1973), 343–46. Cross suggests sixth-century origins for apocalyptic involving reformulations of the prophetic tradition and of the royal ideology. He holds that an important aspect of the new apocalyptic synthesis of the late sixth century was the recrudescence of old Canaanite mythic lore. Hanson took up Cross's suggestion of a new postexilic apocalyptic syncretism with early Israelite and Canaanite roots, and attempted to assign it a social setting. He did this by working into the theory the idea of a prophetic and sectarian impulse behind the oracles of Zechariah 9–14 and Isaiah 56–66.

Hanson attempts to fill in gaps in Plöger's description of a trajectory from prophecy to apocalyptic writings. In part, he does this by looking for the reutilization of ancient Canaanite mythopoetic language by "new prophetic voices" in the postexilic period. Hanson finds such a reuse of myth among postexilic factions in tension with the restored community's leaders. By reconstructing these prophetic factions and their conflicts as the generative matrix of apocalyptic, Hanson tried to describe a development of prophetic eschatology into apocalyptic eschatology.[19]

Specifically, Hanson has maintained that the Third Isaiah prophetic group and their allies (groups of disenfranchised Levites), whose apocalyptic thinking was aimed against those in charge of the temple, were the first to produce Old Testament apocalyptic literature. Subsequently, Zechariah 9–14 was produced by the same antihierocratic circles. This ongoing conflict between prophets-become-visionaries and a Zadokite-led priestly hierocratic group is presented as the social setting of the dawn of apocalyptic eschatology.

Hanson is more explicit than his predecessors about alienation and deprivation as characteristic of the tradents of apocalyptic ideas. He argues that there is a "brooding minority" behind every apocalyptic movement.[20] Hanson's sociological heritage is also more clear than is the case with previous scholars of apocalyptic literature. His study is based on the work of Max Weber, as well as that of Karl Mannheim and Ernst Troeltsch.[21] Hanson's reliance on the sociology of Weber and Mannheim for his view of

19. One of the clearest statements of this latter thesis is in Paul Hanson's *Old Testament Apocalyptic* (Nashville: Abingdon, 1987), 33.

20. Hanson, *Dawn*, 2.

21. See Andrew D. H. Mayes, "Sociology and the Old Testament," in *The World of Ancient Israel: Sociological, Anthropological and Political Perspectives* (Cambridge, England: Cambridge University Press, 1989), 55. Hanson's discussion presupposes Weber's ideal types of the ruling class and the alienated class. For example, *Dawn*, 212, refers to Max Weber, *The Sociology of Religion*, trans. E. Fischoff (Boston: Beacon, 1963; 1st German ed., 1922), 80ff., 106–7; and Talcott Parsons's Introduction to that work, xxix–xxx, xxxv. Then, Hanson draws on Karl Mannheim to show how a "utopian mentality" is characteristic of the alienated ideal-type of group (*Dawn*, 213, refers to Mannheim, *Ideology and Utopia: An Introduction to the Sociology of Knowledge*, trans L. Wirth and E. Shils [New York: Harcourt, Brace and Co., 1936; 1st German ed., 1929], 40, 87, 192–93). Hanson argues that when their expectations for a transformation of society are frustrated, the alienated are drawn to apocalyptic eschatology. Under these circumstances, it is "inevitable that consolation should be sought in genuine otherworldly hopes" (*Dawn*, 214, quotes Weber, *Sociology*, 140). Discussion of Weber, Mannheim, and Troeltsch is resumed below.

deprivation as the causative matrix of apocalyptic eschatology is evident from the following quote:

> Modern sociologists like Mannheim and Weber have demonstrated convincingly that powerful officials ruling over the religious or political structures of a society do not dream apocalyptic visions of the revolutionary overthrow of the existing order of things. Temple priests are not likely candidates for apocalyptic seers.[22]

Although the influence of Weber and Mannheim on Hanson is unambiguous, his use of Troeltsch's church/sect paradigm most strongly informed his scenario of the rise of Israelite apocalyptic eschatology. Troeltsch argued that the medieval church, dependent on the upper classes, kept eschatological teachings to a minimum. By contrast, groups of the sect "type," composed of the marginal and oppressed, adopted eschatological views. The conflict between church and sect, in Troeltsch's view, formed the social matrix for the rise of medieval millennialism as the sect "type" groups adopted "chiliastic" dreams in the face of persecution. Hanson adopts Troeltsch's paradigm to support his description of a postexilic conflict between "hierocratic" and "visionary" elements.[23] Just as Troeltsch saw apocalypticism as the religion of marginal and alienated groups, Hanson places the rise of Israelite apocalyptic eschatology within those postexilic groups oppressed by the priests at the center of society.

The Present Situation

The view that apocalyptic eschatology emerged because of deprivation, particularly that felt by peripheral or disenfranchised factions, is now quite common. Modern discussions of the origins of millennialism in early Jewish history often draw on deprivation theory, especially as found in Plöger and Hanson.[24] For example, Walter Schmithals accepts Plöger's

22. Hanson, *Dawn*, 232.

23. Hanson, *Dawn*, 215, refers to Ernst Troeltsch, *The Social Teaching of the Christian Churches*, 2 vols., trans. O. Wyon (New York: Harper Torchbooks, 1960; 1st German ed., 1911), 336, 995. Hanson, *Dawn*, 216, cites Troeltsch, *Social Teaching*, 337, 380.

24. Besides being presented in the work of Plöger and Hanson, the deprivation view is also found in Morton Smith's hypothetical reconstructions of postexilic religion in *Palestinian Parties and Politics That Shaped the Old Testament* (London: SCM, 1971). Also see such Old Testament Introductions as Norman K. Gottwald, *The Hebrew Bible: A Socio-Literary Introduction* (Philadelphia: Fortress, 1985), 585–90; and Bernhard W. Anderson, *Understanding the Old Testament* (Englewood Cliffs, N.J.: Prentice-Hall, 1986), 502–4, 516, 622. Chapters 2–6 of Theodore Olson's 1982 monograph on the origins of the idea of "progress" provide an example of how widespread the deprivation view is (*Millennialism, Utopianism, and Progress* [Toronto: University of Toronto Press, 1982]).

view of a transition during postexilic times from the eschatology of the prophets to that of apocalyptic. He states that prophetic eschatology was converted to the apocalyptic view by "the heirs of the later prophetic movement, . . . pushed to the fringes of the Jewish community."[25] Schmithals believes that although the advantaged "will hardly denounce history as such," one can envision apocalypticism as arising "on a lower social level."[26]

As one would expect, considering the widespread consensus that apocalypticism originated in Persian period deprivation, proto-apocalyptic texts are often assumed to be the postexilic products of deprived groups. Reflecting this current view, Robert R. Wilson writes, "Postexilic authors seem to have added apocalyptic material to earlier prophetic books such as Isaiah and Ezekiel. The increased use of apocalyptic images suggests that the prophets themselves were part of groups . . . presumably becoming more and more isolated from the central social structure."[27] Reuben Ahroni, another scholar who finds deprivation behind biblical proto-apocalyptic material, argues that Ezekiel 38–39 is a product of distress or trauma in postexilic times.[28] Deprivation approaches are often also applied to texts in Zechariah. Thus, Zechariah 9–14 is treated by William Neil as the product of despair, and by Joseph Blenkinsopp as the probable product of peripheral conventicles.[29]

Interpreters of Joel, furthermore, find deprivation behind its proto-apocalypticism. For example, Hans Walter Wolff's commentary accepts Plöger's view that Joel stems from an eschatological opposition party.[30] Similarly, Paul L. Redditt argues that Joel and the central officials of his society rejected each other, resulting in the Joel group's peripheralization. Redditt's article bases itself on I. M. Lewis's notions about peripheral prophecy and the theory that millennial groups perceive themselves as relatively deprived.[31]

Several studies of full-blown apocalyptic texts are also modeled on the

25. Walter Schmithals, *The Apocalyptic Movement: Introduction and Interpretation*, trans. J. Steely (Nashville: Abingdon, 1975), 136.

26. Ibid., 144–45.

27. Robert R. Wilson, *Prophecy and Society in Ancient Israel* (Philadelphia: Fortress, 1980), 292; cf. 285–86, 290, 308.

28. Reuben Ahroni, "The Gog Prophecy and the Book of Ezekiel," HAR 1 (1977): 24.

29. William Neil, "Zechariah, Book of," *IDB* 4:947; Joseph Blenkinsopp, *A History of Prophecy in Israel* (Philadelphia: Westminster, 1983), 263.

30. Hans Walter Wolff, *A Commentary on the Books of the Prophets Joel and Amos*, Hermeneia (Philadelphia: Fortress, 1977), 10–12, 36, 49, 82, 84–85.

31. Paul L. Redditt, "The Book of Joel and Peripheral Prophecy," *CBQ* 48 (1986): 236–37. Discussion of Lewis is resumed below.

deprivation approach. For example, Schmithals's discussion of apocalypses such as Daniel and *1 Enoch* leads him to conclude: "The apocalyptic groups . . . obviously led an existence as conventicles and, separated from the public religion, cultivated a sect-mentality."[32] In like manner, W. Sibley Towner places Daniel's authors within a dissident apocalyptic tradition, traceable back to those who opposed the triumphant priestly rulers of postexilic Israel.[33]

The recent approaches to apocalyptic literature have overcome many of the problems of the older studies. In doing so, however, they have produced an overarching understanding of the social matrix of apocalyptic literature that, at best, fits only some of the biblical texts. First, this understanding views apocalyptic religion as the child of prophecy. Hanson adopts Plöger at this point, but this view is already found in Rowley and Russell. Rowley had stressed the contribution of prophetic eschatology in the origin of apocalypticism. Russell, in turn, saw postexilic prophecy as the taproot of apocalyptic.[34]

From the beginning there were indications that this view was inadequate to account for all the data. As early as 1919, Gustav Hölscher had argued the opposite idea that *wisdom* is the source of apocalyptic literature.[35] Gerhard von Rad's later elaboration of Hölscher's view has not found wide acceptance, but it does serve as a prominent indicator of unsolved problems.[36] One such unsolved problem is the book of Daniel,

32. Schmithals, *Apocalyptic Movement,* 46.

33. W. Sibley Towner, "Daniel," in *Harper's Bible Commentary,* ed. J. L. Mayes (San Francisco: Harper & Row, 1988), 695–96. At this point, it should be noted that New Testament scholars of apocalyptic texts also use deprivation approaches. Thus, Philipp Vielhauer, drawing on Plöger, accepts the view that apocalyptic literature first originated among the disenfranchised. He writes, "We may accept the view that the home of Apocalyptic is in those eschatologically excited circles which were forced more and more by the theocracy into a kind of conventicle existence" ("Apocalypses and Related Subjects, Introduction," in *New Testament Apocrypha,* ed. E. Hennecke and W. Schneemelcher [London: Lutterworth, 1965], 2:598; cf. 2:595). Vielhauer finds that the temper of Jewish apocalyptic was shared by the early Jewish-Christians, and that apocalyptic expectations were especially cherished in eschatologically stimulated circles in Asia Minor.

34. In this opinion they were following the view set out by Lücke in the nineteenth century (see n. 2 above).

35. Gustav Hölscher, "Die Entstehung des Buches Daniel," *TSK* 92 (1919): 113–38.

36. Gerhard von Rad argued that both apocalyptic and wisdom literature focus on esoteric knowledge divorced from Israel's saving history. See his *Old Testament Theology,* trans. D. Stalker (New York: Harper and Row, 1965), 2:301–15; and

which was more likely produced by wisdom circles than by prophetic circles.[37] If groups such as wisdom circles were millennial, this suggests that other circles, such as priestly groups, are also possible sources of apocalyptic literature.[38]

Second, the newer approaches' overarching understanding reads the apocalyptic texts as the literary expressions of alienated factions in the restored community. These groups are seen as disenfranchised and deprived by a hierocratic group in power. This reading cannot account for the biblical evidence and must be corrected. Left unexplained are those texts often identified as proto-apocalyptic that occur in books from central priestly circles of exilic and postexilic times. It is necessary to move beyond deprivation approaches in order to understand these texts.

Sociological Research on Millennialism

The basic problems raised by Hanson and Plöger's conventicle approach cannot be redressed by simple recourse to sociological and anthropological theory. Like the work of Plöger and Hanson, the sociological discipline itself accepts a generalizing and overarching understanding of the social matrix of apocalyptic literature.

In particular, sociological theory parallels Plöger and Hanson in putting forward alienation and deprivation as the cause of millennialism. The similarities in the approaches to apocalypticism of sociological theory and biblical studies, however, are largely due to a shared foundation. Sociologists' understandings of millennial groups are often rooted in Weber's and Mannheim's paradigms, the same paradigms that also form the foundation of Hanson's thesis.[39]

In the early twentieth century, Max Weber and his friend Ernst Troeltsch[40] argued that millennial type groups consisted of the powerless

---

Wisdom in Israel, trans. J. Martin (New York: Abingdon, 1973), 263–83. Also see Koch, *Rediscovery,* 45–46.

37. The court tales of Daniel 1–6 are replete with wisdom concepts and vocabulary. See the discussion in Robert R. Wilson, "From Prophecy to Apocalyptic: Reflections on the Shape of Israelite Religion," *Semeia* 21 (1981): 87–93.

38. See R. Wilson, *Prophecy and Society,* 308.

39. Max Weber's most important contribution on the rise of millennialism is found in his 1922 treatise *The Sociology of Religion* (e.g., 106, 109, 140, 175). Weber's influence on figures such as Troeltsch predated the publication of this work, however. For Hanson's reliance on Weber, Troeltsch, and Mannheim, see pp. 8–9 above.

40. See Troeltsch, *Social Teaching,* 336–37, 380, 995.

and deprived ("pariah groups").[41] Karl Mannheim, writing in the late 1920s, was influenced both by Marxist categories and by the thought of Weber. Mannheim argued that millennialism is the religion of deprived groups, the lower strata of society, and oppressed and persecuted minorities.[42] Weber and Mannheim are cited both by Hanson, as shown above, and by later sociological studies that Hanson did not employ.

From the 1930s on, sociologists studying group psychology and acculturation reintroduced Weber's view that powerless, persecuted, or dissatisfied groups are the source of apocalyptic ideas. Harold Lasswell, writing in 1935, tried to understand millennialism in terms of psychopathology, and Philleo Nash, writing in 1937, linked millennial groups to the experience of deprivation.[43] Then, in 1941, Bernard Barber argued that millennialism is one of several alternative responses to harsh times: "The messianic movement is comprehensible only as a response to widespread deprivation."[44]

Among anthropologists, Ralph Linton was one of the first to synthesize a complete theory of millennialism based on the deprivation idea.[45] In his pioneering 1943 article, Linton was concerned with movements that result from a culture's contact with other cultures that threaten its integrity. According to Linton, when a culture is dominated, the conditions of hardship, or at least of extreme dissatisfaction, that result can give rise to millen-

41. Of course, pre-Weber scholarship often pictured the members of millennial groups as peripheral, antisocial, or psychologically troubled people. For discussion, see Hillel Schwartz, "Millenarianism, An Overview," in *The Encyclopedia of Religion* (New York: Macmillan, 1987), 9:531–32. Schwartz notes that seventeenth-century works about millennial groups described them as composed of fanatics and even deluded and possessed people. Then, eighteenth-century accounts suggested millennialism was a medical problem. A loss of memory and sense of time was suggested as its cause (ibid., 531). Similarly, nineteenth-century articles looked to chemical imbalances or money-making schemes as explanations for millennialism.

42. Mannheim, *Ideology and Utopia*, e.g., 40, 87, 192–93.

43. Harold D. Lasswell, "Collective Autism as a Consequence of Culture Contact: Notes on Religious Training and the Peyote Cult at Taos," *Zeitschrift für Sozialforschung* 4 (1935): 232–47; Philleo Nash, "The Place of Religious Revivalism in the Formation of the Intercultural Community on Klamath Reservation," in *Social Anthropology of North American Tribes*, ed. F. Eggan (Chicago: University of Chicago Press, 1937), 377–442.

44. Bernard Barber, "Acculturation and Messianic Movements," *American Sociological Review* 6 (1941): 667.

45. Ralph Linton, "Nativistic Movements," *American Anthropologist* 45 (1943): 230–40.

nial movements.[46] Because he held that millennialism originates in times of stress as an irrational flight from reality, Linton helped establish the then-current idea that stress and deprivation give rise to this type of religion.

Like Linton, and Barber before him, Fred W. Voget saw millennial movements as the result of deprivation and frustrations consequent to contact with a dominant society. In addition, Linton's idea received support from Raymond W. Firth, who also viewed millennial groups as composed of the deprived.[47] Anthony F. C. Wallace was another early influential millennialism theorist.[48] Wallace also emphasized stress due to needs not being satisfied as a major cause of millennial groups.[49]

The same year that Wallace's article appeared, Leon Festinger published his theory of cognitive dissonance.[50] Festinger's social psychological study (1956) was concerned to discover why millennial groups continue despite the psychological conflict caused by the disconfirmation of their beliefs and perceptions of the world. Scholars have since used the cognitive dissonance notion, however, to add sophistication to the theory of deprivation.[51] Wayne A. Meeks, for example, has surmised that the "deprivation"

46. Ibid., 233. Linton's theory of cultural deprivation was actually a refinement of F. E. Williams's view that cargo cults result from the imposition of Western culture and the destruction of native ceremonies. Williams made this observation based on his work on the "Vailala Madness" in the 1920s. See his "The Vailala Madness in Retrospect," in *Essays Presented to C. G. Seligmann,* ed. E. E. Evans-Pritchard, et al. (London: K. Paul, Trench, Trubner, 1934), 369–79.

47. Fred W. Voget, "The American Indian in Transition: Reformation and Accommodation," *American Anthropologist* 58 (1956): 249–63; Raymond W. Firth, *Elements of Social Organization* (New York: Philosophical Library, 1951), 113.

48. Anthony F. C. Wallace, "Revitalization Movements," *American Anthropologist* 58 (1956): 264–81.

49. Wallace draws upon Max Weber at several points. For example, Wallace cites Weber's concept of charismatic leadership in characterizing the organization of revitalization movements (ibid., 273).

50. Leon Festinger, Henry W. Riecken, Stanley Schachter, *When Prophecy Fails: A Social and Psychological Study of a Modern Group That Predicted the Destruction of the World* (New York: Harper & Row, 1964; 1st ed., 1956). "Cognitive dissonance" involves a person having two cognitions (pieces of knowledge, beliefs, or feelings) that are inconsistent with each other, thus causing the person to experience interior conflict. Festinger argued that the presence of this sort of dissonance gives rise to pressure on the individual to reduce or eliminate the dissonance.

51. For example, Weston La Barre notes that acculturation theories of millennialism posit "a 'cognitive dissonance' between competing systems which the syncretic [millennial] cult somehow resolves" ("Materials for a History of Studies of Crisis Cults: A Bibliographic Essay," *Current Anthropology* 12 [1971]: 20). (It should be noted that La Barre criticizes the acculturation theory, arguing that mil-

behind Pauline Christian millennial groups can be described in terms of cognitive dissonance. The groups' members found themselves "in an ambiguous relation to [their society's] hierarchical structures." The interior conflict resulting from this perceived "status inconsistency" pressured these people to seek relief from their stress. Appealing to Festinger's theory, Meeks suggests they found relief when millennialism's fundamental images accounted for their cognitive inconsistencies with its view of the world as just as out of kilter as they felt it to be.[52]

Old Testament scholars have also adopted the cognitive dissonance refinement of the deprivation theory. Thus Paul Hanson's 1976 article on apocalypticism seems to adopt a cognitive dissonance approach in its argument that an apocalyptic symbolic universe resolves inner contradictions between religious hopes and experience. This argument's strong link to the deprivation thesis is clear from Hanson's contention that the symbolic universe in question is opposed to that of the dominant society, and that the experience causing inner contradiction is always the group experience of alienation.[53]

It is unfortunate that scholars have so closely linked the dissonance theory with deprivation theory. Dissonance can occur even when groups are not at all deprived or frustrated. As Meeks shows, not all early Christians were objectively deprived; some also belonged to the upper levels of the social structure. Some even had wealth and high prestige.[54] Besides occurring among such people of prestige, cognitive dissonance can also

---

lennial groups can also be caused by socially endogenous conflict.) A cognitive-dissonance explanation for millennialism is also found in Charles Y. Glock and Rodney Stark, *Religion and Society in Tension* (Chicago: Rand McNally, 1965).

52. Wayne A. Meeks, *The First Urban Christians: The Social World of the Apostle Paul* (New Haven: Yale University Press, 1983), 173–74.

53. Paul Hanson, "Apocalypticism," *IDBSup*, 28–31. Other students of apocalyptic groups, such as Robert P. Carroll and Paul L. Redditt, are more explicit than Hanson in their reliance on cognitive dissonance theory. Carroll argues that the rise of Israelite apocalypticism is an example of how "dissonance gives rise to hermeneutic." In his view, postexilic deprivation accompanied by a collapse of prophetic hopes gave rise to dissonance. As a response, apocalyptic reinterpretation of earlier prophecies attempted to eliminate the dissonance (*When Prophecy Failed* [New York: Seabury, 1979], 88, 110, 160, 205, 219). Carroll writes, "With its roots in prophecy, apocalyptic became the resolution of the dissonance caused by the lack of fulfillment of prophecy in the early post-exilic period" (*Prophecy,* 205). Redditt similarly argues for cognitive dissonance behind Zechariah 9–14, resulting in "a revised eschatology in which the old prophecies could still come true" ("Israel's Shepherds: Hope and Pessimism in Zechariah 9–14," *CBQ* 51 [1989]: 640).

54. Meeks, *Urban Christians,* 52, 57, 73.

be experienced by a society's leaders. For example, a group in power can experience psychological turmoil when confronted with an important omen or the message of a persuasive teacher. One would normally consider such psychological turmoil as cognitive dissonance, but not as deprivation. To identify it as such is special pleading. A rehabilitated understanding of cognitive dissonance helps us understand millennialism's background (see below, chapter 2), but there is no need to link it to deprivation.

David F. Aberle's modification of the deprivation thesis helped pave the way for including phenomena like cognitive dissonance under the deprivation rubric. Writing in 1959, a few years after Festinger's book was published, Aberle strongly renewed the argument for deprivation as the cause of millennialism.[55] Although dependent on Lasswell's, Nash's, and Barber's causal theories of deprivation, Aberle's refined deprivation theory was distinctive.[56] His modified theory broadened the deprivation thesis by introducing the notion of relativity. In relative deprivation theory, deprivation is not considered an objective condition that any neutral observer would recognize. Rather, the deprivation consists of people's *perception* of their present condition relative to their expectations.[57] For example, a multimillionaire would have a feeling of relative deprivation if he lost all but his last million. Although Aberle's notion of deprivation clearly covers more millennial groups than previous versions, it is a more difficult con-

55. David F. Aberle, "The Prophet Dance and Reactions to White Contact," *Southwestern Journal of Anthropology* 15 (1959): 74–83.

56. For discussion, see La Barre, "Materials for a History," 24; Weston La Barre, *The Ghost Dance: Origins of Religion* (Garden City, N. Y.: Doubleday, 1970), 287; Virginia H. Hine, "The Deprivation and Disorganization Theories of Social Movements," in *Religious Movements in Contemporary America*, ed. I. Zaretsky and M. Leone (Princeton, N.J.: Princeton University Press, 1974), 651; R. Wilson, *Prophecy and Society*, 78; R. Wilson, "Prophecy to Apocalyptic," 85; and Meeks, *Urban Christians*, 172.

57. See David F. Aberle, "A Note on Relative Deprivation Theory as Applied to Millenarian and Other Cult Movements," in *Millennial Dreams in Action: Essays in Comparative Study*, ed. S. Thrupp (The Hague: Mouton, 1962), 209. Like Aberle, Charles Y. Glock has tried to refine the concept of deprivation to make it more useful. Glock writes, "Deprivation, as we conceive it, refers to any and all of the ways that an individual or group may be, or feel, disadvantaged in comparison either to other individuals or groups or to an internalized set of standards" ("The Role of Deprivation in the Origin and Evolution of Religious Groups," in *Religion and Social Conflict*, ed. R. Lee and M. W. Marty [New York: Oxford University Press, 1964], 27). Glock applies deprivation theory to the origin of religious movements in general. Thus, in his view, religion often compensates for feelings of deprivation ("Role of Deprivation," 29).

cept to apply objectively, and it permits almost any group to be described as deprived.

Other modern sociologists also use deprivation theory in more or less refined forms to account for millennialism. A few of the better known deprivation theorists may be mentioned. Drawing on Weber, Barber, Linton, and Firth, Vittorio Lanternari describes millennial movements as "the religions of the oppressed." These movements, Lanternari argues, convey a message of salvation and hope in the face of crisis and deprivation. "Everywhere, in primitive as in highly developed societies, the messianic movement emerges from a crisis, to offer spiritual redemption."[58]

Norman Cohn employs Weber's theories and a refined deprivation approach in an attempt to find the social and economic causes of millennial movements.[59] Cohn focuses not on poverty as such, but on marginalization or loss of traditional ways of life as the cause of millennialism. Although recognizing that millennialism may appeal to people in various social strata, he argues that discontent or lack of material and emotional support is present in each case. And in the final analysis, Cohn stresses the tendency of medieval millennialism to occur among the lower strata and the radical fringe, arguing that its general context was widespread dissatisfaction with the establishment.[60] Alienated people adopted millennialism to "hold their anxieties at bay" and make themselves feel important and powerful.[61]

As a final development, note I. M. Lewis's work on marginal groups and deprivation cults. Although concerned with a broader category of phenomena than just millennialism, Lewis clarifies peripheral groups and the religion found among them.[62] His investigations have made the scholarly discussion of the differences between peripheral and central groups and institutions more precise and enhance the deprivation thesis.

A New Cross-disciplinary Approach

The present scholarly situation requires not only a correction of Plöger and Hanson's conventicle thesis in light of recent sociological thinking but

58. Vittorio Lanternari, *The Religions of the Oppressed*, trans. L. Sergio (New York: Knopf, 1963), 309.

59. See Thrupp, "Millennial Dreams in Action: A Report," 20. Norman Cohn often draws on Weber in his *The Pursuit of the Millennium* (New York: Oxford University Press, 1970).

60. See Cohn, *Pursuit*, 10, 37, 50–52, 282, 284.

61. Ibid., 87–88.

62. See I. M. Lewis, "Spirit Possession and Deprivation Cults," *Man* n.s. 1 (1966):307–29; and *Ecstatic Religion* (New York: Routledge, 1971).

also a critique of the sociological theory of deprivation. Retreatment of the apocalyptic texts in the Old Testament is in order based on such a reassessment, especially retreatment of central-priestly apocalyptic texts. In addressing this task, I shall make use of sociological studies of millennialism,[63] particularly the efforts at comprehensive treatment that began with the work of Linton and Wallace.[64]

The sociological and anthropological study of millennial groups has been advancing since the end of the nineteenth century, when James Mooney carried out his work on the Ghost Dance religion among Native Americans.[65] These studies constitute relevant sources already used in dealing with some of the aforementioned problems in the study of biblical apocalypticism.[66] As noted above, past sociological study of millennialism parallels the study of apocalyptic religion by biblical scholars. The notion that millennial groups are deprived is common and has a long history in scholarship. Deprivation theory, however, has not been held universally, and several millennial groups have been described that are *not* peripheral or alienated in any obvious sense. I shall make direct use of these sociological descriptions in the hope of avoiding the pitfalls that result from drawing exclusively on the theoretical constructs of sociologists. When the relevant Israelite groups are compared to millennial groups in power, several problems in the study of biblical apocalyptic literature can be solved.

63. A comprehensive review of the anthropological scholarship is unnecessary here. The history of deprivation theory has already been outlined above. Beyond this, several good bibliographic essays are available reviewing the general study of millennialism. See H. Schwartz, "Millenarianism," 531–32; Hillel Schwartz, "The End of the Beginning: Millenarian Studies, 1969–1975," *RelSRev* 2/3 (1976): 1–14; La Barre, "Materials for a History"; Yonina Talmon, "Millenarism" [*sic*], in *The International Encyclopedia of the Social Sciences* (New York: Macmillan Company and Free Press, 1968), 10:349–62; and Ted Daniels, *Millennialism: An International Bibliography* (New York: Garland, 1992).

64. Linton, "Nativistic Movements"; and Wallace, "Revitalization Movements." See the discussion above, and Gary W. Trompf, "Introduction," in *Cargo Cults and Millenarian Movements: Transoceanic Comparisons of New Religious Movements* (Berlin: Mouton de Gruyter, 1990), 1–5.

65. James Mooney, *The Ghost-Dance Religion and the Sioux Outbreak of 1890* (Lincoln: University of Nebraska Press, 1991). The first edition of this work was published as Part 2 of the *Annual Report of the Bureau of American Ethnology* 14 (Washington: Government Printing Office, 1896).

66. For example, see the several related articles in *Semeia* 21 (1981).

2

The Sociology of Apocalyptic Groups

Robert R. Wilson has listed a number of guidelines for using comparative material to elucidate aspects of Israelite religion,[1] and these guidelines are central to the methodology used in this book. Following them, I rely only on twentieth-century sociological work and base my results on a survey of as many societies as possible,[2] collecting information on the history of millennial groups and their ideas, leadership, and recruiting.[3] The results of this survey will help to form hypotheses about apocalypticism, hypotheses that I shall subsequently test with respect to the relevant biblical texts. The exegesis of the texts will control the use of comparative material.

The first problem is deciding how to select millennial groups for analysis. As Norman Gottwald has noted, some criteria for selective grouping

1. Robert R. Wilson, *Prophecy and Society in Ancient Israel* (Philadelphia: Fortress, 1980), 15–16.

2. This examination of groups and societies for later comparison with the biblical material will not be limited to groups and societies that presently exist. Andrew D. H. Mayes refers to both Max Weber's and Emile Durkheim's work as justification for associating sociology and history and for using sociology in trying to understand ancient Israel (*The Old Testament in Sociological Perspective* [London: Marshall Pickering, 1989], 1). Authors such as Sylvia L. Thrupp also argue for the validity of comparing the results of both field and historical studies ("Millennial Dreams in Action: A Report on the Conference Discussion," in *Millennial Dreams in Action: Essays in Comparative Study,* ed. S. Thrupp [The Hague: Mouton, 1962], 13).

3. See the list in Thrupp, "Millenial Dreams in Action: A Report," 13.

are needed.[4] This issue of criteria is important, because using too narrow criteria in the selecting process would prejudice the study from the start.[5] Thus, rather than presupposing a causality, or assuming that millennial groups are to be found in only one type of social milieu, I remain open to consider all groups whose members share certain ideas about the world.[6]

Based on a survey of groups with apocalyptic beliefs and ideas, I shall first describe the phenomenon of apocalypticism. Then, armed with a clarified understanding of apocalypticism, I shall critique deprivation theory and present a more critical view of the origins of millennialism.

The Problem of Definition

The imprecision and ambiguity of the term *apocalyptic* in biblical scholarship make it necessary to define our terms before discussing eschatology[7]

4. Norman Gottwald, "Problems and Promises in the Comparative Analysis of Religious Phenomena," *Semeia* 21 (1981): 111.

5. The thesis that deprivation theory cannot account for many millennial groups will be impossible to demonstrate if we begin by defining a millennial group as one that arises out of a causal matrix of deprivation. Further, there are good empirical warrants against defining millennial groups in terms of one type of social arena. Groups with a millennial worldview are found in many social contexts, and this will be made clear below. Thus Kenelm Burridge writes, "Unless an apocalyptic message is defined by the conditions which supposedly produced them, apocalyptic events [i.e., occurrences of apocalyptic messages or group activities] also occur in quite different conditions" ("Reflections on Prophecy and Prophetic Groups," *Semeia* 21 [1981]: 99–100). Therefore, attempts at definition of the sociology of millennial groups that presuppose a causality will be avoided here. Weston La Barre tries to avoid a similar problem in choosing between terms for millennial groups such as *adjustment movements, revitalization movements,* and *messianic movements* ("Materials for a History of Studies of Crisis Cults: A Bibliographic Essay," *Current Anthropology* 12 [1971]: 11). Unfortunately, even the term *crisis cult,* which La Barre chooses, presupposes too much.

6. See T. Stern's comments in the "Responses" to La Barre, "Materials for a History," *Current Anthropology* 12 (1971): 34.

7. Because even the term *eschatology* is understood differently by different authors, its meaning should also be examined. Thus, Stanley B. Frost's terminology differs from that used here in that for him, the pre-apocalyptic envisioning of a telos within history is not true eschatology ("Apocalyptic and History," in *The Bible in Modern Scholarship,* ed. J. P. Hyatt [Nashville: Abingdon, 1965], 105). The term *eschatology,* from the Greek ἔσχατος meaning "the furthest, the last," is used by biblical scholars to refer to views or positions about a coming time of fulfillment, or a coming consummation of the present course of events. Eschatology as expressed in apocalyptic literature refers to God's decisive or final visit — not within the course of history, but as a radical disjunction with history (see 2 Esd. 11:44;

and apocalypticism.[8] The term *apocalyptic* is from the Greek ἀποκᾰλύπτω, "uncover, reveal." The English adjective generally refers to a revelatory disclosure about the end time, describing an intervention from another, supernatural world. Because more specific definitions of this adjective are needed, some have suggested that the genre apocalypse should be distinguished from apocalypticism and apocalyptic eschatology.[9] It remains unclear, however, whether these particular distinctions really help us better clarify apocalypticism.[10] I think it is more helpful to distinguish between apocalypticism as a literary phenomenon, as a *Weltanschauung* (worldview) or type of (religious) thinking, and as a historical and social phenomenon.

The term *apocalyptic* has been applied to a literary phenomenon, a worldview, and a social phenomenon, and I shall develop characterizations

---

Dan. 7:26-27). Frost states that "the eschaton interrupts the history, it is not anything which the history prepares for or in any way causes to occur" ("Apocalyptic and History," 112). Often, complete irrationality and absolute chaos separate this age from the next (e.g., Rev. 4:1 – 19:21).

8. For discussion of this imprecision and of the ongoing lack of a generally accepted description of apocalypticism, see Bruce Vawter, C. M., "Apocalyptic: Its Relation to Prophecy," *CBQ* 22 (1960): 33–34; Hartmut Gese, "Anfang und Ende der Apokalyptik, dargestellt am Sacharjabuch," *ZTK* 70 (1973): 20; Klaus Seybold, *Bilder zum Tempelbau: Die Visionen des Propheten Sacharja*, SB 70 (Stuttgart: Verlag Katholisches Bibelwerk, 1974), 105; Michael E. Stone, "Lists of Revealed Things in the Apocalyptic Literature," in *Magnalia Dei: The Mighty Acts of God*, ed. F. M. Cross, W. Lemke, and P. D. Miller, Jr. (Garden City, N.Y.: Doubleday, 1976), 439–43; Peter R. Ackroyd, "Apocalyptic in Its Social Setting," *Int* 30 (1976): 412; Wayne A. Meeks, *The First Urban Christians: The Social World of the Apostle Paul* (New Haven: Yale University Press, 1983), 172; and Willem S. Prinsloo, *The Theology of the Book of Joel* (New York: Walter de Gruyter, 1985), 86. Disagreement is especially great over what constitutes proto-apocalyptic literature. Thus, Baruch Halpern refers to proto-apocalyptic as a "crepuscular realm" ("The Ritual Background of Zechariah's Temple Song," *CBQ* 40 [1978]: 167). This latter term is discussed below.

9. Paul Hanson, "Apocalypticism," *IDBSup*, 29–30; Klaus Koch, *The Rediscovery of Apocalyptic* (Naperville, Ill.: Allenson, 1972); and John J. Collins, *Daniel with an Introduction to Apocalyptic Literature*, FOTL 20 (Grand Rapids: Eerdmans, 1984), 2–5.

10. For example, Hanson ("Apocalypticism") does not explain why he singles out apocalyptic eschatology, rather than, e.g., apocalyptic dualism. Further, the relationship between Hanson's categories is unclear. Thus, he fails to explain his view that apocalypticism grows out of apocalyptic eschatology. For discussion, see Robert R. Wilson, "From Prophecy to Apocalyptic: Reflections on the Shape of Israelite Religion," *Semeia* 21 (1981): 83. For evidence that the definition of apocalypticism remains unstable, see the references cited in n. 8 above.

of these three aspects of apocalypticism. In each case, I shall not attempt to give any one overarching definition. Instead, borrowing a concept of "family resemblance" from Ludwig Wittgenstein, I shall sketch various resemblances that overlap and crisscross so that the various examples of apocalyptic surveyed form a family. Kenelm Burridge suggests a way of comparing aspects of millennial phenomena reminiscent of Wittgenstein's family resemblance idea:

> Rather than strive for uniformities . . . it would surely be more fruitful to look for pertinent differences. In one situation, for example, factors a,b,c,d,e,f, might seem to be present; in another situation factors c,e,g,h,f, might seem to be present, in a third situation we might find factors a,f,h,i, to be present. . . . Carrying on with such a procedure, looking for differences, specific relations — of which, as yet, we really have small knowledge — might be adduced.[11]

This Wittgensteinian approach is taken up here, and it is used in opposition to the argument that presenting characteristic features of apocalypticism fails to clarify this phenomenon's essential or intrinsic nature.[12] Apocalypticism does not exhibit invariably fixed ingredients, but neither does it have a statable essence. Rather, apocalyptic phenomena share certain specific overlappings and differences, and it is these that I seek to describe.

The Literary Phenomenon

Apocalyptic literature is the aspect of apocalypticism most accessible to the biblical scholar. It is nonetheless difficult to identify and classify apocalyptic biblical and closely related texts. An important advance has been the classification of the genre "apocalypse" as a subcategory of apocalyptic literary phenomena. John J. Collins, who has defined the apocalypse

11. Burridge, "Reflections," 102.

12. For such an argument, which refers to apocalyptic's ideal nature, see Paul Hanson, *The Dawn of Apocalyptic* (Philadelphia: Fortress, 1979), 6–7. In contrast, Wittgenstein found a concept of "family resemblance" helpful in his argument that a word or expression cannot be clarified by trying to state its ultimate essence. Some words do not have a universal definition but are used for a number of referents, which may not have any one feature in common. For example, suppose that *A, B, C, D,* and *E* are five features or elements. The combinations *ABCD, ABCE, ABDE, ACDE,* and *BCDE* may all be called by the same name, even though they have no one of these ingredients in common. They are not classified together based on any statable essence but based on complicated but objective overlappings and differences. See Ludwig Wittgenstein, *Philosophical Investigations,* 3d ed., trans. G. Anscombe (New York: Macmillan, 1958), 32.

genre in terms of form and content, identifies fifteen apocalypses written between 250 B.C.E. and 150 C.E.[13] The Jewish apocalypses include: Daniel 7–12, the *Animal Apocalypse,* the *Apocalypse of Weeks, Jubilees* 23, 4 Ezra, *2 Baruch,* the *Apocalypse of Abraham, 1 Enoch* 1–36, the *Heavenly Luminaries,* the *Similitudes of Enoch, 2 Enoch,* the *Testament of Levi* 2–5, *3 Baruch,* the *Testament of Abraham* 10–15, and the *Apocalypse of Zephaniah.*

Unfortunately, the larger literary category or macro-genre, "apocalyptic literature," is much more fluid than the genre "apocalypse."[14] Nevertheless, within this fluidity certain characteristics recur. These include the major features of dualistic language and the expression of futuristic but imminent eschatology as well as secondary features such as numerology and pseudonymity. Employing the "family resemblance" approach, I shall attempt to describe these features as the best basis for this literature's generic classification.[15]

Dualistic language is seen in such clear distinctions as that between the "Sons of Light" and the "Sons of Darkness" in the Qumran War Scroll and 1 Thessalonians 5:5. 2 Esdras 6:5 also speaks of two groups of people — those who now sin, and those who stored up treasures of faith and are secure for eternity. Besides picturing two opposing moral forces, this literature often contains a metaphysical dualism. Daniel 7, for example, dualistically distinguishes between heavenly and earthly planes of existence, and

---

13. Collins defines apocalypse as "a genre of revelatory literature with a narrative framework, in which a revelation is mediated by an otherworldly being to a human recipient, disclosing a transcendent reality which is both temporal, insofar as it envisages eschatological salvation, and spatial, insofar as it involves another, supernatural world" (John J. Collins, "The Jewish Apocalypses," *Semeia* 14 [1979]: 22).

14. On the idea that genres can be defined both broadly and specifically, see Gene M. Tucker, *Form Criticism of the Old Testament,* Old Testament Guides to Biblical Scholarhip (Philadelphia: Fortress, 1971), 3.

15. It might be objected that this is a return to the approach of D. S. Russell (*The Method and Message of Jewish Apocalyptic* [Philadelphia: Westminster, 1964]; and *Apocalyptic: Ancient and Modern* [Philadelphia: Fortress, 1978], 22). (Cf. Koch, who lists both formal/literary characteristics and typical moods and ideas of apocalyptic literature [*Rediscovery,* 23–33].) Hanson criticizes Russell's approach, arguing that "long lists of random features" fail to describe apocalyptic literature adequately. For Hanson, such lists are confusing and also misleading in that no apocalyptic work incorporates all the features included in such lists (*Dawn,* 6–7). The Wittgensteinian approach taken here, however, is not vulnerable to such an objection. Those texts within the apocalyptic "family" are not argued to share all their features in common. What they share is a "family resemblance." See n. 12 above.

Daniel 10:20 speaks of a battle on the heavenly plane that will affect events on earth.[16] Finally, apocalyptic literature often expresses a dualism between this temporal world and the world to come. Thus, Revelation 21 pictures the present heaven and earth passing away, and the coming of a new heaven and earth and a new Jerusalem.

Eschatology in apocalyptic literature involves an imminent inbreaking by God inaugurating a future age qualitatively different from this age. The eschatology described in Daniel 7:26-27 is thus one of radical transformation and discontinuity. Similarly, the Qumran War Scroll lays out a plan for a coming doomsday battle that will usher in the new world. Apocalyptic literature often contains descriptions of chaos and wars separating this age from the next (for example, 2 Esd. 5:4f.; Rev. 4:1—19:21). A final judgment concludes these battles, determining who will enter the new kingdom and who will not. *1 Enoch* 1:1 refers to this end-time judgment as the "day of distress for the removal of all the wicked." 1 QM 1:5 states that the final judgment will mean the "eternal annihilation of all the lot of Belial."[17]

Other features often found in apocalyptic literature include a visionary manner of revelation. Thus, *1 Enoch* 1:2 speaks of "a holy vision in the heavens which the angels showed me." Apocalyptic visions are reported using extraordinary and exotic images, such as the arrogant goat sprouting many horns in Daniel 8:1-14 or the living creatures with six wings and full of eyes in Revelation 4:6-8. Further, apocalyptic literature frequently expresses notions of determinism and predestination. Apocalyptic texts may thus present an outline of history's predetermined stages. For example, Daniel 7 presents a blueprint for the world's future. The use of numbers and coded terms is also unique, especially in full-blown apocalyptic literature. Revelation 4:4 mentions twenty-four elders; Revelation 5:1

16. The cosmological and mystical tendencies of apocalyptic literature result in its having a different view of heaven and earth than that typically found in ancient Near Eastern literature (e.g., 1 Kings 22, Kirta, and Aqhat). In contrast to Near Eastern texts in general, apocalyptic literature ontologically differentiates heaven and earth and views them as planes of existence that mirror each other. Thus, in apocalyptic literature, terrestrial happenings have a supernatural backdrop. As a result, the earth's problems can be dealt with by actions (such as celestial battles) in the heavenly plane. (See John J. Collins, *The Apocalyptic Imagination: An Introduction to the Jewish Matrix of Christianity* [New York: Crossroad, 1984], 8, 32, 82.) Further, celestial archetypes exist in heaven that provide the patterns for what is to come on earth. (See Gerhard von Rad, *Old Testament Theology*, trans. D. Stalker [New York: Harper & Row, 1965], 2:288.)

17. See Collins, *Apocalyptic Imagination*, 37, 129.

mentions seven seals; in Revelation 8:8 one-third of the sea becomes blood; and in Revelation 13:18 the number of the beast is 666.[18] Angelology, demonology, and an emphasis on a messiah are additional frequent features of apocalyptic literature.

The Worldview

Apocalyptic literature comes from an apocalyptic *Weltanschauung* or type of (religious) thinking.[19] It is not merely a consciously chosen style or literary device. I am not suggesting any easy move from a type of biblical language to the minds of those using the language. We must, however, explain how the mythic-realistic, sometimes even wildly bizarre, language of apocalyptic writings could have been intelligible and important to the groups that wrote and read them.[20]

The form-critical assumption that genres are related to certain social phenomena sheds some light on this question.[21] Worldviews themselves are one facet of such social phenomena because they are created by groups, not individuals.[22] It is within groups that members share and support worldviews.[23] If the mythic and bizarre language and beliefs of biblical and

18. For examples of the tendency of apocalyptic texts to speculate about secret wisdom, see Stone, "Revealed Things," 414–39.

19. Many sociologists explain what is meant by a worldview. For example, see Anthony F. C. Wallace, "Revitalization Movements," *American Anthropologist* 58 (1956): 266–67; La Barre, "Materials for a History," 27; and Mayes, *Old Testament*, 132–33. John Lofland describes a worldview as "an order of things taken for granted about the attributes of objects, events, and human nature . . . [a view of] the real, the possible, and the moral" (*Doomsday Cult* [Englewood Cliffs, N.J.: Prentice-Hall, 1966], 1).

20. Thus, Meeks assumes that the frequent use of end-time language in a document implies that this language was "intelligible and important" to its readers (*Urban Christians*, 171).

21. Discussion of form criticism of apocalyptic literature is resumed below.

22. Thus, Kenelm Burridge argues (against La Barre) that symbols are *not* "adaptive man-made artifacts," but come into being unbidden. See his comments in the "Responses" to La Barre, "Materials for a History," *Current Anthropology* 12 (1971): 28. Graham Allan also stresses that worldviews are not created from a void by individuals but are social phenomena ("A Theory of Millennialism: The Irvingite Movement as an Illustration," *British Journal of Sociology* 25 [1974]: 298).

23. Thus, Mayes writes, "It may be said that the individual's perception of reality depends upon the ongoing support of the social group to which he belongs. . . . This means that the individual cannot maintain a particular view or understanding of reality in complete isolation; without supporting structures, coming to expres-

related apocalyptic writings are to be explained satisfactorily, they must be related to a social setting with a millennial worldview.

We lack knowledge about the social aspect of the apocalyptic texts from the Mediterranean and ancient Near Eastern world. But because the beliefs expressed by biblical and ancient biblically related apocalyptic literature bear such a strong family resemblance to those of groups sociologists refer to as "millennial," we may safely assume that this literature presupposes a parallel millennial *Weltanschauung*. Further, we can begin to flesh out the type of worldview behind biblical apocalyptic texts by outlining the resemblances among the sociological family of millennial groups.

The worldview of millennial groups combines a linear view of history with a futuristic eschatology that pictures an imminent radical change in the way things are.[24] This radical change may involve the expectation of a coming judgment,[25] often including world or cosmic destruction or at least the destruction of a wicked enemy. The millennial Native American group known as the Smohalla cult, for example, claimed that the aging "Earth woman" would soon be destroyed and all whites would be annihilated at the end of time. Similarly, Melanesian cargo-cult prophecies predicted tidal waves that would destroy all Europeans.[26] No matter how the eschaton is

---

sion in meeting, conversation, ritual and so on, beliefs lose their quality of objective reality and so also their claim on the individual" (*Old Testament,* 133). See also Allan, "A Theory," 299.

24. The question of the exact relationship between a millennial worldview and a given viewpoint on eschatology remains problematic. There may be a trajectory from certain eschatological positions to an apocalyptic symbolic universe. Alternatively, a position on eschatology and the worldview may evolve together. (For Hanson's view, see his "Apocalypticism," 30.)

25. For discussion or descriptions that picture a Last Judgment belief as part of a millennial worldview, see Vittorio Lanternari, *The Religions of the Oppressed,* trans. L. Sergio (New York: Knopf, 1963), 204; Justus van der Kroef, "Messianic Movements in the Celebes, Sumatra, and Borneo," in *Millennial Dreams,* 102; and Norman Cohn, *The Pursuit of the Millennium* (New York: Oxford University Press, 1970), 212. By way of contrast, there was little emphasis on a Last Judgment in the Taiping Rebellion, even though this movement had other millennial aspects (see Eugene P. Boardman, "Millenary Aspects of the Taiping Rebellion [1851–64]," in *Millennial Dreams,* 70).

26. See Bryan R. Wilson, *Magic and the Millennium* (New York: Harper & Row, 1973), 279, 334. For discussion and more descriptions that picture this belief as part of millennial worldviews, see ibid., 234, 300; Weston La Barre, *The Ghost Dance: Origins of Religion* (Garden City, N.Y.: Doubleday, 1970), 310; Mircea Eli-

conceived, it is believed imminent,[27] although often presaged by a period of tribulation or messianic "birth pangs."[28] Cosmic portents also act as harbingers of the end.[29]

According to apocalyptic worldviews, this radical changing of the world is accomplished by another, ontologically separate world. This intervention is by a deliverer from outside the world; a resurrection of the dead who may fight alongside the living; or the arrival of a messiah. The millennial Manseren cult in Melanesia, for example, expected the imminent arrival by boat of Manseren Mangundi, a messiah figure who had gained great power by capturing the Morning Star.[30] Whether or not it expects a messiah, the apocalyptic worldview focuses on divine agency in bringing the eschaton.[31]

---

ade, "'Cargo Cults' and Cosmic Regeneration," in *Millennial Dreams*, 139–40; and Lanternari, *Religions of the Oppressed*, 132.

27. For sample illustrations, see Norman Cohn, "Medieval Millenarism: Its Bearing on the Comparative Study of Millenarian Movements," in *Millennial Dreams*, 31; René Ribeiro, "Brazilian Messianic Movements," in *Millennial Dreams*, 56; and B. Wilson, *Magic*, 213.

28. For sample illustrations, see John L. Phelan, *The Millennial Kingdom of the Franciscans in the New World*, 2d ed. (Berkeley and Los Angeles: University of California Press, 1970), 99; Theodore Olson, *Millennialism, Utopianism, and Progress* (Toronto: University of Toronto Press, 1982), 15; van der Kroef, "Messianic Movements," 111; Eliade, "Cargo Cults," 143; and Cohn, *Pursuit*, 136, 212. Illustrations of groups believing in imminent catastrophes heralding doomsday are also found in Kenelm Burridge, *New Heaven, New Earth: A Study of Millenarian Activities* (New York: Schocken, 1969), 78; Lanternari, *Religions of the Oppressed*, 132; and Thomas W. Overholt, *Prophecy in Cross-Cultural Perspective: A Sourcebook for Biblical Researchers* (Atlanta: Scholars Press, 1986), 130.

29. For example, a nineteenth-century millennial cult among the Xhosa in South Africa held that two suns in the sky, a great darkness, and a violent gale would precede the end (B. Wilson, *Magic*, 239). The radical disjuncture between this age and the next may even be marked by the world being turned upside down (see Burridge, *New Heaven*, 50).

30. See Peter Worsley, *The Trumpet Shall Sound: A Study of "Cargo" Cults in Melanesia*, 2d ed. (New York: Schocken, 1968), 127, 131–36; B. Wilson, *Magic*, 202. For other examples and discussion, see George Shepperson, "Nyasaland and the Millennium," in *Millennial Dreams*, 146; van der Kroef, "Messianic Movements," 110; Cohn, *Pursuit*, 111, 136, 142; and Lanternari, *Religions of the Oppressed*, 135.

31. See Bernard Barber, "Acculturation and Messianic Movements," *American Sociological Review* 6 (1941): 663. For discussion or sample illustrations, see Cohn, "Medieval Millenarism," 31; Ribeiro, "Brazilian Messianic Movements," 65; Olson, *Millennialism, Utopianism*, 112; and B. Wilson, *Magic*, 286, 344.

In an apocalyptic worldview, the coming radical change in the world ushers in a qualitatively different existence. Either a cosmic renewal occurs, or a golden age arrives, or the earth is transformed into a paradise. Often, this new world is one in which wishes and hopes are fulfilled.[32] One account of the message of the millennial Native American Ghost Dance of 1890 reads, "Next Spring Big Man (Great Spirit) come. He bring back all game of every kind . . . nobody but Indians everywhere and game all kinds thick."[33] This ushering in of paradise may be a return to the *Urzeit* (primordial time), and the descriptions of the new age may recall old creation myths known to the group.[34] The new-age hope also often expects a resurrection of the dead so the departed will dwell alongside the living in the new world. The message of the 1890 Ghost Dance, for example, included the belief that "Pretty soon . . . all dead Indians come back and live again. They all be strong just like young men, be young again."[35]

Finally, a moral or ethical dualism is usually part of millennial worldviews. The elect are distinguished from the damned "as white from black."[36] They see themselves as a moral elite, qualitatively different from the rest of humanity.[37] This elite may be pictured as a remnant that will

32. For discussion or examples, see van der Kroef, "Messianic Movements," 110; Barber, "Acculturation," 664; Shepperson, "Nyasaland," 146; Burridge, *New Heaven*, 23; and Lanternari, *Religions of the Oppressed*, 205.

33. Quoted in Overholt, *Prophecy in Cross-Cultural Perspective*, 125. For more sample descriptions and discussion of this belief as part of millennial worldviews, see Barber, "Acculturation," 663; Thrupp, "Millennial Dreams in Action: A Report," 12; Eliade, "Cargo Cults," 139, 141; Cohn, *Pursuit*, 108, 213; and B. Wilson, *Magic*, 332.

34. For examples, see Eliade, "Cargo Cults," 142; B. Wilson, *Magic*, 205; and Burridge, *New Heaven*, 50. For illustrations of how millennial groups often recall the old myths or traditions of their culture, see Peter Lawrence, "The Fugitive Years: Cosmic Space and Time in Melanesian Cargoism and Mediaeval European Chiliasm," in *Millennialism and Charisma*, ed. R. Wallis (Belfast, Northern Ireland: Queen's University, 1982), 291; Ribeiro, "Brazilian Messianic Movements," 57; Eliade, "Cargo Cults," 143; Cohn, *Pursuit*, 145; B. Wilson, *Magic*, 209, 300; and Lanternari, *Religions of the Oppressed*, 170, 173, 220, 231, 242, 261.

35. Quoted in Overholt, *Prophecy in Cross-Cultural Perspective*, 125, cf. 128. For further sample illustrations and discussion, see Barber, "Acculturation," 663; van der Kroef, "Messianic Movements," 110; Eliade, "Cargo Cults," 140; B. Wilson, *Magic*, 239, 279, 300; Burridge, *New Heaven*, 79; Lanternari, *Religions of the Oppressed*, 207; and Worsley, *Trumpet*, 95, 102.

36. Burridge, *New Heaven*, 147. See also Cohn, *Pursuit*, 83, 86, 173.

37. See Cohn, "Medieval Millenarism," 38; Cohn, *Pursuit*, 60, 85; and van der Kroef, "Messianic Movements," 111.

survive the imminent judgment or be refined and tested in the coming tribulation. Thus in the millennial Ghost Dance of Tavibo (1870) it was taught that only "believing" Native Americans would be resurrected in the end time.[38] In contrast, millennial groups hate or at least fear those on the other side of the ethical dualism.[39]

The Social Phenomenon

Groups that hold apocalyptic worldviews have definite sociological family resemblances. A third rubric for defining apocalyptic — that of the apocalyptic social institution — should therefore be distinguished from the apocalyptic literary form and the apocalyptic worldview.[40] As with millennial worldviews, my understanding of the social phenomenon of apocalypticism relies on a survey of millennial groups. I did not presuppose any one type of social matrix in choosing groups included in this survey, allowing that any family resemblances might not be at the level of the larger social matrices of the groups examined.[41] Indeed, it is at the group level, rather than at the level of the larger social contexts of the groups, that sociological family resemblances appear.[42]

Robert R. Wilson has outlined the family resemblances between millennial groups.[43] Millennialism is first of all a group phenomenon. Wilson states, "Apocalyptic religion is not an individualistic phenomenon but one which always appears in the context of a cohesive and relatively well organized group. Members of the group think of themselves as a group and

38. See Thomas W. Overholt, *Channels of Prophecy: The Social Dynamics of Prophetic Activity* (Minneapolis: Fortress, 1989), 40. The remnant belief is also seen in the descriptions of millennial worldviews in Cohn, *Pursuit*, 223; B. Wilson, *Magic*, 286; Lanternari, *Religions of the Oppressed*, 132; Overholt, *Prophecy in Cross-Cultural Perspective*, 125; Worsley, *Trumpet*, 135–36; and La Barre, *Ghost Dance*, 212.

39. For discussion or examples, see van der Kroef, "Messianic Movements," 120; Shepperson, "Nyasaland," 145; B. Wilson, *Magic*, 300; and George Simpson, "The Ras Tafari Movement in Jamaica in Its Millennial Aspect," in *Millennial Dreams*, 161.

40. For one good attempt to keep this distinction clear, see Olson, *Millennialism, Utopianism*, 15. Philip R. Davies makes a good argument for confining the term *apocalyptic* to a literary category and using the term *millenarian* or *millennial*, a recognizable social-scientific category, for the associated social construct. See his "The Social World of Apocalyptic Writings," in *The World of Ancient Israel*, ed. R. E. Clements (Cambridge, England: Cambridge University Press, 1989), 253.

41. See n. 5 above.

42. See the discussion on p. 46 below.

43. R. Wilson, "From Prophecy to Apocalyptic," 84–87.

seek to maintain and preserve its structure."[44] The use by many millennial groups of initiation rituals helps strengthen this group identity.[45] Other millennial groups secure a group commitment by requiring that members sell their possessions before joining.[46]

If the group is a highly organized one, it will have orders of personnel within it. This organizational hierarchy often includes a so-called millennial prophet or catalyst figure, a clique of special disciples, and an outer group of followers.[47] In chapter 3 I shall show how tensions and challenges can arise within the group's organization as part of the group's history.

The worldviews of many millennial groups include a vision of the coming new era including specific goals for the group.[48] In settings involving acculturation, the group's goals often include revival or perpetuation of especially valued aspects of their own society's culture.[49] At the same time, the future vision often anticipates that the millennial group will inherit the secrets and abundance of its enemies. Thus, Peter Worsley writes that in the case of the cargo cults, "Melanesians by no means rejected European culture *in toto:* they wanted the White man's power and riches, but they did not want the perpetuation of his rule."[50]

Millennial groups usually believe that their vision and goals will be

44. Ibid., 84. Cf. Olson's comment, "Millennialism's characteristic form is as an organized force within its society, a movement rather than a literary effort undertaken by individuals" (*Millennialism, Utopianism,* 15). That millennialism is a group phenomenon is not surprising given the uniqueness of the millennial worldview and the above argument that such views are not the product of individuals in isolation (see n. 23 above). Further, it can often be inferred from millennial beliefs themselves that they are the product of a group. For example, millennial worldviews expect the coming salvation to be collective, encompassing all the faithful. See Cohn, "Medieval Millenarism," 32; and Boardman, "Taiping Rebellion," 70.

45. For examples of initiation rituals as part of the sociology of some different millennial groups, see Howard Kaminsky, "The Free Spirit in the Hussite Revolution," in *Millennial Dreams,* 167; Worsley, *Trumpet,* 106; Cohn, *Pursuit,* 143; Burridge, *New Heaven,* 27, 65; Ribeiro, "Brazilian Messianic Movements," 66; Boardman, "Taiping Rebellion," 78; van der Kroef, "Messianic Movements," 103; and Shepperson, "Nyasaland," 149.

46. For sample illustrations, see Kaminsky, "Free Spirit," 170; and Cohn, *Pursuit,* 157, 212.

47. See Wallace, "Revitalization Movements," 273; and the references in n. 134 below.

48. See R. Wilson, "From Prophecy to Apocalyptic," 85.

49. For discussion or examples, see Ralph Linton, "Nativistic Movements," *American Anthropologist* 45 (1943): 230–31; Eliade, "Cargo Cults," 142; B. Wilson, *Magic,* 306; and Ribeiro, "Brazilian Messianic Movements," 57.

50. Worsley, *Trumpet,* 44.

realized within a framework provided by a supernaturally revealed timetable of past and future events. Wovoka, the Native American millennial catalyst figure associated with the Ghost Dance of 1890, had such a schema, which contained a description of past events including the creation. His blueprint for the future involved a "renewal" of all good people in the fall of 1890 and a subsequent renewal of everyone in the spring of that year. A resurrection and an enlargement of the earth would follow.[51]

As Robert R. Wilson argues, to realize its goals and find a way of living in the last days of history, the millennial group develops a practical program for action.[52] This practical program may fall anywhere along a continuum from a passive to an active response. A passive program merely provides for the organization of group life, while an active program organizes collective action to help bring on, or at least prepare for, the eschaton. For example, Melanesian cargo cults actively prepared for the arrival of cargo shipments from the ancestors by building wharfs, airstrips, and storehouses.[53]

Another active response involves the performance of special rituals,[54] sometimes involving the creation or readaptation of special temples or cult objects.[55] Thus, in the Ghost Dance millennial movement associated with

51. Overholt, *Prophecy in Cross-Cultural Perspective,* 128; Burridge, *New Heaven,* 79. For further examples of the group vision, chronological schema, or apocalyptic instruction of millennial groups in several different cultures, see Olson, *Millennialism, Utopianism,* 15, 111, 120; Cohn, *Pursuit,* 108; and van der Kroef, "Messianic Movements," 111.

52. R. Wilson, "From Prophecy to Apocalyptic," 86. For examples and discussion, see Donald Weinstein, "Millenarianism in a Civic Setting: The Savonarola Movement in Florence," in *Millennial Dreams,* 199; Cohn, *Pursuit,* 136; Olson, *Millennialism, Utopianism,* 16; B. Wilson, *Magic,* 19; and Gary W. Trompf, "The Cargo and the Millennium on Both Sides of the Pacific," in *Cargo Cults and Millenarian Movements: Transoceanic Comparisons of New Religious Movements,* ed. G. W. Trompf (Berlin: Mouton de Gruyter, 1990), 74–75.

53. See B. Wilson, *Magic,* 312; and Worsley, *Trumpet,* 115, 151, 178, 247.

54. For discussion and examples, see Barber, "Acculturation," 663; Ribeiro, "Brazilian Messianic Movements," 57, 64–65; van der Kroef, "Messianic Movements," 111; Burridge, *New Heaven,* 79; Lanternari, *Religions of the Oppressed,* 132, 153; Overholt, *Prophecy in Cross-Cultural Perspective,* 129; Cohn, *Pursuit,* 133; and B. Wilson, *Magic,* 248, 284, 288, 319. Not all millennial groups center on rituals and rites, however, and not all of these groups can be labeled cults. For an illustration, see Karlene Faith, "One Love — One Heart — One Destiny: A Report on the Ras Tafarian Movement in Jamaica," in *Cargo Cults and Millenarian Movements,* 329–30.

55. For sample illustrations, see B. Wilson, *Magic,* 319; Worsley, *Trumpet,* 84; Burridge, *New Heaven,* 17; and Lanternari, *Religions of the Oppressed,* 254.

Wovoka, groups performed a ceremony in which the members moved slowly around a central tree. During this dance many of the participants experienced a trance state in which they visited the world of the dead.[56] In other cultures, glossolalia is often reported to be a part of millennial ritual practices.[57]

The practical program of millennial groups may involve the partial or almost complete separation of the group from their world. Sometimes, but not always, groups physically separate from society to build rafts or move into shelters.[58] Other millennial groups leave their communities to hold an extended vigil while awaiting the eschaton.[59] Alternately, millennial groups may separate themselves in preparation for doomsday by refusing to work, destroying stockpiles of food, or spending all their savings. For example, in late-nineteenth-century New Guinea, a millennial catalyst figure named Tokeriu predicted a gigantic tidal wave that would submerge the whole coast. In response to his message, the people killed and ate three hundred to four hundred pigs, exhausting their reservoirs of wealth.[60] This action was an act of faith in the belief that the end had almost arrived, that God would provide abundant food for them once the new era began.

Because the eschatology of millennial groups stresses the total sovereignty of God in the coming cataclysm or war, these groups often do not take up arms.[61] Nevertheless, the practical programs of active millennial

56. Overholt, *Prophecy in Cross-Cultural Perspective,* 123.

57. See van der Kroef, "Messianic Movements," 102–3, 116; B. Wilson, *Magic,* 203, 249; and Jean Guiart, "The Millenarian Aspect of Conversion to Christianity in the South Pacific," in *Millennial Dreams,* 124.

58. For examples of millennial groups that built shelters or rafts, see Worsley, *Trumpet,* 101, 102, 139. For discussion or examples of millennial groups that do not physically separate themselves, see Simpson, "Ras Tafari Movement," 161; and Cohn, *Pursuit,* 160–61.

59. See van der Kroef, "Messianic Movements," 89; Simpson, "Ras Tafari Movement," 162; Kaminsky, "Free Spirit," 170, 171; Cohn, *Pursuit,* 212, 216; Burridge, *New Heaven,* 23; B. Wilson, *Magic,* 334; and David F. Aberle, "A Note on Relative Deprivation Theory as Applied to Millenarian and Other Cult Movements," in *Millennial Dreams,* 214.

60. Worsley, *Trumpet,* 51–53; cf. 69, 111. For discussion and further examples of giving up work or consumption of savings, see Eliade, "Cargo Cults," 142; Simpson, "Ras Tafari Movement," 162; Cohn, *Pursuit,* 217; B. Wilson, *Magic,* 201, 239, 316, 332; Burridge, *New Heaven,* 23; Lanternari, *Religions of the Oppressed,* 172–73, 246; and La Barre, *Ghost Dance,* 213, 306.

61. See B. Wilson, *Magic,* 196, 275, 285–86, 311; Faith, "One Love," 329; and Worsley, *Trumpet,* 232.

groups sometimes stress preparation for military action.[62] Sometimes the end-time war is still understood as fought by God, the group's military preparations being viewed as merely symbolic.[63] In other cases where group members make preparations for actual fighting, the group at least believes that the coming conflict will be carried out under supernatural control and protection. Thus, Sioux millennial groups involved in military conflicts with whites wore so-called ghost shirts, believed invulnerable to bullets.[64]

With respect to the relationship of ethical concern to millennialism, millennial groups tend to exhibit either blatantly unethical behavior and antinomianism or extreme self-control and discipline. Thus, some millennial group programs encourage members to engage in activities (such as orgies, drinking, or stealing) that go against their culture's norms.[65] Burridge understands such experimentation with "no rules" as compatible with the millennial self-understanding of being in a transition phase between this world and the next.[66] Thus, some millennial groups see themselves as living in an inverted world, or as already beginning to enjoy an existence that transcends the social conventions of this age.

It would be untrue to argue, however, that millennial groups characteristically lack morality. Millennial group programs, in fact, often stress ethical diligence.[67] Because the end-time judgment and new age are imminent, such diligence can be seen as especially warranted. Thus, apocalyptic language is frequently attested as a context of parenesis.[68] Wayne Meeks

62. For millennial group programs involving preparation for a battle, see Boardman, "Taiping Rebellion"; Simpson, "Ras Tafari Movement," 162; Cohn, *Pursuit,* 75, 139; B. Wilson, *Magic,* 221–71; and Lanternari, *Religions of the Oppressed,* 241, 254–55, 260.

63. See Ribeiro, "Brazilian Messianic Movements," 66; and Gary W. Trompf, "Introduction," in *Cargo Cults and Millenarian Movements, 7.*

64. Overholt, *Prophecy in Cross-Cultural Perspective,* 132 n. 7.

65. See van der Kroef, "Messianic Movements," 111; Eliade, "Cargo Cults," 142; B. Wilson, *Magic,* 334; Burridge, *New Heaven,* 65, 112; and Cohn, *Pursuit,* 217.

66. Burridge, *New Heaven,* 166.

67. See B. Wilson, *Magic,* 226, 232, 307, 332; Burridge, *New Heaven,* 79; Lanternari, *Religions of the Oppressed,* 152; Overholt, *Prophecy in Cross-Cultural Perspective,* 128, 130–31; Ribeiro, "Brazilian Messianic Movements," 66; and van der Kroef, "Messianic Movements," 103. New Testament apocalyptic texts that stress ethical behavior include 1 Thess. 4:6; 5:1-8; and Rom. 14:10.

68. As Collins writes, "By evoking a sense of awe and instilling conviction in its revelation of the transcendent world and the coming judgment, the apocalypse

notes how ethical behavior sometimes also results from the community cohesion generated by an apocalyptic worldview. When group members are disposed to act for the community's well-being, internal discipline and obedience of leaders result.[69]

"Proto-Apocalyptic"

The term *proto-apocalyptic* has arisen from attempts to trace the origins of Jewish apocalyptic eschatology. Paul Hanson sees proto-apocalyptic eschatology as part of a continuum from prophetic eschatology into apocalyptic eschatology.[70] I do not assume such a continuum, but I retain the term *proto-apocalyptic* for the following reason.[71]

Some Persian-period Israelite literature exhibits the family resemblances found in more elaborate form in the Jewish apocalyptic texts written after 250 B.C.E. At the same time, this literature is different from subsequent apocalypses. The regularities and accepted features of these later works only developed with time. Further, the early biblical apocalyptic texts were not informed by many of the significant ideas and motifs found in the Hellenistic apocalypses. For example, Persian-period texts such as those in Isaiah and Zechariah do not emphasize a general resurrection (but see Isa. 26:19) or a judgment of the dead (but see Isa. 24:21-22), as Daniel and *1 Enoch* do.[72] For these reasons, the earlier literature requires a special designation recognizing its distance both from nonapocalyptic visionary literature (such as Amos's vision-cycle) and full-blown apocalyptic literature (such as the visions of Daniel).[73] I accept the term *proto-apocalyptic* as this designation.

I shall therefore use the term *proto-apocalyptic* to describe those Persian-

---

. . . creates the preconditions for righteous action" (*Apocalyptic Imagination*, 46, cf. 5, 7).

69. Meeks, *Urban Christians*, 175.

70. Hanson, *Dawn*, 27; "Apocalypticism," 32; *Old Testament Apocalyptic* (Nashville: Abingdon, 1987), 33.

71. See chapter 1 for discussion of the problems of viewing prophetism as the mother of apocalypticism.

72. E.g., Dan. 12:2 and *1 Enoch* 90:31-36 (see Collins, *Apocalyptic Imagination*, 20). Such differences are due in part to Hellenistic influence. Collins writes, "It is important that several of the most prominent aspects of the [full-blown] apocalypses involve modifications of biblical tradition that are in accord with widespread ideas of the Hellenistic age" (*Apocalyptic Imagination*, 28).

73. See Seybold, *Bilder zum Tempelbau*, 105; Robert North, "Prophecy to Apocalyptic via Zechariah," VTSup 22 (1972): 70–71; and Samuel Amsler, "Zacharie et l'origine de l'apocalyptique," VTSup 22 (1972): 229.

period religious texts, viewpoints, and practices that have clear affinities with the full-blown apocalypticism found in the subsequent Hellenistic and Roman periods.[74] The use of this term here, however, should not be taken as implying acceptance of any typology presupposing a trajectory from prophetism to apocalypticism.

A Critique of the Causal Theory of Deprivation

Problems with the Original Concept of Deprivation

The sociological concept of deprivation originally had to do generally with unsatisfactory economic conditions or at least the existence of a social setting involving other observable lacks or stresses.[75] Deprivation commonly involves a group's being dispossessed or kept from those things that it needs and expects to have. Early deprivation theorists viewed this observable type of social matrix of deprivation as the cause of millennialism. When biblical scholars examine biblical apocalyptic groups as alienated and disenfranchised, they are presupposing this original causal explanation.

It has become clear that this general concept of deprivation is inadequate to account for the phenomenon of millennialism. Too many millennial groups are not observably deprived. List 1 provides examples of millennial groups that cannot be accounted for by the original concept of deprivation. Many such millennial groups that are associated with the upper echelons of society have been overlooked by anthropologists. This is because, as Worsley notes, these groups are not usually associated with mass movements, which may appear more interesting to study.[76]

List 1. Examples of Nondeprived Millennial Groups

1. The Free Spirit millennial sects, which arose in Europe from the thirteenth century onward, included people from the privileged strata of society as well as less affluent members of the intelligentsia. For example, some of the Free Spirit Brethren came from wealthy, well-established family backgrounds.[77] The Free Spirit millennial prophets

---

74. See Collins, "Jewish Apocalypses," 29.

75. In 1941, Bernard Barber defined deprivation as "the despair caused by inability to obtain what the culture has defined as the ordinary satisfactions of life" ("Acculturation," 664).

76. Worsley, *Trumpet*, xl.

77. Cohn, *Pursuit*, 159.

appealed especially to idle women from the elite of urban society.[78] This is not a case of the uprooted or the poor banning together in order to compensate for their frustrations.

2. A little-known millennial group was that headed by the Wirsberg brothers in Europe in the 1450s and 1460s. These brothers, Janko and Livin of Wirsberg, acted as millennial catalyst figures despite the fact that they were rich and powerful.[79]

3. Members of every class and occupation were involved in the millennialism that spread through Florence at the end of the fifteenth century. The millennial catalyst figure here, the famous civic reformer Savonarola, put forward a worldview that spoke to political officials and the upper class as well as to the poor.[80] Donald Weinstein, a major expositor of Savonarolan millennialism, writes that it was surely "a case of millenarianism that did not arise out of the protests of the poor and cannot be explained by economic crisis."[81] In this case, millennialism was not the religion or worldview of the deprived. Rather, Savonarola's millennial group instruction was taken up as the basis for the civic program of the Florentine republic itself.

---

78. Cohn, "Medieval Millenarism," 37. Even though these women were from the upper class, some will argue that their gender placed them among the deprived. Often, deprivation approaches interpret millennialism among women as their means of compensating for their lack of power in a male-dominated culture. As Hillel Schwartz writes, "Deprivation theories maintain that women, an injured group, use religion as a means to power otherwise denied them by patriarchies" ("Millenarianism, An Overview," in *The Encyclopedia of Religion* [New York: Macmillan, 1987], 9:528). In Schwartz's view, however, this judgment represents an injustice in that it reduces females' religion in general to something merely reactive and compensatory. One could counter deprivation approaches here by pointing out that several female millennial catalyst figures have exercised an active and creative religion (e.g., Guglielma of Milan, Donna Beatrice, Joanna Southcott, Ellen Gould White, Jacobina Maurer, and Kitamura Sayó).

79. Cohn, *Pursuit,* 233.

80. Donald Weinstein writes: "Florentines of every class and occupation — former friends of Lorenzo and Piero de'Medici, . . . patricians as well as *popolani* — were among those who ardently believed that Savonarola spoke with divine authority and that his prophecy of world renewal radiating from Florence was soon to be fulfilled, indeed within the lifetime of many who heard him" (*Savonarola and Florence: Prophecy and Patriotism in the Renaissance* [New Jersey: Princeton University Press, 1970], 30).

81. Weinstein, "Civic Setting," 187, cf. 203.

4. A well-known brand of millennialism of the Middle Ages was that of Joachim of Fiore (c. 1135–1202 C.E.). No special deprivation or crisis occurred in Calabria, where Joachim revived Christian millennialism. As Theodore Olson writes, "At most, one can suggest that Joachim found the exegetical practices of the period inadequate to support his need to understand the shape of the scriptures as a whole."[82] This situation hardly counts as deprivation. The rise of Joachimism, the movement that based itself on Joachim, was not associated with deprivation either. Rather, the Franciscan Spirituals who were at the center of the movement were made up largely of people who had abandoned great wealth.[83] Norman Cohn writes, "The Spirituals were drawn mainly from the more privileged strata of society, notably from the mixture of noble and merchant families which formed the dominant class in Italian towns."[84]

5. Joachimite millennialism spawned a millennial group among the sixteenth-century Spanish colonizers of New Spain. Gerónimo De Mendieta, a Franciscan friar, led this millennial group, which acted on behalf of Spain's monarchy. During the reign of Charles V, Mendieta's group held episcopal, governmental, and economic power.[85] Far from being deprived or oppressed, Mendieta himself described the Spaniards as the "whales" and the natives as the "sardines."[86]

6. The Skoptzi millennial sect in Russia, as well, did not arise among peripheral groups or among the economically marginalized. The sect included noblemen, state officials, and the rich among its members.[87] Even though the sect was not caused by economic or class-status deprivation, its worldview was clearly millennial. The group expected an

---

82. Olson, *Millennialism, Utopianism,* 119.

83. The assumption of many deprivation approaches that poverty always involves discontent and resentment is open to criticism. Sometimes, as in Joachimism, the rich believe it is blessed to be poor. The Kshatriyas' conversion to Jainism involved a similar dissatisfaction with wealth (see the discussion on pp. 51–52 below). Of course, discontent is not always the reason why people abandon wealth. Thus, the belief that wealth will be unnecessary in the imminent new world often motivates millennial groups to abandon money and possessions (see the references cited in n. 60 above). Note that such abandonment of wealth by those joining a millennial group secures their group commitment (see n. 46 above).

84. Cohn, "Medieval Millenarism," 35.

85. Phelan, *Franciscans,* 54.

86. Ibid., 61, 97.

87. La Barre, *Ghost Dance,* 256.

imminent judgment that would usher in the millennial kingdom. One uniqueness of the group's beliefs was their conviction that the millennial kingdom would be sexless. As a preparation for this, the group's millennial plan included the castration of all males.[88]

7. The seventeenth-century Jewish messianic movement led by Sabbatai Ṣevi is another group whose cause cannot be explained either in terms of economic deprivation or in terms of observable stresses such as class tensions.[89] After Sabbatai Ṣevi revealed himself as the Messiah in May 1665, he attracted a following that included burghers and elders, wealthy merchants, and rabbinic scholars.[90] It cannot be argued that persecution of Polish and Russian Jews was an important cause in the rise of the movement.[91] Rather, as Gershom Scholem states, "The messianic wave swept no less over communities that had had no immediate experience of oppression and bloodshed than over those which had."[92] For example, in the prosperous Jewish community in Amsterdam, the messianic enthusiasm was just as great as in other communities. In fact, it was precisely those communities that were least poor or persecuted that led in the propagation of the Sabbatian millennial beliefs.

8. The well-to-do Irvingite Catholic Apostolic Church, which formed in nineteenth-century Britain, was not caused by deprivation; its general membership was of the middle or upper class.[93] The leaders of the

---

88. Cohn, "Medieval Millenarism," 40. Cf. Gal. 3:28.

89. The basic source for understanding this movement is Gershom Scholem, *Sabbatai Ṣevi: The Mystical Messiah 1626–1676* (Princeton, N.J.: Princeton University Press, 1973).

90. Ibid., 391–92. Yonina Talmon comments, "We find among the adherents members of all strata of society, ranging from wealthy merchants, who offered to donate their entire fortune to the Messiah, to the poorest of the poor" ("Millenarism" [sic], in *The International Encyclopedia of the Social Sciences* [New York: Macmillan Company and Free Press, 1968], 10:358).

91. The view that the persecution and massacres of Polish Jewry were instrumental in causing the Sabbatai Ṣevi movement is found in Cohn, "Medieval Millenarism," 32–33.

92. Scholem, *Sabbatai,* 461.

93. See George Shepperson, "The Comparative Study of Millenarian Movements," in *Millennial Dreams,* 49. For discussion of the Irvingite movement as contradicting the usual assumptions made about millennialism, see Allan, "A Theory," 296–311. For a thorough description of the Irvingites, see P. E. Shaw, *The Catholic Apostolic Church Sometimes Called Irvingite: A Historical Study* (Morningside Heights, N.Y.: King's Crown, 1946).

group in particular belonged to the elite of society and some were members of the wealthiest classes. P. E. Shaw describes these leaders, the so-called Irvingite apostles, as follows: "Were they a persecuted company of people, or such as had not made good in the world, it would be easy to account for [their belief that they would be rulers in the millennium] in terms of psychological compensation."[94] In fact they were neither poor nor persecuted: One of these so-called apostles, Frank Sitwell, owned Barmoor Castle in Northumberland, and John Bate Cardale, held to be the founder of the group, was affluent too.[95] A third "apostle," Henry Drummond, was one of the wealthiest persons in England. Further, Drummond was a member of Parliament and belonged to aristocratic circles.[96] Even more than wealth, membership in England's gentry or aristocracy meant great status, and several Irvingite leaders shared this distinction with Drummond. Thus, Spencer Perceval, another Irvingite "apostle" who served in Parliament, was also of aristocratic family.[97] He was descended from the fourth earl of Northampton. His fellow Irvingite Thomas Carlyle joined the titled gentry when he received the dormant title of Baron Carlyle in 1824.

9. Modern Western culture also provides examples of millennial groups that have not suffered empirically observable deprivations. For instance, the Brotherhood of the Sun, a late-twentieth-century millennial group in Santa Barbara, California, owned a chain of supermarkets and warehouses as well as a central headquarters on a 4,000-acre ranch. The millennial catalyst figure of the group, Norman Paulsen, had an annual personal salary of $150,000.[98] Burridge writes, "By and large, the participants in Californian apocalyptic, charismatic, and prophetic movements do not reveal those relative deprivations, frustrations, etc. so beloved by so many students of the phenomena."[99]

94. Shaw, *Catholic Apostolic Church*, 231.

95. Ibid., 82, 72. Cardale's father, William Cardale, was a solicitor who possessed considerable property.

96. Ibid., 73–74, 83. Originally a wealthy commoner, Drummond married Lady Henrietta Hay, eldest daughter of the ninth earl of Kinnoull. Further, Drummond's grandfather was Lord Melville, and his son-in-law was Lord Lovaine, Duke of Northumberland.

97. Ibid., 78, 80. Note that Perceval was the eldest son of the British prime minister (1809–1812) of the same name. The prime minister, who was the son of the second earl of Egmont, was shot May 11, 1812.

98. Trompf, "Cargo and the Millennium," 35–57.

99. Burridge, "Reflections," 102.

10. Former President Ronald Reagan has received much publicity for his great interest in the apocalyptic sections of the Bible and his belief in an imminent global cataclysm.[100] Reagan is held to have identified elements of the international scene during his tenures in public office with biblical apocalyptic figures and references. G. Clark Chapman, Jr., reports that "While governor of California, in 1971 Reagan startled guests at a formal dinner by launching an interpretation of Ezekiel 38–39: . . . 'Gog must be Russia' . . . 'It can't be long now.'"[101] Later when president of the United States, Reagan said in a 1983 phone conversation: "I turn back to your ancient prophets in the Old Testament and the signs foretelling Armageddon . . . believe me, they certainly describe the times we're going through."[102]

"Relative" Deprivation as Also Inadequate

In 1959, in an attempt to add sophistication to deprivation as an explanatory principle, David F. Aberle developed his notion of relative deprivation. By adding the term *relative,* he widened the concept of deprivation to encompass any uneven relation between expectations and means for satisfaction as well as objective hardship or oppression.[103]

Aberle defined relative deprivation as "a negative discrepancy between legitimate expectation and actuality."[104] He contended that this new concept of relative deprivation accounts for much more of the data than previous concepts of objective deprivation. I want to argue that this more sophisticated concept of relative deprivation is still inadequate for understanding the cause and nature of millennialism.

An initial problem with relative deprivation theory is that of *nonoccurrence:* Aberle's concept is unable to predict millennialism.[105] Even docu-

---

100. Yehezkel Landau, "The President and the Prophets," *Sojourners* 13/6 (June-July 1984): 24–25; and Danny Collum, "Armageddon Theology as a Threat to Peace," *Faith and Mission* 4/1 (1986): 61–62.

101. G. Clark Chapman, Jr., "Falling in Rapture Before the Bomb," *The Reformed Journal* 37/6 (June 1987): 13.

102. Quoted in Landau, "The President," 24.

103. David F. Aberle, "The Prophet Dance and Reactions to White Contact," *Southwestern Journal of Anthropology* 15 (1959): 74–83; Aberle, "A Note on Relative Deprivation Theory."

104. Aberle, "A Note on Relative Deprivation Theory," 209; see also Aberle, "Prophet Dance," 79.

105. Already in 1941 Barber admitted there was no "one-to-one relation" between deprivation and millennialism ("Acculturation," 667). See also Burridge,

mented disasters that cause objective deprivation may not provoke a millennial response. Typhoon Ophelia, which hit Ulithi in Micronesia in 1960, did not provoke any millennial groups.[106] Social arenas displaying economic and social deprivation may not produce millennial groups either. René Ribeiro notes that millennial movements have not formed among blacks in Brazil, although this group is at the lower end of the social ladder and has endured severe deprivations.[107] Similarly, the Sabbatian movement (see List 1, item 7) did not gain more supporters or spread more quickly in areas of persecution or economic deprivation than in prosperous and free areas.[108] If objective deprivation has little predictive value for millennialism, relative deprivation, which is more common, has even less. In my judgment, the problem of nonoccurrence weakens the strength of the correlation between deprivation and millennialism and suggests that, at best, deprivation may merely precipitate other more direct causes of millennialism.[109]

New Heaven, 74; H. Silvert (contributor), "Current Anthropology Book Review: The Religions of the Oppressed: A Study of Modern Messianic Cults by Vittorio Lanternari," *Current Anthropology* 6 (1965): 456; Thrupp, "Millennial Dreams in Action: A Report," 26–27; Michael Adas, *Prophets of Rebellion: Millenarian Protest Movements against the European Colonial Order* (Chapel Hill: University of North Carolina Press, 1979), 92–93; and Virginia H. Hine, "The Deprivation and Disorganization Theories of Social Movements," in *Religious Movements in Contemporary America,* ed. I. Zaretsky and M. Leone (Princeton, N.J.: Princeton University Press, 1974), 653. Aberle recognizes this problem with relative deprivation theory: "The fact of deprivation is clearly an insufficient basis for predicting whether remedial efforts will occur, and, if they occur, whether they will have as aims changing the world, transcending it, or withdrawing from it" ("A Note on Relative Deprivation Theory," 211).

106. See the discussions of an article by W. A. Lessa in La Barre, "Materials for a History," 22; and *Ghost Dance,* 281.

107. Ribeiro, "Brazilian Messianic Movements," 64.

108. Talmon, "Millenarism," 358; Scholem, *Sabbatai,* 461.

109. On the problem of lack of correlation, see Hine, "Deprivation," 653. Critics of Aberle have suggested other possible precipitating factors for millennialism besides deprivation and distress. Leslie Spier, Wayne Suttles, and Melville J. Herskovits query, "Is there no other possibility [than relative deprivation]? Aberle admits such a possibility but it would seem that he holds it merely theoretical. But there is no reason why, without deprivation, a cult may not originate and flourish for the sake of realizing the desire for the return of the beloved dead or for the return of an earlier day" ("Comment on Aberle's Thesis of Deprivation," *Southwestern Journal of Anthropology* 15 [1959]: 86).

An even stronger problem with relative deprivation theory involves its inherent elasticity, which raises the problem of circular argument.[110] The theory is much too easily applied: almost any group can be seen as relatively deprived.[111] This being the case, it is too easy for adherents of deprivation theory to apply their interpretation in every case of millennialism, even when empirical warrants are not obvious.

The deprivation explanation becomes not an empirical observation but a principle of interpretation: on principle, some basis for a group feeling of relative deprivation is teased out of each millennial group examined, because millennial groups are defined from the outset as relatively deprived. This criticism of circularity is put forcibly by Sylvia L. Thrupp: "As with Freudian theory, proponents [of the deprivation explanation] have to base their case on faith that if we had perfect information, all of the facts would fall consistently into place as they wish."[112]

110. This problem becomes clear from Bryan Wilson's discussion of what he sees as a difficulty in applying relative deprivation theory. He writes, "The external and objective indices of deprivation stand in uncertain relationship to the sense of deprivation which individuals experience. The only evidence for such 'felt' deprivation, in [some cases may be] . . . the behavior that follows" (*Magic*, 289). But there is a great danger of circular argument if group behavior is used as the evidence of a preceding feeling of deprivation, and the latter is then evoked to explain the former.

111. Burridge makes the same point when he describes the difficulty in suggesting conditions in which a millennial movement might seem unnecessary. Burridge writes, "In short, since the central issue is the ennoblement of the nature of man, there are no known conditions which would render millenarian activities unnecessary" (*New Heaven*, 117). Thus some authors even stretch the elastic "deprivation" category to include the person "who becomes satiated with the economic and social rewards of life" (see the discussion in Hine, "Deprivation," 654).

112. Thrupp, "Millennial Dreams in Action: A Report," 26. An illustration of the problem of elasticity and circularity can be taken from the anthropological debate over millennialism (here, the Plateau Prophet Dance) among Coast Salish tribes living near Vancouver Island. As part of this debate, Aberle defended his deprivation interpretation by appealing to the *possibility* of indirect as well as direct contacts with Western culture ("Prophet Dance," 82). In a response to Aberle's defense, Spier, Suttles, and Herskovits argued that there was no positive evidence backing up Aberle's suggestion of the possibility of deprivation due to contact with whites. Neither epidemics nor acculturation were present in the data base as obvious sources of a feeling of relative deprivation. Thus, Aberle's critics argued that his position amounted merely to an argument that whites at a remote distance *may* have had some "ill-defined" effect on the native tribes (Spier, Suttles, and Herskovits, "Comment," 85). In other words, Aberle was applying a principle of interpretation, teasing out the possibility of deprivation. Aberle's critics agreed that, of

A final major problem with relative deprivation theory is its reductionism. Advocates of the theory often assume that millennialism is an unhealthy or pathological phenomenon within a closed social system. Many Western scholars, especially those with a naturalistic worldview, consider the millennial belief in a new world a delusion.[113] These scholars then logically search for a crisis situation, or at least a feeling of frustration or deprivation, that can account for such a "pathological" response.[114] This assumption is open to criticism.

First, there is no evidence that those holding millennial worldviews must suffer from a psychopathology.[115] This view is a kind of prejudice in which scholars take their own established position as an assumed healthy norm.[116] Thus, Burridge, reacting against this view of millennialism as a

---

course, the Coast Salish may well have had unfulfilled dreams and wishes. They held, however, that the only way to argue that these latter types of feelings constituted "deprivations" would be to extend the meaning of deprivation "so as to make it nearly synonymous with any kind of frustration" ("Comment," 87).

113. The naturalistic presupposition of many scholars can be illustrated by the statement of Bryan Wilson that "Magic does not work; the millennium will not come" (*Magic*, 500). Given this presupposition, scholars such as Aberle, Cohn, and Lanternari tend to explain millennial beliefs as some sort of delusion or compensatory mechanism (see Olson, *Millennialism, Utopianism*, 84 n. 2). Hillel Schwartz has stressed that this problematic presupposition is rampant in millennial studies. Schwartz counters, "One can no longer type apocalyptic feelings as pre-modern or dysfunctional" ("The End of the Beginning: Millenarian Studies, 1969–1975," *RelSRev* 2/3 [1976]: 6). For an attempt to get beyond naturalism and positivism in the use of sociology in biblical studies in general, see Mayes, *Old Testament*, 120–28.

114. For cases where millennialism is viewed as unhealthy, irrational, or deluded, see Cohn, *Pursuit*, 88; B. Wilson, *Magic*, 317, 327, 337; and La Barre, *Ghost Dance*, 317. An example can again be taken from the remarks of B. Wilson: "Millennialism must be irrational, of course: the causal explanation of what is predicted makes leaps beyond the bounds of legitimate inference, and presents prospects which defy all previous experience (when objectively viewed and with full knowledge). The fantasies of fairy stories persist in western society, and now demythologized, religious representations of man's past and future are tolerated: these are the repositories of millennial dreams in the western world" (*Magic*, 338). For discussion of the "irrationality" issue, see Worsley, *Trumpet*, lxvi; and Burridge, *New Heaven*, 123–24.

115. See Ribeiro, "Brazilian Messianic Movements," 68; Burridge, *New Heaven*, 122; Thrupp, "Millennial Dreams in Action: A Report," 17; and Schwartz, "Millenarian Studies," 5.

116. See Overholt, *Channels*, 35 n. 23; and Worsley, *Trumpet*, lxvi, 266–72.

kind of social pathology, states that the "vocabulary of relatively deprived, frustrated, and so on" is a view "to be expected of scholars securely ensconced in an established station."[117]

Second, the assumption that millennialism as a pathological effect must have a material cause (that is, some imbalance within the social system) is misguided. This argument is based on a positivistic conception that all phenomena within a social system can be explained by ironclad laws of cause and effect. But this conception is an example of blatant reductionism. To cite Hillel Schwartz, such a view has no room for the paradoxical and for imbalances within society.[118] It incorrectly sees society as a closed system in which social "energy" is never created or destroyed.

Schwartz argues that millennialism is not an effect, balanced against an actual or perceived wrong in society, within such a closed universe.[119] Millennial "outbursts," like the new wealth created by an entrepreneur, may stem from newly emergent creative "energy." This more holistic approach allows that a millennial group may result from something as simple as a group realization of the variety of available worldviews. Such a realization would allow for the propagation of a new and radically different symbolic universe. In other cases, the emergence of a millennial worldview may be best described in terms of religious motives. Genuine beliefs and motives caused the Sabbatian movement. Because people believed that the Messiah had come, their whole world waxed and waned.[120]

When biblical scholars infer from deprivation theory that a particular social milieu *causes* the millennial groups that produce apocalyptic literature, they adopt from this reductionistic model a view of the relationship between a literary form and its setting foreign to the assumptions of traditional form criticism.[121] Form criticism does not presume to address the

117. Burridge, "Reflections," 100.

118. H. Schwartz, "End of the Beginning." Cf. Olson's remark about relative deprivation theory: "The growth and renewal of millennialism in both ancient and modern times is far too complex to be dealt with adequately at this simple level of causation" (*Millennialism, Utopianism,* 84 n. 2). Similarly, La Barre insists that "crisis cults" have complex causes ("Materials for a History," 26–27).

119. H. Schwartz, "End of the Beginning," 7. Also see the discussions in Mayes, *Old Testament,* 126, 129; and Vittorio Lanternari, "Nativistic and Socio-religious Movements: A Reconsideration," *Comparative Studies in Society and History* 16 (1974): 497.

120. Scholem, *Sabbatai,* 392, 462–63. Savonarolan millennialism (see List 1, item 3) was also due more to "real faith" than to a social crisis, according to Weinstein (*Savonarola,* 59).

121. Ferdinand Deist, for example, can be criticized along these lines. See his "Prior to the Dawn of Apocalyptic," in *The Exilic Period: Aspects of Apocalypticism,*

ambitious question of the "cause" of specific genres or forms (*Gattungen*). The relationship between a linguistic convention and its setting is too complex to be reduced to setting as cause and *Gattung* as effect.[122] Form criticism has the more modest task of identifying the repeating social occurrence in which a particular linguistic form achieves an intention.[123]

Consider the relationship of the prophetic announcement of judgment to its *Sitz-im-Leben*. The form of a prophet's judgment announcement and the way it is delivered *are* affected by the delivery setting and society's constructs and expectations, but the society and setting are not the cause or basis of the message's transmission. The message results from a perceived experience of a divine revelation or contact with the supernatural. Because prophetic activity occurs in different environments and locales, it cannot be viewed as caused by any one of these settings. Neither a specific socioeconomic environment nor a given locale (such as a street corner or a

---

OTWSA 25/26 (1982/1983), 14. The early form critics did not talk about the *Sitz-im-Leben* as a causative matrix. Indeed, Hermann Gunkel never resolved the issue of the exact relationship of form and setting. For example, it is not clear from his writings whether places always generate sagas or whether preexisting sagas sometimes only later get tied down to places. Similarly, though Hugo Gressmann held sagas to be place-bound, his work shows nuances in how various sagas are attached to given places. See Hermann Gunkel, "Fundamental Problems of Hebrew Literary History," in *What Remains of the Old Testament* (London: George, Allen & Unwin, 1938), 57–68; "Die Israelitische Literatur," in *Die Kultur der Gegenwart, Teil I, Abteilung VII: Die Orientalischen Literaturen,* ed. P. Hinneberg (Berlin: Teubner, 1906), 51–102; *Genesis,* 5th ed. (Göttingen: Vandenhoeck & Ruprecht, 1922); and Hugo Gressmann, *Mose und seine Zeit* (Göttingen: Vandenhoeck & Ruprecht, 1913), 121ff., 291ff.; "Sage und Geschichte in den Patriarchenerzählungen," *ZAW* 30 (1910): 1–34.

122. Certain behaviors, speech, and literary genres do have conventional or stereotypical status within recurring situations. The conventions are not simply effects of their settings, however. Cross-cultural variation in conventions calls into question the existence of such a cause-and-effect relationship. For example, the mealtime situation does not "cause" the fork to be held in the right hand: in England, one holds the fork in the left hand while eating. Further, the fact that genres can migrate weakens the idea that they are causally linked to their settings. The setting of a form's language may be different from the setting where it is employed. Here, the new setting cannot be the cause of the stereotypical or generic aspects of the language employed. Finally, although settings help determine linguistic forms, linguistic forms also have a determining effect on their settings (see Klaus Koch, *The Growth of the Biblical Tradition: The Form-Critical Method,* trans. S. M. Cupitt [New York: Macmillan, 1969], 27). Again, there is no simple cause-and-effect relationship here.

123. See Koch, *Growth,* 27; and Tucker, *Form Criticism,* xi.

temple) can be claimed as the cause of prophetic messages. We do not ask what setting "causes" phenomena such as prophecy or preaching. Similarly, we are asking the wrong question if we inquire what setting causes an apocalyptic vision.

A More Critical View of the Origins of Millennialism

The Proper Level of Focus Is the Millennial Group. The deprivation approach to the form criticism of apocalyptic texts has oversimplified the relationship between text and setting, and also adopted from sociology too broad an understanding of setting.[124] Form criticism, for its part, does not focus on the question of the wider socioeconomic factors and environments that may influence or, in some philosophies, even cause human actions and thoughts. It is concerned with the narrower sphere of life or institution, whose regulations and needs influence and form associated manners of speech and writing.[125] To understand the sermon genre, one does not look for commonality among the various denominations and societies within which worship occurs. Rather, one looks to the narrower institution of worship itself. By the same token, form-critical analysis of apocalyptic literature should concern itself with the institution of the millennial group as the sociological level that exhibits the most commonality among the many examples of millennial religion.

Positive Motivating Factors Must Be the Focus of Investigation. Different types of social arenas harbor millennial groups — commonality is found only at the narrower group level. Therefore, millennial groups cannot be characterized as always arising in *reaction* to a situation of deprivation. This discovery helps us do justice to millennial groups' creative and *active* aspects. This is an important corrective, because deprivation theory has too long viewed millennial religion only in negative or compensatory terms.[126] By the same token, the factors motivating millennialism have been viewed too one-sidedly as lacks or negative elements. Constructive or active moti-

---

124. For a cautious approach to using sociology to facilitate the form-critical task, see Robert R. Wilson, *Sociological Approaches to the Old Testament,* Old Testament Guides to Biblical Scholarship (Philadelphia: Fortress, 1984), 24, 82.

125. See Koch, *Growth,* 27; and Hermann Barth and Odil Hannes Steck, *Exegese des Alten Testaments: Leitfaden der Methodik* (Neukirchen-Vluyn: Neukirchener Verlag, 1971), 56.

126. For discussion, see H. Schwartz, "Millenarianism," 9:528. Similarly, Hine writes, "In refining the concept of deprivation, both Aberle and Glock seem at times to be going out of their way to avoid the possibility of positive motivation!" ("Deprivation," 654).

vating factors are characteristically present behind millennial groups, and these have been insufficiently explicated. Therefore, future investigation should focus on millennial groups and their positive causes. After all, the creative activity of the millennial institution, not an amorphous deprivation void, is what produces apocalyptic literature.

One actual positive factor allowing for millennialism is a belief predisposition. Simply put, a millennial group will not form unless the belief that apocalyptic events can happen is allowed.[127] Thus, the traditions or literature carried by the group must allow for a radical inbreaking of God. At the least, the group must have a linear view of history and believe in a God outside of history.[128]

Beyond this, potential millennial groups are often further predisposed.[129] Events can call currently held worldviews into question creating cognitive dissonance — a situation ripe for millennialism. For example, the Irvingites (see List 1, item 8) arose in an atmosphere predisposed toward millennialism.[130] As the millennial group was coming into existence, an outbreak of glossolalia occurred in Scotland. At the same time, eschatological expectations were raised by the sermons of Rev. James Stewart, a traveling preacher.[131] Finally, the recent revolutions in Europe were taken as a sign of a great apostasy that God would not tolerate. The French Revolution aimed at "liberating" humanity from religion and royal authority. The Revolution, which ushered in years of instability in the rest of Europe, horrified the upper-class supporters of the English crown.[132] Indeed, the events they observed around them contradicted their mundane view of the world, creating a mood of apocalyptic tension.

Similarly, before Sabbatian millennialism arose, a predisposition for belief in the imminence of the Messiah's arrival was excited by kabbalism. Indeed, by the seventeenth century, kabbalism had created a widespread

127. Cf. R. R. Wilson's related discussion of the social prerequisites of intermediation (*Prophecy and Society*, 28–32).

128. Linton's observation is correct: "A devout society will turn to nativism . . . long before a skeptical one will" ("Nativistic Movements," 238).

129. See B. Wilson, *Magic*, 315.

130. Shaw, *Catholic Apostolic Church*, 26.

131. Ibid., 64.

132. Ibid., 65–67; Ernest R. Sandeen, "Millennialism," in *The New Encyclopaedia Britannica*, 15th ed. (Chicago: Benton, 1974), 12:203; and Allan, "A Theory," 304. The French Revolution became, in fact, a European revolution that involved many national movements against royal authority. For example, Greece revolted against the Ottoman Empire, Hungary created a nationalistic government, and riots against Austrian imperial rule occurred in Vienna.

expectation that apocalyptic events were imminent.[133] As a result, a predisposition toward millennial belief was rife both among the common people and in the writings of leading rabbis.

Given such a predisposition, a catalyst such as an influential literary work, or a teacher, or a visionary is often a second positive motivating factor in the rise of millennialism.[134] Such a catalyst brings any latent eschatological expectations to the surface, acts as a symbol for the group, and helps to bring an apocalyptic group-vision to a focus.[135] The millennial

---

133. Saadia Gaon's *Book of Beliefs and Opinions* (written c. 935 C.E.) was an important source of the much later excitement. It was translated into Hebrew in 1186 and was influential until the eighteenth century. For discussion, see Scholem, *Sabbatai*, 8, 12; and Talmon, "Millenarism."

134. For discussion or examples of the millennial catalyst figure, see Linton, "Nativistic Movements," 232; Wallace, "Revitalization Movements," 270; Cohn, "Medieval Millenarism," 38, 42; Ribeiro, "Brazilian Messianic Movements," 56; van der Kroef, "Messianic Movements," 117–18; Adas, *Prophets of Rebellion*, 92–93; and B. Wilson, *Magic*, 201, 223, 327. Thomas W. Overholt writes, "While I acknowledge the complexity of this problem and would not want to be party to the kind of 'reductionism' La Barre finds to be 'rampant in crisis cult studies' . . . I find myself wondering whether the presence of a prophetic-type leader is not the critical element in the emergence of a 'crisis cult'" ("Model, Meaning, and Necessity," *Semeia* 21 [1981]: 129). Against Overholt, I prefer to speak not of a prophet or leader, but of a catalyst. A catalyst is not always necessary for a reaction to take place, but is an agent that hastens this result. Further, the catalyst is not always a person, nor do all millennial groups have an extraordinary leader at their center. On these latter points, see George W. E. Nickelsburg, "Social Aspects of Palestinian Jewish Apocalypticism," in *Apocalypticism in the Mediterranean World and the Near East*, ed. D. Hellholm (Tübingen: J. C. B. Mohr, 1983), 648; Roy Wallis, "Introduction," in *Millennialism and Charisma*, 2; and Faith, "One Love," 328–29.

135. See Meeks, *Urban Christians*, 173; Burridge, *New Heaven*, 29, 98, 111, 164; and Worsley, *Trumpet*, xiii, xvii. The problems with relative deprivation theory become even more apparent when it is realized that sometimes a millennial catalyst or recruiter himself creates the so-called feeling of deprivation in prospective group members through sharing and promoting a millennial view. For example, Howard Kaminsky has argued that in Taborite millennialism, stress and tension were created by the movement itself and were not causal factors that preceded it. (Kaminsky's claim was part of the conference discussion reported by Thrupp, "Millennial Dreams in Action: A Report," 21.) By the same token, observers have reported that recruitment in Sun Myung Moon's Unification Church often involves teasing out and amplifying any dissatisfactions with life that can be found in a prospective member. For example, see Wallis, "Introduction," 7. Hine similarly reports a study

catalyst figure often seizes upon the ancient myths of the group and integrates them into a linear view of world history. An apocalyptic worldview is generated as mythic paradigms are fused with a futuristic type of world-historical thinking.[136] Alternatively, if apocalyptic traditions are accessible to the group, catalysis may involve giving these traditions a central place in the group's consciousness. Thus, the worldview of an older apocalyptic writing may undergo recrudescence when the work is drawn on for guidance at a time of worldview reconstruction. Because familiarity with apocalyptic traditions and writings usually reflects systematic study, scribalism can be an important factor in the formation of a millennial group.

In the case of the Irvingites, Edward Irving's preaching of a coming cataclysmic end provoked a new universe of meaning among his predisposed group. This new symbolic universe better fit the group's experience, accounting for the glossolalia and the European revolutions. At the same time, it also consisted of beliefs and values incompatible with the group members' older worldview.

Advantages of a Worldview Theory over Deprivation Theory. A focus on positive factors that allow for a group's new apocalyptic worldview overcomes the deprivation model's tendency toward psychological explanation. This tendency is reductionistic, making millennialism look like a coping mechanism. Also, because *deprivation* is a psychological term, focusing on individuals' feelings and psyches, by itself deprivation theory does not allow sociologists to discuss group issues and group formation. Thus, scholars have tried to combine deprivation theory with other approaches, like cognitive dissonance theory, in order better to move from individuals' psychological states to group attempts at resolving psychological turmoil

---

showing that deprivation is an effect of millennial group dynamics and not a precondition that can explain millennialism ("Deprivation," 655).

136. Apocalyptic thinking projects the *Urzeit* into a future beyond history. Thus, since Gunkel's time, apocalyptic thinking has been described as eschatologized myth (see Frost, "Apocalyptic and History," 99). Frost accepts this view, seeing apocalyptic thought as caused by a blending of "historiological" thought and "mythological" thought (ibid., 105). Similarly, Talmon describes apocalyptic worldviews as created by "a merger between a historical and a non-historical conception of time" ("Millenarism," 10:351–52). Also see Collins, *Apocalyptic Imagination,* 40. It is important to distinguish this cognitive phenomenon from the use of mythic images in the pre-apocalyptic sections of Ezekiel and Isaiah 40–55. These sections still have faith in history.

through worldview reconstruction.[137] Scholars' new sociological sophistication, however, in fact renders deprivation theory unnecessary.
Worldviews, the creation of groups, not individuals, are indeed social phenomena;[138] but groups re-create worldviews for various reasons and not
only in reaction to conditions of deprivation. Thus, focusing on what facil-
itates a group's creation of a new apocalyptic worldview helps push our
sociological understanding of millennialism forward, as long as we remem-
ber that deprivation is not always at issue.

Data such as that of List 1 above show that deprivation is not a necessary cause of a group's creation or adoption of an apocalyptic worldview.
The evidence shows that a change in worldview can take place among
many kinds of groups, even among groups in power who do not feel resentment like those in a setting of deprivation. This is not incredible. Sociological studies reveal that people with power and high social rank often
develop and hold worldviews seemingly inconsistent with their status.[139]
Thus Andrew D. H. Mayes can note the suggestion that, "In the framework of a differentiated society, it may be that apocalyptic eschatology is
an ideology quite incongruent with the social status of those who adhered
to it, since people can and do hold belief systems inconsistent with their
place in society."[140] Furthermore, though the elite of a society are most
well-off, their hopes and wishes often transcend a mere desire to maintain
the realized status quo. Upper-echelon figures are quite capable of desiring

137. See the discussion above in chapter 1, pp. 14–16.

138. See n. 22 above. Thus, the sociologist will find focusing on millennial
worldviews helpful in linking apocalyptic beliefs and thinking to a millennial
group's vision and plan of action. In the case of the Irvingites, it is easy for the
researcher to see a logical sociological chain leading from their millennial
worldview to their group vision and calculations about the end of time (see Shaw,
Catholic Apostolic Church, 186) to their practical plans for living in the final days of
the universe (see ibid., 234).

139. For example, B. Wilson notes that magical patterns of thought may persist
among a society's elite stratum: "The belief in 'money-doubling' among Cabinet
ministers in Ghana was revealed in some of the political intrigues during the government of Kwame Nkrumah" (*Magic,* 193 n. 42). The Cable News Network has
reported that the president of Bolivia similarly holds a mythical perspective (news
report, May 28, 1991). By the same token, astrology was found to have played a
role in some of President Reagan's decision-making. See S. Roberts, "White House
Confirms Reagans Follow Astrology, Up to a Point," *New York Times,* May 4, 1988,
p. A. 1, col. 5; and the editorial by N. Wade, "Your Stars for the 80's: The Age of
Aquarius Isn't Over Yet," *New York Times,* May 5, 1988, p. A. 30, col. 1.

140. Mayes, *Old Testament,* 16–17.

major changes in or even the overthrow of the system they control.[141] These figures may come to embrace a worldview that anticipates such changes.

A paradigm illustration of how a central and power-holding group can adopt a radically new religion or worldview is found in Burridge's discussion of the founders of Jainism.[142] The founders of Jainism in the sixth century B.C.E. were from the upper strata of society. They were aristocrats drawn from the Kshatriya category of persons, which was composed of warrior and ruler. Further, Jains were part of the financial elite of society. They were the bankers of India and had always been extremely wealthy people. Despite the fact that the Kshatriyas were in power, they were led to question their current assumptions so radically that a group of them underwent a reconstruction of their worldview.

The integrity of the Kshatriya universe of meaning began to break down due to purely internal and subjective factors. According to their worldview, their own category of persons did not have access to *Moksha,* the religious goal of absorption into Being itself. External oppression or deprivation was not at issue; rather, interior turmoil arose as members of this elite stratum of society began to experience revulsion at their own social category. Burridge describes Jainism as a "revulsion on the part of Kshatriyas against continuing to be Kshatriyas."[143]

Kshatriya predisposition for a worldview change manifested itself objectively in the successive appearance of new religious teachers propounding new ideas. Eventually, a catalyst figure arose who disseminated a religious view that embodied the new assumptions and convictions about redemption increasingly necessary to many Kshatriyas. The catalyst figure here was Mahavira, a founder of Jainism, who is described by Burridge as a guru, a prophet or teacher.[144] In holding that *Moksha* was open to anyone,

---

141. David Rockefeller, for example, has founded a private group known as the Trilateral Commission, which is trying to alter radically the world economic system. As originally conceived, the Trilateral Commission was bent on uniting East and West into a new world-system. It is now concentrating on the task of drawing the Japanese into a closer relationship with their American and European counterparts. Clearly, although the group members are an elite group of capitalists from upper-echelon international circles, they are trying to alter the present world-system. For reports on some group meetings, see L. Silk, "Trilateralists' Confident Tone," *New York Times,* May 21, 1986, p. D. 2., col. 1; and "Global Appeal of Capitalism," *New York Times,* May 23, 1986, p. D. 2, col. 1.

142. Burridge, *New Heaven,* 86–96.

143. Ibid., 93.

144. Ibid., 151.

Mahavira paved the way for a new religion, Jainism, for the Kshatriyas. Conversion to Jainism involved a radical change in orientation for the aristocrats. It involved substituting unworldliness for worldliness and the giving up of wealth so as to become mendicants. The founding of Jainism may thus serve as a paradigm of how a group in power may undergo a radical change in their symbolic universe.

Implications for Analysis of Millennial Groups in Power

The discussions of this chapter prepare us to move ahead in our study of millennial groups. The definitions and descriptions worked out in the first section will help determine whether selected biblical texts are proto-apocalyptic literature and allow us to fill in gaps in our knowledge concerning the groups and worldviews behind these texts.

The groundwork for a more critical analysis of those biblical proto-apocalyptic texts that may have been produced by millennial groups in power was offered in the second section. The examples of List 1 show that we need not assume that all biblical proto-apocalyptic texts were produced by marginal or disenfranchised groups. Even a setting of relative deprivation need not be at issue for all biblical apocalyptic texts. The millennial group, the *Sitz-im-Leben* of apocalyptic literature, is motivated by factors that occur with or without deprivation.

This result is allowed for by the general findings and results of form criticism. Form criticism allows that recurring situations or settings will involve both constant and variable elements. The variability can often be a function of the different communities and the different religious and political conditions in which recurring settings are found. In other words, form criticism links a genre to a given kind of institution, social occurrence, or group, but the concrete occurrence of an actual institution or group will vary in accordance with its social environment or arena.[145] Deprivation is a variable that may or may not be part of an arena in which millennialism occurs.

---

145. Form criticism identifies the *Sitz-im-Leben* with what is common and typical among a group of comparable concrete situations, which at the same time may be various and indeed quite different. See Hans Werner Hoffmann, "Form — Funktion — Intention," *ZAW* 82 (1970): 342; and Koch, *Growth*, 28. Koch gives the example of the mission sermon with its setting in early Christian missionary preaching. He notes that this setting never occurred in the abstract, but only in different communities under varying circumstances.

The following schematization summarizes these observations.[146] Because *Sitze-im-Leben* do not occur in the abstract, but as concrete situations, we must allow that such situations will vary. In the schema, the capital letters *A, B,* and *C* designate the variety of social environments or arenas that accounts for some of this variableness. I therefore define a social arena as a spectrum of social, economic, religious, and political components that will affect the concrete expression of a *Sitz-im-Leben*. One way to think of such an arena is as an overarching context for concrete situations.

Chart 1. Components of Setting in Form Criticism

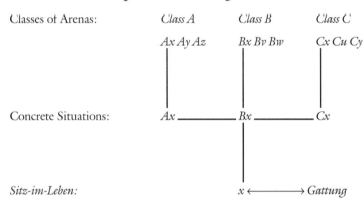

Classes of Arenas: *Class A*   *Class B*   *Class C*

                                    Ax Ay Az   *Bx Bv Bw*   *Cx Cu Cy*

Concrete Situations: *Ax* ———— *Bx* ———— *Cx*

Sitz-im-Leben: $x \longleftrightarrow$ *Gattung*

Note that concrete situations are designated in the schema by a combination of an upper- and lowercase letter. The lowercase letter, the same in each situation, represents the *Sitz-im-Leben*. Form criticism links a given *Gattung* to a specific *Sitz-im-Leben*. The term *Sitz-im-Leben* designates what is constant or common (represented here by the element x) among a group of comparable concrete situations.[147] By designating the concrete situations as *Ax, Bx,* and *Cx* in this way, the schema also illustrates the argument that recurring concrete situations may appear in a variety of social arenas. The influence of the larger arena is indicated by the capital letter in each of the respective designations.

This form-critical schematization provides a framework for understanding the fact that millennial groups can occur in social arenas that lack observable deprivations including the upper strata of a society. The millennial group, like the other social occurrences, institutions, and groups that constitute the *Sitze-im-Leben* of form criticism, will occur in a variety of

146. The schematization here was inspired by the somewhat different one in H. Hoffmann, "Form — Funktion," 343.

147. Ibid., 342.

larger social arenas. No social stratum or type of social contact configuration can be ruled out *a priori* as a possible social arena or matrix for millennialism. When the positive factors discussed above occur, groups undergo millennial catalysis within a variety of larger social environments (arenas like those designated by *class A, class B,* and *class C* in the above schema).

3

Millennial Groups in Power

The reassessment in chapter 2 of deprivation theory has paved the way for the constructive task of elucidating the sociology of millennial groups in power. Clarification of these particular millennial groups should provide several working hypotheses about their nature and sociology. These hypotheses can then be tested against biblical proto-apocalyptic texts apparently produced by groups in power in late-exilic and postexilic Israelite society.

Before elucidating their sociology, I must clarify what it means to consider certain millennial groups to be power-holding or socially central. This question, however, leads to the discovery that millennial groups may be so considered in a variety of ways. Defining and mapping this variety will prepare us to identify biblical power-holding millennial groups and to designate and distinguish their social matrices more precisely.

Although a major task is thus to explicate the variety of possible social arenas for millennial groups in power, further questions are at issue as well.[1] In this chapter I shall also investigate the question of the leadership of millennial groups in power. Evidence here provides an important correction to Paul Hanson's position, outlined in chapter 1, because it shows that a society's priests can be involved in the leadership of millennial groups. Another important topic involves the question of the relation of

---

1. For discussion of the kinds of information to be collected and compared when analyzing millennial groups, see Sylvia L. Thrupp, "Millennial Dreams in Action: A Report on the Conference Discussion," in *Millennial Dreams in Action: Essays in Comparative Study,* ed. S. Thrupp (The Hague: Mouton, 1962), 13.

power-holding millennial groups to other groups both inside and outside their own society. Finally, there is the question of the career of millennial groups in power, specifically, the kinds of ways these millennial groups change over time.

Varieties of Social Arenas

As I showed in chapter 1, a major question in understanding the sociology of the biblical proto-apocalyptic texts is whether the groups that produced these texts were central or peripheral. This issue is more complicated than is often supposed. Usually the terms *central* and *peripheral* designate a social position relative to the basic institutions of one's own society.[2] Central institutions maintain the traditional values and uphold the order of that society.[3] In situations where one's own society encounters or clashes with another, however, the concepts of central and peripheral may be viewed from another perspective. In a situation involving one society dominating another, the central institutions of the dominated society may well appear (to both the dominated and the dominating) as peripheral over against those of the dominating society.[4] Clearly in such cases, the centrality issue depends very much on the perspective one takes. Thus, in order to avoid ambiguity, the social context relative to which a group is central or peripheral must be stated when categorizing the group's milieu.

2. I. M. Lewis provides some important parameters for understanding the concept of *peripheral* in his discussions of possession cults. See his *Ecstatic Religion* (New York: Routledge, 1971), 27–31. Lewis states, "Our own contemporary experience of fringe protest groups and cults should help us to appreciate what is involved here" (p. 27). See also Lewis's "Spirit Possession and Deprivation Cults," *Man* n.s. 1 (1966): 307–29. David L. Petersen sums up Lewis's concept of peripheral as meaning, "Of secondary importance when compared with the central institutions of society, and when compared with the classes of highest status in the society" (*The Roles of Israel's Prophets*, JSOTSup 17 [Sheffield, England: JSOT Press, 1981], 44).

3. See Robert R. Wilson, *Prophecy and Society in Ancient Israel* (Philadelphia: Fortress, 1980), 83–85. Also important is his discussion in *Sociological Approaches to the Old Testament*, Guides to Biblical Scholarship, ed. G. Tucker (Philadelphia: Fortress, 1984), 74–75.

4. Cf. the interesting discussion of the Ghost Dance as both central and peripheral in Thomas W. Overholt, *Prophecy in Cross-Cultural Perspective: A Sourcebook for Biblical Researchers* (Atlanta: Scholars Press, 1986), 16–18. Charles H. Long considers that indigenous cultures become part of the periphery of "the great mercantile Western centers" as a consequence of Western impact ("Cargo Cults as Cultural Historical Phenomena," *JAAR* 42 [1974]: 406).

It seems clear that at least two main logical divisions must be considered in categorizing millennial groups as either central or peripheral. The first is based on whether the social environment of a group involves one culture alone (an endogenous condition) or two cultures in contact (an exogenous condition). The other main logical division is based on the social position of a group in its own society. Chart 2 schematizes millennial groups' social environments based on these two divisions. In the pages following the chart, the categories or classes that result from these divisions will be illustrated by the actual examples named in the chart:

Chart 2. *Classes A through F*

	Endogenous Condition	Exogenous Condition	
		dominating/ colonizing	dominating/ colonized
	Class A	*Class B*	*Class C*
Group is Central in Own Society	Irvingites Coast Salish Sabbatian Movement	Spanish Franciscans	Ghost Dance The Dreamers Savonarola's Florence
	Class D	*Class E*	*Class F*
Group is Peripheral in Own Society	Doomsday Cult Medieval Flagellants	Early American Puritans	Wodziwob's Initial Group

Exogenous Conditions

Probably the most commonly discussed social arena of millennial groups is the exogenous one in which two different cultures come into contact (the second and third columns of Chart 2). Unlike some authors, I do not use the term *exogenous condition* as part of any argument that a clash between cultures causes millennialism.[5] Rather, I delineate one perspective from which a group may be seen as either central or peripheral: those cases where a millennial group's social matrix involves a conflict with

---

5. As is clear from the preceding chapter, acculturation or contact crises cannot be said to be the general cause of millennialism; however, such crises can be aspects of arenas in which millennial worldviews are found. For discussion, see Weston La Barre, *The Ghost Dance: Origins of Religion* (Garden City, N.Y.: Doubleday, 1970), chap. 9.

another, often ethnographically distinct, society or culture.[6] In such cases, one of the two cultures is often considered oppressed or marginalized by the other that has dominated or colonized it.

A study of groups in this type of arena produces at least two significant findings. The first is that millennial groups *do* occur on the dominating or colonizing side of clashes between two societies. The second is that even millennial groups that are part of dominated cultures may be groups in power nonetheless, central from the perspective of their own society.

Class F (Dominated and Peripheral — see Chart 2). Class F appears as one logical category, if one considers possible arenas for millennial groups in terms of a group's status within its own society and that society's possible relationship to alien societies. Like class D, discussed below, a group in a class F arena cannot be considered as central or in power from either per-spective.

The first Ghost Dance of 1870 began in a class F social environment. The Ghost Dance was a nineteenth-century millennial movement with a distinctive dance ritual that arose in the western United States among Na-tive Americans. The catalyst figure of the first Dance, Wodziwob (also known as Tävibo), was a Paiute from near Virginia City, Nevada. An exog-enous milieu is indicated because this millennial movement arose in the midst of years of increasing interference in native culture by whites. At the same time, the millennial catalyst figure here arose within the periphery of his Native American society, and his worldview was not at first accepted by that society.[7] Clearly, such a class F arena does not help explicate the sociology of millennial groups in power.

6. Vittorio Lanternari develops such a distinction between endogenous and ex-ogenous conditions in "Nativistic and Socio-religious Movements: A Reconsidera-tion," *Comparative Studies in Society and History* 16 (1974): 483–84.

7. While in the mountains, Wodziwob was given a vision by the Great Spirit of an imminent huge earthquake. The earthquake would supernaturally destroy all white people but would leave their material goods, houses, and possessions for the Native Americans (see La Barre, *Ghost Dance,* 227). This vision formed the basis for a worldview that expected a coming millennium that would include the restora-tion of scarce game animals and other necessary components of traditional Paiute life (see Thomas W. Overholt, *Channels of Prophecy: The Social Dynamics of Prophetic Activity* [Minneapolis: Fortress, 1989], 82). Returning from the mountains, Wod-ziwob received largely negative feedback from his own society. Apparently, too much faith was required to believe that such a massive earthquake could destroy all the whites and yet leave the Native Americans alive. Wodziwob's society by and large was even more skeptical that any earthquake could destroy the whites but

Class C (Dominated but Central). The predominance of deprivation theory has diverted attention from the fact that millennial groups under dominated conditions may, from the perspective of their own society, be central groups that hold political or social power. That this has not been emphasized is especially disturbing because a great many millennial groups may be considered central in this fashion. For example, many of the millennial groups associated with the Ghost Dance — which, next to the cargo-cult phenomenon, is probably the best known variety of millennialism — occur within a class C social environment.[8]

As part of the second, so-called Great Ghost Dance of 1890, representatives from many different tribes came to learn the message of the messiah, Wovoka. These representatives brought the message of this Native American savior back home, and the accounts of informants imply that whole tribes received it well.[9] From at least one perspective, then, the Ghost Dance can be considered central, for it became the majority voice in the society.

One well-known example of a Native American chief who was also a millennial catalyst figure spreading the second Ghost Dance movement was Sitting Bull. Sitting Bull, chief of the Hunkpapa band of the Teton Dakota Sioux, definitely held central military and political power in his society.[10] At the same time, he promulgated the Ghost Dance worldview and stubbornly advocated military action by his group against the whites.[11]

---

leave the whites' dwellings and goods for the Paiutes. It took Wodziwob at least two more trips to the mountains in order to modify his proclamation before he gained a respectable following within his society. In sum, in its beginnings Wodziwob's millennial group must be seen as peripheral in a society that in turn was peripheral over against white society.

8. Even the Melanesian cargo cults often originate in class C arenas, in that their catalyst figure is usually a potential "big man" who has high status in the society. See Bryan R. Wilson, *Magic and the Millennium* (New York: Harper & Row, 1973), 315; and Overholt, *Prophecy in Cross-Cultural Perspective*, 306 n. 9. For discussion of cargo movements as having central functions (such as reasserting central values), see Overholt, *Prophecy in Cross-Cultural Perspective*, 298.

9. Overholt records an informant's account that two to four representatives came from each of fifteen or sixteen different tribes to see Wovoka. Mooney observed that Wovoka's worldview spread to four-fifths of the tribes of the mountains and the great plains. See the texts reprinted from Mooney's accounts in Overholt, *Prophecy in Cross-Cultural Perspective*, 125–35.

10. See La Barre, *Ghost Dance*, 230, 232.

11. See Vittorio Lanternari, *The Religions of the Oppressed*, trans. L. Sergio (New York: Knopf, 1963), 63, 155.

The fact that he had participated in the Custer massacre helped to reinforce his conviction that a Native American victory was possible. This belief was proved false by the Native American massacre at Wounded Knee.

The class C type of arena for millennial groups is also attested by the cult of the Dreamers that arose in Washington and Oregon in the nineteenth century.[12] The beginnings of this group are found in the preaching of Chief Smohalla, a millennial catalyst figure. Smohalla envisioned a coming resurrection of the dead, who would greatly aid in a military victory over the whites. This victory would usher in a millennium in which the Native Americans' land would be restored.[13]

Smohalla's nativism reinforced central Native American values. He advocated Native American social patterns while opposing white agriculture and domesticated animals: "You ask me to cut grass and sell it, and be rich like white men! But how dare I cut off my mother's hair?"[14] The claim to central status of this case of millennialism was strengthened when its worldview was taken up by a large number of Native Americans and gained the support of Chief Joseph of the Nez Percé. Under Chief Joseph's direction, Smohalla's worldview was actualized as the military plan of a group of tribes. These tribes conducted a well-known war in Idaho in 1877, a war they eventually lost.

Savonarola's Florence (noted in the preceding chapter) provides a different type of example of millennialism in a central group holding power in a threatened or dominated society.[15] Savonarola was a millennial catalyst figure who came to prominence in Florence in the late fifteenth century. The fact that Florentine territory was threatened at the time by a more powerful French government suggests that we are dealing with a class C arena, although the issue here is not acculturation but military threat.

12. This cult was one of the offshoots of the Prophet Dance of the Northwest, the movement that also lay behind the Ghost Dance of 1870 (Wodziwob's movement) and the Ghost Dance of 1890 (Wovoka's movement). See La Barre, *Ghost Dance*, 215–16.

13. For a description, see Lanternari, *Religions of the Oppressed*, 127.

14. Quoted in La Barre, *Ghost Dance*, 219.

15. See Donald Weinstein, "Millenarianism in a Civic Setting: The Savonarola Movement in Florence," in *Millennial Dreams*, 187–203; and *Savonarola and Florence: Prophecy and Patriotism in the Renaissance* (New Jersey: Princeton University Press, 1970). Hillel Schwartz has noted that Weinstein's portrait of Savonarola reveals the "complexity of millenarian hopes" ("The End of the Beginning: Millenarian Studies, 1969–1975," *RelSRev* 2/3 [1976]: 4). Also see the description in La Barre, *Ghost Dance*, 255–56.

Savonarola himself may be considered to have been a central figure in Florentine society. Even before the military crisis of 1494 in which the French invaded Italy and threatened Florence, Savonarola was a revered public figure. He headed an influential church body and cooperated closely with the regime of Piero de' Medici, the head of the Florentine republic.[16] Although a central priest of Florentine society, Savonarola saw the French invasion of 1494 as an apocalyptic doomsday event associated with the outpouring of God's wrath. Indeed, before the actual invasion, Savonarola had been making predictions of a coming period of end-time tribulations for Florence. Later, Savonarola looked back on the invasion as "the opening of the fifth age of the world, the age of Antichrist and of the universal conversion to Christianity."[17]

A second stage in the career of Savonarolan millennialism began as the old Medici regime disintegrated in the wake of the French invasion. When the political leaders of Florence began to revolt against Medici's government, they sent Savonarola to negotiate with the invading French king, Charles VIII.[18] Savonarola successfully averted a military confrontation through these negotiations, greatly increasing his prestige. This placed Savonarola in a position to influence the formation of the new republic that replaced Medici rule. Many of the elite of Florentine society supported Savonarola's rise to power. Donald Weinstein writes of Savonarola's millennial support group, "They had been prominent under the Medici regime, they were active in the Savonarolan republic, and they remained in the forefront of public life."[19]

Savonarola's decisive millennial influence on the central planning of a sovereign territory is significant in any attempt to understand millennial groups in power. Savonarola achieved the status of statesman and lawgiver in the new post-Medici republic.[20] In fact, Savonarola saw his role as akin to that of Haggai and Zechariah in the Old Testament. Just as these leaders

---

16. Savonarola may be considered to have been a central priest within Florence in that he held a powerful and dignified church post and had close relations with the Archbishop of Florence (see Weinstein, *Savonarola,* 110). On Savonarola's support by the royal court and his access to the Medici circle, see ibid., 100, 128.

17. Weinstein, "Civic Setting," 194.

18. For details, see Weinstein, *Savonarola,* 72, 115.

19. Weinstein, "Civic Setting," 187.

20. For this assessment, see Weinstein, *Savonarola,* 77. Weinstein argues that Savonarola was involved politically in the new regime to a great extent, though he did not take on a political post (ibid., 272–74).

rebuilt the temple, Savonarola saw himself leading the Florentines to a new civic order.[21] He did indeed have a decisive influence on the creation of the new constitution in Florence.

There is no doubt that Savonarola's civic plan was a millennial group program based on his millennial vision. This vision included at its center the expectation of an imminent millennial kingdom in which Florence would hold center stage, even upstaging Rome in political and religious importance. Savonarola proclaimed that in the imminent golden age, "Florence will be more glorious, richer, more powerful than she has ever been."[22] Savonarola thus had a clearly millennial view of a coming eschatological reign of the Spirit in which Florentine leadership would play a decisive role, and this vision became the basis for the civic plan of a sovereign republic.

Class E (Dominating but Peripheral). The class E type of arena of millennial groups is an important counterexample to the common understanding of millennialism as a religion only of the oppressed.[23] In some modern theories, millennial groups are thought of as contact cults, groups within a dominated or colonized society. In fact, however, such groups may occur among a *dominating* people as well. The existence of such reverse contact cults shows that it is not only the conquered or colonized who can exhibit millennialism but also the colonizers. Weston La Barre suggests this possibility when he writes, "If, on the one hand, crisis cults are common among the deprived and dispossessed, on the other hand, even politically dominant nations and elites are not untroubled by eschatological anxieties."[24] Hillel Schwartz goes even farther than La Barre when he states: "If millenarianism is the religion of the oppressed, it is no less the religion of the oppressor. What prompts the oppressed to envision a new moral order is likely to be the same as what, some decades earlier, prompted the oppressor to move on or over."[25]

The seventeenth-century English Puritans in America illustrate how a millennial group can be both colonizing in relation to another society and

21. See ibid., 142, 168.

22. Quoted in Weinstein, "Civic Setting," 195.

23. As in the English title of Lanternari's *The Religions of the Oppressed* (see n. 11 above).

24. Weston La Barre, "Materials for a History of Studies of Crisis Cults: A Bibliographic Essay," *Current Anthropology* 12 (1971): 15.

25. Hillel Schwartz, "Millenarianism, An Overview," in *The Encyclopedia of Religion,* ed. Mircea Eliade (New York: Macmillan, 1987), 9:525.

peripheral in relation to the institutions of its own society. That the Puritans held a peripheral position while still in Europe is well known: they were the nonseparating Congregationalists who were antagonized by those in authority in England. As a result of their powerless status, they understood their relationship to England as akin to that between the Israelite exiles and Babylon in the sixth century B.C.E. Thus, their exit from England under John Winthrop was compared by Cotton Mather to the exiles' return to Israel from Babylon.[26]

Although the Puritans were peripheral from one perspective, they may be considered central from another angle (as with class C). From the perspective of the context of North American society, English Puritan colonization may be viewed as central, establishing itself while at the same time pushing Native American culture to the periphery. In view of the general scholarly assumption that it is within peripheral, "contacted," cultures that millennial groups form, it bears repeating that the Puritans were the colonizers, not the colonized, in New England. Within the exogenous context of contact between the English and the Native Americans, the Puritans had the upper hand.

Sacvan Bercovitch has emphasized the millennial worldview of these early American Puritans: the emigrants had a vision of themselves and of the New World as an apocalyptic miracle.[27] For them, their journey to the New World was a sign they were living in the end times. Cotton Mather stressed the eschatological importance of the Puritans' having come to New England: "[The World of Noah's time] was destroy'd, because the grand Prophecy of our SAVIOUR was forgotten in it, and a *New World* brought on for the Revival of that Prophecy. . . . [Now, a new greater family of] *Noah* is the Reviver of the *New World*."[28]

The writings of several Puritan clergymen demonstrate that their undertaking to prepare a New World so God's kingdom would come had

26. See Sacvan Bercovitch, *The Puritan Origins of the American Self* (New Haven: Yale University Press, 1975), 63, 89.

27. Ibid., 90.

28. Quoted ibid., 99. The Puritans' dynamic view of history emphasized their own leading role in preparing for the kingdom of God. The Puritans had felt called to this role at least as early as their rise to power in England under Oliver Cromwell in the 1650s. Transferred to New England, Puritan "postmillennialism" strove to make the New World a preparation for the world to come. New England was to be a model and stimulus leading Europe to prepare for the eschaton. Thus, it had to be made a perfect garden, manicured as no chosen people before had been able to maintain (A. W. Plumstead, *The Wall and the Garden* [Minneapolis: University of Minnesota Press, 1968], 29).

several of the family resemblances of apocalypticism. An apocalyptic moral dualism can be seen in the clergy's stress on the difference between the wicked and the righteous. Also apparent in their works is a belief in apocalyptic determinism, as can be illustrated by a line from Increase Mather's *The Day of Trouble Is Near* (1674): "Our most dismall Providence . . . was decreed before the world began."[29] Further, note that the emigrants saw the "dismall" hardships they experienced in New England as the birth pangs of the millennium.[30]

Apocalyptic expectation among the Puritans seems to have reached its height at the time of King Philip's War, in which the Wampanoag and Narraganset tribes were almost exterminated by them. King Philip's War (1675–76), a war in which six hundred English settlers and three thousand Native Americans lost their lives, was the bloodiest conflict in seventeenth-century New England. Note that the apocalyptic interpretation of the conflict took place not among the Native Americans but among the English, who were fighting to expand their settlement into Native American territory across southern New England. The millennial worldview of the Puritans saw this war as the Dreadful Day, pictured at the end of the book of Malachi, when those who fear God are drawn into the action of apocalyptic judgment. The colonial leadership saw the New England army as executing this judgment by treading down the wicked (Mal. 4:1-3).[31]

What makes the Puritans so important for understanding the sociology of millennial groups in power is that it was the colonial clergy, at the center of the New England theocracy, who led this millennial group in the New World. Theocratic leaders are here attested as capable of holding a millennial worldview. In this case, the clergy's Puritan church-state of New England represented the apocalyptic remnant of the last days: the religious nationalism of New England orthodoxy took the position that the formation of their theocracy was a major step in the culmination of the ages and the coming of the parousia.[32]

---

29. Quoted in Bercovitch, *Puritan Origins*, 54.

30. John Eliot, a missionary to the Native Americans, wrote in 1664: "The hour of temptation, wch Christ hath foretold, Re. 3.10, shall come upon all the world, to try them y^t dwell upon the earth, is in p^rt come, and still coming upon us; and the true state of every man, in the sight of God, is that, as he is found to be upon tryall" ("Letter from Rev. John Eliot, 1664," in *The New England Historical and Genealogical Register* [Boston: Drake, 1855], 9:131). In contrast to the situation of the Melanesian cargo cults, here millennialism is the religion of the missionaries, not the natives!

31. See Bercovitch, *Puritan Origins*, 65.

32. Ibid., 62.

One implication is that clerics at the center of society should not be viewed as necessarily lacking eschatological expectations. The idea that realized eschatology goes along with theocracy cannot stand sociologically as a rule of interpretation. Rather, the literature of the Puritans shows that a theocracy may instead proclaim a futuristic expectation of an imminent radical change in the world.

Class B (Dominating and Central). Several anthropologists now recognize that even central representatives of leading nations and elites who colonize or conquer other societies may be impelled by a millennial worldview.[33] The Spanish conquest of the New World provides some good examples of groups with this type of social matrix. Parties among the Spanish Franciscans, for example, were both colonizing millennial groups and part of the establishment in their own Spanish society.[34] The sixteenth-century Franciscan missionary-historian, Gerónimo De Mendieta, is representative of one such group of colonizers that held to a millennial understanding of their conquest.[35]

Mendieta's group was millennial. They held that the New World was to be the End of the World.[36] In fact, New Spain was to be the physical location of the coming millennial kingdom. Millennial dualism is seen in Mendieta's view of the Spaniards as the new chosen people. Other millennial features include the notion of a period of tribulation to precede the millennial kingdom, and the idea that a messiah would come as a future king of Spain, as well as the belief that the world was on the eve of the last judgment.[37]

John L. Phelan argues that Mendieta's millennialism is quite different from that of exploited groups. Phelan describes Mendieta as an "apocalyptic

33. Thus, F. Sierksma cites the Aztecs as especially interesting because they were infamous conquerors who also were "haunted by the fear of a periodical world catastrophe" ("Current Anthropology Book Review: The Religions of the Oppressed: A Study of Modern Messianic Cults by Vittorio Lanternari," *Current Anthropology* 6 [1965]: 455).

34. A major source for understanding millennialism among the Franciscans in the New World is John L. Phelan, *The Millennial Kingdom of the Franciscans in the New World,* 2d ed. (Berkeley and Los Angeles: University of California Press, 1970).

35. Phelan notes that Mendieta's apocalyptic convictions were shared by a group of influential members of the "pro-Indian" party among the Franciscans (*Franciscans,* 74).

36. See ibid., 110.

37. Ibid., 11, 104–5, 106.

elitist."[38] Rather than advocating violence against the Spanish colonial order, Mendieta wanted the natives to accept the new imposed order as a preparation for the millennial kingdom. Mendieta thus created "an eschatological rationale for the universal monarchy of the Spanish Habsburgs."[39] Under his millennial program, political and religious control of New Spain was to be exercised from the top down. The imminent end was not to be achieved by a revolution of the disenfranchised and alienated, but prepared for by the Spanish conversion of all peoples, preeminently the "pagans" (meaning the Native Americans of the New World). When the king of Spain had accomplished the conversion of humankind, God would allow the last judgment to commence.

It is clear that, from the perspective of their own society, Mendieta's group was part of the Spanish establishment. Already by the late fifteenth century, the millennial ideas of Joachimism had found royal patronage in Spain.[40] The reforms of Ximénez de Cisneros, Queen Isabella's confessor, imposed the Joachimite paradigm on the queen's clergy. Thus, by the 1490s, the way was prepared for monarchic support for Franciscan Joachimite millennialism.[41] As a result, in the sixteenth century, at the beginning of the Franciscan involvement in the New World under Charles V, the friars acted as direct representatives of the crown.

Under Charles, the Franciscans enjoyed the complete confidence of the monarch and were given extensive privileges in order to convert the natives. They held episcopal, governmental, and economic powers given to them directly by the king.[42] Thus, in contrast to the situation of the Puritans in North America, the Franciscans did not flee from Europe, but came as the colonizing representatives of their own society's central establishment.[43] To be sure, the Franciscans lost a good amount of central power after the age of Charles V, when Philip II rose to power. Even though

38. Ibid., 74, 124.

39. Ibid., 16, 53, 106, 108; cf. Bercovitch, *Puritan Origins,* 140.

40. As mentioned in the preceding chapter, Joachimism was a millennial movement of the Middle Ages associated with a group known as the Franciscan Spirituals who often came from the elite of society. On the Spirituals, see Norman Cohn, *The Pursuit of the Millennium* (New York: Oxford University Press, 1970), 14; and "Medieval Millenarism: Its Bearing on the Comparative Study of Millenarian Movements," in *Millennial Dreams,* 35. On Joachim of Fiore, see Theodore Olson, *Millennialism, Utopianism, and Progress* (Toronto: University of Toronto Press, 1982), 110–27; and Cohn, *Pursuit,* 108–10.

41. See Phelan, *Franciscans,* 45.

42. Ibid., 54.

43. Bercovitch, *Puritan Origins,* 140.

Mendieta's group became only one of the voices the king heard, however, Mendieta still viewed himself as a royal adviser.[44] Eventually, Mendieta found himself no longer able to operate effectively as part of Philip's court, and his group began to withdraw from it. By this time, however, his group's millennial worldview was already well established.

Endogenous Conditions

A second possible type of social arena of millennial groups is the endogenous one (see the first column of Chart 2). In endogenous social environments, a conflict with an alien culture does not seem to be a significant element in the social arena of a millennial group; rather, the group's social milieu is best described in terms of factors internal to its own culture and society.[45] The fact that endogenous arenas are attested for millennial groups shows that anthropologists, such as Bernard Barber and Ralph Linton, who associate millennial groups with social matrices involving clashes with other societies have too narrow a view.[46] Our knowledge of the sociology of millennial groups will be enlarged by examining groups in endogenous arenas as well as those experiencing acculturation.

Class D (Endogenous and Peripheral). Class D from Chart 2 represents an endogenous arena in which the millennial group is peripheral, disenfranchised, or alienated within its own society. Norman Cohn has argued that this is an extremely common social arena of the medieval European millennial groups.[47] Because this type of social matrix seems all too well understood by biblical scholars (this is the setting that Paul Hanson and Otto Plöger see behind "the dawn" of biblical apocalyptic eschatology), it will not be treated here in detail.[48] One illustration of the class D arena would be that of the Doomsday cult described by John Lofland.[49] Other

44. Phelan, *Franciscans,* 81.

45. For discussion, see La Barre, *Ghost Dance,* 277; and "Materials for a History," 20.

46. Bernard Barber, "Acculturation and Messianic Movements," *American Sociological Review* 6 (1941): 663–69; Ralph Linton, "Nativistic Movements," *American Anthropologist* 45 (1943): 230–40.

47. Cohn, *Pursuit,* 10, 37, 50–52, 282, 284.

48. For discussion, see chapter 1 above, and Philip R. Davies, "The Social World of Apocalyptic Writings," in *The World of Ancient Israel,* ed. R. E. Clements (Cambridge, England: Cambridge University Press, 1989), 258.

49. John Lofland, *Doomsday Cult* (Englewood Cliffs, N.J.: Prentice-Hall, 1966). Although Lofland does not name the cult in question and changes the names of the principals, his book is based on observations of an actual millennial

examples include the social environments of several of the medieval flagellant groups.[50]

Class A (Endogenous and Central). Class A from Chart 2, like class B,
represents an arena of millennial groups that is most difficult to explain in
terms of deprivation theory. Millennial groups in this class are not deprived
either in comparison to an alien culture or with respect to other groups
within their own culture. Here are endogenous arenas in which millennial
groups are central in their own society in terms of economics, social class,
or political power.

The nineteenth-century Irvingite Catholic Apostolic Church, discussed in the previous chapter, though not encompassing the entire elite of
English society, certainly drew its membership from the middle and upper
classes. Very few members of the group were underprivileged.[51] P. E. Shaw
writes: "The Catholic Apostolic leaders do not manifest . . . variety. . . .
They belong rather to the upper or middle class, not to the poor or the
underprivileged. . . . All of these were men of culture and of education,

---

cult. (In fact, the cult was an early phase of the Unification Church.) This group
had its endogenous context in modern-day America; and within American society,
the cult was clearly peripheral. The group membership was an extreme minority
within society and included people who had been less than successful at various
aspects of social life. Further, the group's recruiting efforts repeatedly failed to increase their numbers. The group had no central political authority, and in terms of
religion, it defined itself against the standard American denominations.

50. For example, a major flagellant movement arose around the year 1260, the
date of the eschaton according to prophecies falsely attributed to Joachim of Fiore
(see n. 40 above). Like other flagellant movements, this one took place within
medieval society with no other cultures involved. Although members of other
classes sometimes participated, these movements were largely composed of the
poor and the destitute. Mass flagellation was the group millennial program undertaken in order to secure group eschatological salvation in the imminently expected
cataclysmic judgment. Cohn describes the flagellant procession as follows: "The
movement was launched in 1260 by a hermit of Perugia and spread southwards to
Rome and northwards to the Lombard cities with such rapidity that to contemporaries it appeared a sudden epidemic of remorse. . . . Men, youths and boys
marched day and night, with banners and burning candles, from town to town.
And each time they came to a town they would arrange themselves in groups before
the church and flog themselves for hours on end" (*Pursuit,* 128).

51. See George Shepperson, "The Comparative Study of Millenarian Movements," in *Millennial Dreams,* 49; and Graham Allan, "A Theory of Millennialism:
The Irvingite Movement as an Illustration," *British Journal of Sociology* 25 (1974):
296.

and most were persons of some social importance."[52] Further, the previous discussion showed that several of the leaders of the Catholic Apostolic Church belonged to aristocratic circles and some, such as Henry Drummond and Spencer Perceval, also served in Parliament. They were not anti-establishment or counterculture advocates but had roles in English society's central institutions and were known for loyalty to the crown.

Despite their central status, the group was clearly millennial, as demonstrated above. A former adherent of the Irvingites, who may be considered an informant, criticized the group for "the continual use which is made of the doctrine of the second advent of our Lord. . . . The nearness of it, its suddenness, and the fearful judgments which would accompany it."[53]

The idiom of a millennial group's worldview is often colored by local differences or reflects the culture or status of the group in which it arises.[54] One interesting aspect of the Irvingite group is that the idiom of their millennial worldview can be seen to reflect their high status in society. For example, the prophecies of Robert Baxter of Doncaster, an early member of Irving's group, reflected his support for and participation in society's central institutions as a lawyer. Specifically, his utterances reflected his support for the monarchy, nobility, and the Church of England.[55] One of Baxter's prophecies denounces denominations that reject episcopacy. He declared to Irving "their offence against God in the popular constitution of their churches, and the rejection of bishops as the standing sign of the apostolic office."[56] As another example, note that the liturgy of the Irvingite group had a High Church, Anglican character.[57] The fact that the Irvingites used incense and the high altar demonstrates not only that millennial groups will retain their own traditions and forms but also that a

52. P. E. Shaw, *The Catholic Apostolic Church Sometimes Called Irvingite: A Historical Study* (Morningside Heights, N.Y.: King's Crown, 1946), 237.

53. Quoted ibid., 46.

54. For discussion or descriptions of millennial worldviews where coloring by local differences is noticeable, see Robert R. Wilson, "From Prophecy to Apocalyptic: Reflections on the Shape of Israelite Religion," *Semeia* 21 (1981): 86; Anthony F. C. Wallace, "Revitalization Movements," *American Anthropologist* 58 (1956): 268; Justus van der Kroef, "Messianic Movements in the Celebes, Sumatra, and Borneo," in *Millennial Dreams,* 81, 89; Mircea Eliade, "'Cargo Cults' and Cosmic Regeneration," in *Millennial Dreams,* 142; Barber, "Acculturation," 663 n. 4; Weinstein, "Civic Setting," 196; Overholt, *Channels,* 33 n. 14; and B. Wilson, *Magic,* 214, 307 n. 110, 312.

55. Shaw, *Catholic Apostolic Church,* 38.

56. Quoted ibid., 43.

57. Ibid., 241.

starchy atmosphere of pomp emphasizing a traditional cultic performance can infuse these groups.

The most interesting endogenous millennial groups are those that also have control over the political power of their society. The Prophet Dance movement among the Coast Salish, the aforementioned native tribes of Canada living around the Puget Sound and the Georgia Strait, provides an attestation of this type of class A social background for millennialism.[58] Strong arguments can be made for seeing the Prophet Dance in its occurrence among the Salish as having an endogenous arena. Wayne Suttles's studies support the position outlined by Melville J. Herskovits that viewing this movement as caused by the stress of contact with another culture misconstrues its social environment.[59] Suttles argues that the appearance of the Plateau Prophet Dance on the Coast occurred before much contact with white society, which only began to happen in the late 1830s.[60]

The arena class of the Coast Salish Prophet Dance must be considered not only endogenous but also central in that the Coast Salish chieftainship was persistently associated with the millennial cult. The Coast Salish tribes were not highly structured politically. Nevertheless, their society did include persons holding political authority, and these chiefs were often, but not always, in leadership positions in the millennial Prophet Dance.[61] The involvement of one such chief in a millennial group that became active in the early 1840s is described as follows by an old Clayoquot man: "The chief would hold the white tail of an eagle in his hand and make sweeping motions with it. . . . Then the chief sang a song. . . . They danced, and during the second repetition of the song some would fall in a faint."[62] Later

58. See chapter 2, n. 112. This group is related to the original Prophet Dance of the Northwest (see n. 12 above). The worldview of the Prophet Dance included a belief in the coming resurrection of the dead and of imminent world destruction.

59. In 1938, Melville J. Herskovits stressed that indigenous aboriginal phenomena were the sources of the Ghost Dance movements. His arguments opposed anthropologists such as Philleo Nash who stressed white influence in explaining the Ghost Dance's cause. For discussion of the early anthropological debate, see Wayne Suttles, "The Plateau Prophet Dance among the Coast Salish," *Southwestern Journal of Anthropology* 13 (1957): 391; David F. Aberle, "The Prophet Dance and Reactions to White Contact," *Southwestern Journal of Anthropology* 15 (1959): 75; and chapter 2, n. 112 above.

60. Suttles, "Plateau Prophet Dance," 358; also see Suttles's later reflection on this position in his *Coast Salish Essays* (Seattle: University of Washington Press, 1987), 198.

61. Suttles, "Plateau Prophet Dance," 383.

62. Quoted ibid., 374.

in the 1860s, a chief among the Lummi tribe is reported to have been the first to believe in the imminent activity of a "transformer" deity. The chief, known as David Crockett, became the leader of the Prophet Dance group among the Lummi, and most of his people joined it.[63]

The involvement of the upper class in the medieval messianic movement led by Sabbatai Ṣevi can also be considered to illustrate the type A class of arena.[64] Unlike many of the medieval movements described by Cohn, the Sabbatian movement was not caused by the disenfranchised of society creating mob pressure for a mass awakening (although some later writers tried to argue this).[65] The rise of the Sabbatian movement was not caused by any social or class tensions or the eruption of class struggle within medieval Jewry. Rather, from the beginning, the movement included rich merchants and those from the ruling class. Gershom Scholem writes:

> All the more surprising is the real proportion of believers and unbelievers within the ruling classes. . . . the majority of the ruling class was in the camp of the believers, and the prominent and active part played by many of them is attested by all reliable documents.[66]

The millionaires of Amsterdam who offered their fortunes to Sabbatai Ṣevi are an example of the fact that a millennial group can form among the prominent members of a society.

Leadership, Priesthood, and Millennialism

Sociological evidence allows for the catalyst figure leading millennial groups to be drawn from persons having varying roles within a society, including the role of priest.[67] That the so-called millennial prophet may

63. Ibid., 359.

64. This movement was discussed in chapter 2. See Lawrence Fine, "Medieval Jewish Apocalyptic Literature," in *The Encyclopedia of Religion*, ed. M. Eliade (New York: Macmillan, 1987), 1:344; and Gershom Scholem, *Sabbatai Ṣevi: The Mystical Messiah 1626–1676* (Princeton, N.J.: Princeton University Press, 1973).

65. Scholem, *Sabbatai*, 392.

66. Ibid., 5.

67. Max Weber defined the priest as a specialist who regularly participates in a cult. Although this definition is useful, Weber's sharp distinction between the priest and other religious functionaries, such as prophets, must be rejected. (It was Weber's methodological use of ideal types that caused him to view priests as ontologically different from prophets; see, e.g., *The Sociology of Religion*, trans. E. Fischoff [Boston: Beacon, 1963; 1st German ed., 1922], 46.) As R. Wilson states, "The fact that priests sometimes have other religious functions prevents sharply distinguishing the priest from other religious specialists" (*Prophecy and Society*, 26–27).

actually be a priest is shown by such a figure as Te-Ua, the leader of the Hau-hau millennial movement in New Zealand that started in 1826. Te-Ua was the priest of a native Maori cult who began announcing that the British would be expelled from New Zealand. Te-Ua's millennial worldview included the idea that the millennium would be ushered in when the British were cast out as well as a belief that the dead would soon rise again.[68] The program of the Hau-hau movement involved a holy war against the British colonizers.

Priests, such as Te-Ua, who lead offshoot movements away from the central cult of a society are not the only kind of priests who become millennial prophets. The leadership of millennial religion may also be the priesthood at the center of society (compare Mendieta's group described above). One illustration of this possibility is the Nuer priest Gwek's authority over his group of followers.[69]

In the 1920s Gwek led a large native group among the Lau Nuer in the southern Sudan in military conflict against white colonizers. His group had several characteristics that would place it in the class C type of social arena discussed above. The arena was exogenous in that Gwek and his followers were involved in a struggle against a colonial administration. At the same time, Gwek had central status within his own society as a leopard-skin priest, a member of the most prominent group of ritual experts in that society.[70] Far from being peripheral to Nuer priestly institutions, Gwek's family and followers built the Pyramid of Dengkur, a central cult site for the Lau where sacrifices took place. Besides his role as a central priest, Gwek's central status was buttressed by his membership by birth in a class ranked as leaders in the Nuer hierarchy.

Chiefs and elders from other Nuer groups recognized Gwek's author-

---

Thus, it is now recognized by some scholars that several of Israel's writing prophets functioned within the Jerusalem cult. This view is buttressed by Petersen's discussion of role enactment and the possibility of one person taking on multiple roles, one of which is that of priest (*Roles of Israel's Prophets*, 21). Unfortunately, despite the growing acceptance of the idea of priestly prophets, little scholarly attention has been given to the possibility of a millennial catalyst figure functioning within the central cult. (For an introduction to the scholarly literature and debate on the relationship between the biblical writing prophets and their possible functioning within the cult, see H. H. Rowley, "Ritual and the Hebrew Prophets," *JSS* 1 [1956]: 338–60; and R. Wilson, *Prophecy and Society*, 8–10.)

68. See Lanternari, *Religions of the Oppressed*, 253, 256.

69. A convenient source describing Gwek's group is Overholt, *Prophecy in Cross-Cultural Perspective*, 215–30.

70. See ibid., 217.

ity, recognition that in turn enabled Gwek to mobilize both his own and neighboring tribes in a military millennial-like movement.[71] Gwek called to his followers' minds previous prophecies of a coming time of invasion by the whites. He held that at the time the invading whites reached the Nuer border, his people would rise and drive them out forever, ushering in Nuer sovereignty. As in similar movements, Gwek convinced his followers of their invulnerability to their enemy's bullets during the climactic battle. He held that the bullets of the enemy's rifles would become like water falling to the ground rather than hurting the Nuer.[72]

Gwek's claim to supernatural power, his charismatic authority, and his leadership role in the military movement suggest he played several roles within Nuer society. His uniting of the people in military involvement indicates that besides the role of priest, he also had the role of another Nuer institution, that of *ruic* or "spokesman."[73] Further, insofar as Gwek commanded spiritual powers, such as the knowledge that his people were invulnerable to bullets, he should also be considered a prophet. Given the above facts, it can be concluded that Gwek's activities suggest that the roles of priest, millennial prophet/catalyst figure, and spokesman overlapped in him. For the purposes of the present discussion, because Gwek played both the role of priest and that of millennial prophet, he may serve as a paradigm for the possibility of a priest at the center of his society also having the role of a catalyst figure for millennialism.

Another illustration documenting the existence of a society's central priesthood playing a leading role in millennial religion is provided by the Mamaia cult in Polynesia. The millennial character of the Mamaia group is shown by such features as prophecies of the coming expulsion of the whites, the expectation of the appearance of a new era, and the idea of the imminent return of the dead. Its social arena is best described as class C: The movement had an exogenous arena in that it involved a march against the Christian missions. At the same time, like other millennial groups in Polynesia, the Mamaia movement was backed by native royalty and the

---

71. Ibid., 225–26.

72. Ibid., 230. For discussion or descriptions of the idea of supernatural protection during war as a characteristic belief in militant millennial groups, see Peter Worsley, *The Trumpet Shall Sound: A Study of "Cargo" Cults in Melanesia*, 2d ed. (New York: Schocken, 1968), 141; Kenelm Burridge, *New Heaven, New Earth: A Study of Millenarian Activities* (New York: Schocken, 1969), 39, 79; B. Wilson, *Magic*, 303; Lanternari, *Religions of the Oppressed*, 254 n. 1, 255 n. 4; and La Barre, *Ghost Dance*, 230, 308.

73. Overholt, *Prophecy in Cross-Cultural Perspective*, 217.

native aristocratic class.[74] In this case, the movement was supported by Queen Pomare and King Tapoa of Tahaa. The native priesthood played a leading role beside these monarchs. Far from being isolated from the central cultic institutions of the society, the movement had as its shrine of worship the traditional sanctuary of Opoa in Marae Taputapuatea.

Unlike the case of peripheral cults, which often worship gods other than the central gods of a society,[75] the native god Oro was worshiped by his own native priesthood at the center of the Mamaia millennial movement. The millennial program of the priesthood involved revitalizing the society's own practices and traditions within the cult's framework. Vittorio Lanternari states that in the Mamaia cult, traditional rituals were restored as the natives sought to "bring the power of their traditions to bear on the teachings of the missionaries with sufficient force to crush them."[76]

Effects of Millennialism on Factions

Estrangement

The rise of millennialism in a society may either accompany further alienation between factions or it may create more unity and cooperation between them. The former possibility may occur in the class D arena discussed above.[77] Such an arena of conflict between the disenfranchised and those in power is the type of matrix often assumed to underlie the factional polemics sometimes found in proto-apocalyptic literature. Cross-cultural

74. For discussion, see Lanternari, *Religions of the Oppressed*, 236–55. Note that the Hau-hau movement, described above, was also supported by local chiefs such as Hepanaia.

75. For discussion, see Petersen, *Roles of Israel's Prophets*, 44.

76. Lanternari, *Religions of the Oppressed*, 243.

77. An illustration could be drawn from the thirteenth-century medieval European millennial movement of Pseudo-Baldwin in Flanders. The rise of Pseudo-Baldwin as a millennial prophet in 1224 polarized the oppressed masses on the one hand and the French king and the followers of the countess Joanna on the other. Civil war broke out between those who saw the prophet as the resurrected Baldwin IX who had come at last as the messiah of popular expectation, and those who remained loyal to Joanna, Baldwin's daughter. Cohn notes the increase in alienation between classes caused by the growth of the millennial movement: "While the rich tended to look askance at the new sovereign, the poor were all convinced that it was indeed Baldwin who had appeared amongst them. . . . [With the rise of the millennial movement] the better-off and rich people got a bad deal everywhere. The poor folk said they would have gold and silver" (*Pursuit*, 92). In sum, the millennial group under Pseudo-Baldwin was a disenfranchised faction that became alienated from those at the center of society.

evidence indicates, however, that this assumption does not always hold. When factional alienation is associated with millennialism, it may alternatively involve a struggle between two or more factions that are all central groups in power in a society. That strife between two central or elite factions may be associated with millennialism is attested by the social background of the Java War of 1825–30 in Indonesia.[78]

The Java War involved a military millennial movement against Dutch colonizers led by Prince Dipanagara, a member of the Javanese royal house. Dipanagara's followers believed he was the *Ratu Adil,* a messiah figure.[79] According to the worldview of the group, the *Ratu Adil* was to appear at a time of great wickedness near the end of the world. This ruler would defeat the forces of darkness and establish the millennium.[80]

The military conflict between Dipanagara's group and the Dutch must be considered as a major part of the social background of the group's millennial beliefs; however, the career of the group also involved a Javanese inner-establishment struggle. A member of the royal family that governed most of the island, Dipanagara held power in the area of religious affairs on Java. He commanded a following that included royal relatives and palace troops. Events within court politics thrust Dipanagara's group into conflict with the followers of his younger brother who was much more worldly in orientation. As a result of what he saw as an increasingly intolerable situation at court aggravated by Dutch interference, Dipanagara eventually abandoned the court at Yogyakarta and expanded his group into a military force that came to number in the hundreds of thousands.[81] Thus, the sociology of a millennial group is here seen to have involved an alienating quarrel between factions, both of which were at the royal center of society.

Unification

Distortions will arise if a situation involving conflict between factions is generalized to all millennial groups,[82] because the alternative possibility

78. The Java War is conveniently described by Michael Adas, *Prophets of Rebellion: Millenarian Protest Movements against the European Colonial Order* (Chapel Hill: University of North Carolina Press, 1979), 3–11, 94–99.

79. For discussion of Indonesian messianic beliefs, see van der Kroef, "Messianic Movements," 117–21.

80. Adas, *Prophets of Rebellion,* 97–99.

81. Ibid., 11.

82. It was seen in chapter 1 that Otto Plöger describes the social matrix of early biblical apocalyptic literature in terms of F. Tönies' distinction between "community" (*Gemeinschaft*) and "society" (*Gesellschaft*). Plöger finds the origins of apocalypticism in factional conflict between an underground community and those at

exists in which millennialism is accompanied by a banding together of dissociated factions or groups that may even have been previously hostile.[83] Such banding together, often in response to calamity, may be orchestrated by central millennial groups (here, those in arenas A, B, and C) and is often accompanied by a group reemphasis on central values.[84] Central morality and authority is not threatened but validated in this type of situation.[85] This alternative type of social pattern was already seen in the above discussion of the millennial movement among the Lau Nuer in the Sudan in the 1920s. Taking on the Nuer role of *ruic,* or "spokesman," Gwek united previously independent groups for military conflict against the colonizers. His millennial worldview provided ideational symbols capable both of uniting his own tribe and providing for federation between adjacent tribes.

The effect of central millennialism in uniting groups is also attested in other cultures and especially in several Native American groups. The millennial military movement of 1690 among the Pueblo tribes in the Southwest of North America is one example.[86] This movement took place within the C type of social arena involving native leaders heading a millennial group within a society that was facing massive contact with European Spaniards.

In 1690, a millennial catalyst figure arose among the Pueblo in the person of a Tewa medicine man named Popé. He claimed to have visited the land of the dead, and on the basis of his communications with the spirits, he advocated a millennial group plan of revolt. Popé's millennial worldview, combined with his ability to work wonders, united the Pueblo chiefs against the colonizing Spanish priests. Each of the chiefs received cords tied with knots. The chiefs untied one knot per day until all the knots

---

the center of society. See Andrew D. H. Mayes, *The Old Testament in Sociological Perspective* (London: Marshall Pickering, 1989), 7–17.

83. Several anthropologists describe how millennialism can unite separate or hostile groups. See Worsley, *Trumpet,* 230; B. Wilson, *Magic,* 223–24; and Lanternari, *Religions of the Oppressed,* 320–21.

84. For the response of central prophets in general to natural and political calamities, see the discussion in Petersen, *Roles of Israel's Prophets,* 64–65.

85. Cf. Jean Chesneaux's view that the unifying role of millennialism in class C arenas is very significant. In this type of milieu, according to Chesneaux, millennial groups are frequently movements of "national unity" and "national character" ("Current Anthropology Book Review: The Religions of the Oppressed: A Study of Modern Messianic Cults by Vittorio Lanternari," *Current Anthropology* 6 [1965]: 449).

86. For discussion of this movement, see La Barre, *Ghost Dance,* 205.

were gone, whereupon they led the Pueblo tribes in a united insurrection that drove out the Spanish priests and soldiers. The success of the Pueblo revolt of 1690 was made possible only by the intervention of the millennial catalyst figure, Popé, which produced intertribal cooperation.[87] Such cooperation was new to the region before the rise of millennialism.

In eighteenth-century America, the millennial worldview associated with the Delaware Prophet served as another focal point that unified various groups of Native Americans. Neolin, the Delaware Prophet, had an important influence on Chief Pontiac, the leader of the Ottawas.[88] Chief Pontiac drew on the prophet's worldview in uniting the Chippewas and probably the Miamis, Piankashaws, and the Weas into a military alliance. In 1763, Pontiac summoned the chiefs to a council near Detroit where they worked out a military group plan based on the millennial group-teachings of the Delaware Prophet.[89] Bryan R. Wilson states, "The religious response of the Delaware Prophet was a valuable, perhaps in some respects a necessary ideological basis for even temporary nascent union of otherwise dispersed peoples."[90] The movement ended when Pontiac lost the military struggle and was eventually assassinated.

A final Native American example of millennialism uniting factions comes from the early nineteenth century. This case involves a Shawnee millennial prophet named Tenskwatawa who united several different tribes of Native Americans. B. Wilson quotes the prophet as having told the white governor of Ohio:

> The religion which I have established in the last three years, has been attended to by the different tribes of Indians in this part of the world. Those Indians were once different peoples; *they are now but one:* they are all determined to practice what I have communicated to them, that has come immediately from the Great Spirit through me.[91]

Tenskwatawa's millennial beliefs upheld central native customs and values while also expecting the imminent arrival of the Master of Life. This Master was expected to bring a cataclysm destroying all white men and ushering in the millennium. Tenskwatawa was taken on as an adviser by his brother Tecumseh, an important Shawnee military leader. Tecumseh was inspired by his brother's millennial visions to form a great Native American confederacy. Here again millennialism is attested as forming a focal point

87. See ibid., 263.

88. See B. Wilson, *Magic*, 228; Lanternari, *Religions of the Oppressed*, 131; and Barber, "Acculturation," 663 n. 5.

89. La Barre, *Ghost Dance*, 208.

90. B. Wilson, *Magic*, 229.

91. Ibid., 233.

for uniting factions or groups under a single plan of action.[92] Eventually, Tenskwatawa was discredited by a major Native American defeat at Tippecanoe in 1811.

The Career of Millennial Groups

Sociological evidence indicates that millennial groups, including those in power, are not static entities. Changes take place in a group over time in response to such factors as changes within the group's social milieu. Exigencies may lead a millennial group to pursue different goals than those it had at first. In other cases, the leader of a millennial group may be forced into a new role or his followers may even turn against him.[93] One of the most interesting facts about millennial groups is that the feedback that the leader or leaders get from the group and the larger society over a period of time will affect the extent to which a group is millennial. This as well as other factors may result in a change in a millennial group's composition over time.[94]

Routinization

Routinization of a millennial group takes place when the group's worldview becomes more mundane than at first and the group program is altered so that group activities take on a more routine character, allowing them to be sustainable over an extended or indefinite period of time. In such cases, what was once a major millennial movement may dwindle to a small sect within society.[95] Such a change in the group worldview is one

92. Thus, B. Wilson writes, "The millennialist ideas that Tenskwatawa learned and disseminated were a valuable stimulus to tribal unity" (ibid., 235).

93. See R. Wilson, *Prophecy and Society*, 79–80. Wilson's discussion is reminiscent of Thrupp's statement: "At a certain stage of success the [millennial] movement tends to force the leader into a new role that may not be congenial to him" ("Millennial Dreams in Action: A Report," 23). Thus, in the career of the Irvingite movement, Edward Irving himself found his role being stipulated by the new "apostles" whose authority was growing at the time (see Shaw, *Catholic Apostolic Church*, 51–59). For other cases where a leader's exclusive dominance is challenged, see Burridge, *New Heaven*, 168; and B. Wilson, *Magic*, 300. On the phenomenon of millennial leaders being turned against after disconfirmation of their prophecies, see van der Kroef, "Messianic Movements," 89; Lanternari, *Religions of the Oppressed*, 125; and Overholt, *Prophecy in Cross-Cultural Perspective*, 303.

94. See Roy Wallis, "Introduction," in *Millennialism and Charisma*, ed. R. Wallis (Belfast, Northern Ireland: Queen's University, 1982), 8.

95. See the discussion in Worsley, *Trumpet*, xlvii.

possible result of repeated disconfirmations of the members' apocalyptic expectations.[96] Thus, when the millennium expected in the Ghost Dance never materialized, the apocalyptic elements in its message were deemphasized. Thomas W. Overholt writes:

> The fact that Mooney spoke with Wovoka himself does not guarantee us an accurate account of the original message, since that interview took place in early 1892, after the occurrence of two important events which may have been responsible for certain modifications in the teaching, viz., the failure of the millennium to arrive in the spring of 1891, as had been widely expected, and the violence among the Sioux which culminated in Wounded Knee. It is possible that by 1892 Wovoka had modified his message in the direction of a decreased emphasis on the destruction of the whites through some natural catastrophe and an increasing elaboration of its ethical content (do not fight, cooperate with the whites, etc.).[97]

In the end, in his old age, this famous millennial prophet of the Ghost Dance functioned basically as a tired healer.[98]

Radicalization

Radicalization of a millennial group takes place when, in response to events and feedback, its members' apocalyptic expectations become more fervent than at first and its practical program is altered in ways that separate the activities of the group further and further from the mundane routines of everyday social existence.[99] An example of radicalization is seen in the changes that the Ghost Dance worldview underwent as it spread among the Sioux. Among this group, the sense of the imminence of the end

---

96. Note, however, that often disconfirmations do not have important effects on the fervency of a group's apocalyptic expectation. Worsley argues that in many cases this is due to the "spongy" quality of millennial prophecies, whereby all events, both local and international, can be interpreted as confirmations of the group's beliefs (*Trumpet,* xix). For example, in the Doomsday cult described by Lofland, events deleterious to the group were interpreted as products of the powers of evil at work in the end times. See n. 49 above. In Puritan America, setbacks such as King Philip's War served to intensify apocalyptic expectation. See Bercovitch, *Puritan Origins,* 103; and n. 30 above.

97. Overholt, *Prophecy in Cross-Cultural Perspective,* 124.

98. Overholt, *Channels,* 42, 38 n. 36.

99. As I will argue in the next subsection, even millennial groups that end up being attacked by those in power may start out in community with them. For example, the Rodeador movement did not intend any break with the Catholic church at its beginning (see René Ribeiro, "Brazilian Messianic Movements," in *Millennial Dreams,* 65–66). Divisions within society and breaks with dominant institutions may be relatively late events in the career of a millennial group.

increased sharply. Short Bull, a Sioux leader of the Ghost Dance, pro-claimed that the millennium was coming much sooner than expected.

Further, the millennial message of the Ghost Dance began to involve much more hostility toward the whites than was the case with the move-ment among other native groups.[100] The reason the message became more radical seems to have been an increase in the exogenous tension. The mil-lennium would be coming more quickly, according to Short Bull, because "the Whites are interfering so much."[101] The millennial group among the Sioux was experiencing mounting tension with government agents. Fur-ther, they were increasingly opposed by white residents living on and near their reservations. Thus, as Overholt argues, factors in the historical-cultural situation probably account for the hostile turn of the Ghost Dance doctrine as it was preached among the Sioux.[102]

Radicalization within a millennial group is also attested by the career, over the first half of the twentieth century, of the millennial movement in Dutch New Guinea associated with the Mansren myth.[103] In the early phase of this millennial movement, in the years after about 1908, white influence in the area was increasing. At this time, millennial catalyst fig-ures began interpreting the Mansren myth, a native myth centering on a messiahlike magical figure, in an apocalyptic fashion. An inversion of soci-ety was expected in which the Papuans would become like whites, and the whites would have to perform menial tasks such as weeding gardens.

As time went on, the worldview associated with the Mansren myth became more radical, until a drastic alteration of the whole cosmos was expected by the Papuans. Peter Worsley describes the changed expectations of the natives:

> Not only was the order of society to be inverted, but even the order of Nature itself. Yams, potatoes and other tubers would grow on trees like fruit, while coconuts and other fruit would grow like tubers. Sea-creatures would become land-creatures, and vice versa.[104]

In all likelihood, this radicalization of the worldview of the natives should be correlated with the constant white interference with native life in the decades leading up to World War II. This white disturbance of native life,

---

100. Overholt, *Prophecy in Cross-Cultural Perspective*, 133–34.

101. Quoted in Overholt, *Channels*, 44 n. 58.

102. Ibid., 49.

103. See the description in Worsley, *Trumpet*, 126–40; and the discussion in chapter 2 above.

104. Worsley, *Trumpet*, 136.

which included suppression of native institutions, placed increasing stress on the Papuans.

A final stage in the radicalization of the movement occurred in the years following 1939. The time of the return of Mansren and the Deluge of the world was moved up in the natives' expectation. As a result of the heightened anticipation of an imminent end, the millennial program of the movement became more active. For example, many rafts were built in expectation of the coming flood.[105] Millennial vigils took place with hundreds dancing so as to hasten Mansren's arrival.[106] As radicalization continued, the group plan of the millennial movement lost its harmless character and the movement became violent.

In general, radicalization does not continue indefinitely. If the expected millennium does not eventually arrive, there are three usual results. The group may simply die of disillusionment when its members disband. If the group manages to stay in existence, perhaps with a smaller membership, it may undergo the type of routinization described above. A third alternative, which often occurs when the fervor of a group becomes threatening to its opponents, is that the group may be destroyed by military force.

Changes in Group Composition and Group Orientation

In certain instances it is possible for the career of a millennial group to include a change in its composition or in the alliances it forms with other groups in its society. For example, a millennial worldview may spread out from those among the privileged of society and be embraced by groups among the common people. Worsley has described how the millennialism of a "coterie-cult," a sort of upper-class millennial club or set, can be taken up by the masses and turned into an activist movement.[107] Examples of

105. Shelters, rafts, or storehouses are frequently built as part of a millennial group's practical plan. For some cross-cultural comparisons, see B. Wilson, *Magic,* 316, 286; Lanternari, *Religions of the Oppressed,* 135, 139, 170, 215; and Worsley, *Trumpet,* 102, 139.

106. For discussion or descriptions of vigils as an important part of many millennial groups' plans, see van der Kroef, "Messianic Movements," 112; Eliade, "Cargo Cults," 142; B. Wilson, *Magic,* 201, 212; Burridge, *New Heaven,* 23, 27; and Lanternari, *Religions of the Oppressed,* 136 n. 4, 246.

107. Worsley, *Trumpet,* xl–xli. Worsley argues that it makes sense for a millennial group scheme to develop among those with the culture and facilities of money and leisure. Max Weber himself argued that the charismatic millennial prophet must have a certain amount of intellectual culture that in some cases could result

this are found among the Melanesian cargo cults. These groups may start as microsects led by a big-man of high social stature in Melanesian society. They become movements when the native masses see the big-man's worldview as embodying their own needs and demands. In such a way, millennialism can find a new center in its pervasive acceptance among a native people.[108]

When radicalization of a millennial group or an influx of new recruits occurs, members with power in society may abandon the group. Such a change in group composition and orientation occurred among the revolutionary flagellants in Germany in the fourteenth century.[109] In the early stages of the career of this group, its membership included nobles and rich burghers. With time, however, the group became more radical, and this was accompanied by a change in the composition of the group with new members being taken in from the masses of society. In this particular case, the nobles and burghers dropped out when the flagellant group turned into a messianic mass movement. Presumably, their power and riches impeded them from continuing with the movement, which would have meant abandoning their social positions.

In other cases, members of a millennial group do in fact abandon the power they hold in society. It was noted above how some of the millionaires of Amsterdam gave their whole fortunes to the messiah figure Sabbatai Ṣevi. By the same token, many of the Franciscan Spirituals abandoned great wealth in order to join ascetic millennial groups.[110] In these cases, it was possible for an alliance to form between disenfranchised groups and those from the upper strata who were willing to abandon their wealth.

Millennial group members may abandon not only money but also political influence and position. As stated above, in the course of time Mendieta's priestly group became increasingly unhappy with the policies of the Spanish royal court under Philip.[111] In fact, Mendieta began to abandon his expectation of an immediate Spanish Habsburg millennium. He interpreted Philip's reign as a tribulation period or even an apocalyptic catastro-

---

from the figure's being associated with the privileged strata. For discussion, see Cohn, *Pursuit,* 51.

108. See Worsley, *Trumpet,* xli. Although Worsley's accounts of changes in millennial group composition are very instructive, his Marxist view of cargo cults as prepolitical is obviously not accepted here. For one critique of Worsley, see Michael Hill, *A Sociology of Religion* (New York: Basic Books, 1973), 211–16.

109. For discussion of this group, see Cohn, *Pursuit,* 137.

110. See n. 40 above.

111. See the discussion at p. 67 above.

phe that would now have to be endured before any millennium appeared.[112] As their worldview became more radical, the members of
Mendieta's group found themselves relinquishing their advisory capacities
at the royal court. After about 1580, they aligned themselves with other
"pro-Indian" parties against the secular clergy and the crown officials who
increasingly became their opponents. By 1595, Mendieta's group had dis-
tanced themselves even farther from the policy of Philip. They broke with
the mendicant moderates who merely did not want the natives exploited,
and joined forces with the mendicant extremists who argued that Philip
should stop using native labor altogether.[113]

Significance for Interpretation of the Biblical Texts

Together with the preceding critique of deprivation theory, the discussion in this chapter makes clear the validity of inquiring whether some
biblical proto-apocalyptic groups may have held social and political power.
By attesting to the existence of nondeprived millennial groups in other
societies, the sociological evidence shows that we cannot assume when we
encounter a biblical proto-apocalyptic group that its members must have
been peripheral or marginalized in their society. The scholar must be willing to follow the evidence of a biblical text if it suggests that the group
that produced it was socially central.

Broadly speaking, there are four arenas within which a millennial
group may be considered central: classes A, B, C, and E. Some of these
social arenas are not obvious categories in which to place biblical millennial
groups. Unlike the class B arena, for example, Israel in the Persian period
was not involved in the conquest of another people. Nevertheless, Mendieta's class B situation in New Spain is still of interest. Like the Zadokites of
the Persian period in ancient Israel, Mendieta represents a faction within a
hieratic leadership that was sometimes in tension with other groups. His
concrete example is sure to prove helpful in elucidating Zadokite millennialism.

The sociological evidence shows that priests can form the leadership
of millennial groups, and cult functions can be a crucial part of a millennial
group's program. In Mamaia millennialism the priesthood of the native
god played a leading role, and traditional cult rituals formed an important
part of the practical program of the group. Proto-apocalyptic texts within
biblical books associated with Zadokites should be reexamined based on

112. Phelan, *Franciscans,* 108.
113. Ibid., 102.

this and similar data. These texts may have been written by central priests, and their cultic and liturgical idioms may reflect priests' group programs.

The sociological material also suggests the need to reevaluate the view, held by several biblical scholars, that a sociology of hostile factions formed the social arena of early biblical apocalyptic literature. The parallels show an alternative possibility; namely, that millennialism in the postexilic period would have been able to support central morality and authority and indeed rally various hostile factions around the central leadership in a time of crisis. This is what happened in the case of the millennial movement among the Lau Nuer, the Pueblo revolt of 1690, the Delaware Prophet movement, and the millennial movement surrounding Tenskwatawa. Whether this possibility in fact best explains the social background of some biblical proto-apocalyptic texts must now be tested. Of special interest is a careful study of proto-apocalyptic texts that show evidence not of intergroup conflict but of cooperation.

The discussion of the career of millennial groups should also prove helpful in understanding the biblical data. Form-critical and redactional studies of early biblical apocalyptic literature may indicate an increase in the language of tension and expectation in successive layers of a biblical text. Such changes in language may reflect a millennial group's apocalyptic expectations becoming more fervent than at first, and its program being altered so as to become more radical. Such a process of radicalization in some cases could have been accompanied by changes in group composition or in the relations between factions in the society. Thus, a postexilic group initially comfortable with its members' roles within the central institutions of the society might have begun to urge them to withdraw from such roles. I shall inquire in chapter 5 whether such a process can be traced in Zechariah.

4

Ezekiel 38 and 39

The prophecy against Gog of the land of Magog (Ezekiel 38–39) may well be one of the earliest examples of biblical proto-apocalyptic literature. Twentieth-century scholars have tended to miss the significance of this passage, however, partially because it is often not treated as an authentic part of the message of Ezekiel and his school.[1] Scholars in the first half of this century argued that Ezekiel 38–39 was not written during the exile. It was assumed that Ezekiel would not have spoken of cosmic catastrophes or used imagery found elsewhere mostly in postexilic writings. Thus, because of its eschatology and its concern with a future after the restoration, the text was dismissed as an extraneous accretion. For example, in 1929 Hugo Gressmann argued that Ezekiel could not have written Ezekiel 38–39 because the exilic prophets viewed the exile itself, not some future event, as Israel's final catastrophe.[2] Gressmann located the Gog piece historically nearer to the locust-prophecy (*Heuschreckenweissagung*) of Joel than to the exilic prophecies of Ezekiel.[3] William A. Irwin similarly argued in 1943

---

1. See the discussion in Walther Zimmerli, *Ezekiel 2,* trans. J. D. Martin, Hermeneia (Philadelphia: Fortress, 1983), 302; the summary of scholarship in Daniel I. Block, "Gog and the Pouring Out of the Spirit," *VT* 37 (1987): 257; and the discussion of Ezekiel in Robert North, "Prophecy to Apocalyptic via Zechariah," VTSup 22 (1972): 66–67.

2. Hugo Gressmann, *Der Messias* (Göttingen: Vandenhoeck & Ruprecht, 1929), 124. For the problematic assumption here, see n. 6 on Paul Hanson below.

3. Gressmann, *Der Messias,* 134.

that only one formula and ten words in Ezekiel 38–39 could be attributed to the prophet of the exile.[4]

Modern scholars who espouse deprivation theory have overlooked the Gog text or supported these early radical critiques of it. If they had recognized Ezekiel 38–39 as congruent with the book as a whole, it would have contradicted their deprivation approach to the development of apocalyptic literature. The Gog text has thus not been given particular attention in the major treatments of the rise of apocalypticism by Otto Plöger and Paul Hanson.[5] Hanson argues that chapters 38–39 are not relevant in a discussion of Ezekiel and apocalypticism, because he assumes that a central priest such as Ezekiel would not have had an apocalyptic worldview. Rather, he sees Ezekiel 38–39 as the product of a postexilic apocalyptic circle that tried to make sense of Ezekiel's prophecies. Hanson writes:

> In a sense, Ezekiel 38–39 serves to reinterpret Ezekiel 1–37, 40–48 even as Isaiah 56–66 seeks to interpret Isaiah 40–55. Why have the dazzling promises of the prophets not taken place? Because the evil remaining in the land necessitates further destruction and judgment, after which the restoration will finally occur.[6]

Other modern scholars also follow this approach, considering Ezekiel 38–39 as a late, postexilic intrusion into the book of Ezekiel. Reuben Ahroni argues that the Gog passage was added to Ezekiel in the period after Zechariah, that it is a "self-contained entity" that "differs widely" from the rest of the book.[7] Ahroni, adhering to deprivation theory, argues that the Gog prophecy arose out of some distressful or traumatic experience in postexilic times that released the bitter emotions of Israel.[8]

---

4. William A. Irwin, *The Problem of Ezekiel* (Chicago: University of Chicago Press, 1943), 172ff.

5. As B. Erling has stated, "One wonders how a closer analysis of Ezek 38–39 would fit into the explanations of the Jewish origins of apocalyptic which [Plöger and Hanson] offer" ("Ezekiel 38–39 and the Origins of Jewish Apocalyptic," *Ex Orbe Religionum Studia Geo Widengren* [Leiden: E. J. Brill, 1972], 1:106).

6. Paul D. Hanson, *The Dawn of Apocalyptic* (Philadelphia: Fortress, 1979), 234 n. 47. This reading misses the point that the destruction in Ezekiel 38–39 is of the enemies of Israel. The judgment is not at all related to any evil in Israel itself. Hanson repeats his opinion that Ezekiel 38–39 was added to the sayings of Ezekiel by a later apocalyptic circle in his more recent works: *The People Called: The Growth of Community in the Bible* (San Francisco: Harper & Row, 1986), 270; and *Old Testament Apocalyptic* (Nashville: Abingdon, 1987), 37.

7. Reuben Ahroni, "The Gog Prophecy and the Book of Ezekiel," HAR 1 (1977): 2.

8. Ibid., 24.

Joseph Blenkinsopp similarly sees Ezekiel 38–39 as a mosaic of biblical references and motifs fitted together by a late apocalyptist. He states, "What we have, then, is an apocalyptic tract from long after the time of Ezekiel inspired by the prophetic Day of Yahweh (Ezek 39:8) and, more specifically, the prediction in Jeremiah and elsewhere of the coming of a foe from the north (Ezek 38:17)."[9]

Recent form-critical treatments, however, contradict the earlier radical critiques of Ezekiel and suggest that the core of Ezekiel 38–39 comes from the prophet Ezekiel himself. This core was expanded within the Zadokite school of Ezekiel.[10] If the Gog prophecy can indeed be shown to be a product of exiled Zadokite priests, we would have in Ezekiel 38–39 an example of early apocalyptic literature produced by a priestly elite.

To show how Ezekiel 38–39 thus contradicts deprivation theory, I shall first have to establish that the Gog prophecy is indeed proto-apocalyptic literature. The questions of the passage's authorship and its congruity with the book as a whole can then be addressed in order to show that it is a Zadokite product, not an incongruent, late addition to the book. On the basis of these analyses, I shall suggest an alternative social arena for the millennial group behind the text that does not involve deprivation.

The Genre of Ezekiel 38–39

Apocalyptic literature has certain identifying features (see chapter 2), marked especially by a radical, imminent eschatology and by dualism.

---

9. Joseph Blenkinsopp, *A History of Prophecy in Israel* (Philadelphia: Westminster, 1983), 205. Happily, Blenkinsopp gives a more cautious reading of Ezekiel 38–39 in his commentary (*Ezekiel*, Interpretation [Louisville: John Knox, 1990], 179–91).

10. Michael C. Astour states that there is little reason to deny the Gog passage to Ezekiel's pen: "The style and imagery of its basic parts are not different from those of the chapters which are generally accepted as genuine writings of Ezekiel" ("Ezekiel's Prophecy of Gog and the Cuthean Legend of Naram-Sin," *JBL* 95 [1976]: 567). Even if all of Ezekiel 38–39 cannot be assigned to Ezekiel, modern form critics do assign at least a core within these chapters to him (see Zimmerli, *Ezekiel 2*, 304). Thus, Frank L. Hossfeld notes that nowadays the older two-source hypothesis for Ezekiel 38–39 has been replaced by the idea of a *Kernelement* usually seen as authentic Ezekiel material that has been expanded in a complex growth process (*Wachstumsprozess*) within the Ezekiel school (*Untersuchungen zu Komposition und Theologie des Ezechielbuches*, FB 20 [Würzburg: Echter, 1977], 403). On the Ezekiel school as the tradents of the Gog passage, see Zimmerli, *Ezekiel 2*, 310.

These are usually accompanied by such secondary features as bizarre imagery, determinism, and numerology.

Radical Eschatology

Ezekiel 38–39 pictures a radical inbreaking by God that inaugurates a future age. In describing this eschatological inbreaking, the Gog passage emphasizes the total sovereignty of YHWH in war. It is God who defeats Gog through superhuman means (Ezek. 38:19-23):[11] the Israelites are not part of the battle.[12] Israel merely handles the mop-up operations — clearing the battlefield and burying the dead enemy (Ezek. 39:9-16). The apocalyptic battle fought by God ends the present order (though the new secure order pictured is not without continuities with the present age).[13] The defeat of Gog marks the beginning of millennial security for Israel (Ezek. 39:7, 26) and a new life inaugurated by the pouring out of God's Spirit (Ezek. 39:29).

To express this apocalyptic eschatology, the passage uses the ancient divine-warrior myth of the holy-war tradition.[14] This is consistent with the heavy use of the divine-warrior motif in the early history of the development of Israelite apocalyptic religion.

In biblical proto-apocalyptic literature, the motif of the wars of YHWH is transformed so that historical victory becomes apocalyptic final judgment.[15] Thus, Ezekiel 38–39 uses the images of cloudbursts and hail-

11. Ronald M. Hals correctly finds that the burning of the weapons after the battle (Ezek. 39:9-10) implies that the victory and plunder are YHWH's (*Ezekiel*, FOTL 19 [Grand Rapids, Mich.: Eerdmans, 1989], 282). The old holy-war pattern is taken up, according to which everything of the enemy's is burned after a battle as devoted material.

12. See Zimmerli, *Ezekiel 2*, 318. As Astour notes, the Israelites emerge enriched, although they will not have had to strike a single blow ("Cuthean Legend," 567).

13. This view is in keeping with the worldviews of several of the millennial groups that have been discussed. Thus, Smohalla's vision of the postvictory world of the Native Americans was a land where they could dwell securely (cf. Ezek. 39:26). Savonarola's Florence of the coming golden age was to have great renown (cf. Ezek. 39:13), but at the same time it was still to be Florence.

14. On the importance of the ancient Near Eastern divine-warrior motif in proto-apocalyptic writings, see Frank Moore Cross, *Canaanite Myth and Hebrew Epic* (Cambridge, Mass.: Harvard University Press, 1973), 343f.; Hanson, *Dawn*, 123f.; and Patrick D. Miller, Jr., *The Divine Warrior in Early Israel* (Cambridge, Mass.: Harvard University Press, 1973).

15. For example, Isaiah 13 seems to depict the final destruction wrought by YHWH and his heavenly armies (see Miller, *Divine Warrior*, 136). Joel 4:9f. (cf.

stones, borrowing terminology from the old stories about the wars of
YHWH (*Jahwekriegserzählungen*) such as Joshua 10:10-11 and 1 Samuel
7:10-11.[16] Along with the participation of nature, the motif of the self-
slaughter of the enemy (Ezek. 38:21) is another holy-war element (Judg.
7:22; 1 Sam. 14:20)[17] often taken up by (proto-)apocalyptic literature (for
example, Zech. 14:13; Rev. 6:3-4; *1 Enoch* 100:1-2).[18]

Finally, the image of becoming glutted and drunk on the fat and blood
of the slain enemy (Ezek. 39:19-20) has been adapted by Ezekiel from the
divine-warrior myth. In Ugaritic myth (*CTA* 3.2.1-41), for example, the
warrior goddess Anat plunged herself into blood and gore "until she was
satiated" (*'d. tsb'* [*CTA* 3.2.29]; Ugaritic *šb'* = Hebrew *śb'* [Ezek. 39:19-
20]). Isaiah 34:5-7 pictures YHWH's sword satiated and drunk with blood
as part of end-time judgments. The apocalyptic judgment of God's enemies in Isaiah 63:1-6 also continues the image of intoxicating blood, although here YHWH does not become drunk. This aversion to speaking
of YHWH as drunk is taken further by Ezekiel 39:17-20, where it is animals and not YHWH or the sword of YHWH that become intoxicated on
the blood of the slain.[19] Other (proto-)apocalyptic texts connecting intoxicating blood and end-time judgments are Joel 4:13 (Eng.: 3:13); and
Revelation 14:19-20; 19:15.

Ezekiel 38–39 also uses the mythical image of the attack of the many
nations on Jerusalem to express a radical eschatology. YHWH's deliverance
from an attack by the united kings and nations of the world (Pss. 2:1-5;
46; 48; and 75 [compare Ps. 65:7])[20] was taken up in such (proto-)

---

esp. vv. 11b and 12b) refers to the involvement of heavenly warriors alongside its
other apocalyptic elements (see Miller, *Divine Warrior,* 137).

16. See the discussion in Hossfeld, *Untersuchungen,* 460.

17. Blenkinsopp, *Ezekiel,* 187.

18. The *1 Enoch* 100:1-2 text reads, "Brothers one with another shall fall in
death, Till the streams flow with their blood . . . . From dawn till sunset they shall
slay one another."

19. In the Ugaritic texts, there is no such aversion to speaking of the gods as
getting drunk. They drink "wine till sated // must till inebriated." See Marvin Pope,
"Notes on the Rephaim Texts from Ugarit," *Essays on the Ancient Near East in Memory of Jacob Joel Finkelstein,* Memoirs of the Connecticut Academy of Arts and Sciences, v. 19, ed. M. Ellis (Hamden, Conn.: Archon, 1977), 175.

20. Several psalms also make reference to the Israelite king's (e.g., Pss. 45:5 and
110:1) and God's (e.g., Pss. 47:3 and 110:5) subduing of the peoples. Sigmund
Mowinckel argued that psalmic descriptions of the nations' attack on Jerusalem
and their rout and destruction are to be understood as "the 'cultic myth' of the
[YHWH enthronement] festival, which we call the *myth about the fight of nations*"

apocalyptic literary units as Zechariah 12:1-9; 14; and Revelation 20:7-10, and expanded into the judgment at the end of time.[21] Lorenz Dürr argued in 1923 that Ezekiel first used the *Völkersturm* motif this way and incorporated it into the scenario of the end times.[22] The use of this motif with its idea of an attack against the center of the world (Ezek. 38:12) indicates that the eschatology of Ezekiel 38–39 looks forward to a decisive cosmic event.[23]

In Ezekiel's eschatology, the above described Gog event is to happen in the "latter years" (אחרית השנים; Ezek. 38:8) or "latter days" (אחרית הימים; Ezek. 38:16). Here Ezekiel uses an idiom from older eschatology (for example, Num. 24:14; Isa. 2:2; Jer. 23:20)[24] and gives it a use akin to that in full-blown apocalyptic literature as a technical term for the eschatological end-act. The *Damascus Rule* uses the term in this way: "The Sons of Zadok . . . shall stand at the end of days" (CD 4:4; 6:11; see also Dan. 10:14; 1QSa 6:1).

Over against the preexilic meaning of the term, Ezekiel 38–39 adds a universal dimension to this coming judgment.[25] Combined with this added universality is the sense in Ezekiel 38–39 that a culmination of history is intended by the "latter days" idiom.[26] It is important to note that the culmination of the era, not the distance of the eschaton, is stressed.

(*The Psalms in Israel's Worship*, trans. D. R. Ap-Thomas [New York: Abingdon, 1967], 1:152).

21. See Lorenz Dürr, *Die Stellung des Propheten Ezechiel in der Israelitisch-Jüdischen Apokalyptik*, Alttestamentliche Abhandlungen 9:1, ed. J. Nikel (Münster: Aschendorffschen Verlagsbuchhandlung, 1923), 65.

22. Ibid., 65.

23. Zimmerli, *Ezekiel 2*, 311.

24. Dürr argues that the idiom was clearly used before the exile (*Die Stellung*, 100–102).

25. Ezekiel expands the contents of the idiom so that it points to a judgment on the world nations, represented in Ezekiel 38–39 by Gog (Dürr, *Die Stellung*, 103–4).

26. Brevard S. Childs states, "The appearance of Gog falls 'in the latter years' (38:8, 16), which indicates that the events described have passed from the plane of history and entered the apocalyptic age. The battle is considered the final stage before the coming of the new age" ("The Enemy from the North and the Chaos Tradition," *JBL* 78 [1959]: 196). Horst Seebass states that Ezek. 38:16 prepares for the usage's development as a technical term as in Dan. 2:28, where "the outcome of the future is what is intended, and not the future in general" ("אחרית," *TDOT* 1:207).

Ezekiel does not put off the end-time judgment to a distant, abstract future. He had been reproached by his countrymen for this sort of irrelevance before (Ezek. 12:26-28). In contrast here, as Ezekiel 38:8 shows, Ezekiel is concerned with coming events after a restoration, occurring in the near future.[27] Thus, the passage implies that a restoration must now occur first in accordance with Ezekiel's earlier preaching. Nevertheless, this places the next phase of the eschaton only as "an event at one remove."[28]

The above mentioned eschatological features in Ezekiel 38–39 indicate that Ezekiel's concept of the Day of YHWH (ההוא ביום: Ezek. 38:10, 14, 18, 19; 39:11, [22]; היום הוא: Ezek. 39:8) is closer to proto-apocalyptic concepts of the end time than to the preexilic prophetic emphasis on judgment against Israel and Judah.[29] Thus, the Day of YHWH in Ezekiel 38–39 is associated with the same salvific eschatological drama found in Joel and Zechariah.[30] In the proto-apocalyptic eschatology of these prophets, the Day of YHWH involves the attack of many nations (Zech. 12:3-4; 14:1-7) followed by the dawning of the millennial era (Joel 4:18 [Eng.: 3:18]).

Dualism

Ezekiel 38–39 pictures the world locked in a struggle between two opposing moral forces. To express this moral dualism, the Gog passage goes beyond historical referents in using mythic-realistic images.[31] Specifically, the preexilic "enemy-from-the-north" expectation is given a transhistorical

27. Hossfeld notes that Ezekiel's time usages here (such as "after many days") are necessary because the restoration is still about to come in the near future as a first phase. Following this is the second phase, occupied with the emergence of Gog. See Hossfeld, *Untersuchungen,* 441.

28. Zimmerli, *Ezekiel 2,* 307.

29. See Dürr, *Die Stellung,* 86–89. This is not to argue that oracles of salvation are absent in the preexilic prophets. Nevertheless, there is some truth to Dürr's contention that Ezekiel 38–39 reorients the "Day of YHWH" so that it becomes more of an object of hope as in the preexilic popular eschatology that prophets such as Amos condemned (Amos 5:18-20).

30. On the use of the "Day of YHWH" in postexilic prophecy, see M. Sæbø, "יום," *TDOT* 6:31.

31. Erling, "Ezekiel 38–39," 107; Aelred Cody, *Ezekiel with an Excursus on Old Testament Priesthood* (Wilmington, Del.: Glazier, 1984), 183. For the "mythic-realistic" concept, see John J. Collins, *Daniel with an Introduction to Apocalyptic Literature,* FOTL 20 (Grand Rapids, Mich.: Eerdmans, 1984), 6.

existence.[32] The enemy from the north, now Gog and his allies, is a monstrous northern horde, the antithesis of heavenly power (Ezek. 38:4, 6, 9, 15, 22; 39:4, 11-12).[33] Like the "great army" in Joel 2:25, the apocalyptic horde is a חיל רב ("mighty army," Ezek. 38:15; compare 38:4). The Daniel millennial group was also threatened by a "mighty army" from the north (Dan. 11:13).[34]

Other apocalyptic terms and features are associated with the horde in Ezekiel 38–39. Ezekiel uses a metaphor of dark obscurity (*Undurchsichtigkeit*) expressed by the term ענן ("cloud"; Ezek. 38:9, 16) to describe Gog's overwhelming incursion.[35] Joel 2:2 describes the apocalyptic enemy army in the same way.[36] The description of Gog's army as a "tumultuous multitude" (המון; Ezek. 39:11, 15-16) is found elsewhere in apocalyptic literature as part of descriptions of the end-time forces in rebellion against God. The Qumran War Scroll states, "They [the enemy army] are a wicked horde . . . all their multitudinous throng . . . shall not be found" (1QM 15). The warhorse image (Ezek. 38:4) is also an important part of the apocalyptic-horde motif (Joel 2:4; Rev. 9:7; compare 1QM 6:8-16).

Further, the monstrous size of Gog and his horde is clear from the amount of time it takes to bury the multitude (Ezek. 39:11-14)[37] and to

---

32. Childs, "Enemy," 187–98. The genuine Jeremiah passages dealing with the enemy from the north are: Jer. 1:13-15; 4:5b-8, 11b-17a, 19-21; 5:15-17; and 6:1-5, 22-26 (Childs, "Enemy," 190). Childs argues that in apocalyptic eschatology, the enemy from the north takes on superhuman characteristics. "The marked change in the essential nature of the enemy, as well as his function, appears first in Ezekiel 38–39" (ibid., 196).

33. As Dürr notes, Gog is the personification of the world powers hostile to Israel (*Die Stellung*, 94, 97). Indeed, Ahroni states that the central theme of the Gog prophecy is the "final conflict between God and Gog, the embodiment of cosmic evil forces" ("Gog Prophecy," 16). (Although Ahroni appears wrong about the provenance of Ezekiel 38–39, his classification of the Gog prophecy with apocalyptic literature is illuminating [see "Gog Prophecy," 15].)

34. H. Eising, "חיל," *TDOT* 4:352.

35. David Noel Freedman and B. E. Willoughby, "ענן," *TWAT* 6:272 (cf. Lam. 3:44).

36. The idea of the Day of YHWH as dark and gloomy (Zeph. 1:15) may be part of the background of both Joel 2 and Ezekiel 38–39.

37. Pope argues that the corpses of "Gog's Mob" are so many that the crush of the "departed" stops up the Hinnom Valley (Ezek. 39:11), the "terminal depot" for those passing on to the infernal underworld metropolis known as "Crowd-Town" (Ezek. 39:16) ("Rephaim Texts," 174).

burn up its weapons as timber (Ezek. 39:9-10).[38] As with Edom in Isaiah 63:1-6, in Ezekiel's description of Gog the nations are lumped together as the collective Evil opposed to the forces of good. Brevard S. Childs states, "Gog has become the representative of the cosmic powers of the returned chaos which Yahweh destroys in the latter days, powers which cannot be described as historical."[39]

Ezekiel 38–39 also contains a dualism between the present age and the age to come. The text pictures a return to *Urzeit* chaos, which in turn signals an end to the present creation. A. Baumann states that המון, the term for Gog's multitude, itself is "particularly suited for representing everything chaotic."[40] This term also occurs at Qumran in descriptions of the end-time assault of chaos.[41] Further, Ezekiel 38:20 pictures a reversal of creation in the same way that end time is primordial time (Endzeit ist Urzeit) in Isaiah 34:11, part of a postexilic proto-apocalyptic literary unit. In Isaiah 34, YHWH reduces "Edom" to a place just like primordial chaos (תהו + בהו). Similarly, Isaiah 24:1, 20, part of the so-called Isaiah Apocalypse, pictures a return to cosmic tumult. This chaos motif, and especially the idea of mountains collapsing, is developed further in full-blown apocalypses. Thus, *1 Enoch* describes the final judgment as a time when "the lofty mountains shall be shaken; they shall fall and be disintegrated" (*1 Enoch* 1:3-9).

To express this apocalyptic return to chaos, which dualistically separates this world from the world to come, Ezekiel 38–39 also employs the רעש ("earthquake") motif (Ezek. 38:19-20). Childs has shown how רעש evolved into a technical term within the language of the return to chaos associated with the eschaton.[42] In exilic and postexilic writings, the

38. See Gressmann, who writes that from the seven years it takes to burn the weapons, one realizes the monstrous size (*die ungeheure Grösse*) of the enemy and its terrific armament (*Der Messias,* 126). Also, cf. the description of the aftermath of battle in Ezek. 39:9-16 with that in the proto-apocalyptic text Isa. 66:15-24.

39. Childs, "Enemy," 196. Also see Robert R. Wilson, "Ezekiel," *Harper's Bible Commentary,* ed. J. Mays (San Francisco: Harper and Row, 1988), 692.

40. "המה," *TDOT* 3:416. The root is used to designate both the raging of the sea and of hostile nations. Thus, in Ezek. 39:11, 15-16 the idea of the powers of chaos in rebellion against God is expressed.

41. "המה," *TDOT* 3:417. See 1QH 2:12, 16, 27; 3:13-16, 31-34. 1QH 3:32; 6:24 associate the root המה with תהום.

42. Childs, "Enemy," 189. The importance of this argument has apparently escaped Hals, who does not see Ezekiel 38–39 as apocalyptic literature (*Ezekiel,* 284). Hals's arguments lose much of their force when the distinction between "apoca-

"enemy-from-the-north" tradition (just discussed) and the "great-shaking" motif become fused together as part of the development of apocalyptic eschatology.[43] Thus, Joel uses the verb רעש twice with respect to a final judgment through a returned chaos (Joel 2:10; 4:16 [Eng.: 3:16]). The verb is also joined to the chaos motif in Isaiah 13:13; 24:18; and Zechariah 14:4-5.[44] By New Testament times, the earthquake motif was a standard part of the picture of the birth pangs of the new age (Mark 13:8; Matt. 24:7-8; Luke 21:11; Rev. 6:12-14; 11:13; 16:18, 20). In these texts, σεισμός ("earthquake") is clearly part of the end-time tribulation. The earthquake motif also recurs in full-blown Jewish apocalyptic literature: The *Assumption of Moses* states, "The Heavenly One will arise . . . and the earth will tremble" (10:3-7). A sign of the end of the present age in 2 Esdras 6:11-17 is that "the foundations of the earth . . . will tremble and be shaken."

Secondary Features

The Ezekiel 38–39 passage exhibits several secondary features of apocalyptic literature described in chapter 2 above. For example, Ezekiel 38–39 contains notions of apocalyptic determinism. God first brings Gog against Israel (Ezek. 38:4). This, combined with the use of terms expressing inevitability (for example, ונהיתה "and it will happen," Ezek. 39:8), pictures Gog as a pawn, predestined to his own destruction.[45]

The Gog passage also exhibits the beginnings of apocalyptic determinism by making steps toward a blueprint or timetable of future events. One of the remarkable features of the Gog passage is that it looks two stages beyond the present. The gathering of the exiles is expected as a first stage (Ezek. 38:8, 12; 39:27, 28); then, as a second stage, Gog attacks and is defeated.[46] From this Walther Zimmerli concludes, "A first step is taken on

---

lypse" and "apocalyptic literature" is kept clear. On this distinction, see John J. Collins, "Introduction: Towards the Morphology of a Genre," *Semeia* 14 (1979): 10, and the discussion in chapter 2 above.

43. Childs, "Enemy," 197–98.

44. On the earthquake motif as part of the "ultimate theophany" in Isaiah 13; 24; and Joel 4 (Eng.: 3), see Günther Bornkamm, "σείω, σεισμός," *TDNT* 7:198.

45. See Astour, "Cuthean Legend," 568. Ralph W. Klein writes, "As the account makes clear from beginning to end, the coming of Gog and his defeat are totally under Yahweh's control" (*Ezekiel: The Prophet and His Message* [Columbia: University of South Carolina Press, 1988], 163).

46. See n. 27 above.

the way to apocalyptic, the aim of which is to set up a sequential order of future events."[47]

Examples of apocalyptic interest in speculative devices and numerology are also present in Ezekiel 38–39. For instance, the number seven, a favorite in apocalyptic writings, occurs several times in the Gog passage. See the time references in Ezekiel 39:9, 12, and 14 and the enumeration of seven kinds of weapons in Ezekiel 39:9.[48] Also note the seven peoples in Gog of Magog's horde (Ezek. 38:2-6). As another example of numerology, Ronald M. Hals argues that the name Magog may "be the result of an alphabetic play on the name Babel by using in reverse order letters one step further along in the alphabet."[49]

Still other secondary apocalyptic motifs occur in Ezekiel 38–39. For example, the passage uses the apocalyptic-sword motif at Ezekiel 38:21. This sword (חרב) of end-time judgment also occurs in such (proto-) apocalyptic texts as Isaiah 27:1; 34:5-6; 66:16; Zechariah 11:17; 13:7; and Revelation 6:3-4.[50] The Qumran War Scroll refers to this apocalyptic sword too: "Blows of a sword which shall not be that of a man, and a sword which shall not be human shall devour him" (1QM 11:11-12). The motif of a bloody punishment (Ezek. 38:22) is also common in (proto-) apocalyptic texts (for example, Isa. 34:1-4; 63:6; Joel 3:3 [Eng.: 2:30]; Rev. 8:7).[51] By the same token, "fire" (Ezek. 38:22; 39:6) often appears in descriptions of apocalyptic final judgment (for example, Isa. 66:15-16; Joel 3:3 [Eng.: 2:30]; Zech. 9:4; 12:6).[52] Finally, Ezekiel 39:17-20 contains the motif of an apocalyptic sacrifice. The sacrificial-feast motif was taken up by both Ezekiel 38–39 and Isaiah 34:5-8 from earlier prophecy

---

47. Zimmerli, *Ezekiel 2*, 304. See also Dürr, *Die Stellung*, 90.

48. Ahroni, "Gog Prophecy," 17; John W. Wevers, *Ezekiel*, NCBC (Greenwood, S.C.: Attic, 1969), 292.

49. Hals, *Ezekiel*, 284; note that the same suggestion that MGG is a cryptogram for BBL was made earlier by Louis Finkelstein (*The Pharisees: The Sociological Background of Their Faith* [Philadelphia: Jewish Publication Society, 1938], 1:338). Hals states "that such far-fetched speculative devices actually were employed is known from the appearance of Sheshach in Jer 51:41 as a code for Babel by using 'athbash,' the replacement of the first letter in the alphabet by the last, the second letter by the second last, etc." (*Ezekiel*, 284).

50. O. Kaiser, "חרב," *TDOT* 5:160.

51. B. Kedar-Kopfstein, "דם," *TDOT* 3:249-50.

52. One might also mention the use of the term גפרית ("brimstone"; Ezek. 38:22) in the apocalyptic description of God's destruction of Edom in Isa. 34:9.

(Zeph. 1:7) to depict the apocalyptic destruction of God's enemies (compare Rev. 19:17-18).[53]

Later Reuse of the Gog Tradition

Ezekiel 38–39 may be one of the earliest examples of biblical apocalyptic literature. That Ezekiel should contain such a passage might have been expected given the book's several general tendencies toward apocalypticism.[54] As Dürr argued, biblical apocalypticism first emerges in the writings of Ezekiel, and the origins of the Gog text are best viewed as a part of this development. Dürr found that it was Ezekiel who took up the early popular conception of the destruction of the nations at Jerusalem and projected it to the end of days. Thus, Dürr argued that Ezekiel was the originator (*Urheber*) of the later eschatological schema found in full-blown apocalyptic thought.[55] Later reuses of the Gog tradition confirm this argument.

Although it is always difficult to determine dependence, it appears that Ezekiel 38–39 lies behind several later examples of this genre of literature.[56] Thus, B. Erling sees Ezekiel 38–39 as "an early stage in the development of the apocalyptic tradition" behind Zechariah 14:1-5; Daniel 11:40-45; and Revelation 20:7-10.[57] Ezekiel 38–39 probably also influenced the picture of the attack of the nations on Jerusalem in Zechariah 12:1-9. The book of Joel also uses Ezekiel 38–39: Dürr sees Joel as an example of how Ezekiel's conception of a great end-time enemy from the north continued in later eschatology. All it took was a devastating locust swarm to rouse the expectation of the "northerners" (הצפוני, Joel 2:20) and the Day of YHWH (Joel 3 and 4 [Eng.: 2:28 — 3:21]).[58] Additionally, Ezekiel 39:29 paves the

53. B. Lang, "זבח," *TDOT* 4:29.

54. Cross writes, "The transformation of classical prophecy into proto-apocalyptic takes place in the oracles of Ezekiel before one's eyes" (*Canaanite Myth*, 223 n. 15). Also see Hanson, *Dawn*, 234.

55. Dürr, *Die Stellung*, 94.

56. Issue is taken here with Gressmann, who does not find traces of the Gog prophecy in later biblical apocalyptic literature. For Gressmann, the Gog material first plays an influential role only in the postbiblical period (*Der Messias*, 133).

57. Erling, "Ezekiel 38–39," 107. Similar arguments are made by Dürr, *Die Stellung*, 99–100. On the use of the Gog tradition in Dan. 11:40-45, see also F. F. Bruce, "The Earliest Old Testament Interpretation," in *The Witness of Tradition*, OTS 17 (Leiden: E. J. Brill, 1972), 42. On Ezekiel's end-time visions as behind Revelation 20–22, see Johan Lust, "The Order of the Final Events in Revelation and in Ezekiel," *L'Apocalypse johannique et l'Apocalyptique dans le Nouveau Testament* (Leuven: Leuven University Press, 1980), 179–83.

58. Dürr, *Die Stellung*, 99.

way for the promise of the pouring out of the Spirit in Joel 3:1 (Eng.: 2:28).[59] The Gog tradition also lies behind nonbiblical apocalyptic texts such as *1 Enoch* 56:5-8; 2 Esdras 13:5-11; and portions of the Qumran War Scroll (for example, 1QM 11).

The Relation of Ezekiel 38–39 to the Rest of the Book

Ezekiel and the school that transmitted and interpreted his book are located sociologically among the priestly upper echelons of Israelite society. The reference in Ezekiel 1:3 to Ezekiel as a priest is confirmed by the book's many priestly interests (Ezek. 4:14; 18:6; 20:12; 36:25; and 43:7-9). Not only was Ezekiel a priest, he was a Zadokite priest.[60] At the time of the exile, the Zadokites controlled the high priesthood and held central-priestly power, if not hegemony, at the temple in Jerusalem — a position they had consolidated since the time of Solomon's dismissal of Abiathar (1 Kings 2:26-27).[61] It was almost certainly from among this central Zadokite group that Ezekiel was taken into exile as part of the first Babylonian deportation of 597 B.C.E. The argument that Ezekiel was a Zadokite priest is confirmed by his book's linguistic resonances with Leviticus 17–26, the Holiness Code (H).[62] As I shall suggest below, H is best understood as stemming from Zadokite circles.

The school of Ezekiel was also within Zadokite circles.[63] This school focused on Israel's sacral worship, the new temple, and the hierarchical ordering of the priesthood.[64] Blenkinsopp states, "In its final form the book is the product of a school which owed allegiance to Ezekiel, which

---

59. See Zimmerli, *Ezekiel 2,* 321, 567.

60. See Robert R. Wilson, *Prophecy and Society in Ancient Israel* (Philadelphia: Fortress, 1980), 282. Ezekiel may even have conceived of himself as the high priest of the coming age. See the comments in Jon D. Levenson, *Theology of the Program of Restoration of Ezekiel 40–48* (Missoula, Mont.: Scholars Press, 1976), 140.

61. On the Zadokites and Jerusalem priestly politics, see Cross, *Canaanite Myth,* 208; Hanson, *Dawn,* 221; and Ferdinand Deist, "Prior to the Dawn of Apocalyptic," in *The Exilic Period: Aspects of Apocalypticism, OTWSA* 25/26 (1982/1983): 13–38. On Ezekiel as a member of the central-cultic elite, see Blenkinsopp, *History of Prophecy,* 206; and Hanson, *Dawn,* 225.

62. See Walther Zimmerli, *Ezekiel 1,* trans. R. E. Clements, Hermeneia (Philadelphia: Fortress, 1979), 16, 46–52, 111.

63. For an overview of the idea of an "Ezekiel school," see Walther Zimmerli, "The Message of the Prophet Ezekiel," *Int* 23 (1969): 133; and *Ezekiel 1,* 68–74.

64. See Zimmerli, *Ezekiel 1,* 65.

was closely associated with the cult, and which inherited the ancient traditions of the priesthood as did Ezekiel himself."[65]

Examination of Ezekiel 38–39 leaves little doubt that it is from this
Ezekielian circle of Zadokite priests. As the following data base (List 2)
shows, numerous linguistic usages and idioms link the Ezekiel 38–39 passage to the rest of the book of Ezekiel.

The following list should be read with two caveats in mind. First, it
does not take into account the question of whether the parallels cited are
to material from the hand of Ezekiel himself or to additions by his tradents.
The argument that these chapters are Zadokite material holds in both
cases.[66] Second, because the relationship of the appendixlike section Ezekiel 39:21-29 to the rest of Ezekiel 38–39 is especially problematic, usages
and idioms particular to these verses within the Gog section will not be
considered here. I shall return to discussion of Ezekiel 39:21-29 below.

List 2. Continuity of Ezekiel 38–39 and Ezekiel as a Whole

1. בֶּן־אָדָם ("Son of man"; Ezek. 38:2, 14; 39:1, 17): This term of address for Ezekiel is characteristic of the book as a whole. See Ezekiel
   2:1, 3, 6, 8; 3:1, 3, 4, 10, 17, 25; 4:1, 16; 5:1; 6:2; 7:2; 8:5, 6, 8, 12;
   11:2, 4, 15; 12:2, 3, 9, 18, 22; etc.

2. שִׂים פָּנֶיךָ אֶל־ ("set your face toward . . . "; Ezek. 38:2): This formula
   of hostile orientation is used repeatedly in Ezekiel and is characteristic
   of his style.[67] See Ezekiel 6:2; 13:17; 21:2 (Eng.: 20:46); 21:7 (Eng.:
   21:2); 25:2; 28:21; 29:2; 35:2. Also compare Ezekiel 4:3, 7.

3. מֶשֶׁךְ ("Meshech"; Ezek. 38:2, 3; 39:1): This term appears as a geo-
   graphical name elsewhere in the Hebrew Bible only in Ezekiel 27:13
   and 32:26. In both cases, Meshech is paired with Tubal as it is here.

4. הִנָּבֵא (Niphal imperative, "prophesy"; Ezek. 38:2, 14; 39:1): This usage occurs frequently in Ezekiel (twenty-seven times), but elsewhere
   only at Amos 7:15.

65. Blenkinsopp, *History of Prophecy*, 195.

66. Even if authors such as Gressmann are correct that Ezekiel 38–39 as a whole
is from a time much later than Ezekiel, the evidence to be presented still shows
that this material comes from Zadokite priests. Gressmann himself states that the
views of Ezekiel 38–39 may very well stem from disciples (*Jünger*) or associates
(*Freunde*) of Ezekiel. He asks, "Why should there not have been more such priests
in prophetic mantle?" (*Der Messias*, 124).

67. See Hals, *Ezekiel*, 361; and Zimmerli, *Ezekiel 2*, 302. Klein notes that even
Ezekiel's setting his face against individuals is not unique to this passage (this also
occurs in Ezekiel 13:17 and 29:2) (*Ezekiel*, 167 n. 7).

5. הנני אליך (the challenge-to-a-duel formula;[68] Ezek. 38:3; 39:1): As Zimmerli notes, "Of the twenty-two Old Testament occurrences of this formula two are found in Nahum ... six in Jeremiah ... and the remaining fourteen in Ezekiel (5:8; 13:8, 20; 21:8; 26:3; 28:22; 29:3, 10; 30:22; 34:10; 35:3; 36:9; 38:3 [here]; 39:1 [here])."[69]

6. חח ("hook"; Ezek. 38:4): This image resonates with that in Ezekiel 19:4, 9; and 29:4.[70] Elsewhere the term occurs only in 2 Kings 19:28 and Isaiah 37:29, where the hooks are in "noses" and not in "jaws" as in the Ezekiel 29:4 and 38:4 passages.

7. מכלול ("perfection, splendor"; Ezek. 38:4): The usage occurs elsewhere in the Hebrew Bible only in Ezekiel 23:12.

8. קהל רב ("a great company"; Ezek. 38:4; compare Ezek. 38:15): Similar usages occur in Ezekiel 26:7 and 32:3.[71] The usage as it occurs in the Psalms (Pss. 22:26; 35:18; and 40:10, 11) has a different meaning (the "great congregation" of Israel).

9. מגן + צנה (the use of "buckler" and "shield" together; Ezek. 38:4; compare Ezek. 39:9): As with item 7 above, there seem to be resonances here with Ezekiel 23 (here with v. 24), although this combination also occurs at Jeremiah 46:3 and Psalm 35:2.

10. מגן + כובע (the use of "shield" and "helmet" together; Ezek. 38:5): This combination occurs elsewhere in the Hebrew Bible only at Ezekiel 27:10 (although 2 Chron. 26:14 does contain both words).

11. אגף ("army"; Ezek. 38:6, 9, 22; 39:4): This usage is unique to Ezekiel (Ezek. 12:14 and 17:21).[72]

12. תגרמה ("Togarmah"; Ezek. 38:6): Togarmah is also mentioned in Ezekiel 27:14. The only other occurrence of the noun is in the Table of Nations (Gen. 10:3 = 1 Chron. 1:6).

13. הכן והכן (the doubling of the verb כון: "be prepared and prepare yourself"; Ezek. 38:7): Zimmerli notes that this type of verbal doubling is "a favorite stylistic feature of Ezekiel."[73] Similar double expressions are found at Ezekiel 14:6; 18:30; 20:4; and 22:2.

---

68. On the *Herausforderungsformel*, see Hals, *Ezekiel*, 359.

69. Zimmerli, *Ezekiel 1*, 175.

70. See Zimmerli, *Ezekiel 2*, 306.

71. Even if these passages in Ezekiel 26 and 32 are secondary as Hossfeld argues, they still stem from the Zadokite tradents of Ezekiel (see Hossfeld, *Untersuchungen*, 437).

72. See Zimmerli, *Ezekiel 2*, 302; and Hossfeld, *Untersuchungen*, 439.

73. Zimmerli, *Ezekiel 2*, 286.

14. מקבצת (the concept of the gathering back [קבץ] of Israel; Ezek. 38:8; the verb also occurs at 39:27; compare 39:28): The important theme of Ezekiel's theology that God will gather back Israel is clearly shared by Ezekiel 38–39. In fact, this restoration to the land may be seen as in fulfillment of promises such as those found in Ezekiel 28:25-26.[74] Other cross-references are Ezekiel 11:16-17; 20:34,41; 34:13; 36:24; and 37:21.

   מאסף (the same concept of gathering back expressed with the root אסף; Ezek. 38:12): The same root is used in Ezekiel 11:17 to express this idea.

15. הרי ישראל ("the mountains of Israel"; Ezek. 38:8; 39:2, 4, 17): Even Ahroni, who argues that Ezekiel 38–39 is a late intrusion, recognizes that this expression represents a usage unique to Ezekiel.[75] The cross-references are: Ezekiel 6:2-3; 19:9; 33:28; 34:13; 35:12; 36:1, 4, 8; 37:22.

16. חרבה ("desolate place"; Ezek. 38:8, 12): Although also common in Jeremiah (for example, Jer. 7:34; 22:5; 25:9), this usage is characteristic of Ezekiel (Ezek. 5:14; 13:4; 25:13; 26:20; 29:9, 10; 33:24, 27; 35:4; 36:4). The usage in Ezekiel 38–39 has especially clear resonances with the Ezekiel cross-references noted at Ezekiel 5:14; 33:24, 27; and 36:4 (compare 36:35, 38 where the adjective הָרֵב "waste" appears).

17. The root ישב used together with בטח ("live securely"; Ezek. 38:8, 11, 14; 39:26; compare 39:6): This linguistic usage is characteristic of Ezekiel (Ezek. 28:26; 34:25, 28; compare 34:27). The usage in Ezekiel 38–39 is in continuity with the theology of the book. As Zimmerli notes, the process of restoration described in Ezekiel 34–37 is presupposed by Ezekiel 38–39 to have been completed.[76]

18. כסה + ענן ("a cloud" used with the verb "cover"; Ezek. 38:9, 16): There are resonances here with Ezekiel 30:18 and 32:7. (This combination as found in passages such as Exod. 24:15 and Lev. 16:13 represents a different order of usage.)

19. בזז + שלל ("capture spoil" used together with "seize plunder"; Ezek. 38:12, 13; 39:10): There are resonances here with Ezekiel 29:19,

74. Erling notes how earlier parallel references in Ezekiel all "stress how Yahweh will manifest his holiness before the nations by bringing his people back to their own land" ("Ezekiel 38–39," 110). The new element in Ezekiel 38–39 is God's further, final demonstration of power. For further discussion of the gathering back of Israel in Ezekiel, see, e.g., Klein, *Ezekiel*, 160.

75. Ahroni, "Gog Prophecy," 6; see his n. 13 for details on the usage. Also see Hossfeld, *Untersuchungen*, 463; and Zimmerli, *Ezekiel 1*, 185.

76. Zimmerli, *Ezekiel 2*, 307.

which also uses both verbs (compare Ezek. 26:12). Elsewhere this combination of verbs is found only in Isaiah 10:6.

20. שבא, דדן, and תרשיש ("Sheba, Dedan, and Tarshish"; Ezek. 38:13): There are echoes here of the trade list in Ezekiel 27. ("Sheba" occurs in Ezek. 27:22, 23; "Dedan" occurs in Ezek. 27:15, 20 [see also 25:13]; and "Tarshish" occurs in Ezek. 27:12.)

21. קהל גדול וחיל רב ("a great assembly and a mighty army"; Ezek. 38:15 [compare also item 8 above]): A similar usage occurs at Ezekiel 17:17 (compare Ezek. 37:10).

22. הגוים + ידע ("the nations" as the subject of the verbal element of the [modified] recognition formula; Ezek. 38:16, 23; 39:[6], 7, 23; compare 39:21): The *Erkenntnisformel* (recognition formula), as is well known, is common in Ezekiel, occurring often with "Israel" as the subject (for example, Ezek. 25:7).[77] It occurs this way in Ezekiel 39:22. The more narrowly defined usage of Ezekiel 38–39 conveying the idea that the "nations will know" has several cross-references with the book of Ezekiel as a whole. See Ezekiel 36:23, 36-38; 37:28 (compare Ezek. 21:10 [Eng.: 21:5]; 26:6; 29:6; and 30:26).

23. קדש (in a reflexive stem) with "God" as subject + "before the eyes" (construct = עיני) ("I [God] shall sanctify myself before [their] eyes"; Ezek. 38:16 [Niphal stem]; 38:23 [Hithpael stem]; 39:27 [Niphal stem]): This formulation also occurs in Ezekiel 20:41; 28:25; and 36:23 (compare Ezek. 28:22).

24. קנאה + דבר ("speak in angry zeal"; Ezek. 38:19): The usage also occurs in Ezekiel 5:13; and 36:5, 6.

25. אש + עברה ("blazing wrath"; Ezek. 38:19): This combination is an Ezekiel expression (Ezek. 21:36; and 22:21, 31).

26. הרס ("throw down"; Ezek. 38:20): The book of Ezekiel is elsewhere fond of this verb (Ezek. 13:14; 16:39; 26:4; 30:4; and 36:35-36).

27. שפט (Niphal stem) + את ("enter into judgment with"; Ezek. 38:22): The usage also occurs in Ezekiel 17:20 and 20:35-36.

28. דבר + דם ("pestilence and blood"; Ezek. 38:22): This combination resonates with Ezekiel 5:17.

29. גשם שוטף ("torrential rain"; Ezek. 38:22): This combination occurs elsewhere in the Hebrew Bible only at Ezekiel 13:11, 13.

30. אלגביש ("hail"; Ezek. 38:22): This term is peculiar to Ezekiel in the Hebrew Bible (Ezek. 13:11, 13).[78]

---

77. For discussion, see Zimmerli, *Ezekiel 1,* 37–40.

78. Here again Ahroni, who disagrees that Ezekiel 38–39 is authentic Ezekiel material, still recognizes that אבני אלגביש ("hailstones") occurs solely in Ezekiel ("Gog Prophecy," 7).

31. נפל (in the Hiphil stem) + a weapon (Ezek. 39:3): The language here resonates with Ezekiel's description of the battle with Pharaoh in Ezekiel 30:22.[79]

32. Give (נתן) for food (אכלה) to wild animals (Ezek. 39:4; compare Ezek. 39:17-20): Frank L. Hossfeld notes the way Ezekiel 39:4b is tightly connected to the "authentic Ezekiel passages" of Ezekiel 29:5 and 33:27.[80] Also compare Ezekiel 15:4,6; 32:4,5; 34:5,8; and 35:12.

33. צפור כל־כנף ("every kind of bird"; Ezek. 39:4, 17): This is one of Ezekiel's idioms (Ezek. 17:23), although similar language occurs in Deuteronomy 4:17.

34. אני דברתי ("it is I [YHWH] who have spoken," a conclusion formula for divine speech; Ezek. 39:5): Hals notes that this formula is a frequent marker in Ezekiel stressing the power of God's word (Ezek. 5:13, 15, 17; 17:21, 24; 21:22 [Eng.: 21:17], 37 [Eng.: 21:32]; 22:14; 24:14; 26:14; 28:10; 30:12; 34:24; 36:36; and 37:14).[81] Zimmerli also finds this formula to be particularly characteristic of Ezekiel.[82]

35. האיים ("the coastlands"; Ezek. 39:6): The term is familiar from Ezekiel 27:3, 6, 7, 35.

36. שם קדשי (concern for "my holy name"; Ezek. 39:7, 25; the same concern is expressed in different terms in Ezek. 38:16, 23; 39:27 [see item 23 above]): This usage, characteristic of Ezekiel, also reflects the theology found elsewhere in the book. The cross-references are: Ezekiel 20:39; 36:20, 21, 22, 23; and 43:7, 8.

37. ולא־אחל את־שם (the problem of the profaning [חלל] of the holy name; Ezek. 39:7): Closely related to the preceding item, this usage occurs here and elsewhere in Ezekiel in contexts where God expresses concern for God's "name." The cross-references to this characteristic Ezekiel usage are: Ezekiel 20:39; 36:20, 21, 22, 23; and 43:7. Further, God's concern for God's name is reflected in worries about the nations' opinion in Ezekiel 20:9, 14, 22 and the concern about the knowledge of Israel in Ezekiel 20:44.[83]

---

79. See Zimmerli's discussion in *Ezekiel 2*, 308.

80. Hossfeld, *Untersuchungen*, 466.

81. Hals, *Ezekiel*, 360.

82. Zimmerli, *Ezekiel 1*, 26–27.

83. Also see the discussion by Zimmerli, who argues that the Gog text reflects the history of the profanation of God's holy name (Ezek. 36:20-23) (*Ezekiel 2*, 315).

38. טהר (Piel stem) ("cleanse, purify"; Ezek. 39:12, 14, 16): The term is a favorite one in the book of Ezekiel (Ezek. 36:25, 33; 37:23; and 43:26).

39. כבד (Niphal stem) ("get honor"; Ezek. 39:13): The usage is also found in Ezekiel 28:22.

40. נשיאי הארץ ("the princes of the earth"; Ezek. 39:18): Zimmerli notes the linguistic resonance here with נשיאי הים ("the princes of the sea") in Ezekiel 26:16.[84]

41. שבעה ("satiety"; Ezek. 39:19): This feminine form occurs elsewhere in the Hebrew Bible only six times, two of which are in Ezekiel (Ezek. 16:28, 49),

42. שלחני ("my table," with YHWH as antecedent; Ezek. 39:20): This expression is attested elsewhere in the Hebrew Bible only in Ezekiel 44:16.

Discussion

Ezekiel 38–39 clearly belongs to the mainstream of the Ezekiel priestly tradition. The idioms, style, and theology of Ezekiel 38–39 match what are common elsewhere in the book. Thus, Dürr's assessment is correct that the whole presentation bears a thoroughly Ezekielian character.[85] Zimmerli states:

> Ezekiel's language is recalled by the elevated prose style, the emphasis by means of the concluding formula כי אני דברתי ("for I have spoken [it]") in 39:5 (see 23:34; 26:5; 28:10) [see item 34 above]. But also the broad development of the image of Yahweh's sacrificial meal . . . in comparison with the briefer mention of it in Zeph 1:7 is in line with [Ezekiel's characteristic development of models found in earlier prophets].[86]

Besides echoing the vocabulary and language of Ezekiel, the Gog passage also parallels other specific passages in the book. For example, Ezekiel 38–39 has close links with the oracle of judgment on Sidon in Ezekiel 28:20-26 (see List 2, items 2, 5, 14, 17, 23, and 29). At points the Gog passage is also reminiscent of the lament over Egypt in Ezekiel 32 (see items 8, 18, and 32).[87] The reference to the humiliation of Meshech and

84. Ibid., 309.

85. Dürr, *Die Stellung,* 65.

86. Zimmerli, *Ezekiel 2,* 302.

87. On the interrelation between Ezekiel 38–39 and Ezek. 32:17-32, see Marco Nobile, "Beziehung zwischen Ez 32, 17–32 und der Gog-Perikope (Ez 38–39) im Lichte der Endredaktion," in *Ezekiel and His Book,* ed. J. Lust (Leuven, Belgium: Leuven University Press, 1986), 255–59. Nobile notes that both of these passages share the funerary motif and the characteristic element "seven" ("Beziehung," 256;

Tubal as underworld denizens in this lament (Ezek. 32:26-27) closely relates to Ezekiel 38–39 (see item 3). Compare also the judgment on Gog
with the judgment on Egypt described in Ezekiel 29 (see items 2, 5, 6, 22,
and 32).[88] Other links include that between Ezekiel 38:13 and the trade
list in Ezekiel 27 (see item 20).

Many links exist between Ezekiel 38–39 and the rest of the book, but
the place of the Gog passage in the book's overall context and message
must be addressed in order to assure that these chapters belong to the
Ezekiel school.

The preceding chapters of Ezekiel have dealt with Israel's restoration,
describing future reversals of wrongdoings and wrong situations. These
chapters of Ezekiel, however, lack a central reversal: Prior to Ezekiel 38–
39, the enemies of Israel are not finally done away with, and God's holiness
is not yet vindicated. In other words, the restoration chapters have not
described any reversal of Israel's destruction in 586 B.C.E. This is now sup-
plied by the Gog prophecy.[89] The Gog text shows that a lack in God's
power was not at issue in the fall of Jerusalem and the ensuing exile. God
could have defeated all the world powers put together in 586 just as God
will defeat them in Gog at the end time.

Thus, the description of Gog in the passage makes use of terms used
elsewhere in Ezekiel to describe the old lover-enemies of Jerusalem who
had destroyed her — usages such as "splendidly attired" and "with buckler
and shield" (see items 7 and 9). Now these enemies in turn will be destroyed in Gog as the final reversal associated with Israel's restoration. This
destruction is depicted in Ezekiel 38–39 by means of judgment language
that recalls expressions used previously in Ezekiel against Israel. For example, the Gog passage contains reversals of the prophecies against Israel
in Ezekiel 5 (see items 5, 16, 24, 28, and 34) and Ezekiel 13 (see items 2,
5, 26, 29, and 30). It may therefore be concluded that the Gog passage has
an important place in the restoration message of the book as the account of
the reversal of the successful invasion of God's land demonstrating God's
true power.

Objections that Ezekiel and his school would not have pictured an
eschatological battle after the start of the restoration age cannot be sup-

---

also see the discussion on p. 95 above). Thus, in its redacted form, Ezek. 32:17-32
describes seven peoples in the underworld.

88. See Nobile, "Beziehung," 257 n. 12. References in the Gog passage to the
oracles against the nations help shape Ezekiel 38–39 into the sequel and climax of
Ezekiel 25–32.

89. See Hals, *Ezekiel*, 288; and Klein, *Ezekiel*, 166.

ported.[90] Millennial groups usually believe that the millennium will be ushered in by a final eschatological battle unlike previous mundane battles (see chapters 2 and 3).[91] The Ezekiel group, which was millennial when the Gog prophecy was written, seemingly came to a similar belief.[92]

The group viewed the (new) belief in a final eschatological battle as in harmony with Ezekiel's earlier prophecies. The Gog prophecy is linked with previous predictions in Ezekiel that the people will be restored (item 14) and dwell securely (item 17). Ezekiel 38–39 has especially close links with the promise of regathering scattered Israel in Ezekiel 36:16-18 (see items 14, 16, 22, 23, 34, 36, 37, and 38). There are also links with the promise of Ezekiel 20:33-44 (items 14, 23, 36, and 37). When these links are kept in mind, it is clear that the account of the end-time invasion and overturning of Gog powerfully reiterates earlier Ezekiel forecasts of the people's coming restoration and inviolability.

Evidence of the Hand of Central Priests in Ezekiel 38–39

The fact that Ezekiel 38–39 reflects the rest of Ezekiel suggests that this text might fruitfully be investigated for the cultic terms and priestly language and theology found in the entire book. In fact, this passage contains specific language indicating that it is indeed priestly.

First, that Ezekiel 38–39 is linked with the Holiness Code (H) demonstrates that it was produced by central priests.[93] H was the legislation at

90. Such an objection is voiced by several of the critics discussed in the introduction to this chapter. For example, Ahroni states: "The resumption of hostilities as well as the need for the reassertion of God's superiority after the restoration, which is the overriding concern in the Gog Prophecy, has therefore no logical place in Ezekiel's scheme for the future, is clearly in disharmony with his intention and spirit, and is alien to the whole picture of the restoration as depicted in the Hebrew Bible [footnote: Cf. Pfeiffer (1948, pp. 562f); Eichrodt (1970, p. 519)]" (Ahroni, "Gog Prophecy," 10).

91. The New Testament book of Revelation pictures two Gog battles associated with the millennium, one ushering it in, and one at its climax (Rev. 19:11-21; 20:7-9).

92. Thus Astour is supported by the cross-cultural evidence when he writes, "The whole point of the Gog prophecy is that the Israelites will, in the event, be saved from that fate; [Ezekiel 38–39] does not contradict but, on the contrary, it strengthens the motif of safety and inviolability of the future Israel" ("Cuthean Legend," 567). Also see Erling, "Ezekiel 38–39," 107; and Klein, *Ezekiel*, 158–59.

93. On the wider question of the relationship between the Holiness Code and Ezekiel as a whole, see the detailed discussion in Zimmerli, *Ezekiel 1*, 46–52. Zimmerli concludes that, "It cannot be denied that Ezekiel has been influenced by

home in Zadokite circles within the exile.[94] Ezekiel 38–39 has several links
with this source. In fact, in the book of Ezekiel, it is precisely at Ezekiel
39:7 that YHWH is described as קדוש ("holy"; see Lev. 19:2; 20:26; and
21:8).[95] The closely related idea that God will be "sanctified" (List 2, item
23) found in Ezekiel 38:16, 23; and 39:27 also has links with H (Lev.
21:8; 22:32).[96] The usage "sight of the nations" in Ezekiel 38:23 and
39:27 is found in H at Leviticus 26:45. In this context, note also that both
Ezekiel 38–39 and H show a concern for God's "holy name" (List 2, item
36). This usage is found both in Ezekiel 39:7, 25, and Leviticus 20:3;
22:2, 32 (compare Lev. 18:21; 19:12; 21:6).

There are several other links between the Gog text and H. For example, the combination of the root ישב and the adverb בטח ("live securely"; List 2, item 17 above: Ezek. 38:8, 11, 14; 39:26), though also
occurring in other places such as Deuteronomy 12:10 and Judges 18:7,
seems here to reverberate with H (Lev. 25:18, 19; 26:5). By the same token, the usage ואין מחריד ("and there will be no one making them afraid")
in Ezekiel 39:26 recalls Leviticus 26:6. Further, the reference to the
"sword" in Ezekiel 38:21 recalls the picture of Leviticus 26:36-37. (The
other "sword" in Ezekiel 39:23, which initiated the exile, seems to be that

---

detailed material built into H, or which already underlies it" (*Ezekiel 1*, 52). Also
see Peter R. Ackroyd, *Exile and Restoration*, OTL (Philadelphia: Westminster,
1968), 88; Millar Burrows, *The Literary Relations of Ezekiel* (Philadelphia: Jewish
Publication Society, 1925), 28–36; and Keith W. Carley, *Ezekiel among the Prophets*,
SBT, 2d Series, 31 (Naperville, Ill.: Allenson, 1974), 62–65.

94. For the view that H was brought by the Zadokites into exile, see Hanson,
Dawn, 225. More recently, Jacob Milgrom and Israel Knohl have argued strongly
that P and H stem from separate priestly schools, and that the original tradents of
H were among the priestly establishment of the Hezekian Jerusalem temple. See
Jacob Milgrom, *Leviticus 1–16*, AB 3 (Garden City, N.Y.: Doubleday, 1991), 13–
35. Unfortunately, a full-length sociological study outlining the Zadokite back-
ground of H over against the Aaronide background of P has not yet been written.
For now, see the discussions of the authorship of H in S. Dean McBride, Jr., "Bibli-
cal Literature in its Historical Context: The Old Testament," in *Harper's Bible Com-
mentary*, ed. J. Mays (San Francisco: Harper and Row, 1988), 20–21; Zimmerli,
Ezekiel 1, 52; Keith W. Carley, *The Book of the Prophet Ezekiel*, CBC (Cambridge,
England: Cambridge University Press, 1974), 260; and Roland de Vaux, *Ancient
Israel* (New York: McGraw-Hill, 1961), 2:376.

95. Zimmerli, *Ezekiel 1*, 48.

96. See the discussion in Avi Hurvitz, *A Linguistic Study of the Relationship
Between the Priestly Source and the Book of Ezekiel* (Paris: Gabalda, 1982), 40.

of Leviticus 26:25.) Finally, the reference to טמאה ("uncleanness") in Ezekiel 39:24 reflects the language of Leviticus 18:19 and 22:3, 5.

The use of the motif of Jerusalem as a bulwark against the attack of the many nations in Ezekiel 38–39 also indicates a central-priestly theology.[97] This component of the royal theology of the Jerusalem cult was carried by Ezekiel into exile and shows itself at several points in Ezekiel 38–39.[98] First, the reference in Ezekiel 38:12 to Israel being at the "center" (טבור) of the world links Ezekiel 38–39 with this central type of ideology.[99] Zion theology also states that God is invested in and protects this center. The usage "mountains of Israel" (see List 2, item 15 above), like the usage הרי ("my mountains") in Isaiah 14:25, is important because it connotes this idea.[100]

Second, as part of the *Völkersturm* motif, the nations attack God's mountain(s), causing chaos, but are trampled.[101] Clearly, Ezekiel 38–39 takes up this picture of a coming chaos and its aftermath found in the Zion psalms. For example, both Ezekiel 38:19 and Psalm 46:4 use the language of earthquake (רעש). Further, Ezekiel's picture of the aftermath of battle (Ezek. 39:9) reverberates with Psalm 46:8-10.[102] Thus, Ezekiel clearly reflects the Jerusalem central theology — the belief of the rulers and priests of Jerusalem that God will protect the temple on Zion. Gressmann correctly observes that Ezekiel 38–39 pictures the assault of the nations against the divine mountain (*Götterberg*) at the navel of the earth.[103]

Ezekiel 38–39, however, does not repeat the Jerusalem central theology; it reactualizes it. Because of the exile, the Jerusalem theology was profoundly called into question.[104] The disappointment after the fall of Jerusa-

97. For discussion of the Jerusalem tradition, see Gerhard von Rad, *Old Testament Theology*, trans. D. Stalker (New York: Harper and Row, 1965), 2:157, and p. 89 above.

98. Levenson, *Restoration*, 14–15. On the links between the Zadokites and the royal theology, see Deist, "Prior to the Dawn," 24.

99. See Levenson, *Restoration*, 16; Zimmerli, *Ezekiel 2*, 311; and Hossfeld, *Untersuchungen*, 446.

100. See Zimmerli, *Ezekiel 1*, 185.

101. See Hossfeld, *Untersuchungen*, 470.

102. See Zimmerli, *Ezekiel 2*, 300; and Hossfeld, *Untersuchungen*, 471. Psalm 46:9 does not picture a state of peace, but an appalling postbattle scene.

103. Gressmann, *Der Messias*, 127.

104. Ralph W. Klein writes that the "temple had gone up in flames, and enemies had raced through the sanctuary in which foreigners were not even to be present. . . . Worst of all, the temple's destruction called God into question: either there

lem in 586 B.C.E. is reflected in the sad dispositions of the people in such passages as Ezekiel 33:10 and 37:11.[105] The genius of Ezekiel was in his taking up the *Völkersturm* motif, associated with the Jerusalem theology, and projecting it as an eschatological event against a new Jerusalem. Ezekiel says the nations will again assault God's city, but this time they will indeed be destroyed.[106] Because Ezekiel was a central priest as well as a millennial catalyst figure, it was natural that he should have been the one to mediate this old hope into the general picture of the eschaton in proto-apocalyptic literature (Isa. 66:6-16; Zech. 12:1-9; Joel 3–4; and Isaiah 24–27).

The concern for the cultic purity of the land in the Gog passage best demonstrates a priestly minded authorship. Apprehension about purity comes across clearly in the burial description in Ezekiel 39:11-16, which reflects a repeated concern to purify the land (Piel stem of טהר; Ezek. 39:12, 14, 16; see List 2, item 38). The Holiness Code contains this same concern in negative terms (using טמא) in Leviticus 18:25, 28, and also in passages concerned with ceremonial cleanness (טהר) in relation to the de-filing effect of corpses: Leviticus 17:15; 22:4, 7. In sum, as Robert R. Wilson states, "The purity of the land was an important issue for the Zadokite priesthood of which Ezekiel was a part, and he wanted to be sure that the dead bodies of Gog and his hoard [*sic*] would not contaminate Jerusalem and render it unfit for ritual purposes."[107]

The concern with the means of achieving this purity is worked out with a precision and technical interest that strongly suggest a priest's mind-set. Thus, Gressmann cites Hans Schmidt's sarcastic remark that what troubles the prophet here is not that so many men die for no reason, but the possibility that even one human bone might remain unburied.[108] To prevent this possibility, a "commission of men with standing orders" (אנשי תמיד)is "set apart for sacral business" (בדל) in order to cleanse the land (Ezek. 39:14).[109]

---

were deities stronger than or superior to Yahweh, or for some reason Yahweh had rejected his own people and his own place" (*Israel in Exile,* OBT [Philadelphia: Fortress, 1979], 3).

105. See Dürr, *Die Stellung,* 93.

106. Ibid.

107. R. Wilson, "Ezekiel," 692.

108. Gressmann, *Der Messias,* 124.

109. On these usages as betraying a priestly *Heimat* (provenance), see Zimmerli, *Ezekiel 2,* 318; and Hossfeld, *Untersuchungen,* 474.

Synthesis: The Sociology of the Apocalyptic Unit Ezekiel 38–39

Ezekiel and his disciples, having gone into exile from central posts in Jerusalem, were among the leaders of the exiled Israelites. In fact, Ezekiel's continuing school provided the theological basis for the program of the late-exilic Zadokite leadership.[110] As Hanson writes: "In exile [the Zadokites] likely renewed their control over the community, and set to work planning for the restoration of . . . the temple cult. . . . This Zadokite ideal was transformed into a program of restoration by . . . Ezekiel. . . . [T]he Zadokite temple theology profoundly influenced [Ezekiel's] thinking."[111] The data suggest that this priest Ezekiel and his school of Zadokites wrote Ezekiel 38–39. Thus, in contradiction to deprivation theory, those at the center of society wrote proto-apocalyptic literature. Modern exegetes have dismissed Ezekiel 38–39 too soon, based on their assumption that Ezekiel, as a "pragmatic priest," could not have had an apocalyptic worldview.[112] In contrast, it has been shown that the priestly interests of Ezekiel were indeed compatible with apocalyptic forms and ideas.[113] Indeed, I shall show

110. For the argument that the postexilic Zadokite temple program based itself on Ezekiel, see Hanson, *Dawn*, 240–45; "Zechariah, Book of," *IDBSup*, 982–83; and cf. David L. Petersen, *Haggai and Zechariah 1–8*, OTL (London: SCM, 1984), 116–19. The interest of the Zadokites in continuing to transmit and interpret Ezekiel (as revealed in such places as Ezek. 40:46b and 48:11) supports this argument.

111. Hanson, *Dawn*, 225. Hanson argues that "a message basically consonant with the aims of the later hierocracy" is found even in the parts of Ezekiel attributable to the prophet (ibid., 233).

112. Ibid., 234–36. The discussion of the Irvingites in chapter 3 showed that a millennial group may indeed have a pragmatically oriented concern with structures and offices. Despite their concern with liturgy, incense, and altars, the Irvingites were certainly characterized by a millennial orientation. Similarly, the discussion in chapter 3 called into question Hanson's assumption that priests are unlikely candidates to be millennial catalyst figures. Hanson's prophet/priest dichotomy is betrayed in his statements that: "The priestly interests of Ezekiel are . . . very visible beneath the visionary forms" (ibid., 238); and "The history of the hierocratic tradition . . . begins with Ezekiel, even as the study of the post-exilic visionary tradition begins with Second Isaiah" (ibid., 226).

113. J. J. Burden has made the similar observation that Ezekiel's language tends to apocalypticism while at the same time favoring the theology of the priests ("Esegiël, Priester en Profeet," *Theologia Evangelica* 18/1 [1985]: 14–21). Unfortunately, this observation does not lead Burden to question the overly neat two-party view that "the sociological background of the exile . . . was dominated by two

below that even at the time they were settling for a rebuilt temple in Yehud that was realistic in human terms, the Zadokites were just as apocalyptically minded as they were in exile. The hypothesis developed in chapter 3 that proto-apocalyptic texts within books associated with a Zadokite group are the work of a millennial group led by central priests fits the data of Ezekiel 38–39. Ezekiel was a central priest who also had the role of catalyst figure for millennialism.[114]

It is now possible to be more specific about the social milieu of the millennial group behind at least the first layers of Ezekiel 38–39. In chapter 3, four possible scenarios were described where millennial groups can be considered central or in power (arena classes A, B, C, and E). The arena of the group that wrote Ezekiel 38–39 is closest to class C: the millennial group is central in terms of its own society, but that society is dominated by another culture. In Ezekiel 38–39 that domination is the continuing captivity in Babylon and the reproach of the foreign nations.[115]

Such an exogenous arena in Babylon is supported by the late-exilic viewpoint implied in Ezekiel 39:25-29, probably part of the last stage of the Gog tradition-history.[116] The use of the future tense in Ezekiel 39:25

---

groups, viz. the hierocrats (i.e., the priests) and the visionary prophets" (ibid., 14). We must go beyond Burden and see the Ezekiel group as a central-priestly circle that was also "visionary."

114. Ezekiel may have been a recognized leader in the exile, but he was not listened to by his contemporaries. In fact, Ezekiel eventually concluded that he would never be able to bring the majority of the exiles to repentance (hence the emphasis in Ezek. 36:22 on God *not* acting for the people's sake). The situation of the British Irvingites was somewhat similar. Although they came from the upper strata of society, the majority of society did not accept their views.

115. It is interesting to compare the class C arena of Ezekiel 38–39 with the class C arena of the Native American millennial group led by Smohalla (see chapter 3, and Vittorio Lanternari, *The Religions of the Oppressed,* trans. L. Sergio [New York: Knopf, 1963], 127–29). Just as the lands of the Native American tribes were being taken away (Lanternari, *Religions of the Oppressed,* 127), Israel had been exiled from its land (Ezek. 38:8; 39:27). Smohalla said the tribes' troubles were because the Supreme Being deplored the way the Native Americans had forsaken their native religion (Lanternari, *Religions of the Oppressed,* 128). Similarly, Israel's defeat is blamed on their forsaking God (Ezek. 39:23-24). Both the Smohalla group and the Ezekiel group had strong religious bonds with and desires for their land (Ezek. 38:8; cf. Ezek. 28:26; 34:25, 27-28; Lanternari, *Religions of the Oppressed,* 129). Finally, both groups expected a final apocalyptic victory over the forces threatening them (Ezek. 39:4; Lanternari, *Religions of the Oppressed,* 127).

116. See the discussion below.

(עתה + an imperfect verb) looks ahead to the completion of the restoration, indicating that it was not too far under way.[117] Thus, the earlier core of the Gog passage probably comes from the end of Ezekiel's ministry in Babylon. Perhaps it was written during the rise of Cyrus (c. 555 B.C.E.).[118] There is no evidence in the book of Ezekiel that this social context involved any suffering or oppression for Ezekiel and the priestly elite.[119] Indeed, the fact that many exiles did not return to Israel as part of the restoration indicates that life was not so bad in Babylon.[120] This conclusion is supported by the fact that there is no anti-Babylonian oracle in Ezekiel. Ezekiel 38–39 does reverse the Babylonian conquest, but specifically not by a divine victory over Babylon.[121]

The practical program of the Ezekiel millennial group within its class C arena was a passive one.[122] It was noted above that in the Gog passage the Israelites take no active part in the apocalyptic battle. They are involved merely in mopping-up operations. This literary description implies that Ezekiel and his group expected to play a passive role in the end times. They expected God to bring the restoration for the sake of God's own name. God would then bring Gog against Israel and destroy him there. At that point, God would make God's holy name known in the midst of Israel

---

117. See p. 120 below.

118. Zimmerli locates the original Gog oracle in the period before the conquest of Babylon by Cyrus. He notes that at this time, the country around Meshech-Tubal was not yet joined to Persia and could plausibly be feared as an independent threat (*Ezekiel 2*, 303). Klein also notes that after 539 B.C.E. there were no longer any grounds for fears of a great eruption in the north (*Ezekiel*, 157). For a similar view, see Hals, *Ezekiel*, 284.

119. See Hanson, *Dawn*, 226 n. 39.

120. Jeremiah 29:5-6 indicates that the exiles became integrated into Babylonian society. Such integration is attested at a later period by the Murashu documents, which show no hints of discrimination or restrictions on Jews living in exile (see Michael Coogan, "Life in the Diaspora: Jews at Nippur in the Fifth Century B.C.," *BA* 37/1 [1974]: 10, 12). For references to the financial prosperity of the exiles, see Ezra 1:6; 2:68-69. For further discussion of exilic conditions, see Klein, *Israel in Exile*, 3; Ackroyd, *Exile*, 32; John Bright, *A History of Israel*, 3d ed. (Philadelphia: Westminster, 1981), 362–63; and J. Maxwell Miller and John H. Hayes, *A History of Ancient Israel and Judah* (Philadelphia: Westminster, 1986), 432–35.

121. See p. 104 above. Hostile attitudes toward Babylon, though present in such texts as Jeremiah 50, Isaiah 13–14, and Daniel, do not appear in Ezekiel and may have been of limited scope. For discussion, see Ackroyd, *Exile*, 37, 222.

122. See the discussion of the programs of action of millennial groups in chapter 2 above.

(Ezek. 39:7). The Ezekiel group — and Israel as a whole — would partici-
pate in the last days of history basically in the role of spectators.

Evidence of Radicalization and Routinization

Thus far the examination of Ezekiel 38–39 has been basically syn-
chronic. Diachronic analysis of Ezekiel 38–39, however, not only further
supports the arguments being made but also reveals much about the history of Ezekiel's millennial group as it carried the Gog material through
the end of the exilic period. The millennial group seems to have undergone
a process of radicalization followed by one of routinization.

Radicalization

Form-critical analysis of Ezekiel 38–39 reveals that the section Ezekiel
38:17-23 is of particular importance for understanding the history of the
Ezekiel millennial group. Ezekiel 38:17, which begins with its own messenger formula (כה־אמר אדני יהוה [“Thus says Lord YHWH”]), stands as a
somewhat independent transition to vv. 18-23.[123] This section begins with
a connecting formula (והיה ביום ההוא [“and it will come about on that day”])
and an oddly placed prophetic utterance formula (נאם אדני יהוה [“utterance
of Lord YHWH”]) in v. 18. The section is concluded by the recognition
formula (וידעו כי־אני יהוה,[“and they will know that I am YHWH”]) in v.
23 (although this formula also marks the conclusion of the larger unit,
Ezek. 38:1-23). Ezekiel 39:1 begins a new section with a new address to
the prophet as “Son of man,” a new direction to prophesy, and a new messenger formula (כה־אמר אדני יהוה). Thus, Ezekiel 38:18-23 can be isolated
as a logical unit within Ezekiel 38–39. This section should probably not
be further subdivided. The oath formula in v. 19 does not mark a separate
section, and the prophetic utterance formula (נאם אדני יהוה) in v. 21 simply
marks an internal logical division separating the description of cosmic ap-
paritions from the direct judgment on Gog.

Despite the relative independence of Ezekiel 38:18-23 as a subsection
within Ezekiel 38–39, these verses are not inconsistent with the rest of the
Gog passage. Certainly, this is not the only part of Ezekiel 38–39 that contains apocalyptic motifs and themes. Apocalyptic usages appear throughout Ezekiel 38–39.[124]

123. Ezekiel 38:17 may be a late addition to the text. See Gressmann, *Der Messias*, 126; and Zimmerli, *Ezekiel 2*, 312.

124. For example, the references to the “latter years” (אחרית השנים) and the
“latter days” (אחרית הימים) are found in Ezek. 38:8 and Ezek. 38:16; the apocalyp-

The sociological evidence also does not support the contention that this section is inconsistent with the surrounding material. I disagree with Hossfeld's argument that the authors of this section ignored the idea that the cosmic events described would disrupt Israel and that the blows of judgment (*Gerichtsschläge*) against Gog would adversely affect Israel and the other witnesses.[125] Wodziwob, the Paiute millennial catalyst figure, envisioned an imminent huge earthquake that would destroy all the whites but leave the Native Americans alive (see chapter 3). *1 Enoch* 1:1-9 describes the coming fall of the mountains but insists at 1:8 that "[God] will protect the elect."[126] Cross-cultural evidence like this shows that an apocalyptic worldview can incorporate the conflicting ideals of God's coming triumph through destruction of the present era and the elect's subsequent enjoyment of a future era of peace.

Despite the continuities of Ezekiel 38:18-23 with the Gog passage as a whole, this section may well mark a diachronic development *within* the Gog tradition-history. The passage is marked as an expanding addition by the introductory והיה ביום ההוא ("and it will come about on that day") at v. 18, a usage often employed to attach supplemental eschatological material (for examples, see Joel 4:18 [Eng.: 3:18] and Zech. 14:6). Further, Gog is now spoken of as a third party. Finally, these verses seem to gravitate together to an extent that marks them off diachronically from the surrounding material.[127] The unit as a whole contains some of the most radical language and imagery of the Gog prophecy in its coherent picture of the dissolution of the cosmos and the destruction of Gog. This radical language probably corresponds to a radicalization of the Ezekiel group.

Ezekiel 38:18-23 reflects radicalization within the Ezekiel millennial group, but these disciples of Ezekiel still are to be characterized as central priests. Like Ezekiel 38–39 as a whole, this section contains idioms and themes that link it to the rest of the book. See List 2, items 11, 22, 23, 24, 25, 26, 27, 28, 29, and 30 (and compare 36) above. These links confirm that Ezekiel 38:18-23 is the product of the same continuing Zadokite circles that produced and transmitted the book of Ezekiel.

The connection of Ezekiel 38:18-23 with Ezekiel 39:11-16 further

---

tic-horde motif is found in Ezek. 38:1-16 and 39:9-16; and the apocalyptic-sacrifice motif is found in Ezek. 39:17-20.

125. Hossfeld, *Untersuchungen,* 461. For similar objections, see Zimmerli, *Ezekiel 2,* 314; Klein, *Ezekiel,* 161; and Carley, *The Prophet Ezekiel,* 260.

126. See also Heb. 12:27.

127. See Hossfeld, *Untersuchungen,* 418.

strengthens the argument that this radicalizing expansion is a product of central priests.[128] Ezekiel 39:11-16 is among the literary appendices following Ezekiel 39:1-5.[129] These verses describing a priestly concern with the burial of the Gog horde are probably part of the same reworking of the Gog passage that added Ezekiel 38:18-23.

Both Ezekiel 38:18-23 and Ezekiel 39:11-16 begin with והיה ביום ההוא ("and it will come about on that day"). Both passages speak of Gog in the third person, whereas the rest of the Gog passage does not.[130] Also, like Ezekiel 38:18-23, Ezekiel 39:11-16 itself radicalizes apocalyptic motifs found in the Gog passage. For example, the statement that it takes seven months to bury Gog (Ezek. 39:12) radicalizes the horde motif. Thus, both passages intensify the Gog presentation into gigantic proportions. Finally, as Hossfeld notes, references to the late Sidon oracle of Ezekiel 28:20-23 are in both sections (Ezek. 38:22 ↔ Ezek. 28:23; Ezek. 39:13 ↔ Ezek. 28:22a).[131]

As discussed above, Ezekiel 39:11-16, with its concern for the purity of the land, clearly betrays a priestly technical interest.[132] This passage is painstakingly serious about Zadokite matters. In view of this fact, Hossfeld places this level of the Gog tradition-history closer to the priestly regulations of Ezekiel 40–48 than to the earlier parts of the book.[133] As the millennialism of the Ezekiel group became more fervent, so did its priestly focus. In the experience of the Ezekiel group, apocalyptic radicalization is linked with an increasing emphasis on central-priestly concerns.

The addition of Ezekiel 38:18-23, 39:11-16 probably occurred in the period of uncertainty at the end of the exile, when an actual return to Israel

128. Hossfeld's form-critical analysis takes Ezek. 38:18-23 and Ezek. 39:11-13, (14-16) as part of the same third reworking (= the fifth redactional level) of the Gog passage. Hossfeld sees this addition as orienting itself to pronouncedly priestly literature such as P and H (*Untersuchungen*, 507, 527).

129. Ezekiel 39:5 concludes the first section of this chapter with a conclusion formula for divine speech (כי אני דברתי ["for it is I who have spoken"]; see List 2, item 34) and a prophetic utterance formula (נאם אדני יהוה ["utterance of Lord YHWH"]). Following this verse is a series of groups of verses that expand upon vv. 1-5. Of these groups, vv. 11-16 represent a complex unit containing an etymological etiology (v. 11), a description of the burying of Gog and his multitude concluding with a prophetic utterance formula (vv. 12-13), and another section dealing with the special case of the bones (vv. 14-16).

130. See Hossfeld, *Untersuchungen*, 418, 432, and 507.

131. Ibid., 507.

132. See p. 108 above.

133. Hossfeld, *Untersuchungen*, 507, 527.

became viable.[134] In this period (c. 539–520 B.C.E.), the Ezekiel group found itself in a unique sociological situation ripe for radicalization of its eschatological hopes. On the one hand, the policies of Cyrus II (559–530 B.C.E.) made tangible the group's hopes for restoration. A first return under Sheshbazzar actually occurred c. 538 B.C.E. On the other hand, the circumstances were extremely nebulous and stressful. It did not appear that a humanly accomplished restoration would fulfill the Ezekiel group's expectation of God's power being made clear to all nations.[135] That the temple and cities of Israel were still in ruins as the restoration began (Isa. 64:10-11; 63:18) was a further cause of stress.[136] A new temple could be built, but the Zadokites would have to settle for much less than the structure depicted in the visions of Ezekiel 40–48, unless God intervened. The sociological situation in which a group has its basic expectations built up as its members' world changes rapidly is often rife with apocalyptic radicalization.

An instructive sociological parallel is Norman Cohn's description of the rise of millennialism that coincided with the expansion of social and economic horizons in Europe starting in the eleventh century. It was not the deprivations of the preceding period that gave rise to millennial groups in medieval Europe. As Cohn states, "If poverty, hardships and an often oppressive dependence could by themselves generate it . . . millenarianism would have run strong amongst the peasantry of medieval Europe."[137] In contrast, millennial groups did appear in the following period of expansion. Millennial groups arose when people saw the possibility for undreamed-of wealth.[138]

The type of experience that Cohn describes requires that the group in

---

134. Hals suggests the period around 520 B.C.E. as an alternate possibility for the dating of Ezekiel 38–39 as a whole (*Ezekiel*, 284).

135. Ezekiel himself may have lived to doubt that the restoration would be enough to impress the nations with God's sovereignty. In any event, as Erling states, "There is little evidence that any of the nations were in fact led to glorify Yahweh out of wonderment over the return of some of the exiles to the post-exilic Jerusalem community" (Erling, "Ezekiel 38–39," 110). Similarly, Theodore Olson writes, "Not even the 12 tribes of Ezekiel's vision, much less the nations, grouped themselves around Jerusalem and its Temple" (*Millennialism, Utopianism, and Progress* [Toronto: University of Toronto Press, 1982], 37).

136. See, e.g., Bright, *History of Israel*, 364; and Olson, *Millennialism, Utopianism*, chapter 3: "The Crisis of Return."

137. Norman Cohn, *The Pursuit of the Millennium* (New York: Oxford, 1970) 55.

138. Ibid., 58.

question must be close to or within the centers of power. Andrew D. H. Mayes even notes the possibility that apocalyptic worldviews in general should be seen as most common among those groups that have some access to rewards or power and thus "see what is possible."[139] I suggest that Ezekiel 38–39 was radicalized in this type of environment. The Ezekiel group was among those in charge of postexilic society, given authority over the restoration by the Persians.[140] As part of the upper echelon of the Diaspora, working out restoration plans, they saw the possibility for their dreams to come true.[141] This central position, however, set them up to

139. Andrew D. H. Mayes, *The Old Testament in Sociological Perspective* (London: Marshall Pickering, 1989), 17.

140. As stated in n. 110 above, several scholars deduce a Zadokite dominance over restoration polity. That the levitical priestly group was not in charge seems clear from their minimal representation in the returnee list of Ezra 2; also cf. Ezra 8:15. For discussion, see Hanson, *Dawn*, 225–27; and also the interesting arguments in Yehezkel Kaufmann, *The Religion of Israel*, trans. M. Greenberg (Chicago: University of Chicago Press, 1960), 190–91. In contrast to the small number of Levites, Ezra 2:36-39 lists a large number of returnees who linked themselves to Eleazar and Ithamar: three of the four priestly groups here are noted in 1 Chronicles 24 as Ithamarites and Eleazarites. Passhur, the exception, may be a subgroup of the sons of Malchijah, 1 Chron. 24:9 (see David J. Clines, *Ezra, Nehemiah, Esther*, NCBC [Grand Rapids, Mich.: Eerdmans, 1984], 54). De Vaux holds that all four of these groups probably claimed Zadokite ancestry (*Ancient Israel*, 2:388). Most certain, however, is the Zadokite identification of the Jedaiah group — Ezra 2:36 indicates that the high priest and his brethren belonged to this phratry. Whether or not de Vaux is right that the other three groups claimed to be Zadokites, it clearly was the Zadokites who held dominance over them. This is indicated by the position of Jeshua/Joshua (Ezra 2:2, 36; 3:2) as high priest (Zech. 3:1-10; 6:11; Hag. 1:1). Joshua was descended through Jozadak from the last preexilic Zadokite chief priest, Seraiah (2 Kings 25:18; 1 Chron. 6:8-15). For discussion, see de Vaux, *Ancient Israel*, 2:375–76, 388. Texts such as Ezek. 44:9-16; 40:46b; and 48:11 indicate that the Zadokites continued to work to maintain their priestly dominance after the return (as suggested in n. 110 above). Against Julius Wellhausen (*Prolegomena to the History of Ancient Israel* [Gloucester, Mass.: Peter Smith, 1973; 1st German ed., 1878], 122–27), the pro-Zadokite stance of these texts no doubt postdates the more inclusive Aaronide system of P.

141. Blenkinsopp writes, "The concentration by the school of Ezekiel on the central issue of cult and divine presence, on which other matters such as land tenure depended (see especially Ezekiel 11:14-21), their familiarity with the old sacral law, their polemic in favor of Diaspora Judaism and of the Zadokite priesthood (e.g., Ezekiel 40:46; 43:19; 44:15-31; 48:11), suggest strongly that we are dealing with a priestly elite, probably in the Babylonian Diaspora, which was actively preparing

experience stress, inner dissonance and, in turn, a radicalization of millennial beliefs. The Ezekiel group must have dreamed of the fulfillment of the promises of Ezekiel 34–37 as the Persian period began, only to fear that they would not be realized.[142] Thus, as stress increased and the group's fears grew, they underwent the type of radicalization described above in the discussion of the career of millennial groups (see chapter 3).

The social arena of this Zadokite millennial group was no longer exogenous when they eventually returned to Yehud. Under the Persians, they were not in a contact situation in the same way as when in Babylonian exile. Nevertheless, contact is not required for a group to look forward to a conflict with enemy forces. After their return the Ezekiel millennial group still believed in the rise of a Gog, much like twentieth-century endogenous millennial groups in the United States speculate that countries such as Russia or Libya will soon become end-time foes.[143]

Routinization

As stated in chapter 3, a millennial group is routinized when its worldview becomes more mundane than at first and group activities are toned down to a level where they can be sustained indefinitely. The addition of the summary appendices of Ezekiel 39:21-29 represents literary evidence of such routinization within the Ezekiel millennial group.

Form-critically, these appendices are marked as a logical unit by the two prophetic utterance formulas (נאם אדני יהוה ["utterance of Lord YWHW"]) in Ezekiel 39:20 and 39:29. The unit is subdivided by the messenger formula (כה־אמר אדני יהוה ["Thus says Lord YWHW"]) and the transitional לכן ("therefore") in Ezekiel 39:25, marking a turn from judgment to promise.

As with the radicalizing units just discussed, this section should be viewed as a contiguous part of the Gog tradition. The following data base (List 3) shows the continuities between Ezekiel 39:21-29, Ezekiel 38–39, and Ezekiel as a whole.

List 3. The Relationship of Ezekiel 39:21-29, Ezekiel 38–39, and Ezekiel as a Whole

1. משפט (the idea that all the nations will see God's "judgment"; Ezek.

---

for the return to Judah" (*History of Prophecy,* 197). On the late layers of the Gog passage as stemming from this historical period, see Zimmerli, *Ezekiel 2,* 310.

142. This type of scenario is suggested by R. Wilson, "Ezekiel," 692–93.

143. As recent primary-source examples basing themselves on Ezekiel 38–39, see John F. Walvoord, "Russia: King of the North," *Fundamentalist Journal* 3/1

39:21): "Judgment" refers back to the judgment on Gog described in Ezekiel 38–39. The appendix here continues the reversal theme of these chapters (Ezek. 5:8 is reversed).

2. יד (the image of God's powerful "hand"; Ezek. 39:21): God's hand has been laid against Gog and the nations, as described in Ezekiel 38–39. The image here of the use of God's hand resulting in recognition (vv. 22-23) is characteristic of Ezekiel as a whole (see Ezek. 6:14; 25:7, 16-17; 35:3-4). On the hand of God used in judgment, see Ezekiel 13:9; 14:9, 13; 16:27; and 25:13. On God's mighty hand used in restoration, see Ezekiel 20:33-34.

3. הלאה ("onward"; Ezek. 39:22): The adverb is also used at Ezekiel 43:27.

4. The recognition formula (Ezek. 39:22, 23, 28): This formula is a link between the appendix and both Ezekiel 38–39 (Ezek. 38:16, 23; 39:7; compare 39:13) and Ezekiel as a whole (see List 2, item 22 above, and especially Ezek. 36:23).

5. מעל ("act faithlessly"; Ezek. 39:23, 26): This usage, with its reverberations with H (Lev. 26:40), is a favorite one in Ezekiel. See Ezekiel 14:13; 15:8; 17:20; 18:24; and 20:27.

6. אסתר פני ("I hid my face"; Ezek. 39:23, 24, 29): The expression echoes Ezekiel 7:22, "I shall also turn (סבב) my face from them." The broader theme here that the exile was caused by Israel's sin is also basic to the thought of the rest of the book.[144]

7. ואתנם ביד צריהם ("and I gave them into the hand of their adversaries"; Ezek. 39:23): With this expression, compare Ezekiel 16:39; 23:28; 30:10, 12; and 31:11.

8. נפל + ב + חרב ("all of them fell by the sword"; Ezek. 39:23): This expression echoes Ezekiel 23:25 (compare Ezek. 6:1-3). Here again, the usages in the Ezekiel 39:21-29 appendix function to reiterate the notion of the reversal of Israel's fate that is portrayed in Ezekiel 38–39 (see also Ezek. 32:26).

9. טמאה ("uncleanness"; Ezek. 39:24): This usage, with its reverberations with H (Lev. 18:19; 22:3, 5), is a favorite one in Ezekiel. See Ezekiel 22:15; 24:11, 13; 36:17, 25, 29.

10. שוב + שבות ("restore fortunes"; Ezek. 39:25): The usage is also found in Ezekiel 16:53 and 29:14.

(1984): 34–38; and Ed Hindson, "Libya: A Part of Ezekiel's Prophecy," *Fundamentalist Journal* 5/6 (1986): 57–58.

144. See the comments by Wevers, *Ezekiel*, 294.

11. כל־בית ישראל ("the whole house of Israel"; Ezek. 39:25): This usage occurs often in Ezekiel: Ezekiel 3:7; 5:4; 11:15; 12:10; 20:40; 36:10; 37:11, 16; 45:6. The expression בית ישראל by itself is even more common in the book (Ezek. 3:1; 4:3; 6:11; 8:6; 10:19; etc.). The idea of the restored "whole house" as comprising the reunited northern and southern kingdoms is found in Ezekiel 37:21-22.

12. שם קדשי ("my holy name"; Ezek. 39:25): This usage is a link between the appendix and both Ezekiel 38–39 and Ezekiel as a whole.[145] See List 2, item 36 above.

13. כלמה ("reproach, shame"; Ezek. 39:26): On God's desire in Ezekiel that Israel bear its shame, see Ezekiel 16:52, 54, 63; 44:13. On the problem of the insults of the nations, see Ezekiel 34:29 and 36:6, 7.

14. בטח + ישב ("live securely"; Ezek. 39:26): This usage is a link between the appendix and both Ezekiel 38–39 and Ezekiel as a whole. See List 2, item 17 above. Note, however, that now, after the defeat of Gog, there is really "no one to make [them] afraid."

15. ואין מחריד ("no one to make [them] afraid"; Ezek. 39:26): This usage, which is shared by H (Lev. 26:6), clearly echoes Ezekiel 34:28.

16. שוב ("bring back" in reference to restoring Israel; Ezek. 39:27): This usage echoes Ezekiel 38:8, which also uses the Polel stem to refer to the restoration of Israel. (Compare also the use of the Polel stem in Ezek. 38:4 and 39:2 in reference to Gog.)

17. קבץ (God will "gather" them from the lands of their enemies; Ezek. 39:27): This usage is a link between the appendix and both Ezekiel 38–39 and Ezekiel as a whole. See List 2, item 14 above.

18. קדש (in a reflexive stem) with "God" as subject + "before the eyes of" (עיני) ("I shall be sanctified through them in the sight of the many nations"; Ezek. 39:27): This usage is a link between the appendix and both Ezekiel 38–39 and Ezekiel as a whole. See List 2, item 23 above.

19. שפכתי את־רוחי ("I shall have poured out my spirit"; Ezek. 39:29): This usage is a development of ideas found earlier in Ezekiel (Ezek. 11:19; 36:26-27; and 37:14).

Discussion

The data of List 3 indicate that the appendix, Ezekiel 39:21-29, was aware of the Gog passage.[146] As List 3, items 1, 4, 8, 12, 14, 16, 17, and 18 show, Ezekiel 39:21-29 presupposes the preceding sections of Ezekiel

145. See Block, "Gog," 262.
146. See Zimmerli, *Ezekiel 2*, 321.

38–39. This unit also takes a wider step back, however, forming a proper conclusion to a larger block of preceding chapters. Thus Ezekiel 39:21-29 was added in one or two stages as a concluding unit both to Ezekiel 38–39 and to the rest of the preceding chapters of Ezekiel. This redaction may constitute one of the last layers in the book, postdating the proto-apocalyptic redaction.[147]

The perspective of the Ezekiel school when this concluding unit was added differs from earlier perspectives in the layers of Ezekiel 38–39. It takes us back to the exiles' "real time," the mundane situation of those still feeling on the verge of restoration. As Daniel I. Block notes, with Ezekiel 39:23 the chronological perspective is focused back on the exile of Israel.[148]

Our concern now focuses on the stage before Gog's appearance (Ezek. 39:25). Block states, "The עתה brings the prophet back to the present."[149] The result is that the second, future stage of the conflict with Gog is emphasized as being in a more distant future. As shown in chapter 2, the sociological evidence indicates that millennial groups tend to focus on the imminent end. Thus, this return to a focus on the present is literary evidence that the writers have lost some of their apocalyptic fervor. Replacing that fervor is a concern by the Ezekiel group to place the Gog oracles within the overall prophetic message of the prophet.[150] There even seems to be an emphasis on the living out of a reinstituted this-worldly covenant relationship (Ezek. 39:28-29).[151]

The social setting of the concluding unit, Ezekiel 39:21-29, was a literary one. Members of the Ezekiel school engaged in editorial activity with

147. It is likely that this section represents one last stage of the tradition-history of the Gog passage. Both Zimmerli and Hossfeld see this section as the product of the final redactors of the Gog material (Zimmerli, *Ezekiel 2,* 324; Hossfeld, *Untersuchungen,* 508). For interesting textual arguments to this effect, see Johan Lust, "The Final Text and Textual Criticism. Ez 39,28," *Ezekiel and His Book,* ed. J. Lust (Leuven, Belgium: Leuven University Press, 1986), 48–54. See also Hurvitz, *Linguistic Study,* 125.

148. Block, "Gog," 261.

149. Ibid., 265.

150. Zimmerli states that for those who added Ezek. 39:23-29, "the Gog incidents signified no new emphasis in the history of Yahweh's dealings with his people . . . [the Gog pericope] is completely integrated into the great proclamation of salvation for Israel" (*Ezekiel 2,* 321). Hossfeld argues that Ezek. 39:23-29 aims at the integration of the hitherto expanded Gog pronouncement in the context of the book of Ezekiel, especially Ezekiel 33ff (*Untersuchungen,* 508).

151. Block stresses this idea of the covenant relationship. For Block, the pouring out of the Spirit here is a sign and seal of the covenant ("Gog," 266–68).

the purpose of producing a coherent edition of the book of Ezekiel. Drawing on a literary and theological study of Ezekiel, especially chapters 34, 36, and 37, the redactors added an appendix to the Gog passage that both summarized the preceding chapters of Ezekiel and functioned to better level the incorporation of Ezekiel 38–39 into the book of Ezekiel as a whole.

5

Zechariah 1–8

The book of Zechariah is a major source for understanding millennialism among the Zadokites after Ezekiel's period. The tradition-history of this book is a potential mine of information for tracing the postexilic development of apocalypticism within at least one Zadokite group. Unfortunately, however, the critical insight that distinguished Zechariah 1–8 from Zechariah 9–14 has in some cases been so radicalized it makes the flow of the Zechariah tradition-history incomprehensible. This modern treatment of the book has its roots in Julius Wellhausen's position that the two halves of Zechariah have opposite ideologies.

On the one hand, Wellhausen argued that Zechariah 1–8 focused on the mundane task of restoring Yehud: "All that [Zechariah 1–8] aims at is the restoration of the temple and perhaps the elevation of Zerubbabel to the throne of David."[1] Zechariah is not viewed as a genuine millennial figure by this interpretation: his major concern was the this-worldly creation of a postexilic theocracy. Redaction in Zechariah 1–8 exhibits even less eschatological concern in Wellhausen's view. According to him, it reflects a priestly oriented community that was accepting of the status quo. For example, Wellhausen argued that redaction camouflaged an original crowning of Zerubbabel in Zechariah 6, focusing the text instead on the high priest.[2] The tradents of Zechariah 1–8 had settled for a sort of realized

1. Julius Wellhausen, "Zechariah, Book of," in *Encyclopaedia Biblica*, ed. T. Cheyne (New York: Macmillan, 1903), 4:5394.

2. Julius Wellhausen, *Die Kleinen Propheten übersetzt und erklärt*, 3d ed. (Berlin: Georg Reimer, 1898), 185.

eschatology, replacing any future messianic hopes of the original prophet with a present theocracy governed by priests.[3]

On the other hand, Wellhausen treated Zechariah 9–14 as entirely different from Zechariah 1–8. He placed Zechariah 9–14 much later in the second century B.C.E. and argued that it was directed against the priests and those who ruled the Jews.[4] Since the time of Wellhausen, many scholars have held that Zechariah 9–14 has nothing to do with chapters 1–8 of the book, that the two sections represent opposing standpoints.[5]

Otto Plöger's and Paul Hanson's treatments of Zechariah take this position almost to an extreme.[6] Hanson maintains that Zechariah 1–8 supported and spoke for a Zadokite hierocratic program.[7] Zechariah 9–14, however, is the product of a dissident group, opposed to the hierocrats and the dominant temple-cult.[8] The Zechariah 1–8 tradition-history moves in a hierocratic and noneschatological direction while Zechariah 9–14, representing a diametrically opposite tradition, moves increasingly in an apocalyptic direction. If Hanson is correct, it would be very difficult to understand how the two halves of Zechariah ever came together.[9]

3. As a result, modern scholars often see Haggai and Zechariah as operating within a framework of realized eschatology. For example, see W. J. Dumbrell, "Kingship and Temple in the Post-Exilic Period," *The Reformed Theological Review* 37 (1978): 33; and Christian Jeremias, *Die Nachtgesichte des Sacharja* (Göttingen: Vandenhoeck & Ruprecht, 1977), 223. Also see the bibliography cited in Adam S. van der Woude, "Serubbabel und die messianischen Erwartungen des Propheten Sacharja," *ZAW* 100 Suppl. (1988): 139.

4. Wellhausen states, "The shepherds are the high priests and ethnarchs of the Jews. . . . They were all of them worthless whether they traced their descent from Zadok or from Tobias" ("Zechariah," 4:5395).

5. For example, see J. Alberto Soggin, *Introduction to the Old Testament*, OTL, trans. J. Bowden (Philadelphia: Westminster, 1976), 347.

6. Otto Plöger, *Theocracy and Eschatology*, trans. S. Rudman (Richmond, Va.: John Knox, 1968), 78–96; and Paul Hanson, *The Dawn of Apocalyptic* (Philadelphia: Fortress, 1979), 209–401.

7. Hanson, *Dawn*, 227, 243, 247, 261.

8. For Hanson, Zechariah 9–14 was produced by circles opposed to the hierocratic program and its Zadokite protagonists ("Zechariah, Book of," *IDBSup*, 983). See also Hanson, *Dawn*, 283, 323; and Hanson's diagram in *The People Called: The Growth of Community in the Bible* (San Francisco: Harper & Row, 1986), 252.

9. The view accepted by Hanson that Zechariah 9–11, Zechariah 12–14, and Malachi were attached at a late date to the minor prophets as separate booklets using משׂא ("oracle") as a heading is untenable (*Dawn*, 292, 400; "In Defiance of Death: Zechariah's Symbolic Universe," in *Love & Death in the Ancient Near East*, Marvin Pope *Festschrift*, ed. J. Marks and R. Good [Guilford, Conn.: Four Quarters, 1987], 173). For critiques of the משׂא-theory, see Brevard S. Childs, *Introduc-*

In contrast, I shall argue that Zechariah 1–8 and 9–14 represent phases within one tradition-history whose tradents were a millennial group of central priests. Once the possibility of a millennial group in power is accepted, the movement of the priestly-and-millennial Zechariah tradition through the redaction of Zechariah 1–8 and the various new compositions of Zechariah 9–14 can be understood.[10]

Zechariah 1–8 as Apocalyptic Literature

Despite its proto-apocalyptic literary features, Hanson argues that Zechariah 1–8 is not apocalyptic literature. It is significant, however, that Hanson's view is not based directly on the evidence of the text itself, but rather on his principle of interpretation that a central-priestly group cannot produce apocalyptic literature.[11] As Robert R. Wilson states:

---

tion to the Old Testament as Scripture (Philadelphia: Fortress, 1979), 491–92; and Julie O'Brien, *Priest and Levite in Malachi,* SBLDS 121 (Atlanta: Scholars Press, 1990), 51–52. For discussion of Zechariah 9–14 as in continuity with Zechariah 1–8, see n. 10 and pp. 133–138 below.

10. If the understanding of the movement of the redaction of Zechariah 1–8 being presented is correct, the Zechariah tradition includes a continuing millennial expectation — an expectation in continuity with the apocalyptic worldview evident behind Zechariah 9–14. The implication is that a continuity of tradition runs from Zechariah 1–8 through the redactional additions to these chapters and on downstream into Zechariah 9–14. Such a continuity is claimed, e.g., by Rex Mason, "The Relation of Zech 9–14 to Proto-Zechariah," *ZAW* 88 (1976): 227–39. See also Rex Mason, *The Books of Haggai, Zechariah, and Malachi,* CBC (Cambridge, England: Cambridge University Press, 1977), 11, 79, 81; and Carroll Stuhlmueller, C. P., *Rebuilding with Hope: A Commentary on the Books of Haggai and Zechariah,* International Theological Commentary (Grand Rapids, Mich.: Eerdmans, 1988), 47, 117. In view of this possibility, a new look at the links between Zechariah 1–8 and Zechariah 9–14 is in order. For now, see the lists of elements of continuity and similarities in style between Zechariah 1–8 and Zechariah 9–14 in the following: Mason, *Zechariah,* 78–79; Ronald W. Pierce, "Literary Connectors and a Haggai/Zechariah/Malachi Corpus," *JETS* 27 (1984): 281–89; Stuhlmueller, *Rebuilding,* 114; Childs, *Introduction,* 482–83; Joyce G. Baldwin, *Haggai, Zechariah, Malachi* (London: Tyndale, 1972), 68–69; and Roland Kenneth Harrison, *Introduction to the Old Testament* (Grand Rapids, Mich.: Eerdmans, 1969), 953–54. On the basis of the many links cited in these references, a strong argument can be made that Zechariah 9–14 comes from the continuing line of the tradition that produced Zechariah 1–8.

11. Hanson defines the social position of apocalyptic groups as "that of powerlessness and disenfranchisement vis-à-vis the controlling powers" (e.g., *Dawn,* 251, cf. 283). Thus, by definition he must argue that if apocalyptic forms and motifs are found in the "hierocratic tradition" (i.e., in the literature of Zadokite priests), they

Hanson experiences . . . difficulties in his treatment of Zechariah 1–8, which he admits contains the literary features of apocalyptic but which he wishes to analyze as a series of visions supporting the Zadokite reform program. He is therefore forced to argue that Zechariah 1–8 does not reflect apocalyptic eschatology, even though the visions contain apocalyptic motifs. . . . This distinction seems difficult to maintain.[12]

The history of scholarship has produced several important arguments that, contrary to Hanson, Zechariah 1–8 is proto-apocalyptic literature. In the nineteenth century, such critics as Heinrich Ewald (1841) and Rudolf Smend (1884) recognized the kinship of Zechariah 1–8 to full-blown apocalyptic literature.[13] Then, in 1901, Ernst Sellin attributed the fatherhood of apocalypticism to Zechariah, setting the visions of Zechariah at "the hour of birth" (*die Geburtsstunde*) of apocalypticism.[14]

More recently, several scholars have stressed that Zechariah's visions are a precursor of later full-blown apocalypses.[15] In Uppsala in 1971, both Robert North and Samuel Amsler argued that Zechariah 1–8 was proto-apocalyptic literature.[16] And in 1973, Hartmut Gese argued that Zechariah 1–8 is the oldest "apocalypse" known to us.[17]

---

cannot be significant as "real" apocalyptic, i.e., as representing the substance of a group's beliefs (*Dawn*, 252, 256, 259). Rather, they are mere "carriers of a very pragmatic program" (*Dawn*, 232, 235). As argued in chapter 2 above, the sociological evidence does not support this logic, which, in fact, begs the question. Hanson's reasoning works only if millennial groups are defined *a priori* as deprived, a position critiqued in chapter 2.

12. Robert R. Wilson, "From Prophecy to Apocalyptic: Reflections on the Shape of Israelite Religion," *Semeia* 21 (1981): 83.

13. Heinrich Ewald, *Die Propheten des alten Bundes* (Göttingen: Vandenhoeck & Ruprecht, 1841), 3:318; Rudolf Smend, "Anmerkungen zu Jes. 24–27," *ZAW* 4 (1884): 199.

14. Ernst Sellin, *Studien zur Entstehungsgeschichte der jüdischen Gemeinde nach dem babylonischen Exil* (Leipzig: A. Deichert, 1901), 2:90. See the history-of-interpretation reviews in Hartmut Gese, "Anfang und Ende der Apokalyptik, dargestellt am Sacharjabuch," *ZTK* 70 (1973): 24; and Samuel Amsler, "Zacharie et l'origine de l'apocalyptique," VTSup 22 (1972): 228.

15. See the surveys in Klaus Seybold, *Bilder zum Tempelbau: Die Visionen des Propheten Sacharja,* SB 70 (Stuttgart: Verlag Katholisches Bibelwerk, 1974), 104–5; and John J. Collins, "The Jewish Apocalypses," *Semeia* 14 (1979): 29f.

16. Robert North, "Prophecy to Apocalyptic via Zechariah," VTSup 22 (1972): 47–71; Samuel Amsler, "L'origine de l'apocalyptique." Note that Hans P. Müller also presented a compatible position at the conference. See his "Mantische Weisheit und Apokalyptik," VTSup 22 (1972): 268–93.

17. Gese, "Anfang und Ende."

Those scholars, such as Gese, who see Zechariah 1–8 as an apocalyptic composition make a strong argument.[18] Radical eschatology, dualism, and several other features of apocalyptic literature are evident in this corpus. The text bears a clear family resemblance to later full-blown apocalyptic literature.

Radical Eschatology

Zechariah's first vision makes it clear that the saving work of God will not come through human history (Zech. 1:11). Rather, final salvation will be brought about by the intervention of the transcendent (*durch transzendenten Eingriff*) into history (Zech. 1:13 16).[19] This view is reinforced by Zechariah 2:13 (Eng.: 2:9), which describes God's hand turning the nations into plunder for their slaves.

Zechariah's vision of the four horns and four workmen, Zechariah 2:1-4 (Eng.: 1:18-21), describes more fully this coming intervention of God. The mythic-realistic image of horns can be identified with the world powers (as in Dan. 7:7-8, 24; 8:3, 5-9; Rev. 13:1; 17:12-13) arrayed in their totality (note the use of the number "four") against Israel. The workmen are agents of holy war, commissioned by YHWH to destroy his enemies. Using the roots חרד ("terrify") and ידה ("throw down"), Zechariah images apocalyptic destruction of the nations by these agents in Zechariah 2:4 (Eng.: 1:21). Although lacking the gory details of some full-blown apocalyptic descriptions, Zechariah's second vision clearly describes the apocalyptic final battle.

Zechariah's eighth vision of the four chariots, Zechariah 6:1-8, again strongly focuses on God's end-time judgment on the nations of the world, especially the ominous "enemy from the north." In Ezekiel 38–39, the Ezekiel group had transformed the expected enemy from the north into a

18. For Hanson's arguments against Gese, see *Dawn*, 230 n. 44. Against Hanson's critique, much of Gese's article will be defended below. The use of Ludwig Wittgenstein's concept of "family resemblance," discussed in chapter 2, meets Hanson's first objection to Gese's methodology. Hanson's second objection is based on his "contextual" method (see *Dawn*, 29), which assumes an overly simple two-party view of postexilic society. The social situation lying behind postexilic apocalyptic texts cannot be described accurately in such dualistic terms (as in, e.g., *Dawn*, 217, 342, 366, 373, 399, 400). Indeed, Hanson's method runs the risk of reverting to the old monolinear evolutionary scheme that characterized Wellhausen's opposition of priest and prophet. Against Hanson's final objection, the organic connection between Zechariah 1–8 and 9–14 is clear from evidence such as that referred to in n. 10 above. This connection will also be defended below.

19. Gese, "Anfang und Ende," 27.

monstrous demonic horde, embodying cosmic evil (Ezek. 38:4, 6, 9, 15, 22; 39:4, 11-12; compare Joel 2:20; Dan. 11:13). Here in Zechariah, these northerners are to be engaged in holy war by God's multicolored chariotry.[20] Note that this use of horses as agents of apocalyptic judgment and destruction (also see Zech. 1:8-11, 15) becomes important in later apocalyptic literature (such as Zech. 10:3; 1QM 6:8-16; Revelation 6). In the Zechariah passage, the divine forces go to the "land of the north" and "appease God's רוּחַ." The term רוּחַ refers to "wrath" or "temper" here (as in Judg. 8:3; Prov. 25:28; 29:11; Job 15:13; and Eccl. 10:4; see Zech. 6:8 in TEV and NASB) so that the meaning of הניחו את־רוחי in Zechariah 6:8 is the same as that of Ezekiel's expression והנחותי חמתי "I will vent my wrath" (Ezek. 5:13; compare Ezek. 24:13).

The apocalyptic wrath of God is even clearer in other passages. As early as Zechariah's first vision, God expresses great anger with the nations who are at ease (Zech. 1:15). This extreme anger is also revealed in Zechariah 8:2-3, "'I am jealous for Zion with great jealousy, and I am jealous for her with great wrath.' Thus says YHWH, 'I will return to Zion, and will dwell in the midst of Jerusalem.'" The implication of both passages is that God's future dwelling in Jerusalem will be predicated on the wrathful destruction of the world-enemies of Jerusalem and Zion.

Zechariah's expectation of God's coming wrathful intervention has a universal dimension. The God behind the coming judgment is אדון כל־הארץ ("the lord of all the earth"; Zech. 6:5; 4:14). God's gaze and control cover the whole world: Zechariah 1:11; 4:10b. Thus, the scope of the planned divine intervention is correspondingly universal. The appearance of four diabolical horns in the second vision shows that all corners of the earth are targets of the coming overthrow. A universal conquest of evil is in view.[21]

Discussion of Zechariah's radical eschatology makes clear his lack of hope in history. In his view, historical processes are going nowhere and will accomplish nothing (Zech. 1:11). The eradication of the perpetrators of evil (Zech. 5:3-4), the overthrow of all the enemies of Israel (Zech. 2:4 [Eng.: 1:21]), the anticipated blazing physical presence of God in the city (Zech. 2:9 [Eng.: 2:5]), and the turning of the many nations to YHWH (Zech. 2:15 [Eng.: 2:11]) are all inconceivable without direct apocalyptic divine intervention from beyond history.[22] Although this intervention is

20. See Hanson, "Defiance of Death," 177.

21. See Gese, "Anfang und Ende," 27.

22. Against Hanson, the Zechariah group could hardly have expected that their millennial group-vision would be realized "within the historical realities of the sixth

imminent, it is still a future hope.[23] With the coming of the sunrise at the end of Zechariah's night of visions, the new era is about to dawn.

Dualism

Associated with Zechariah's radical eschatology is a clear dualism between the present age and the age to come. This dualism is clear from the several glimpses of the coming millennial era in Zechariah.[24] Zechariah 8:1-8 describes this millennial kingdom as including longevity for Jerusalem's elders and children's joyful play. Fertility of the land, abundant rain, and agricultural bounty are described in Zechariah 8:12.

Zechariah also takes up the motif of the pilgrimage of the nations to Jerusalem (Isa. 2:2-3; Mic. 4:2) to describe the millennial age as different from the present age. Zechariah 8:22-23 reads, "Many peoples and strong nations shall come to seek YHWH of hosts in Jerusalem . . . ten men from nations of every language shall take hold of a Yehudite, grasping his garment and saying, 'Let us go with you.'" Zechariah 6:15 describes "those who are far off" as coming to help build the millennial temple.

An ontological dualism is also visible in Zechariah 1–8. Understanding Zechariah's thought requires envisioning two planes of existence. Gerhard von Rad states, "The clear-cut way in which the heavenly world is differentiated from the earthly is important. The eschatological saving orders and offices are already present in the world above . . . the emphasis now placed on the archetypal existence of the final things in heaven is something new."[25]

In many of his visions, Zechariah sees activities of the heavenly plane that will affect the plane of earthly existence. Indeed, entities from the heavenly realm plan imminent activity on earth. Thus, "spirits of heaven" are about to come into the world (Zech. 6:1-5), and stork-women will soon be active in the no-man's-land between earth and heaven (Zech. 5:5-11). They have access to our world via a mythic-realistic locale, the "hollow"/"cosmic deep" of Zechariah 1:8 and the "bronze mountains" of

---

century" (*Dawn*, 258). The text clearly shows that the group did not settle for a position "squarely within the present order" (ibid., 273–74).

23. The content of Zechariah's visions remains "promise." See Seybold, *Bilder zum Tempelbau*, 63, 102.

24. Similar views of cosmic renewal and the arrival of a golden age were seen in the discussion of cross-cultural parallels in chapter 2. The worldview behind the Ghost Dance of 1890 is especially analogous.

25. Gerhard von Rad, *Old Testament Theology*, trans. D. Stalker (New York: Harper & Row, 1965), 2:288.

Zechariah 6:1. (On the mythic references here, see: Gen. 2:10-14; Gil-gamesh Tablet XI.194–96; *CTA* 4.4.20-24; and *ANEP,* 683–85.)

A moral dualism is also present in Zechariah 1–8. The appearance of Ls ("the satan") in Zechariah 3:1-2 is the first element of this feature to strike the modern reader. And indeed, although the term does not here denote the archfiend of full-blown apocalyptic literature, there is a mali-ciousness to the satan's role in Zechariah 3. Unlike other satans of the Old Testament (Ps. 109:6; Job 1–2), this satan is the actual enemy of God and is thus rebuked and disappears from the scene. Other passages of Zechariah 1–8 depict even more clearly the existence of evil as a force opposed to God. As noted above, Zechariah 2:1-4 (Eng.: 1:18-21) pits good against evil in its dualistic picture of "workmen" versus "horns." The figure of horns presents the forces of evil grouped as a totality.[26]

Even more significant is Zechariah's understanding of wickedness as personal with its own face and existence. The image of the woman of wick-edness in Zechariah 5:5-11 is a mythic-realistic one. Zechariah is told that the woman is   ul , Wickedness herself. His apocalyptic worldview envi-sions here what later millennial catalyst figures will call the "whore of Baby-lon" (see Revelation 17).[27]

In Zechariah's worldview, there are only two camps — those who side with God at God's city in Jerusalem, and those who worship Wickedness at her anti-temple in Babylon. The struggle between the two camps is clear from the double use of the root Œ u ("cast down") in Zechariah 5:8. Zech-ariah's audience must choose sides in this struggle. As a millennial catalyst figure, Zechariah encourages an existential response from his hearers, di-recting them to flee Babylon (Zech. 2:10 [Eng.: 2:6]).[28]

---

26. On the adversarial nature of the satan figure in Zech. 3:1-2, see, e.g., the NEB translation and Richard J. Coggins, *Haggai, Zechariah, Malachi,* Old Testa-ment Guides (Sheffield: JSOT Press, 1987), 45. Peggy L. Day has correctly argued for a multiplicity of referents for the term   Ls ("satan") in the Old Testament. However, her suggestion that the idea of an independent personality, Satan, under-stood as an enemy of God was borrowed from Zoroastrianism is overstated (*An Adversary in Heaven: śāṭān in the Hebrew Bible,* HSM 43 [Atlanta: Scholars Press, 1988], 63). On the horns of Zech. 2:1-4, see Gese, "Anfang und Ende," 27. Gese describes the "horn" as nature's fundamental weapon, *die schöpfungsmässige Urwaffe.* Thus, in the mythology of older cultures and in this late tradition, the horn is the symbol of world power (*Weltmacht*).

27. See Gese, "Anfang und Ende," 31.

28. Ibid., 37.

Secondary Features

Its visionary patterning is one of the most obvious formal characteristics of Zechariah 1–8. Zechariah's visions recall actual experiences of the millennial catalyst figure. Although they take place at night they are not dreams, as shown by Zechariah's questions as well as by his arousal at Zechariah 4:1. The figure of an otherworldly mediator interpreting such visions is a frequent secondary feature of apocalyptic literature (see, for example, Dan. 7:16; 8:16).[29] Therefore, it is significant that an angelic intermediary is central to Zechariah's visions: Zechariah 1:9; 2:2 (Eng.: 1:19); 2:7 (Eng.: 2:3); 4:1, 4; 5:5, 10; 6:4. The mediatory role of the angel as interpreter is clear in Zechariah 1:9; 2:4 (Eng.: 1:21); 4:5, 11, 13; 5:6; 6:5.

Zechariah 1–8 also exhibits other secondary features of apocalyptic literature. Zechariah describes several superhuman entities, including the satan (Zech. 3:1-2), stork-women (Zech. 5:9), and multicolored horses (Zech. 1:8; 6:2-3). Numerology can also be glimpsed. The number seven is especially prominent. The original number of visions seems to have been seven (see the discussion of Zechariah 3 below), and "seven" recurs within the visions: Zechariah 3:9; 4:2, 10. There are also indications of an idea of the predetermination of all history and the certainty of expected events. The visions depict events on the heavenly plane that will find their necessary parallels in earthly history. Joyce G. Baldwin writes, "This conviction that God had already worked out His purposes in heaven so that all that remained was for the same pattern to be repeated on earth was to dominate apocalyptic."[30]

Messianism is the most important secondary feature of apocalyptic literature in Zechariah 1–8.[31] Zechariah places a major stress on instituting a diarchic polity at the center of his cycle of visions (Zech. 4:12-14). From the start, the cycle thus highlighted a hope in the coming of a future messianic Davidide and high priest.[32] Further, Zechariah never viewed his messianic hopes for the diarchy as already realized. Rather, by not naming

29. Of course, angelic mediators also figure in prophetic texts (e.g., Ezekiel 8).

30. Baldwin, *Zechariah*, 72. This idea of determination may be emphasized through the use of the recognition formula at Zech. 2:13 (Eng.: 2:9); 2:15 (Eng.: 2:11); 4:9; and 6:15.

31. On Zechariah's messianism, see R. North, "Prophecy to Apocalyptic," 50.

32. See van der Woude, "Serubbabel," 156. Note that some later apocalyptic literature, including that found at Qumran, also looked for both priestly and Davidic messiahs. See, e.g., 1QS 9:11; 1QSb 2:12-14; and *Testament of Levi* 18.

specific individuals, Zechariah looks forward to the expected high priest and prince of the coming millennium (Zech. 4:14).

A significant difference between Zechariah and Haggai is that Haggai does grant a definite messianic status to a contemporary, namely Zerubbabel (Hag. 2:20-23).[33] In contrast, though Zechariah at one time may have looked to Zerubbabel with messianic hopes (see Zech. 4:6-10a, an early addition to the vision),[34] for this prophet he was only a messianic candidate; and the Zechariah tradition soon pointed its hopes to a future Davidide, referred to as the צמח ("sprout, branch").[35] The term צמח in earlier prophecy (Jer. 23:5; 33:15; compare Isa. 4:2; [11:1]) emphasized a coming ideal Davidide who would execute justice on the earth. Zechariah's use of the term is probably based on Ezekiel's reference to these prophecies (Ezek. 17:22-24). Thus, Ezekiel's coming "tender twig" is the "Branch"

33. Zerubbabel was the titular and hereditary leader. The grandson of Jehoiachin (1 Chron. 3:17-19; Ezra 3:2), Zerubbabel was of royal descent: he was the Davidide. Scholars often assume that Haggai and Zechariah both held Zerubbabel to be the Messiah (see, e.g., Hanson, *Dawn*, 255, 261, 279; and the references in n. 35 below). It is true that Zechariah supported Zerubbabel as the first representative of the civic side of his projected diarchy. As the Persian appointed governor of Yehud (פחת יהודה; Hag. 1:1; 2:2), he was the logical Davidide representative at the start of Zechariah's ministry. There is no evidence in Zechariah, however, that the millennial group ever decisively settled on Zerubbabel as the Messiah.

34. The statements about Zerubbabel added to the lampstand vision (Zech. 4:6-10a) may suggest Zechariah at one time viewed him as a messianic candidate (see the discussion in the following section). However, Zechariah 4 probably did not direct itself to Zerubbabel in its original form. See van der Woude, "Serubbabel," 155, 156.

35. Wilhelm Rudolph is correct that the "Branch" is not clearly identified with Zerubbabel in Zechariah. See his *Haggai — Sacharja 1–8 — Sacharja 9–14 — Maleachi*, KAT 13/4 (Gütersloh: Gütersloher Verlagshaus Gerd Mohn, 1976), 100, 108, 130f. In contrast, issue must be taken with those scholars who equate Haggai's and Zechariah's views on Zerubbabel. Thus, Hinckley Mitchell states, "Zechariah follows Haggai in recognizing Zerubbabel as the Messiah" (*Haggai, Zechariah, Malachi and Jonah*, ICC [New York: Scribner's, 1912], 104). Also see, e.g., Gunther Wanke, "Prophecy and Psalms in the Persian Period," in *The Cambridge History of Judaism*, ed. W. D. Davies and L. Finkelstein (Cambridge, England: Cambridge University Press, 1984), 1:182–83; Walter Schmithals, *The Apocalyptic Movement: Introduction and Interpretation*, trans. John E. Steely (Nashville: Abingdon, 1975), 173; and Bernhard W. Anderson, *Understanding the Old Testament* (Englewood Cliffs, N.J.: Prentice-Hall, 1986), 518–19.

predicted at Zechariah 3:8 and 6:12. The Targum correctly saw this Branch as the Messiah.[36]

On the basis of the family resemblances summarized above, the overall genre of Zechariah 1–8 can be identified as proto-apocalyptic literature. Whether Gese is correct that it is an apocalypse as well is moot. The text clearly evidences the same millennial worldview observable in the comparative anthropological evidence. As Samuel Amsler asks,

> This universal perspective, this insistence on the transformation of the world by the destruction of earthly powers, this description of the purification of the people through the judgment of unfaithful members, this intention to comfort and to console (דברים טובים דברים נחמים :1:13), not to mention the literary form itself: hermetic vision, sequence of seven scenes—does not all of this signal the apocalyptic literature that flourished by the second century?[37]

The Continuity of the Zechariah Apocalyptic Tradition

As noted above, since Wellhausen's time, scholars have tended to see the eschatology of the Zechariah tradition as increasingly having settled for a priestly theocracy replacing any original messianic hopes. Thus, Hanson traces in the alterations to Zechariah 1–8 an ending of the incipient messianism of the hierocratic tradition.[38] Expanded and interpreted, the visions are identified with attained institutional realities.[39] Similarly, Rex Mason states that "the tradition has been passed on among those who were anxious to elevate the role of the priesthood and to limit the role of Zerubbabel."[40]

I want to argue that the ongoing Zechariah tradition, rather than abandoning its apocalyptic/messianic features, continued along apocalyptic lines. Redaction points the visions toward the future, not toward any pragmatic community control. Indeed, the redaction of Zechariah 1–8 as well as the composition of Zechariah 9–14 continue Zechariah's messianic focus on a future Davidide.

36. See the Targum on Zech. 3:8 and 6:12 (Alexander Sperber, ed., *The Bible in Aramaic* [Leiden: Brill, 1962], 3:481, 485). For helpful annotations, see Kevin J. Cathcart and Robert P. Gordan, translators, *The Targum of the Minor Prophets,* The Aramaic Bible vol. 14 (Wilmington, Del.: Michael Glazier, 1989), 192, 198.

37. Amsler, "L'origine de l'apocalyptique," 228.

38. Hanson, *Dawn*, 257, 264, 268; "Zechariah," 982–83.

39. Hanson, "Zechariah," 983. Hanson writes, "The apocalypses of Zechariah were re-edited and given a new function as propaganda for the hierocracy and its Zadokite leaders" ("Apocalypticism," *IDBSup*, 32).

40. Mason, *Zechariah,* 28.

Messianic Redaction in Zechariah 1–8

An initial pro-Davidide, messianic redaction is present in Zechariah's fifth vision of the golden lampstand. Whether or not Zechariah 4:6-10a is a simple insertion, these verses clearly exhibit some early reworking of Zechariah 4.[41] The redaction here places emphasis on Zerubbabel and thus holds open the Davidide half of Zechariah's millennial diarchy expectation. Note especially that this messianic hope is held alive even at the risk of underemphasizing the priest's governing role.

At the time of this early redaction, millennial optimism may have hoped that Zerubbabel himself might be the Messiah. Thus, v. 6 speaks of the outpouring of the divine Spirit (רוחי), an Ezekielian apocalyptic motif (Ezek. 39:29) later stressed in Zechariah 12:10. And v. 7 is reminiscent of the language of the leveling of mountains, an apocalyptic motif found in Zechariah 14:4 (and in Ezek. 38:20).[42] Thus, reworking of Zechariah 4 functioned to insure an eschatological interpretation of the fifth vision at a period when Zerubbabel may still have been a messianic candidate in the eyes of the group.

Redaction of Zechariah 1–8 also involved attaching an appendix to the visions at Zechariah 6:9-15. This appendix, describing a prophetic sign-act of crowning, also contains a messianic thrust in its present form. Although the text-history here may be complex, no textual support exists for the suggestion, often adopted since Wellhausen, that the crowning was originally of Zerubbabel but was changed to Joshua (v. 11).[43] Neither can the present text be taken as identifying Joshua or any future priestly officeholder with the Branch at vv. 12-13.[44] Rather, the Zechar-

---

41. Since Wellhausen (*Die Kleinen Propheten,* 182–83), nearly all critics have contested the literary unity of Zechariah 4. See the commentaries and the text re-arrangements in the NEB and NAB.

42. See Childs, *Introduction,* 478.

43. Wellhausen, *Die Kleinen Propheten,* 185, as mentioned in n. 2. The text at Zech. 6:11b is actually emended from "Joshua" to "Zerubbabel" by NAB; see also JB, n. "i," and NEB, n. "g." Commentators espousing this view include: Mitchell, *Zechariah,* 185–86; D. Winton Thomas, "The Book of Zechariah, Chapters 1–8, Introduction and Exegesis," *IB* 6:1080; Karl Elliger, *Das Buch der zwölf Kleinen Propheten,* ATD 25/2 (Göttingen: Vandenhoeck & Ruprecht, 1959), 2:128f.; Samuel Amsler, *Aggée, Zacharie, Malachie,* CAT 11c (Paris: Delachaux & Niestlé, 1981), 108f.; and Erling Hammershaimb, "The Change in Prophecy during the Exile," in *Some Aspects of Old Testament Prophecy from Isaiah to Malachi* (Copenhagen: Rosenkilde og Bagger, 1966), 106. For an excellent critique of this thesis, see van der Woude, "Serubbabel," 138–56.

44. This seems to be the intention of KJV, NIV, and NASB, which at v. 13 read, "He [the Branch] will/shall be a priest." Baldwin interprets Zech. 6:9-15 as

iah 6 appendix exhibits the millennial group's characteristic separation of the priestly and royal offices (as in Zech. 4:14 and 3:8). Thus, Zechariah is instructed to make עטרות ("crowns"), the plural indicating that neither a simple crowning of Zerubbabel nor of Joshua is at issue.[45] The NJPS captures the sense of v. 11: "Take silver and gold and make crowns. Place [one] on the head of High Priest Joshua son of Jehozadak." The other crown is to stay in the temple (v. 14) awaiting the coming of the Branch. This interpretation is clinched by the wording of Zechariah 6:13, which distinguishes between שניהם "the two of them" (the future priest and Davidide). Rather than elevating a contemporary figure, either Zerubbabel or Joshua, the text looks forward to the coming of a future Davidide, the Branch.

If the (reworked?) Zechariah 6 appendix represents a later layer of the Zechariah tradition, it shows that this tradition was not satisfied with a realized eschatology. Wellhausen's assumption of a downfall of the Davidides resulting in a stagnant priestly hegemony over restoration polity is no longer tenable.[46] It has been a misreading to see either a reflection of increasing priestly power, or tendentious pro-priestly editing in this pericope.[47]

---

indicating a future messianic unification of the priestly and royal offices: "Nowhere else in the Old Testament is it made so plain that the coming Davidic king will also be a priest" (*Zechariah*, 137).

45. RSV, NIV, TEV, and NASB emend to the singular, "crown," in Zech. 6:11, and this is supported by LXX[LC] and the Syriac. However, this reading makes no sense in context (see below), and the plural of the MT is to be preferred as more original. The MT is supported by most LXX witnesses and the Targum. (That the Targum's *Vorlage* had "crowns," contrary to the statements of many scholars, is shown by its treatment of the plural as a *pluralis excellentiae* ["a large crown"]. See Cathcart, *Targum*, 198 n. 9.) והעטרת in v. 14 logically refers to only one of these crowns, and should be pointed as the singular "crown," as shown by the tense of the following verb in the MT and supported by the LXX: ὁ δὲ στέφανος. Carol and Eric Meyers argue that this singular noun in v. 14 may have caused the confusion of the LXX[LC] and the Syriac in v. 11. See their *Haggai, Zechariah 1–8*, AB 25B (Garden City, N.Y.: Doubleday, 1987), 349.

46. Hanson continues to accept this assumption (*People Called*, 265–66). See, however, the discussion on p. 163 below.

47. Thus, Hanson is incorrect in arguing that the text "disruptions" in Zech. 6:9-14 are an attempt to degrade the Davidide in favor of the priesthood (*Dawn*, 264, 268). Hanson states, "This textual alteration documents the transformation of the original Zadokite diarchy into the later priestly hierarchy" ("Zechariah," 983). This view is widespread. See, e.g., Lawrence A. Sinclair's statement that "the pericope has been changed by someone who wished to place more emphasis on Joshua, the High Priest" ("Redaction of Zechariah 1–8," *BR* 20 [1975]: 42).

Far from arguing for acceptance of any hierocratic status quo, the text points forward to a coming messianic reign.[48]

Zechariah's entire fourth vision of the cleansing of Joshua the High Priest, Zechariah 3, is probably a later addition to the vision cycle, since it lacks the unique formal features of the other visions.[49] It is significant that futuristic messianic expectations strongly continue in the redaction of this late addition, where purity is the focus of the tradition.

Messianism was stressed through the insertion into Zechariah 3 of vv. 6-10.[50] In v. 8, Joshua and his priestly colleagues are called to listen to a promise. These colleagues are אנשי מופת, "men assigned an omen," and Adam S. van der Woude has plausibly argued that this omen is the Davidic crown of Zechariah 6:14 awaiting the Messiah in the temple.[51] The divine promise is a simple messianic reminder: "I am going to bring my servant the Branch." Together with the Davidic omen, the divine reminder binds a messianic/eschatological perspective to the chapter's central-priestly concern for the cleansing of the land (vv. 4, 9). In its redacted form, Zechariah 3 thus gives Joshua and his colleagues only qualified support. The ongoing Zecharian hope for the future rule of a Davidide tempers the group's enthusiasm for an expanded priestly role in Yehudite society. The Zechariah group clearly endorses the high priesthood, but this priesthood must not lose its apocalyptic vision.[52]

---

48. See Childs, *Introduction*, 478; and van der Woude, "Serubbabel," 151. The temple mentioned in v. 12, then, is the millennial temple (cf. Hag. 2:9; and Ezek. 37:26; 40–48). In this regard, note the use of the term היכל ("Temple") in Zech. 6:12 in contrast to בית ("house"), the latter term being more often used for the mundane temple in Zechariah (Zech. 1:16; 3:7; 4:9; 7:3).

49. Thus the stereotypical ואשא עיני וארא ("then I lifted up my eyes and looked") and המלאך הדבר בי ("the angel who was speaking to me") are both lacking. Zechariah does not inquire about what he sees and indeed is not even addressed. For discussion, see Gese, "Anfang und Ende," 25; Mason, *Zechariah*, 50; van der Woude, "Serubbabel," 146; Amsler, "L'origine de l'apocalyptique," 227; Stuhlmueller, *Rebuilding*, 77; and Seybold, *Bilder zum Tempelbau*, 16–17.

50. See Amsler, "L'origine de l'apocalyptique," 237.

51. Adam S. van der Woude, "Zion as Primeval Stone in Zechariah 3 and 4," in *Text and Context: Old Testament and Semitic Studies for F. C. Fensham*, ed. W. Claassen (Sheffield: JSOT Press, 1988), 244; "Serubbabel," 150, 153.

52. See Childs, *Introduction*, 479. Meyers and Meyers aptly conclude that the supplements to Zechariah 3 employ future-king imagery to help resolve the anomaly of a restored temple without the presence of a monarch. Retention of a messianic hope is crucial for the group. As a result of the supplements, "the view presented in chapter 3 as a whole accords completely with the dyarchic picture painted in chapter 4, where Zerubbabel has been cautiously included again in the Oracular Insertion, and with the dramatic Crowning scene of chapter 6, in which a second

Zechariah 9–14

It is beyond the scope of this discussion to detail all the sharpened apocalyptic features and motifs of Zechariah 9–14.[53] Instead, it is best to concentrate on the one feature of messianism, an emphasis carried over from the redaction of Zechariah 1–8. Discussion of how the Zechariah tradition continues in Zechariah 9–14 its messianic focus on a future Davidide significantly illuminates the Zechariah tradition-history.[54]

The first text to be examined, Zechariah 9:9-10, is one of the best-known messianic pericopes in Zechariah. Zechariah 9:1-8 sets the stage for the entrance of the Messiah by describing God's restoration of the Davidic empire. Then, echoing the liturgical shouts of joy of Zechariah 2:14 (Eng.: 2:10), Zechariah 9:9 depicts the future entrance into Jerusalem of the coming king. Finally, v. 10 describes the millennial era of universal peace this king ushers in. In the end time, God will cut off (כרת) all war implements resulting in harmony and peace (שלום). The description of this verse draws on the cultic language of the royal psalms (Pss. 72:8; 89:26) to describe a universal dominion for the coming king.[55] The belief in a coming universal reign of God had formed the center of the expectation of Zechariah 1–8 and is tellingly reemphasized here.

A second evidence of messianism in Zechariah 9–14 is found in Zechariah 10, which describes the millennial blessings from the Messiah. Within this chapter it is likely that Zechariah 10:4 contains a triple messianic designation.[56] According to this verse, "the cornerstone," the "tent peg," and the "bow of battle" will come from Judah. The Targum's messianic interpretation of these designations is probably on target. This interpretation paraphrases "cornerstone" by "king," and "tent peg" by

---

crown has been set aside for a future Davidide" (Meyers and Meyers, *Zechariah 1–8*, 227, cf. 203).

53. In Zechariah 9–14 the apocalyptic eschatological patterns of Zechariah 1–8 reemerge, but in an expanded and sharper form. See Childs, *Introduction*, 483.

54. It should be noted up front that the expectation of a coming Davidic Messiah in Zechariah 9–14 is contrasted with pictures of the present civic leadership as "antimessiahs." Thus, the Zechariah group's critique of past and present rulers (Zech. 10:2-3; 11:4f.) is extended to include a prediction of a coming evil ruler (Zech. 11:16-17; 13:7-9). Discussion of this expectation resumes below. The idea of antimessiahs is surely an important part of the background of the end time Ἀντίχριστος ("antichrist") of the New Testament (e.g., 1 John 2:18; cf. Rev. 13:1-10).

55. See Magne Sæbø, "Vom Grossreich zum Weltreich: Erwägungen zu Pss. lxxii 8, lxxxix 26, Sach. ix 10b," *VT* 28 (1978): 83–91.

56. See William Neil, "Zechariah, Book of," in *IDB* 4:946; Mason, "Relation," 236; and *Zechariah*, 100.

"anointed One."[57] The term פִּנָּה ("corner [stone]") especially is elsewhere used figuratively of a ruler (Judg. 20:2; 1 Sam. 14:38; Isa. 19:13; Ps. 118:22).

In a deliberate contrast to their description of an antimessiah in Zechariah 11:15-17 and 13:7-9, the Zechariah group in chapter 12 paints a positive messianic portrait of the future Davidic house. Zechariah 12:8 envisages a millennial Davidic reign in which the house of David will be כאלהים . . . לפניהם, that is, like God in the view of the inhabitants of Jerusalem. This verse probably looks forward to an end-time Davidic ruler who, in contrast to the present corrupt governors, will rule perfectly in accordance with God's will.[58] This expectation is buttressed by the emphasis in v. 10 on the house of David as the special object of God's pouring out of the Spirit. Thus, Zechariah 12 continues the Zechariah tradition's messianic, pro-Davidide emphasis. Indeed, the continuing importance of both Davidic and priestly houses for the Zechariah tradents is indicated by their mention in Zechariah 12:12-13.

Zechariah 13 contains a further explicit messianic reference. Verse 1 describes the millennial purification and cleansing of the house of David. As in Zechariah 12, this verse presents a positive Davidic expectation in the face of present corruption within the civic government of Yehud. When the millennium arrives, this sin and impurity will be washed away so "David" can rule in purity.

The above analysis does not support the view that Zechariah 1–8 and Zechariah 9–14 represent two diametrically opposite traditions, the former espousing a realized eschatology, the latter an apocalyptic eschatology. Instead, the evidence points to one Zechariah tradition that was messianic from the beginning.[59] If, indeed, the Zechariah group was millennial from its beginnings, the question arises of its place in society. I suggest that the Zechariah millennial group is best viewed as a group of priests in power within the postexilic Yehudite community.

Zechariah as the Product of a Central-Priestly Group

Various evidence indicates that Zechariah represented the central powers of postexilic Yehudite society. That Zechariah was supported by the Yehudite elders is clear from Ezra 6:13-15. The support mentioned here

---

57. The Targum on Zech. 10:4 reads: "From them will be their king, from them their anointed One." See Sperber, *Bible,* 3:491; and Cathcart, *Targum,* 209 n. 21.

58. See Mason, *Zechariah,* 117.

59. On the basis of the above discussion, issue must be taken with those authors (e.g., Dumbrell, "Kingship and Temple," 40) who see a diminished Davidic interest in Zechariah 9–14.

can also be read from between the lines of Zechariah's writings.[60] Zechariah was not merely supported by those in power, however; he was himself a member of the priestly establishment of the restoration community. As Gese states, apocalyptic literature first emanated from a person who was certainly an official.[61]

Zechariah's Central-Priestly Office

Many scholars argue that the postexilic period saw a strong emphasis on cult prophecy.[62] Chronicles and Joel imply the importance of postexilic cult prophets in Yehudite society (1 Chron. 25:1, 4-8; Joel 1:13-14), an importance that went beyond that enjoyed by their preexilic predecessors (attested, for example, in 2 Kings 23:2).[63] Like Haggai, Zechariah was among these new postexilic temple prophets closely aligned with the priesthood.[64] As R. R. Wilson has noted, Zechariah clearly operated within temple-cult circles.[65]

The account of Zechariah 7:1-7 attests to Zechariah's office as a cult prophet. Here Bethelsarezer (בית־אל־שר־אצר) sends a delegation to ask the temple officials about fasts. That the answer comes from Zechariah (vv. 4-7) shows the close association of priests and prophets in the temple.[66] Zechariah might have even delivered his oracle in the temple itself.[67]

Zechariah was not only aligned with the temple priesthood, he was a priest himself.[68] Zechariah was the grandson of the priest Iddo (Zech. 1:1;

60. Even the many allusions to previous prophetic writings in Zechariah 1–8 probably indicate that he had official backing. Presumably, free access to the temple-library collection—a phenomenon that will be seen again in the discussion of Joel—would not have been granted to someone not supported by the official leadership.

61. Gese, "Anfang und Ende," 40.

62. See the discussion of priestly concern in postexilic prophecy and the bibliographic notes in Thomas W. Overholt, *Channels of Prophecy: The Social Dynamics of Prophetic Activity* (Minneapolis: Fortress, 1989), 152, 156.

63. For bibliography and discussion of postexilic temple prophecy, see the discussion of Joel in the next chapter and Joseph Blenkinsopp, *A History of Prophecy in Israel* (Philadelphia: Westminster, 1983), 232, 251-55.

64. See Stuhlmueller, *Rebuilding*, 151; Neil, "Zechariah," 944; and Hammershaimb, "Change in Prophecy," 102.

65. Robert R. Wilson, *Prophecy and Society in Ancient Israel* (Philadelphia: Fortress, 1980), 289.

66. See the discussion in Blenkinsopp, *History of Prophecy*, 232.

67. See ibid., 248.

68. Such a prophetic role for priests is attested by Mal. 2:7, which applies the term מלאך ("messenger") to the priest's office. See O'Brien, *Priest and Levite*, 147.

Ezra 5:1; 6:14) who was in charge of one of the priestly families that returned to Yehud from Babylonian exile.[69] Nehemiah 12:4, 16 indicate that
Zechariah eventually officiated as head of Iddo's priestly household.[70]

Central-Priestly Usages and Ideology in Zechariah 1–8

Using the idiom of Zechariah 1–8 to confirm its priestly background
is somewhat more complicated than was the case with Ezekiel 38–39 in
the previous chapter. Scholars are increasingly aware of the methodological
problems involved in using distinctive language to identify groups responsible for postexilic literary activity and redaction. For example, although
the language of Deuteronomy was characteristic of one specific minority
group before the exile, Deuteronomistic idioms and themes were taken up
by many groups in the Persian period.[71] Another methodological problem
involves intertextuality issues, which come increasingly into play in postex-

69. It is unclear why the use of בֶּן in Ezra 5:1 and 6:14 with the meaning
"grandson" troubles many commentators. For this usage elsewhere, see Gen. 29:5
↔ 24:15, 29; 31:28, 43; Ruth 4:17; and 2 Kings 9:20 ↔ 2 Kings 9:14.

70. See R. Wilson, *Prophecy and Society,* 288. Also see Wanke, "Prophecy and
Psalms," 1:162–88; Franz Joseph Stendebach, *Prophetie und Tempel: Die Bücher
Haggai — Sacharja — Maleachi — Joel* (Stuttgart: Verlag Katholisches Bibelwerk,
1977), 22; and Wellhausen, "Zechariah," 5390.

71. On the problem of the mixing of language and types of prophecy in the
postexilic period, see R. Wilson, *Prophecy and Society,* 289, 292, 295, and 306. Wilson notes that even the Ephraimite and Judean views of appropriate prophetic
activity had merged by early postexilic times. Because the Deuteronomistic theology contained one of the few adequate explanations for the occurrence of the exile,
it is understandable why this theology and its associated terminology were partially
adopted even by those groups that were opposed to Deuteronomistic thinking
in the preexilic period (cf. Zech. 7:11-14). Wilson states, "The Ephraimite views
advocated by the peripheral prophets provided an acceptable explanation for the
disaster [of 586]. Yahweh had punished the nation for breaking the divine covenant. . . . We may suppose the Deuteronomic views gathered increasing popular
support during the exile. . . . The [resulting] exilic mixing of Deuteronomic and
Jerusalemite traditions is reflected in the prophetic literature of the postexilic period
and in the writings of the Chronicler. The theological views of the prophets of this
period are an amalgam of positions that had been distinct in the preexilic period"
(*Prophecy and Society,* 305–6). An important example of the influence of Deuteronomistic theology on Zechariah 1–8 is the call to repent in Zech. 1:3. (For Zech. 1:1-
6 as a summary of Deuteronomistic teaching, see Blenkinsopp, *History of Prophecy,*
235.) YHWH will return if the people will "return" (שוב) to him. Zechariah here
seems close to the Deuteronomistic/Jeremianic notion of repentance as a prerequi-
site for restoration (Deut. 30:1-10; Jer. 31:19). This view was abandoned by Ezek-

ilic texts. Zechariah 1–8 and Zechariah 9–14 draw on written collections of authoritative prophetic material. It is hard to imagine that the language and motifs in these collections would not have influenced the modes of expression of the Zechariah group. Despite such mixing of traditions evident in the Zechariah 1–8 text, the provenance of this apocalyptic writing can nevertheless still be determined: the text is the product of a central-priestly group.

The very forms and organizing principles of Zechariah 1–8 breathe the atmosphere of the central cult and its authorities. An emphasis on visions is characteristic of those Judean prophetic circles associated with the Jerusalem royal theology,[72] and Zechariah is replete with such an emphasis: Zechariah 1:8; 2:1 (Eng.: 1:18); 2:5 (Eng.: 2:1); 3:1; 4:1,2; 5:1, 5,9; 6:1. Beyond this, the operations of the central cult clearly have furnished the elements that form the very fiber of the symbolism of Zechariah's visions. This evidence is clearly seen in Klaus Seybold's excellent description of the organization of Zechariah's visions in accordance with the "sacral-architectonic structure of the temple."[73] Seybold traces the provenance of the scenes, spatial organization, and movement of the visions. They are bound to sacral precincts and to such elements as altars (Zech. 2:1-2 [Eng.: 1:18-19]), lampstands (Zechariah 4), cultic theophanies (Zech. 2:9 [Eng.: 2:5]), ceremonial curses (Zech. 5:1-4), and judicial sacral procedures (Zechariah 3). Zechariah doubtless borrowed the elements of his presentation from the ritual and liturgy of the temple cult.[74]

---

iel (Ezekiel 36). For Ezekiel, God's name will be restored with Israel as a mere passive instrument (Ezek. 36:22). Thus, the "return" vocabulary of Zechariah may represent somewhat of a middle ground between Deuteronomy/Jeremiah and Ezekiel for reestablishing relationship with YHWH as with the similar language used in Isaiah 44: "Return to me, for I have redeemed you" (v. 22). Meyers and Meyers write: "The reciprocal nature of such a turning [Zech. 1:3] in the relationship between God and his community establishes the potential for full reconciliation. . . . The position adopted by the prophet Zechariah offers another possibility [other than Deut. 30:1-10 and Ezek. 36:24-31] for the reestablishment of Israel's relationship with God, for his generation had already begun, under Haggai's prodding, to exhibit a new spirit of returning centered about the temple project" (*Zechariah 1–8*, 99).

72. R. Wilson, *Prophecy and Society*, 289.

73. Seybold, *Bilder zum Tempelbau*, 36.

74. Ibid., 44, cf. 76–77, 99. In his chapter 8 on temple symbolism and the Zion tradition, Seybold also notes the indebtedness of the vision cycle to the ancient Near Eastern conventions of sacral building/temple construction (ibid., 80, cf. 100). On Zechariah's reverie as bearing a close relationship to Mesopotamian

Material content as well as formal presentation distinguish Zechariah 1–8 as the product of central priests. Significant here is Zechariah's strong advocacy of the theology of the election of Jerusalem. As Rex Mason states, "Zechariah was steeped in the traditions of Zion and the temple which saw Jerusalem as the city which God had chosen for himself."[75] A focus on the Jerusalem temple sanctuary is already clear at Zechariah 1:15-17. Verse 17 emphasizes God's "choice" (בחר) of Jerusalem. Thus, the first of Zechariah's apocalyptic visions makes clear that the vision cycle will be Zion-centered.

In fact, Zion theology is evident at several points in the visions. The third vision of the surveyor (Zech. 2:5-17 [Eng.: 2:1-13]) signifies the assured restoration and blessing of Zion. Verse 14 (Eng.: v. 10) promises God's "dwelling" (שכן) in Jerusalem's midst. God's election of Jerusalem is again explicit at v. 16 (Eng.: v. 12). As in Zechariah 3:2, the root בחר ("choose") is conspicuous here.

God's choice of Zion means that God will dwell in the temple to be built there. As preparation for this apocalyptic event, the visions announce the present building of the mundane temple (Zech. 4:9), which is a type of the millennial temple (Zech. 6:12-13). The descriptions of the building project probably draw on the myth of the cosmic mountain/*Urhügel*, popular in royal and priestly circles, in describing Zion (see Zech. 4:7, which addresses Mount Zion as "temple platform").[76]

Outside of the actual visions themselves, Zion theology is also seen clearly in the glorious picture of Jerusalem in Zechariah 8:2-3: "Thus says YHWH of hosts: I am jealous for Zion with great jealousy, and I am jealous for her with great wrath. Thus says YHWH: I will return to Zion, and will dwell in the midst of Jerusalem." The cosmic-mountain motif here reinforces the pro-Zion image: "Then Jerusalem will be called the City of Truth, and the mountain of YHWH of hosts, the Holy Mountain."

The concern for purity in Zechariah 1–8 also marks this text as central-

---

temple-renovation liturgies, see also Baruch Halpern, "The Ritual Background of Zechariah's Temple Song," *CBQ* 40 (1978): 167–90.

75. Mason, *Zechariah*, 28. Also see Stuhlmueller, *Rebuilding*, 49.

76. See van der Woude, "Primeval Stone," 237–48; and Meyers and Meyers, *Zechariah 1–8*, 228, 244–46. Seybold points out the probable mythological connection of Zechariah's temple and the entrance point of the chariots of Zech. 6:1-8 at the omphalic center of the four winds (*Bilder zum Tempelbau*, 80). The organization of the vision cycle, which places the temple at the center of the cosmos from which God's eyes range throughout the earth (Zech. 4:10b), similarly reinforces the omphalos myth (Seybold, *Bilder zum Tempelbau*, 81).

priestly. In the millennium, Zechariah states, Zion will be known as the "Holy Mountain" (Zech. 8:3) and Yehud will become the "holy land" (אדמת הקדש; Zech. 2:16 [Eng.: 2:12]). This concern for the purity of the land is at the heart of Zechariah's sixth vision of the flying scroll and his seventh vision of the woman in the ephah. These visions exhibit Zechariah's stress on holiness and cleanness with reference to the whole land. The vision of the flying scroll, Zechariah 5:1-4, describes the coming purge (Niphal stem of נקה) of sinners from the land. The vision of the woman in the ephah, Zechariah 5:5-11, goes even further in describing the removal of Evil herself. This cleanness/purity emphasis in Zechariah is reminiscent of the comparable Zadokite interest found in Ezekiel.

Priestly Emphases in Zechariah's Polity

From the first, Zechariah emphasized Zadokite prominence and participation in the highest levels of authority.[77] This position, a clear clue to Zechariah's social placement, is best illustrated by his vision of the golden lampstand in Zechariah 4. The centrality of the lampstand vision is emphasized through literary devices such as rhetorical techniques (vv. 5, 13) and the pericope's original central position in the vision cycle. Gese notes that this vision required a special rousing (עור, v. 1), indicating an expansion of the visionary's consciousness allowing deeper perception.[78]

As discussed above, the polity envisioned is a diarchy. The two olive trees flanking the cultic lampstand in the Zechariah 4 vision must be the two community leaders, the high priest and the Davidide. Since the two figures are not named, they represent ideal officials. For Zechariah, in the millennial age there will be two central administrators. The reference to the flow of oil in v. 12 indicates that both leaders will support the temple and the new cult community.

The cultic lampstand that the two leaders flank symbolizes God's presence. Its spouts represent the eyes of YHWH ranging throughout the earth: in the coming age, God's glory will emanate from the temple into

---

77. Specifically Zadokite prominence is inferred from Zechariah's focus on Jeshua/Joshua. It should be recalled that Joshua was the first priestly leader of the postexilic period (Ezra 2:2, 36; 3:2), the high priest (Hag. 1:1; Zech. 3:1; 6:11) who had come from Babylon. This Joshua, the son of Jehozadak (Zech. 6:11), and the grandson of Seraia, was descended from the last Zadokite chief priests at Jerusalem before the fall of the city in 587 B.C.E. (2 Kings 25:18; 1 Chron. 6:8-15). For discussion and references, see chapter 4, n. 140 above. Joshua was clearly the Zadokite head who was to reestablish Zadokite control of the temple.

78. Gese, "Anfang und Ende," 28.

the world (v. 10b). The vision thus connects the two leaders with the divine essence, full of eyes, seen by Ezekiel (Ezek. 1:18; 10:12).[79] The priestly and Davidic "sons of oil" are here pictured in interrelationship with the awesome divine presence itself.

The vision's picture of the high priest linked to God clearly emphasizes the authority and importance of the Zadokites. At the same time, there is no evidence that the Zechariah group supported any narrow Zadokite dominance over the Yehudite community. Rather, the vision presents Zechariah's idealized hope for an egalitarian relationship between high priest and Davidide.[80] The Zechariah group's emphasis on a future Davidide, the coming Branch, resists any pretensions to hegemony on the part of their fellow priests. As argued above, the redaction visible in vv. 6-10 functions as a strong reminder of the importance of the Davidide half of the diarchy in the original vision.

The Continuing Zechariah Tradition

There are strong signs that Zechariah 1–8 was transmitted and interpreted (still messianically) within circles of the Jerusalem priestly leadership.[81] Significant here is the redactional addition of the fourth vision of Joshua the High Priest (Zechariah 3), which best illustrates the focus on Zion theology and the priesthood in the continuing tradition. That Zechariah 3 was a later addition to the vision cycle indicates that the central-priestly focus of the Zechariah group was an ongoing emphasis, not a position soon abandoned in the history of the group.[82] Zechariah 3:2 continues Zion theology's stress on the divine election of Jerusalem, and Zechariah 3:3-5 emphasizes the importance of the high priest within Zion. The robes of state (מחלצות; v. 4) given to Joshua further indicate the Zechariah tradents' support of a (tempered) leadership role for the Zadokites. Zechariah 3:7 even states that Joshua is to be given access to the divine council.[83]

79. See ibid., 29.

80. David L. Petersen has shown how this "twoness" works itself out in "symmetric and heraldic fashion" (*Haggai and Zechariah 1–8*, OTL [London: SCM, 1984], 232).

81. See Mason, *Zechariah*, 10.

82. See n. 49 above.

83. If v. 7 is redactional, it is further evidence that the polity of the continuing Zechariah millennial group remained in support of Zadokite authority over the temple. Redaction at Zech. 6:13 had already extended this priestly authority into the messianic era, at which time והיה כהן על־כסאו, "there will be a priest upon his throne." The unusualness of this hieratic image in which a throne is allocated to a

This vision also clearly engages the central-priestly concern that the high priest be ritually clean (Zech. 3:4, 9; compare Ezek. 36:25; Exod. 29:4-6; Lev. 16:4). Joshua's feculent garments are removed and replaced with robes of state. The vocabulary here recalls Ezekiel 4:9-17. When ordered to perform a sign-act prefiguring the exile, Ezekiel had begged God not to be defiled (מטמאה) by the kind of fecal contact to which Joshua has now become exposed (Ezek. 4:12 and Zech. 3:3 both use the root צוא ["be filthy"]). In removing Joshua's feculence (Zech. 3:4), God thus reverses the ritual defilement caused by what the Zadokites viewed as excrementitious exilic conditions (Ezek. 4:13). Joshua is also given a pure turban (צניף טהור; Zech. 3:5). Use of the root טהר ("cleanse, purify") here further reflects the Zadokite concern for ceremonial cleanness that was observed in Ezekiel (see List 2, item 38). Future priestly ritual and the sacrificial cult (משמרתי; v. 7) can be efficacious for Zechariah because God is officially granting cultic purity to the high priest.

The central-priestly language and motifs characteristic of the Zechariah tradents are also apparent in Zechariah 9–14. Thus, these chapters continue to stress the need for the ritual purity of the community. For example, Zechariah 9:7 states that before the Philistines' end-time incorporation into Judah, they will have to be made ritually clean.[84] The Jerusalemites will also be purified. The language of Ezekiel 36:17, 25 is used in Zechariah 13:1 to describe the millennial cleansing of Jerusalem's inhabitants. This verse looks forward to God's end-time cleansing of the city in which a fountain will spout salvation. Note especially the use of Ezekiel's menstrual term נִדָּה ("impurity") here (Ezek. 7:19-20; 18:6; 22:10; 36:17; and H: Lev. 18:19; 20:21). Zechariah's millennial fountain will fully deal with this Zadokite concern. Zechariah 13:2 describes the removal of "the unclean spirit" (רוח הטמאה) from the land: In the millennium, God will even remove the supernatural causes of impurity.[85]

The central-priestly focus on the divine election of Zion and the temple

---

priest was toned down in the LXX: καὶ ἔσται ὁ ἱερεὺς ἐκ δεξιῶν αὐτοῦ ("and the priest will be at his [the Davidic Messiah's] right hand"). Brian A. Mastin argues that the LXX did not have a different *Vorlage* here, but was probably influenced by the picture of 1 Kings 2:19: "The high priest is said to be 'at the right hand' of the prince, in the same way that Bathsheba's כסא ['throne'] is placed at Solomon's right hand when Solomon sits on his throne" ("A Note on Zechariah 6:13," *VT* 26 [1976]: 115).

84. See Neil, "Zechariah," 947.

85. The central-priestly character of Zechariah 13 is so clear that Plöger sees the program of the theocratic leadership here (*Theocracy*, 87).

is just as clear in Zechariah 9–14 as it is in Zechariah 1–8 (see Zech. 9:8, 12 [where Jerusalem is referred to as a בצרון, a "stronghold"]; 12:3, 8; 13:1; 14:10, 16).[86] Heavy use of the *Völkersturm* motif of Ezekiel 38–39 in Zechariah 12 makes this dependence on the Zion tradition especially clear.[87] Zechariah 12:1-9 places Jerusalem at the center of the end-time cosmic battle. The many nations of the earth gather against Jerusalem in an Armageddon-like campaign (v. 3) but are severely defeated by the divine warrior. The description of the enemy's defeat uses the holy-war motif of supernatural confusion and panic (v. 4) frequent in apocalyptic literature (compare Ezek. 38:21-22). Thus, Jerusalem emerges here as the inviolable and eternal city.

The *Völkersturm* motif of Zion theology is picked up again and elaborated in a somewhat different way in Zechariah 14. Note the usage הרי ("my mountains") in v. 5 as in Ezekiel 38:21. Indeed, Zechariah 14 uses the cosmic-mountain/*Götterberg* motif at several places to describe the future Zion. Thus, v. 8 draws on the idea of the cosmic mountain as the source of all the waters of the world (Gen. 2:10-14). The associated motif of a perennial stream flowing from the temple (compare Zech. 13:1) was preserved in the royal cult (Ps. 46:4; 36:9; 65:10-14) and was stressed by the Ezekielian Zadokites (Ezek. 47:1-12).[88] Verse 10 describes a millennial physical alteration of Israel's geography involving Jerusalem's literal elevation to the *axis mundi*. The result will be that Zion's physical height will correspond to its cosmic-mountain identity.

It is significant that Zechariah 14, usually considered the most apocalyptic chapter of the book,[89] exhibits more central-priestly concern than

86. See Stuhlmueller, *Rebuilding,* 142–45; and Mason, "Relation," 227–31.

87. See the discussion of the "Later Reuse of the Gog Tradition" in chapter 4 above. David L. Petersen writes that in Zech. 12:1-9, "the Zion tradition appears in the motif of an inviolable city in which the deity dwells" ("Zechariah," *Harper's Bible Commentary,* ed. J. Mays [San Francisco: Harper and Row, 1988], 751).

88. See Hanson, *Dawn,* 377–78; van der Woude, "Primeval Stone," 244–45; and Stuhlmueller, *Rebuilding,* 150.

89. See Hanson, *Dawn,* 369; and Patrick D. Miller, Jr., *The Divine Warrior in Early Israel* (Cambridge, Mass.: Harvard University Press, 1973), 140. Apocalyptic elements in this chapter include the cosmic struggle of the divine warrior (vv. 2-3) and the splitting of mountains (v. 4) followed by a millennium, including such elements as continuous daylight (v. 7) and the flow of living waters (v. 8). Petersen summarizes the apocalyptic descriptions of this chapter: "Fantastic changes [will happen] in the natural world. There will be a radically new time when human experience of this age will be abrogated — no more cold, but presumably pleasant

any other chapter in the Zechariah corpus. While clearly an apocalyptic text, Zechariah 14 shares with the Holiness Code a view of the importance of the cultic celebration of the Feast of Booths (Lev. 23:34-43). That Zechariah 14:16-19 so vehemently insists on the necessity of all the nations going to the Jerusalem temple to celebrate the Feast of Booths indicates an especially strong focus on the centrality of Jerusalem's temple cult (compare Zech. 8:22).[90]

The ritual prescriptions of the feast in Zechariah 14:20-21 clearly betray a priestly concern for cultic purity (compare Zech. 8:3). For our priestly millennial group, legitimate ritual cannot take place without it, especially in the age to come. But the purity concern here is not limited to priestly altar service performed in the midst of the temple complex. The holiness of the temple extends outward to the temple courts, where sacrificial meat was cooked, and beyond into the rest of Jerusalem. The Zechariah tradents' continuing concern for purity here extends to everything in Jerusalem and in Judah — down to the bells on the horses' harnesses.

Despite Walter Harrelson's attempt to limit the YHWH-enthronement liturgy of the Feast of Booths to the preexilic period, its themes were probably borrowed directly from the postexilic central cult by the Zechariah group.[91] That the group would have performed this liturgy is indicated by several texts. Ezra 3:2-4 indicates the Feast of Booths was celebrated by the returnees, including the Zadokites, even before the temple was built. Verse 5 implies an ongoing observance of it thereafter. Nehemiah 8:13-18, which may predate Zechariah 14, also stresses the

---

warmth, no more night but continuous light. . . . Eden-like living waters (cf. Joel 4:18 [Eng.: 3:18]) will presumably lead to marvelous fertility" ("Zechariah," 751).

90. The world-importance of the Feast of Booths at Jerusalem in Zechariah 14 contrasts with the lesser role it had in other periods and for other groups. Thus, the early injunction of Exod. 23:17 that all *Israelite* males appear for the feast does not specify a centralized celebration. Indeed, even after cult centralization, an annual pilgrimage to Jerusalem was not emphasized in every period. See Neh. 8:16-17, and George W. MacRae's observation that at a later time, "Jesus apparently had a free choice about whether to celebrate Tabernacles in Jerusalem or not (cf. John 7, 2-10)" ("The Meaning and Evolution of the Feast of Tabernacles," *CBQ* 22 [1960]: 269).

91. Walter Harrelson first states that the Zecharian authors were influenced by actual cultic proceedings, but then seems to take back the implications of this by denying enthronization themes to the postexilic cult ("The Celebration of the Feast of Booths According to Zech xiv 16-21," *Religions in Antiquity*, Goodenough *Festschrift*, ed. J. Neusner [Leiden: Brill, 1968], 91 n. 2).

importance of the Feast of Booths in the postexilic period.[92] The feast's postexilic observance is further demonstrated in that some YHWH-enthronement psalms employed in its celebration are of a late date. An example is Psalm 96, which is dependent on Second Isaiah and shows considerable borrowing from other psalms.[93]

Because the Feast of Booths emphasized the *Völkersturm* motif in its liturgy, it is natural that Zechariah 14 argues for this feast's yearly celebration after YHWH's apocalyptic final victory.[94] The associated motif of rain and fertility (Deut. 16:15; Ps. 65:9-13)[95] was readily interpreted in Zechariah 14:17-19 in terms of the Yehudites' much-hoped-for millennial prosperity (Hag. 1:10; Zech. 8:12; 10:1). The cultic Feast of Booths and its motifs thus logically shaped the apocalyptic expectations and expressions of the Zechariah millennial group. YHWH's eschatological kingship and this cultic feast are properly linked at Zechariah 14:16.[96] A central-cultic emphasis is found even at the tail end of the Zechariah tradition-history.

Restoration in Zechariah 1–8 Compared with Ezekiel

The discussion thus far strongly suggests that the Zechariah millennial group was composed of priestly officials. The label *priest,* however, like the label *visionary,* does not adequately define a Persian-period group. Several different priestly groups existed in the postexilic period, and part of the sociological task is to find where the Zechariah group best fits in among them. This requires comparing the idiom and viewpoint of Zechariah with those of other biblical texts, so as to uncover any possible connections.

Several places where Zechariah echoes Zadokite and Ezekielian language and ideas have already been mentioned. These linguistic and thematic reverberations suggest it may be near Ezekiel's priestly school that the Zechariah group would best be located.

---

92. Verse 17 cannot mean the feast was not observed since the days of Joshua. See, e.g., 1 Kings 8:65. The issue here must be lack of "proper" observance, e.g., the failure to dwell *everywhere* in actual "booths," or to include the "entire assembly."

93. Sigmund Mowinckel saw the enthronement *Gattung* associated with the Feast of Booths as preexilic, but admitted that some of the actual enthronement psalms were of postexilic origin. See his *The Psalms in Israel's Worship,* trans. D. Ap-Thomas (Nashville: Abingdon, 1967), 117–18.

94. See W. J. Dumbrell, "Some Observations on the Political Origins of Israel's Eschatology," *The Reformed Theological Review* 36 (1977): 37.

95. Mowinckel, *Psalms,* 1:119; MacRae, "Feast of Tabernacles," 269.

96. See Mowinckel, *Psalms,* 1:119.

Indeed, investigation reveals that the visions of Zechariah correspond closely to the writings of Ezekiel and his tradents.[97] An actual dependence is seen in Zechariah's borrowing terminology from Ezekiel. For example, Zechariah's description of God as having great "jealousy" (קנאה; Zech. 1:14; 8:2) resonates with Ezekiel's prophecy (Ezek. 5:13; 23:25; 36:5-6; 38:19; compare 39:25), as does Zechariah's use of the verb זרה to describe the past "scattering" of Judah (Zech. 2:2, 4 [Eng.: 1:19, 21]; Ezek. 5:10, 12; 12:14; 20:23; 22:15; compare H at Lev. 26:33).

The influence of Ezekiel is also apparent from shared ideas, motifs, and even literary and structural characteristics in the two literatures. Zechariah takes from Ezekiel the association of God's Spirit and the four winds of the cosmos (Zech. 6:4-8; Ezek. 37:9-10). The flying scroll of Zechariah 5:1-4 that functions as a curse is reminiscent of the scroll mentioned in Ezekiel 2:9-10, which contained lamentations, mourning, and woe (also written on both sides). The personification of wickedness and impurity as a woman in Zechariah 5:8 may draw on Ezekiel's simile in Ezekiel 36:17, "when the house of Israel lived on their own soil . . . their conduct in my sight was like the uncleanness of a woman in her menstrual period."[98] Finally, Zechariah is clearly influenced by the broad visionary emphasis of Ezekiel. Like those of Zechariah, Ezekiel's visions are filled with temple symbolism and explicate the Zion theology.[99]

Reverberations between the reconstruction programs of Zechariah 1–8 and Ezekiel[100] further suggest a dependence of the Zechariah group on the

97. The influence of Isaiah 40–55 is also noticed occasionally, but this is only sporadically demonstrable. See Seybold, *Bilder zum Tempelbau*, 84; and Petersen, *Zechariah 1–8*, 122.

98. Also see Ezekiel's parable of the adulterous woman (Ezekiel 16), and his parable describing the unfaithfulness of Oholibah (Ezekiel 23).

99. See Seybold, *Bilder zum Tempelbau*, 85.

100. There are several indications that the Hebrew Bible preserves evidence of Zadokite temple-reconstruction programs in Ezekiel 40–48 and Zechariah 1–8. Hammershaimb argues that the exiles "gave intensive thought to the problems which would be caused by the revival of the cult, and . . . drew up a complete plan . . . as the exiles' programme of reform for their native land" ("Change in Prophecy," 103; see also R. Wilson, "From Prophecy to Apocalyptic," 87). For Hanson, Zechariah's visions "functioned in the activity of Zechariah as a prophetic endorsement of the Zadokite temple program" worked out by their "patron saint" Ezekiel, and a good deal of evidence suggests that this view is not far wrong (see Hanson, "Zechariah," 982; *Dawn*, 233, 245 [also n. 53]; and *People Called*, 256–57). Stendebach writes, "In his interest in the rebuilding of the temple, Zechariah proves himself—like Haggai—to be a genuine follower (*Nachfolger*) of Ezekiel, who laid

writings of the Ezekiel group. Both blocks of literature, for example, use similar language to describe the return of God's glory to Zion and the temple. Indeed, God's promise to Zechariah that God will return to Jerusalem and God's house (Zech. 1:16) fulfills Ezekiel's vision of the return of YHWH's glory (Ezek. 43:1-5).[101] Note that Zechariah 2:9 (Eng.: 2:5) and 2:12 (Eng.: 2:8) draw on Ezekiel's כבוד־יהוה ("YHWH's glory") terminology (Ezek. 1:28; 11:23; 43:4; 44:4). Further, like Ezekiel, Zechariah 2:14 (Eng.: 2:10) and 8:3 use the root שכן ("to dwell") to describe God's future dwelling with Israel (see Ezek. 37:24-27; 43:7-9).[102] Even Zechariah's portrayal of the preparation of Zion for God's return (Zech. 2:5-6 [Eng.: 2:1-2]) makes use of the surveyor's measuring line of Ezekiel 40:3.

Ezekiel's emphasis that repossessed Jerusalem will include restoring a Davidide also heavily influenced Zechariah.[103] Ezekiel's Davidide concern is most clear in Ezekiel 34:20-24 and 37:24-28. As in Zechariah 3:8, God describes the coming Davidide in Ezekiel as עבדי, "my servant" (Ezek. 34:24; 37:24). Although the Davidide is emphasized to a lesser extent in Ezekiel 40–48, this does not mean that these later passages of Ezekiel, in contrast to Zechariah, give him a negative evaluation. Special promise is still set on the prince even in Ezekiel 40–48. The prince is given a special allocation of land (Ezek. 48:21; compare 45:7-8), and he has the further (albeit somewhat token) privilege of using rooms inside the east-gate structure of the temple.[104]

---

out in chapters 40–48 of his book a grand program for the future, centering on the new temple and the creation of a new people" (*Prophetie und Tempel*, 23).

101. See Mason, *Zechariah*, 38; and Baldwin, *Zechariah*, 100.

102. See Hanson, *Dawn*, 249 n. 56; and Seybold, *Bilder zum Tempelbau*, 85.

103. Ezekiel's views on the Davidide are somewhat complex. First, rather than using the title מלך ("king"), Ezekiel describes the one shepherd as a נשיא ("prince"), e.g., Ezek. 34:23-24. (Walther Zimmerli argues that Ezekiel is using a genuine ancient Israelite title here [*Ezekiel 2*, Hermeneia, trans. J. D. Martin (Philadelphia: Fortress, 1983), 218].) Nevertheless, the prince is king (Ezek. 12:10; 37:22, 24-25). Second, the figure of the Davidide changes somewhat between the earlier references in Ezek. 34:23 and 37:25 and the later references in Ezekiel 40–48. The former texts picture the Davidide's return as ushering in the era of salvation in a comparable picture to that of Zechariah. Ezekiel 40–48, in contrast, examines the Davidide in terms of his concrete tasks for the near future. A trend toward deemphasizing the king becomes apparent here, and restraints are placed on the prince's power (Ezek. 46:16f.).

104. More strongly than Zechariah, Ezekiel 40–48 stresses the separation of priestly and Davidic prerogatives. Petersen's reference to the prince as a "priest-monarch amalgam" in Ezekiel is misleading (*Zechariah 1–8*, 118). Ezekiel 43:8 stipulates that the temple is no longer to be a subelement of the palace complex

Ezekiel and Zechariah are closely linked, but this does not mean that their viewpoints are identical.[105] Zechariah 1–8 sometimes significantly deviates from Ezekiel, attempting to come to grips with problems not anticipated by him. Thus, whereas Ezekiel's visions did not prepare for apostasy after Israel's restoration (see Ezek. 43:7), Zechariah deals with the problem of postexilic disorder in his vision of the flying scroll. The implication is that his group's program had to deal with the reality of a not yet perfect society (Zech. 5:1-4). Further, whereas Ezekiel's Jerusalem has walls (Ezek. 48:30-35 refers to "three gates"), Zechariah's Jerusalem without walls (Zech. 2:5-9 [Eng.: 2:1-5]) may have been a concession to the present impracticality of any wall building in preparation for the eschaton.

Zechariah's third vision of a Jerusalem without walls also alerts us to an important variation in the understanding of holiness in Zechariah and Ezekiel. Since Zechariah 2:9 (Eng.: 2:5) envisions YHWH permeating Jerusalem, the temple is not emphasized as the locus of YHWH's presence as it is for Ezekiel (Ezek. 43:7).[106] This contrast regarding localization of YHWH's presence relates to a contrast between gradation and nongradation of holiness. Ezekiel's vision emphasizes the themes of separation and gradation of holiness (see Ezek. 42:20, 44:23).[107] Ezekiel 43:12 epitomizes these themes.[108] Still emphasizing holiness, the Zechariah tradition

---

(contrast 1 Kings 7:2-12 and 2 Kings 11; see John W. Wevers, *Ezekiel*, NCBC [Greenwood, S.C.: Attic, 1969], 216; and Zimmerli, *Ezekiel 2*, 552). Whereas in monarchic times the king might even officiate at the altar (2 Kings 16:12f.), for Ezekiel, the king, like all the laity, is excluded from this priestly bailiwick (see Moshe Greenberg, "The Design and Themes of Ezekiel's Program of Restoration," *Int* 38 [1984]: 206; and Dumbrell, "Kingship and Temple," 35–37). Thus, Ezekiel 46 stipulates that the prince is not to enter the inner court or take part in the sacrifice. Rather, in the cultic sphere, the נשיא ("prince") is to be no more than the chief representative of the community. As such he may merely sit in the closed outer east gate of the sanctuary for a sacrificial meal (Ezek. 44:1-3).

105. Thus, Petersen finds eight categories of contrasting restoration views between Ezekiel and Zechariah, suggesting that "Zechariah has presented an alternative to or a revision of the notions of restoration present in Ezek 40–48" (*Zechariah 1–8*, 119, cf. 116f.; also see his "Zechariah's Visions: A Theological Perspective," *VT* 34 [1984]: 195–206). The examples given here are from Petersen's discussion.

106. With regard to Zechariah's view, Petersen writes, "Yahweh's holiness will be accessible throughout this city of weal—it is described as on the perimeter, the walls, and inside the city [Zech 2:9 (Eng.: 2:5)]" (*Zechariah 1–8*, 171).

107. See Greenberg, "Ezekiel's Program," 203.

108. See Ronald M. Hals, *Ezekiel*, FOTL 19 (Grand Rapids, Mich.: Eerdmans, 1989), 306; and Greenberg, "Ezekiel's Program," 192.

moves away from a gradation stress. Thus, the final development of the tradition sees all of Jerusalem sanctified. The horses' bells and every pot in Jerusalem and Judah are holy to YHWH (Zech. 14:20-21).[109] Thus, in both Ezekiel and Zechariah, the central temple assures that Jerusalem is sacred. However, in Zechariah, the temple extends its sacred character outward in a way not anticipated in Ezekiel 40–48.

The most interesting variation between the polities of Ezekiel and Zechariah is that Ezekiel does not discuss a "high priest."[110] Zechariah, in contrast, sees the position of the high priest as very much a reality (Zech. 3:1; 4:14; 6:11): this office constitutes half of Zechariah's joint civil-religious leadership.[111] A related variation is that the strong distinction between Zadokites and Levites in Ezekiel 40–48 is not present in Zechariah. Zechariah does not wish to elevate the Zadokites above the Levites; no priestly groups are earmarked as subservient.

In summary, the above discussion has indicated the special dependence of the Zechariah group on Ezekiel. Their views differ in some respects, however. The situation is not as simple as Hanson's view that Zechariah 1–8 supports Ezekiel's program (whereas Zechariah 9–14 vehemently attacks it). Zechariah draws on Ezekiel's language and program but also differs from Ezekiel. Behind the Zechariah literature was a group trying to work with Ezekiel's restoration framework while remaining independent from some of Ezekiel's views.

Ezekiel also seems to preserve a Zadokite restoration program in the form it took before encountering the hard facts of the actual return. Variations from Ezekiel, then, may involve more than the different emphases of the Zechariah group. This group also interprets Ezekiel for their own time in the face of contemporary problems. Zechariah presents a revision of Ezekiel's restoration plans in light of postexilic realities.[112]

Finally, the variations between Ezekiel and Zechariah do not mean

109. Whereas Ezek. 46:21-24 depicts the people's having their sacrifices boiled by Levites in kitchen areas within the temple courts, these levitical functionaries are not mentioned in Zech. 14:20-21. Clearly, the Zechariah tradition has a different form of expressing the Zadokite holiness concern than does Ezekiel 40–48.

110. See Petersen, "Zechariah's Visions," 205. Greenberg finds it hard to tell if Ezekiel's omission is "accidental," or if it implies "annulment" ("Ezekiel's Program," 208). A third possibility would be that the position of high priest only achieved prominence after Ezekiel's period (see Petersen, *Zechariah 1–8*, 189).

111. Petersen writes, "The [Zecharian] visions . . . make clear that the high priest is to have an important leadership role, and this is in contrast to Ezek 40–48" (*Zechariah 1–8*, 118).

112. See Petersen, "Zechariah's Visions," 202.

that the Zechariah group belonged to a different, non-Zadokite, priest-hood over against Ezekiel's group. Zechariah has stronger links with Ezek-iel than with the texts of other priestly groups (such as Second Isaiah). It is just that the Zechariah and Ezekiel groups were not identical. Rather, the Zadokite priesthood must have encompassed several subgroups with somewhat different views. The holiness and separatist emphases in Ezekiel 40–48 may represent the polemic of a hard-line faction within a larger Zadokite priesthood.

Synthesis: The Sociology of the Zechariah Group

Study of Zechariah does not confirm the idea of Plöger and Hanson that apocalyptic eschatology arose out of increasingly deprived prophetic circles. Rather, Zechariah 1–8 evidences a millennial and messianic worldview among priests in power in the early days of the restoration. As Gese states, "Zechariah belonged to the priestly upper class (*Priesteraristok-ratie*), he supported the building of the temple."[113] It must be concluded that an apocalyptic worldview need not be a fringe phenomenon. In the case of Zechariah 1–8, apocalyptic literature was produced from the center, both theologically and sociologically. Plöger's thesis that the priestly elite had a noneschatological theology which opposed the views of opposition circles cannot be maintained.[114] Indeed, the whole generalization, traceable to Max Weber and Ernst Troeltsch, that nobility and priests are "dedicated to the preservation of the status-quo" so that "eschatological teachings are kept at a minimum" does not fit the evidence of Zechariah.[115]

113. Gese, "Anfang und Ende," 40. Cf. von Rad's statement that Zechariah's message culminates in "the imminent establishment of [God's] kingdom, but, to the great embarrassment of not a few of the commentators, this message is linked closely to the rebuilding of the Temple in Jerusalem" (*Theology*, 2:281, cf. 2:285). Also see Coggins, *Zechariah*, 55, 58.

114. Plöger, *Theocracy*, 89, 93–94, 111. Also note at this point the thesis of Robert G. Hamerton-Kelly, who views Zechariah as a compromise treatment at-tempting to mediate both eschatological and institutional concerns ("The Temple and the Origins of Jewish Apocalyptic," *VT* 20 [1970]: 1–15). Although Hamerton-Kelly's analysis better explains the data of Zechariah than does that of Plöger and Hanson, he still holds to a two-party view of "a theological stalemate between the theocrats and the eschatologists" ("Temple," 14). We must go beyond this author and accept that a theocrat may also have an apocalyptic worldview.

115. Hanson adopts these generalizations (*Dawn*, 214–15, 247). Thus, he ar-gues that the hierocratic party was virtually indifferent toward eschatology (*Dawn*, 284).

The priestly center of postexilic society, to which the Zechariah group was tied, was not homogeneous. Both similarities and differences can thus be observed between Zechariah and Ezekiel, the major known representative of a Zadokite restoration perspective. These variations demonstrate that Ezekiel's language and viewpoint were unique. Not all Zadokites would have copied or imitated him completely, nor should we expect homogeneity among a large priestly group like the Zadokites.

The Zechariah community's differences with some views of Ezekiel indicate the existence of subgroups or branches of the Zadokite priesthood involved in a shared discourse. In contrast to some hard-liners, the Zechariah subgroup did not stress gradations of holiness within Jerusalem or the limitation of the temple priesthood to Zadokites. Although closely associated with other Zadokite temple priests, they were an independent coterie, identifiable vis-à-vis the other priests of the house of the Lord. Thus, in Zechariah 7:1-7 the delegation sent by Bethelsarezer inquires of the temple priests and prophets (v. 3), but Zechariah's answer addresses not only the people of the land but also other priests (v. 5).

The Millennial Group Program of Zechariah 1–8

The practical program behind Zechariah 1–8 does not lend itself to the analysis of Plöger that was taken up by Hanson.[116] This approach assumes that millennial group programs are hostile to society's law and cult. In contrast, sociological evidence undercuts these assumptions and helps explain how the Zechariah messianic group adopted a practical program of rebuilding the temple, reinstating the central cult, and forming a community observant of the central legal codes of the society.[117]

---

116. Recall that according to Plöger, postexilic society began to "limit" faith to the cultic sphere where it could not find full expression (*Theocracy*, 35–46). This situation produced a reaction involving the formation of eschatological communities/conventicles (ibid., 46–48). Plöger understands the Zechariah tradition against the background of this scenario. Thus, he holds that the purified remnant of Zech. 13:8-9 "seems to be those who think and hope eschatologically . . . in contrast [to those who] . . . expect the purification in a formal, ritualistic manner" (ibid., 89). Behind Zechariah 12–14, Plöger sees a setting in which "the cultic community is of the opinion that it can remain untouched by historical afflictions if it resorts to the approved cultic-ritual measures, [whereas] the eschatological group proclaims that judgment is being meted out against Jerusalem" (ibid., 107).

117. In chapters 2 and 3, sociologically parallel millennial group programs were discussed that focus on central-cult priests and their sanctuaries. One such group, the Mamaia millennial group in Polynesia, was based in the society's central shrine. The native priesthood played a leading role in this central cult, which was also

A specific example of such evidence is Savonarola's millennial program for fifteenth-century Florence (discussed in chapters 2 and 3 above). Although a central priest of Florentine society, Savonarola was a millennial catalyst figure with an apocalyptic view of a coming reign of the Spirit in Florence.[118] He used his status as statesman and lawgiver in the post-Medici republic to implement a civic plan preparing Florence for a central role in the imminent millennial kingdom. Like Zechariah in Jerusalem, Savonarola viewed his role as showing the Florentines how to build a new eschatological order in Florence, God's chosen city, that would usher in the new age.[119] His order for the new era was based on an apocalyptic worldview but at the same time was central-cult centered. Like Savonarola's civic plan for Florence, Zechariah's practical program centered around rebuilding temple and city.

Zechariah's millennial program for action was not just central-cult focused, it was also nationalistically royalist. Again, certain parallels help to clarify the sociology behind this pro-Davidide stance of the Zechariah millennial group. For example, like the priests of the Zechariah group, the early American millennial clergy also supported a governor who had emigrated with them from a "second Babylon." Cotton Mather's millennialism saw John Winthrop, the first governor of the Massachusetts Bay Colony, as a messiah, a "micro-christus."[120] Winthrop was to lead the Massachusetts Bay theocracy into the "age of miracles" that Mather announced was dawning. Like Zerubbabel, Winthrop was thus caught up in theocratic millennialism. In 1629 the governor wrote that the settlers' undertaking "appears to be a worke of God."[121]

---

millennial. See Vittorio Lanternari, *The Religions of the Oppressed,* trans. L. Sergio (New York: Knopf, 1963), 240. The Nuer millennial group headed by Gweck Wundeng also had its base in the society's central shrine, the Pyramid of Dengkur. See Thomas W. Overholt, *Prophecy in Cross-Cultural Perspective: A Sourcebook for Biblical Researchers* (Atlanta: Scholars Press, 1986), 219, 226. Finally, note that the *Testament of Levi* 2–7 seems to have lent legitimation to the Hasmonean royal priesthood, just as Zechariah 1–8 supported the Zadokites and their central-cult-based restoration program (see Hanson, "Apocalypse, Genre," *IDBSup.,* 28).

118. See Donald Weinstein, *Savonarola and Florence: Prophecy and Patriotism in the Renaissance* (New Jersey: Princeton University Press, 1970), 110, 146, 168.

119. Ibid., 142, 168.

120. Sacvan Bercovitch, *The Puritan Origins of the American Self* (New Haven: Yale Press, 1975), 58.

121. Quoted ibid., 61; see also 53, 55, 63. Other millennial groups have also looked to governors or even kings in messianic expectation. Thus, Spanish-Franciscan millennialism believed that a Messiah would come as a future king

Hanson assumes that, unlike the group behind Zechariah 1–8, "true" millennial groups do not take the real events of history and politics seriously. For him, existing structures are "matters of indifference" to millennial groups, which lack a "sense of vocation" within the present order.[122] I disagree. Millennial groups have a program for action that gives them a clear vocation preparing for the eschaton. Although some of these millennial group programs are passive, they are hardly indifferent to contemporary events and structures. It was seen in chapters 2 and 3 that a millennial group's vocation may involve creating or restoring temples, cult objects, and rituals. Millennial group programs also often stress ethical behavior.

The Zecharian messianic group program passively disavowed use of human force and power in bringing in the millennium (Zech. 4:6; 6:7-8).[123] This practical program, however, actively stressed purified worship and ethical behavior, including penitential practices.[124] The group believed the human work of rebuilding and purifying would pave the way for a coming divine intervention that would have dramatically real historical consequences.[125]

Arena Class and Historical Background

The wider social environment of the Zechariah millennial group was a class A arena: the group held central power within an endogenous environment. Their environment can be considered endogenous because, rather than threatening the group, the Persian Empire guaranteed a relatively peaceful existence for the Yehudite community. Although its "toleration" is often overstated,[126] the Persian patrimonial system did insure their

---

of Spain. As a result, the Franciscans supported Spanish-Hapsburg imperialism in preparation for their monarch's rule over the millennial kingdom. See John L. Phelan, *The Millennial Kingdom of the Franciscans in the New World*, 2d ed. (Berkeley and Los Angeles: University of California Press, 1970), 16, 53, 106, 108.

122. E.g., Hanson, *Dawn*, 232, 281, 286.

123. See Mason, *Zechariah*, 55.

124. See Blenkinsopp, *History of Prophecy*, 245.

125. As Gese notes, the alleged disconnection with history of apocalyptic is conditioned by the totality of the salvation, achieved only by an *Einbruch* ("inbreaking") from the Beyond ("Anfang und Ende," 37).

126. See the arguments in Amélie Kuhrt, "The Cyrus Cylinder and Achaemenid Imperial Policy," *JSOT* 25 (1983): 94.

subjects' cultural and social patterns.[127] The Persians did not oppose or trouble the Yehudites religiously under this system.[128]

Indeed, the Persians actually supported Zechariah's temple rebuilding project and the central cult where his group held power.[129] Darius prevented interference with the project and provided material help (Ezra 5:6—6:15). The Zechariah group and the Persians also cooperated in support of the importance of the Davidide in restoration polity (see Ezra 1:8).[130] Hanson sees so much cooperation between the Persians and the Zadokites that he considers the Zadokites "compromised" themselves, although there is no support for this assumption.[131]

Political "crises" can no more explain the formation of the Zechariah millennial group than can arguments about "stressful contact" with the Persians.[132] The apocalyptic worldview of Zechariah 1–8 did not arise from the jolts of the political tumult that shook the Persian Empire between 522

127. See Meyers and Meyers, *Zechariah 1–8*, xxxii.

128. See Wellhausen, "Zechariah," 5392; Gese, "Anfang und Ende," 21; Baldwin, *Zechariah,* 17; Stuhlmueller, *Rebuilding,* 50; and Peter R. Ackroyd, *Exile and Restoration,* OTL (Philadelphia: Westminster, 1968), 165.

129. Persian support of their subjects' cults is attested by Udjahorresne's Inscription. Udjahorresne, "chief physician" in Egypt, reconsecrated the temple of Neith for Cambyses (530–522 B.C.E.). See J. Maxwell Miller and John H. Hayes, *A History of Ancient Israel and Judah* (Philadelphia: Westminster, 1986), 450; and Meyers and Meyers, *Zechariah 1–8,* xxxii. Continuing Persian interest under Darius in the Egyptian cult is attested from a later time by the Demotic Chronicle. See Geo Widengren, "The Persian Period," in *Israelite and Judaean History,* ed. John H. Hayes and J. Maxwell Miller (Philadelphia: Westminster, 1977), 515.

130. Thus Hammershaimb notes that Zerubbabel's position as governor (Hag. 1:1) would have been based on nomination by the Persian king, a nomination made despite the fact that he was descended from Jehoiachin ("Change in Prophecy," 101).

131. Hanson, *Dawn,* 219, 226, 262. See Meyers and Meyers, *Zechariah 1–8,* 223.

132. For these sociological terms, see the discussion of relative deprivation in chapters 2 and 3. On the basis of the discussion of the previous two paragraphs, the situation of the Zechariah group appears relatively endogenous, at least when compared, e.g., to the exogenous interference that occurred in the wake of the conquests of Alexander the Great. (The possibility of millennial groups in a class A arena renders unnecessary the hypothesis of those authors who date Zechariah 9–14 to Alexander's period so as to make it the product of a contact cult.)

and 520.[133] Scholars such as Peter R. Ackroyd and Samuel Amsler note that, although Zechariah 1–8 may well preserve earlier material, the historical context for Zechariah's visions given by Zechariah 1:7 (c. February 15, 519)[134] is probably correct. If so, this gives a date for Zechariah's proto-apocalyptic corpus after Darius had restored order in 520.[135] This historical setting agrees with the statement of Zechariah 1:11 that כל־הארץ ישבת ושקטת, "all the earth is peaceful and quiet."[136] Thus, the origins of the apocalyptic worldview of Zechariah are to be dated not to a period of crisis and deprivation, but to the peaceful period after 520.

The Zechariah Tradents and Social Change

Gese's discussion of Zechariah 1–8 as apocalyptic literature makes the important observation that these chapters lack a presentation of end-time travail (*Wehen*) and the final-battle descriptions characteristic of later apocalypses. In Zechariah 1–8 humanity between the old and new eons is basi-

---

133. In a well-known article, Leroy Waterman argued that Zechariah's prophecies originally represented a messianic conspiracy inspired by this Persian crisis. A crown was even made for Zerubbabel, but the Persians arrived and purged Zerubbabel, Zechariah, and Haggai from the scene. See his "The Camouflaged Purge of Three Messianic Conspirators," *JNES* 13 (1954): 73–78. See also Hanson, "Zechariah," 983; and *Dawn*, 244f. It will be remembered from chapter 2 that some sociologists, such as Weston La Barre, think of all millennial groups as crisis cults. See La Barre, "Materials for a History of Studies of Crisis Cults: A Bibliographic Essay," *Current Anthropology* 12 (1971): 11.

134. See Meyers and Meyers, *Zechariah 1–8*, xlvi, 108.

135. Peter R. Ackroyd, "Two Old Testament Historical Problems of the Early Persian Period," *JNES* 17 (1958): 13–27; Samuel Amsler, "L'origine de l'apocalyptique," 230. Also see Neil, "Zechariah," 944; and Seybold, who writes, "As for Zechariah's visions, they are above all intensively concerned with the problem of the already consolidated, all-powerful, and omnipresent Persian reign of universal peace (*Weltfriedensreiches*)" (*Bilder zum Tempelbau*, 95). It has been argued that the Persian restoration of order should not be connected with any "purge" of Zerubbabel. Wellhausen's thesis of a downfall of Zerubbabel is an unnecessary hypothesis.

136. See Amsler's lexical work, which shows the terms here may imply a postcrisis calm ("L'origine de l'apocalyptique," 230 n. 3). Unfortunately, Amsler is still able to argue that the Zecharian proto-apocalyptic literature was produced by a kind of deprivation: the world upheaval had not given the Zechariah group the hoped-for salvation ("L'origine de l'apocalyptique," 230–31). As is the case with other similar arguments, this view overstretches the elastic deprivation rubric. See the discussion in chapter 2 above.

cally calm, not enmeshed in an end-time military crisis.[137] In contrast, in Zechariah 9–14 we get the messianic woes, purges, and battles characteristic of later, more "pessimistic" apocalyptic literature.[138] Sociological evidence is available to help explain this radicalizing shift in the Zechariah tradition from an optimistic to a pessimistic apocalyptic worldview.

The changes undergone by the sixteenth-century Spanish Franciscan group surrounding Gerónimo De Mendieta significantly illuminate the course of Zechariah's group. As noted in chapter 3, Mendieta's millennial group was originally in power (it was in a class B arena: dominating and central). Like the Zechariah group, in its early phases Mendieta's group had what John L. Phelan calls an "apocalyptic elitist" character, rather than a "revolutionary chiliast" one.[139] As Haggai and Zechariah looked to the royal head of society for the Messiah, Mendieta thought first that the Messiah might be the king of Spain.[140] During his period of apocalyptic optimism before 1580, Mendieta envisioned a coming millennial universal monarchy of the Spanish Hapsburg rulers (compare Zech. 2:15-17 [Eng.: 2:11-13]).

Mendieta's early optimism, however, was not characteristic of the entire course of his group's history. His apocalyptic worldview changed as his relationship to his establishment supporters changed. Although the reign of Charles V was a golden era for Mendieta, he became increasingly unhappy with Spanish policy under Philip II. The divine plan for the end of history and establishment policy could no longer be optimistically equated in his mind.

Examination of the Zechariah corpus reveals a polemical tradition-

---

137. See Gese, "Anfang und Ende," 41.

138. Use of the term *pessimism* does not mean the millennial group was not still looking forward to the coming kingdom and their participation in it. Rather, the term refers to the emphasis on cosmic catastrophe as ushering in the hoped-for era. See Klaus Koch, *The Rediscovery of Apocalyptic* (Naperville, Ill.: Allenson, 1972), 29. Already in Zechariah 9–11, God's coming intervention is described as violent, involving Israel in war: Zech. 9:11-17; 10:5 (see Gese, "Anfang und Ende," 42). However, a change of tone is seen especially in Zechariah 12–14, the so-called Trito-Zechariah (see Mason, *Zechariah*, 122, 134; and Gese, "Anfang und Ende," 43). These chapters see the whole community as in need of renewal (Zech. 13:1-2). Thus, a remnant theology is invoked, whereby large parts of the Zechariah group's own community will be weeded out (Zech. 13:8-9). Indeed, Zion theology itself is modified so that Jerusalem is actually allowed to be captured before God intervenes (Zech. 14:2).

139. Phelan, *Franciscans*, 74.

140. Ibid., 11.

stream corresponding to Mendieta's increasing dissatisfaction with his establishment backers.[141] The disappointing nonarrival of the millennium with the completion of the temple in Jerusalem may have been blamed on this perceived increasing moral failure. By the time of Zechariah 9–14, the group's dissatisfactions with people and governors allowed for a very pessimistic view.

From its beginnings the Zechariah group was concerned with the possibility that YHWH's flock could doom itself to slaughter. Already in the visions of Zechariah 1–8 the Zechariah group is concerned with the failure of the people and their leaders. The vision of the flying scroll, Zechariah 5:1-4, symbolizes God's coming judgment against sinners in the community. The prose sermons of Zechariah continue this concern about lack of covenant fidelity. The present generation's ancestors are characterized as sinners, and there is the danger that such disobedience may continue (Zech. 1:4-6; 7:11-14).

Indeed, before the ministry of Zechariah's group, there was ethical chaos (Zech. 8:10). Thus, ethical exhortation is deemed necessary by the Zechariah group for the contemporary Jerusalem community, and in preparation for rebuilding the temple a call to repentance was issued (Zech. 1:1f.).[142] These ethical pleas continue even as the temple is being rebuilt (Zech. 7:8-10; 8:16-17), and the latest layers of Zechariah 1–8 continue the charge to covenant fidelity (Zech. 3:7; 6:15). Ronald W. Pierce thus observes that at the end of Zechariah 1–8 the reader is left pessimistic about the character of the restored remnant.[143]

Further, Zechariah 1–8 advances Ezekiel's pessimism about civil rulers (Ezek. 22:27; 34:1-10; 45:8-9; 46:18), already foreshadowing the attacks against the "shepherds"/leaders of the people in Zechariah 9–14. Bethelsarezer, who in Zechariah 7:2 sends a delegation to the temple authorities on

---

141. Cf. the discussion of Ronald W. Pierce, who traces an increasing concern with the moral character of the restored community through the last three minor prophets ("A Thematic Development of the Haggai/Zechariah/Malachi Corpus," *JETS* 27 [1984]: 401–11).

142. Rex Mason has described this Second Temple preaching as upholding both the rules of the cult community and messianic expectation: "If these preachers could marry continuing eschatological expectation with pastoral concern for the continuing life of the theocratic community, still further doubt is cast on the views of those who have held that 'theocracy' and 'eschatology' represent two distinct, and indeed, opposed views in post-exilic Judaism" ("Some Echoes of the Preaching in the Second Temple? Tradition Elements in Zechariah 1–8," *ZAW* 96 [1984]: 234).

143. Pierce, "Thematic Development," 407.

behalf of the people of the land, must have been a civil or community leader.[144] The polemical reply to him recorded in Zechariah 7:5-6 indicates that already before the temple is completed, the Zechariah group is contending with the people and their governors.[145] These notes of controversy are expanded in Zechariah 9–14 — especially in the attack on the shepherds in Zechariah 10:1-3; 11:4-17; and 13:7-9.

Redaction in Zechariah 1–8

Mendieta's apocalyptic worldview became more and more pessimistic in the 1580s and 1590s as his dissatisfaction with the Spanish establishment increased. Among the sociological factors involved was Mendieta's resistance to the Spaniards' system of forced paid labor.[146] As the greed of the Spanish establishment became increasingly apparent to Mendieta's pro-Native party, Mendieta became more and more a doomsday prophet. A similar social situation probably resulted in Zechariah's millennial group making redactional modifications to the visions and oracles of Zechariah 1–8.

It has been argued that the Zechariah community was largely responsible for the insertions in Zechariah 1–8, which update the visions in light of the group's experience. These additions may have been motivated by the adverse reactions of this group against their society's wrongdoing, against the civil leadership, perhaps, even against their increasingly powerful fellow Zadokites.[147] The group increasingly expressed their expectation of a future Davidic rule in the face of present societal failings. The coming Davidide would not share the faults of the present civil leadership; his coming would establish the Zechariah group's ideal of justice, set firmly in their ideal diarchic governmental power structure. If the behavior of their fellow priestly leaders was in fact a problem for the group, their emphasis on the coming Davidide may have also been intended to temper hierocratic ambitions by preserving a place for the coming Davidide (Zech. 3:8), while directing parenesis against any priestly abuse (Zech. 3:7).[148]

144. See Neil, "Zechariah," 944; and Mason, *Zechariah*, 66.

145. One implication of the Zechariah text is that religious rites and festivals displeasing to God, such as those of Isa. 58:3-7, are not necessarily those sponsored by the Zadokites in charge of the temple.

146. See Phelan, *Franciscans*, 104f.

147. On the latter possibility, see Petersen, *Zechariah 1–8*, 125.

148. The Zechariah group never opposed temple authority in principle, even though they may have eventually come to believe that their fellow religious leaders had compromised themselves. (On this distinction, see Blenkinsopp's discussion of "Third Isaiah" in *History of Prophecy*, 251.) That by the time of Zechariah 9–14 their

New Literature in Zechariah 9–14 and Changes in Group Orientation

Like Mendieta's group (and Dipanagara's Javanese group as well), the Zechariah group may have remained members of the establishment for a time while not necessarily agreeing politically and religiously with other power-holding members. Even Zechariah 9 lacks the evidence of strong polemic that would indicate the members of the Zechariah group may have started to abandon their establishment positions. The optimism of Zechariah 1–8 is still present: salvation comes to the nation as a whole.[149] As of Zechariah 9, the composition and orbit of the Zechariah group has not yet changed significantly.

A change in this group situation and arena class may be indicated, however, by those texts that attack Israel's "shepherds." To understand such a change, one must identify these shepherds, a complicated task.

The shepherds of Zechariah 9–14 probably represent civil, not religious, leaders.[150] In the ancient Near East and Hebrew Bible, shepherds generally symbolize monarchs or rulers.[151] Thus the Targum naturally takes the shepherds to be kings, not priests (see the Targum on Zech. 10:2, 3; 11:3; and 13:7). Further, as Brevard S. Childs notes, Zechariah's shepherd

---

fellow Zadokites may, nevertheless, have been de facto deserving of their rejection is suggested by such texts as Neh. 13:29-30 and Mal. 2:1-9. See O'Brien, *Priest and Levite,* 124. Note also Mason's interesting suggestion that if the book of Malachi was accepted into the Haggai-Zechariah-Malachi corpus as congenial to the Zechariah tradents, then Malachi's attack on the priesthood was not objectionable to the Zechariah group at that point (*Zechariah,* 11, 139).

149. See Hanson, *Dawn,* 324.

150. Issue is taken here with Plöger and Hanson, who see the evil shepherds in Zechariah 9–14 as the leaders of the hierocratic establishment. Plöger states that in the framework of the Jewish theocracy, nothing precludes thinking of the high priest as the shepherd attacked in Zech. 13:7-9. "This earthly pinnacle of the theocracy is overturned by Yahweh himself" (Plöger, *Theocracy,* 88). Hanson argues that Zech. 11:4-17; 13:7-9 stems from the struggle between visionary and hierocratic elements, and represents an attack on the leaders of the temple cult (*Dawn,* 342, 345f.). Paul L. Redditt's view must also be critiqued. He argues that the group behind Zechariah 9–14 is anti-priestly, and that the evil shepherds include the priests ("Israel's Shepherds: Hope and Pessimism in Zechariah 9–14," *CBQ* 51 [1989]: 632, 638). There is little data to support this argument.

151. For רעה ("shepherd") as a specifically royal title in the ancient Near East and Hebrew Bible, see Lester V. Meyer, "An Allegory Concerning the Monarchy: Zech 11:4-17; 13:7-9," in *Scripture in History and Theology: Essays in Honor of J. Coert Rylaarsdam,* ed. A. Merrill and T. Overholt (Pittsburgh: Pickwick, 1977), 228. Important references include: Num. 27:15-23; 2 Sam. 5:2; Jer. 23:4-5; Ezek. 34:23-24; 37:24; Mic. 5:1-3; Ps. 78:70-72; and *ANET,* 164, 443.

allegory owes much to Ezekiel 34, where again the kings are the "shepherds."[152]

The objection that it was the priests, not civil leaders, who were in charge of Persian-period Yehud, having ascended to governmental hegemony, is now known to be overstated.[153] Nehemiah 3:7 and 5:15 indicate that various civil governors ruled the restoration community long after the tenure of Zerubbabel.[154] In Nehemiah 5:15, Nehemiah states: "The former governors who were before me laid heavy burdens on the people, and took food and wine from them . . . Even their servants lorded it over the people." The reference to a פחה ("governor") in Mal. 1:8 indicates that such a civil leader was still in power c. 520–400 B.C.E. The Yehud seals and coins published by Nahman Avigad support the biblical data, refuting the idea that Yehud was theocratically managed in the Persian period.[155]

It can be concluded that the Zechariah group's attack on the shepherds

152. Childs, *Introduction*, 481.

153. This view was held by Wellhausen, who argued that the postexilic period marked the final entrenchment of the ruling priestly party (see also the references in n. 3 above). Note that this assumption of increasing postexilic priestly hegemony also lies behind Wellhausen's theory that Zerubbabel has dropped out of the text as the one crowned in Zech. 6:9-15, thus elevating the high priest (see nn. 2 and 43 above). Thus, Hammershaimb argues that though a crown was to be set on Zerubbabel's head, "we may guess that the king of Persia intervened and removed [Zerubbabel] in order that the high priest might from then on become the leader of the Jewish people" (Hammershaimb, "Change in Prophecy," 106). This is Hanson's position. He describes an "intervention of the Persians due to the pretentious nationalistic claims [surrounding Zerubbabel]" (*Dawn*, 247). He goes on to state that "the downfall of Zerubbabel was used to increase the power and prestige of the high priest, leading to the exclusive rule of the Zadokites over the post-exilic Jewish community" (*Dawn*, 258, cf. 262).

154. See Widengren, "The Persian Period," 522; van der Woude, "Erwartungen," 139 n. 2, 148; and the bibliographic references in O'Brien, *Priest and Levite*, 118.

155. Nahman Avigad, *Bullae and Seals from a Post-Exilic Judean Archive*, Qedem 4 (Jerusalem: Hebrew University Institute of Archaeology, 1976). Other governors of Yehud between Zerubbabel and Nehemiah known from the seals and jar handles include: Elnathan, Yeho'ezer, and Ahzai (local Yehudites). See Miller and Hayes, *History*, 460f.; Peter R. Ackroyd, "Archaeology, Politics and Religion: The Persian Period," *Iliff Review* 39/2 (1982): 11–12; Sean E. McEvenue, "The Political Structure in Judah from Cyrus to Nehemiah," *CBQ* 43 (1981): 361; Meyers and Meyers, *Zechariah 1–8*, xl, 12–14, 370; and Widengren, "The Persian Period," 502, 510. Eric Meyers argues that at least one of these governors may have married into the house of David ("The Shelomith Seal and Aspects of the Judean Restoration: Some Additional Reconsiderations," ErIsr 17 [1985]: 33–38).

represents a polemic against Israel's civic rulers, not her religious ones. This attack, with its anti-shepherd expectation (Zech. 11:16-17; 13:7),[156] is best interpreted as part of the pessimism of the later course of the group. This pessimism clearly involved a psychological abandonment of the contemporary civil establishment, and it could have been accompanied by corresponding changes in the position and composition of the Zechariah group. Little direct evidence exists for any alienation from the religious establishment. Nevertheless, tension with some Zadokite establishment supporters may perhaps be assumed.[157]

Eventually Mendieta was no longer able to reach a modus operandi with the Spanish establishment.[158] He viewed Philip II's reign as an apocalyptic catastrophe and completely separated himself from those mendicants who cooperated with the crown. By the time the Zechariah group pessimistically expected a terrible tribulation period (Zech. 13:8-9) and the cutting off of half of Jerusalem (Zech. 14:2), its members also may have separated themselves from the ruling non-Davidic civic establishment and those priests who cooperated with it. If so, their arena would now be best labeled class D, at least insofar as alienation from the civic leadership is

156. Comparison should be made with Jer. 23:1-8, which attacks the shepherd rulers of Judah (vv. 1-3) but also looks forward to the "Branch," the coming righteous Davidide (vv. 3-6). In contrast to Jeremiah, however, the governors attacked by the Zechariah group were probably non-Davidides.

157. Compare the change in Mendieta, in which his apocalyptic worldview took on more and more gloomy elements. By 1595, Mendieta's worldview was permeated by a mood of apocalyptic doom. In Mendieta's case, this increasing emphasis on doomsday tribulation went along with an important sociological change in which he broke with mendicant moderates and joined forces with mendicant extremists. See Phelan, *Franciscans*, 102. It is conceivable that Zechariah's followers may have undertaken a similar change of alliance. Whether at such a point the Zechariah group incorporated other priestly elements, such as some of the tradents of Isaiah, is a problematic question. Petersen finds evidence all along of a "shared discourse between the prophetic traditionists of the Isaianic circle, the prophet Zechariah, and those preserving Zechariah's visions and oracles" (*Zechariah 1–8*, 122). Nevertheless, definite differences of perspective exist between these groups, differences that mitigate against the suggestion of an eventual joining of forces. It is especially unclear whether the Isaianic group would have been accepting of the Zechariah group's emphasis on a coming Davidide (see Stuhlmueller, *Rebuilding*, 8). Isaiah 40–55 and Isaiah 56–66 do not lament over the fall of the Davidic monarchy, nor do they express the type of messianic hope found in Zechariah (see Blenkinsopp, *History of Prophecy*, 245).

158. Phelan, *Franciscans*, 102.

involved. Even if this was the case, however, the group certainly did not become anti-cult and anti-temple.[159] The discussion above showed that the Zechariah group became more concerned with cult and temple as it underwent radicalization, culminating in the focus on cult and ritual in Zechariah 14. The group never lost its central-cult focus and was perhaps able to continue its activities within the temple throughout its history.[160]

159. For the possibility that dissident segments of an establishment may break away, see R. Wilson, *Prophecy and Society*, 83. For discussion of millennialism involving such a socially endogenous conflict but where both sides make appeal to traditional, central values, see chapter 3 above and Weston La Barre, *The Ghost Dance: Origins of Religion* (Garden City, N.Y.: Doubleday, 1970), 278.

160. If the attack against the shepherds in Zechariah 9–14 is focused on the civic leadership of the restored community, there is no direct evidence here of alienation from the temple establishment (see Blenkinsopp, *History of Prophecy*, 263). Indirect arguments that the Zadokites were the ultimate source of corruption behind the contemporary civic leadership cannot be sustained either (e.g., Hanson, *Dawn*, 347, 351, 393; cf. Mason, *Zechariah*, 109).

In one such indirect argument, Hanson interprets the prophet's casting of the silver into the temple in Zech. 11:13 as "an incredibly harsh indictment of the hierocratic leaders" (*Dawn*, 347). However, it is not necessary to see this act as intended to identify the priestly officials as in league with the governors. Since temples in this period may have functioned as banks accepting private accounts as they did at a later time (2 Macc. 3:6-40, especially vv. 10-11, 15), the prophet may be merely making a deposit of the measly sum. Alternatively, the prophet may be making an offering at the temple, perhaps signifying that it is God whom the people have dishonored. Thus Robert C. Dentan writes, "Since it is not himself, but God, who has been so ignominiously treated by the people and their foreign rulers, the prophet symbolically deposits the wages in the temple treasury" ("The Book of Zechariah, Chapters 9–14, Introduction and Exegesis," in *IB* 6:1105).

In another indirect argument, Hanson, followed by Redditt, draws on the distinctions between Judah and Jerusalem that seem to occur in certain texts in Zechariah 9–14 (e.g., 12:2). Hanson identifies "Judah," viewed favorably in Zech. 12:2, 7, with his visionaries, whereas Jerusalem represents the hierocrats (*Dawn*, 361, 363). (In a similar position, Redditt argues that the group behind Zechariah 9–14 "seems to speak for the relatively oppressed persons of the towns and villages of Judah" ["Shepherds," 640].) This argument has important holes. For example, Zech. 12:8-9 sides with Jerusalem, indicating that it, not the clans of Judah, is to be exalted. Hanson's contention that this section is "likely from the hand of a later editor writing from the viewpoint of the hierocratic party" is certainly a case of special pleading (*Dawn*, 365). The "clans-of-Judah" argument does not work well for Zechariah 14 either. If Zech. 14:14 is interpreted as meaning Judah fights "against," not "at," Jerusalem, Zech. 14:15 indicates Judah will be destroyed. This is an unlikely prediction for a group identifying itself with the clans of Judah.

6

Joel

The book of Joel is an important witness to the recurrence of millennialism within the Zadokite priesthood of Yehud long after the completion of the temple in 515 B.C.E. A drought and locust plague, viewed as harbingers of the Day of YHWH, ignited apocalyptic fears within the priestly center of postexilic society.[1] The response of Joel and his group to fears of apocalyptic destruction was appropriate for cult officials and functionaries. Unfortunately, most exegetes have missed the significance of Joel's attestation to a millennial group in power in Jerusalem during the Persian period. This is partly because many critical analyses divide Joel into two sections, one "historical" (Joel 1–2 [Eng.: 1:1 — 2:27]) and the other "apocalyptic" (Joel 3–4 [Eng.: 2:28 — 3:21]).[2] Such a division obscures the significance of the

---

1. A postexilic dating is indicated by probable references to the fall of Jerusalem and the exile in Joel 4:1, 17 (Eng.: 3:1, 17); the lack of mention of a king; and Joel's dependence on earlier written prophets (e.g., Isaiah 13; Ezekiel 38–39; Obadiah 7). Late vocabulary in Joel provides general support for this dating: מתלעות ("teeth") in Joel 1:6; (מ)מגרה ("granary") in Joel 1:17; the roots אנח ("sigh") and בוך (Niphal, "be confused") in Joel 1:18; שלח ("weapon") in Joel 2:8; the phrase חנון ורחום ("gracious and compassionate") in Joel 2:13; and סוף ("end," a late synonym of קץ) in Joel 2:20. Further, the picture of an operational central cult in the book (e.g., Joel 1:14; 2:17) indicates a date for Joel after 515 B.C.E. A more specific late Persian-period dating may be indicated by such evidence as the possible quotation of Mal. 3:2 by Joel 2:11, and the possible reference to the walls of Jerusalem (post-433 B.C.E.) in Joel 2:7-9.

2. A word of clarification is in order concerning the verse and chapter enumeration of the book of Joel. Chapter 4 of Joel in the MT is the same as chapter 3 in

cultic measures taken in Joel 1–2 as the millennial group program of central priests in the face of the imminent Day of YHWH. Further obscuring
the significance of Joel, scholars such as Otto Plöger have assigned the
apocalyptic sections of Joel to peripheral groups, seen as opposed to those
in power in the temple.

Maurice Vernes first questioned the unity of Joel in 1872. This questioning was expanded by J. W. Rothstein in 1896, and by Julius Bewer,
who in an elaborate analysis of the book in 1911, attributed its references
to the Day of YHWH to a later "apocalyptist."[3]

Bernhard Duhm's questioning of Joel's unity in 1911, however, laid
the foundation for much of the later work on this text.[4] According to
Duhm, Joel was formed by a Maccabean synagogue preacher preoccupied
with the Day of YHWH. This apocalyptic writer incorporated earlier historical material into his eschatological work, Joel 3–4 (Eng.: 2:28 – 3:21).
Duhm attributed the earlier material, including most of Joel 1:1 – 2:17,
to the original prophet. However, references to the Day of YHWH in the
original poetry were, Duhm believed, apocalyptic interpolations (Joel
1:15; 2:1b, 2a, 11b). Many scholars have adopted Duhm's two-stage formation thesis.[5]

Otto Plöger agrees with Duhm that the book of Joel represents a historical message embellished and expanded from an eschatological-
apocalyptic perspective.[6] Plöger, however, reconstructs a more complex development for the book, which must be understood within his scenario of
postexilic factional conflict over the issue of realized eschatology. Plöger

---

most English translations. The other difference is that Joel 3:1-5 in the MT is the
same as Joel 2:28-32 in English versions.

3. Maurice Vernes, *Le peuple d'Israël et ses espérances relatives à son avenir depuis les
origines jusqu'à l'époque persane* (*Ve siècle avant J. C.*) (Paris: Sandoz et Fishbacher,
1872); *Einleitung in die Literatur des Alten Testaments,* a German version of S. R.
Driver's *An Introduction to the Literature of the Old Testament* (Edinburgh: T. & T.
Clark, 1894), translated and annotated by J. W. Rothstein of Halle in 1896; and
Julius A. Bewer, *A Critical and Exegetical Commentary on Obadiah and Joel,* ICC
(New York: Scribner's, 1911).

4. Bernhard Duhm, "Anmerkungen zu den Zwölf Propheten: X. Buch Joel,"
ZAW 31 (1911): 184–88.

5. Those who have adopted Duhm's thesis include Ernst Sellin, *Das Zwölfprophetenbuch,* KAT 12/1 (Leipzig: A. Deichert, 1922); Theodore H. Robinson and
Friedrich Horst, *Die Zwölf Kleinen Propheten,* HAT 1/14 (Tübingen: J. C. B. Mohr,
1938); and Johannes Lindblom, *Prophecy in Ancient Israel* (Philadelphia: Fortress,
1962). Also see the works discussed in the following paragraphs.

6. Otto Plöger, *Theocracy and Eschatology,* trans. S. Rudman (Richmond, Va.:
John Knox, 1968), 97–106.

holds that Joel's message was early embellished with eschatological reflections in Joel 2:1b, 2, and 2:11. Unfortunately, according to Plöger, "statements about the day of Yahweh that were previously understood eschatologically" were then "adopted by a later period" and given a noneschatological cultic form.[7] Plöger's eschatological circle, reacting against this theocratic liturgical use of Joel, added chapters 3 and 4 (Eng.: 2:28–3:21) to Joel 1 and 2. Those who added Joel 3 and 4 belonged to the party identified by Plöger as still respecting the "old prophetic word." Unlike the theocrats, they still believed the eschatological meaning of Joel's prophetic message.[8] Unique to Plöger's reconstruction is his view that significant parts of Joel 4 (Eng.: 3) were added to Joel 1–2 before the addition of Joel 3 (Eng.: 2:28-32). This latter chapter was added as a third stage, he believed, to limit eschatological salvation to the small circle of its peripheral, antitheocratic authors.[9]

In his influential commentary, Hans Walter Wolff adopts Plöger's sociological view of an antitheocratic conventicle behind Joel's eschatology.[10] Even though Wolff reads Joel as a unity containing both liturgical and apocalyptic sections, curiously he sees the book stemming from a fourth-century eschatological opposition party. Despite Joel's temple-based language, Wolff believes the book is a product of an antihierocratic sect. Having the social function of "literary opposition," the book of Joel "engages the task of effecting a revival within the stiffening, religiously self-assured theocratic cultic community."[11] This revival emphasizes that YHWH's reign will come to Zion in the future, that the divine goal is not realized in the present cult.[12]

---

7. *Theocracy*, 100. Plöger argues that although ideas in Joel about the Day of YHWH were once understood eschatologically, "within the cultically based community of the post-exilic period they served simply to illustrate present afflictions, which could be withstood and overcome by the approved path of cultic observances" (ibid., 102).

8. Ibid., 100.

9. Plöger argues that the later insertion of Joel 3 restricts the hopes of Joel 4 to the Israel "which draws its life from the eschatological faith and which is characterized as eschatological by the outpouring of the spirit" (ibid., 106, also see 103–4).

10. Thus, Hans Walter Wolff cites Plöger to argue that Joel belongs to "those 'eschatological groups' who are still expecting completely new acts of Yahweh" (*A Commentary on the Books of the Prophets Joel and Amos*, Hermeneia [Philadelphia: Fortress, 1977], 12).

11. Wolff, *Joel*, 10. Wolff writes, "An extremely critical word is spoken in veiled manner against the cultic community of Jerusalem which has constituted itself theocratically" (ibid., 36, cf. 49, 85).

12. Ibid., 82, 84.

Gosta W. Ahlström's interpretation of Joel is somewhat similar to Wolff's. Like Wolff, Ahlström both assumes Joel's unity and argues that Joel critiqued prevailing institutions and worked for revival. Joel worked for a "right" cult and tried to get the people to turn from worshiping other gods.[13] Unlike Wolff, however, Ahlström sees Joel as operating within the structures of the temple.

Not all scholars agree with Ahlström and Wolff that Joel can be read as a unity. Joseph Blenkinsopp, following Duhm, argues for an eschatological rereading of Joel that reinterpreted the locust plague as heralding the consummation of history.[14] In his view, long after the time of Joel's historical plagues, a later writer transformed them "into a proleptic symbol of final judgment to take place on the Day of Yahweh."[15] "It is widely accepted," the author writes, "that Joel 2:28 – 3:21 (MT: 3:1 – 4:21) belongs to the later stratum, probably also 1:15; 2:1b-2a, 11b."[16] Blenkinsopp agrees with Plöger and Wolff in identifying the group responsible for Joel's later stratum. He finds it probable that "this kind of work emanated from associations or conventicles" that clung to an eschatological faith.[17]

Like Blenkinsopp, Paul Hanson sees a postexilic dissident group behind Joel.[18] Indeed, he is much more confident than Blenkinsopp in asserting that the group criticized the Zadokite hierocracy and viewed the central institutions of their society as defiled.

As a final development, note Paul L. Redditt's article on Joel, which attempts to trace the history of the tension that Plöger, Ahlström, and Wolff find between Joel and the Jerusalem cultus.[19] Drawing on I. M. Lewis's categories of peripheral and central prophecy, Redditt traces the original prophet moving away from a role in the central cult. Joel's tradents are placed among those in society's periphery critical of the Jerusalem priest-

---

13. Gosta W. Ahlström, *Joel and the Temple Cult of Jerusalem* (Leiden: Brill, 1971), 25–27.

14. Joseph Blenkinsopp, *A History of Prophecy in Israel* (Philadelphia: Westminster, 1983), 253.

15. Ibid., 258.

16. Ibid., 278 n. 66.

17. Ibid., 263. Blenkinsopp writes, "The effect of the final judgment will be to reveal the true Israel, those who call on the name of Yahweh [Joel 3:5 (Eng.: 2:32)] or, in other words, those who share the writer's eschatological faith" (ibid., 258).

18. Paul D. Hanson, *The People Called: The Growth of Community in the Bible* (San Francisco: Harper and Row, 1986), 252, 312–14. Hanson's analysis relies closely on Plöger's views here.

19. Paul L. Redditt, "The Book of Joel and Peripheral Prophecy," *CBQ* 48 (1986): 225–40.

hood. Redditt states, for example, that Joel "attacked the Jerusalem priest-hood for allowing the daily sacrifices to cease, with the consequence that the priests relegated the community gathered around Joel . . . to the periphery of postexilic Judah's religious life. This peripheral group became sectarian, envisioning a new day when the group would survive any catastrophe associated with the Day of Yahweh."[20]

I want to challenge the idea that a group opposed to the central cult produced the apocalyptic texts in Joel. Joel's apocalyptic texts clearly stem from the pro-temple priestly center of postexilic society. This is clear in that an apocalyptic worldview, catalyzed by a drought and locust desolation, is already visible behind Joel 2:1-11. The cultic measures and temple rites pictured in Joel 1–2 must therefore be the temple authorities' conscious reactions to a looming apocalyptic threat. Since Joel 2:1-11 is closely connected structurally and thematically both with its immediate context and with Joel 3 and 4 (Eng.: 2:28—3:21), the book emerges as a unity, an apocalyptic text produced by temple officials.

The Genre of Joel 2:1-11; 3–4

The book of Joel, especially Joel 2:1-11 and 3–4 (Eng.: 2:28—3:21), exhibits the identifying features that characterize proto-apocalyptic literature. Indeed, the major theme of the book is its presentation of the Day of YHWH as a decisive apocalyptic event.[21] Joel carefully develops this

---

20. Ibid., 225.

21. Joel exhibits a radical, imminent eschatology, dualism, and other features of apocalyptic genres such as determinism, use of ciphers, and an emphasis on the ideas of fire and blood. When taken together these features compel recognition of the family resemblance of Joel to apocalyptic literature. This argument that Joel contains proto-apocalyptic literature takes issue with the views of a number of scholars. For example, Siegfried Bergler argues that Joel is not yet an "*Apokalyptiker.*" He finds that the book does not contain a calculation by stages and a revealing of the end-time drama. Further, Bergler thinks that because Joel employs typological categories and pictures continuities between the present and future ages, he is merely describing an inner-historical progression. See his *Joel als Schriftinterpret,* Beiträge zur Erforschung des Alten Testaments und des Antiken Judentums 16 (Frankfurt am Main: Verlag Peter Lang, 1988), 347. Ahlström also argues that Joel's ideal future is still in the continuum of this world (*Temple Cult,* 90–91, 96). Other scholars vacillate on the question. Willem S. Prinsloo states, "Depending on one's definition of eschatology and apocalyptic one could classify this pericope [3:1-5 (Eng.: 2:28-32)] under either one or the other!" (*The Theology of the Book of Joel* [New York: Walter de Gruyter, 1985], 86).

apocalyptic picture of the Day of YHWH (יום יהוה: Joel 1:15; 2:1, 11; 3:4 [Eng.: 2:31]; 4:14 [Eng.: 3:14]; compare 4:1, 18 [Eng.: 3:1, 18]).[22] Stating that nothing can compare to this day (Joel 2:2), he views it as having a radical ultimacy. According to Wolff, this is the same view found in full-blown apocalyptic texts. Wolff comments that Joel "demonstrates that passionate interest in determining the incomparable which apocalyp-ticism developed beyond the sapiential propensity for the ordering and comparing of phenomena."[23] The Qumran literature also tries to describe the incomparable Day of YHWH. According to 1QM 18, when God has prevailed against the multitude of Belial, the priests are to bless God and say, "[You have done] wondrously, and the like of this has not been from of old."

Joel saw the imminent eschatological Day as ultimately decisive; as in Malachi 3:23 (Eng.: 4:5), the Day is both גדול ("great") and נורא ("awe-some") (Joel 2:11; 3:4 [Eng.: 2:31]). At the same time, for this millennial catalyst figure and his group, the Day-of-YHWH theme was fraught with ambiguity. Joel believed the Day could bring either decisive destruction or decisive salvation for Yehud (Joel 2:14).[24] Joel 1–2 (Eng.: 1:1 — 2:27) thus expresses fear of possible apocalyptic desolation; Joel 3–4 (Eng.: 2:28 — 3:21) hope for apocalyptic salvation. Wolff is correct when he states, "By developing the theme in both directions, Joel stands at the threshold be-tween prophetic and apocalyptic eschatology."[25] Wolff's statement, how-ever, is misleading when it implies that the destructive view of YHWH's Day in Joel 1–2 is merely prophetic. Joel's description of possible desola-tion for Yehud (Joel 2:1-11) is definitely developed using apocalyptic ideas and terms.

Radical Eschatology

Joel's Day-of-YHWH theme presents the radical eschatology that char-acterizes proto-apocalyptic literature. In both parts of the book, Joel's es-

---

22. For a discussion of the Day of YHWH in prophetic literature, see Yair Hoffmann, "The Day of the Lord as a Concept and a Term in the Prophetic Litera-ture," *ZAW* 93 (1981): 37–50. Also note that the usage ביום ההוא ("on that day") in Joel 4:18 (Eng.: 3:18) is associated with the tradition of the Day of YHWH. Cf., e.g., Ezek. 38:10, 18; 39:11; and see Magne Sæbø, "יום," *TDOT* 6:31. Joel 3:2 (Eng.: 2:29) and 4:1 (Eng.: 3:1) also make reference to the Day of YHWH through the usage בימים ההמה ("in those days").

23. Wolff, *Joel*, 45.

24. Thus, Prinsloo notes that Joel's present catastrophe could turn into either blessing or judgment (*Theology*, 60).

25. Wolff, *Joel*, 12.

chatological scenario centers on the same event: the apocalyptic attack of the nations on Jerusalem that overturns the order of the cosmos and causes writhing and anguish. Although Joel 2:1-11 describes destruction and Joel 3–4 (Eng.: 2:28 — 3:21) salvation, both presuppose this same *Völkersturm* motif drawn from Ezekiel 38–39. Walther Zimmerli states:

> The book of Joel . . . clearly makes quite specific use of Ezekiel 38f. A locust and drought catastrophe becomes for this prophet an omen of the nearness of the Day of YHWH, which, with cosmic traits (2:10), is described as the invasion of an enemy which in the retrospective 2:20 is called the "northern" (הצפוני). "Day of Yahweh" and "northerner" are here completely linked.[26]

Joel 3–4 (Eng.: 2:28 — 3:21) further specifies the threat of 2:1-11 as the attack by the united kings and nations of the world envisioned by Ezekiel 38–39 and Zechariah 12:1-9; 14:1-5. Ezekiel 38–39 and Zechariah 9–14 took up this *Völkersturm* motif from the mythical imagery of the royal psalms (for example, Psalms 2 and 110)[27] and expanded it in depicting the judgment at the end of time. Joel represents a further expression of this tradition.

The people and earth writhe at the approach of the apocalyptic army because of its fearsomeness, and because it brings cosmic portents altering the fabric of reality.[28] Indeed, the army's very nature as chaos means the actual overturning of the world. Thus, both Joel 2:10 and 4:15 (Eng.: 3:15) state that the sun and moon are about to grow dark, and the stars will lose their brightness (also see Joel 3:4 [Eng.: 2:31]). This picture parallels other (proto-)apocalyptic texts. See Isaiah 13:10, Jeremiah 4:23,

---

26. Walther Zimmerli, *Ezekiel 2,* Hermeneia, trans. J. D. Martin (Philadelphia: Fortress, 1983), 321.

27. Arvid S. Kapelrud, rejecting the dependence of Joel on Ezekiel 38–39 because of his early dating of the book, argues that Joel relied directly on ancient cultic tradition for his view of the defeat of an assembly of nations. "The judgement which we find recorded in Joel 4:12 [Eng.: 3:12] has its prototype in the judgement upon the enemies which was enacted at the enthronement festival" (*Joel Studies* [Uppsala: Lundequistska Bokhandeln, 1948], 160).

28. Joel's first description of the Day of YHWH in Joel 2:1-11 depicts both the earth and its people as quaking (רגז) before the coming desolation (vv. 1, 10). Other proto-apocalyptic texts use the same verb to describe the trembling of the nations at God's advent (Isa. 64:1), and the shaking of the heavens and the earth at the time of the final cosmic punishment of evil (Isa. 13:13). Joel 2:6 continues this picture of apocalyptic anguish using the verb חיל ("writhe"). Again, the same usage is found in other proto-apocalyptic texts. Isaiah 13:8 states that at the Day of YHWH, people will "writhe like a woman in labor." The usage is also found in Jer. 4:31 and Zech. 9:5.

Zechariah 14:6, Mark 13:24, Revelation 6:12, and 8:12 — all envision the darkening of the sun and moon at the eschaton. Similarly, the idea of the stars losing their brightness is recurrent in (proto-)apocalyptic descriptions of the end. Isaiah 13:10 and 34:4, Daniel 8:10, and Mark 13:25 all describe the wearing away or the destruction of the host of heaven at the eschaton. Isaiah 13:10, for example, says that at that time, "the stars of heaven and their constellations will not flash forth their light."

Although the motif of the nations' attack is central in Joel, both sections of the book make clear that God is the actual force causing the radical world changes of the end times. Joel 1–2 (Eng.: 1:1 — 2:27) describes a totally sovereign God acting through the apocalyptic army, using it as God's agent.[29] In contrast, Joel 3–4 (Eng.: 2:28 — 3:21) draws on the divine-warrior motif of the holy-war tradition to describe God's radical intervention. The tables are turned, and the sovereign warrior destroys the attacking armies. Thus, in Joel 4:11 (Eng.: 3:11), God is called on to come with God's mighty ones (הנחת יהוה גבוריך) to fight the attacking nations.[30]

Joel 4:13 (Eng.: 3:13) continues to use holy-war motifs. Here the warrior's host is commanded to execute his annihilating judgment. This verse has clear parallels with the proto-apocalyptic description of the divine warrior in Isaiah 63:1-6. Apocalyptic judgment in both texts is expressed using the image of the "wine press" (גת: Joel 4:13 [Eng.: 3:13]; Isa. 63:2). The notion of the treading down of peoples is also found in both descriptions (Joel 4:13 [Eng.: 3:13] and Isa. 63:6; compare Zech. 10:5). This image of a bloody "harvesting" of the earth reappears in such full-blown apocalyptic descriptions as that in Revelation 14:14-21 (cf. Rev. 19:15).

Finally, Joel's *Endzeit* description of divine judgment in a valley (Joel 4:14b [Eng.: 3:14b] reads: כי קרוב יום יהוה בעמק החרוץ ["For near is the Day of YHWH in the valley of decision"]) also draws on mythological

29. Thus, Joel 2:11 makes clear that the coming apocalyptic army is under God's authority. A corresponding view is found in Joel 4 (Eng.: 3), which, in contrast, emphasizes the sovereignty of YHWH in carrying out end-time judgment on this attacking army. It is YHWH who calls the army into existence in Joel 4:9 (Eng.: 3:9; cf. Ezek. 38:7). YWHW then directs it against Jerusalem (Joel 4:2 [Eng.: 3:2]) as in Ezek. 38:8, 16-17; and Zech. 14:2. After this, God sits to judge the army (Joel 4:12 [Eng.: 3:12]) as in Ezek. 38:22. As a result of the end-time judgment, it is finally clear that YHWH is God (Joel 4:17 [Eng.: 3:17]; cf. Ezek. 38:23; 39:28).

30. See Patrick D. Miller, Jr., *The Divine Warrior in Early Israel* (Cambridge, Mass.: Harvard University Press, 1973), 137; and Kapelrud, *Joel Studies,* 162–63.

divine-warrior imagery like that found in Joshua 10:12-13 and the Ugaritic texts. Thus, Ahlström compares the warrior Anat's slaughter "in a valley" (*bʿmq*) between two cities (*CTA* 3.2.1-41).[31]

The apocalyptic eschatology of Joel describes God's definitive end-time intervention as a universal judgment. The international and even cosmic extent of the end-time crisis is evident in the escalating reactions pictured in Joel 2:1-11. Commenting on Joel 2:10, Willem S. Prinsloo states, "The לפניו ['before them'] refers to the עם עצום ['powerful army,' v. 2], and hence 10a and 10b describe a cosmic reaction, enhanced by the climactic structure of the pericope. First we have a local, *national* reaction in 2:1b; this is followed by an *international* (2:6), and finally by a *cosmic* reaction (2:10ab) to the עם עצום."[32]

Although Joel 3 and 4 (Eng.: 2:28 — 3:21) promise salvation for Yehud, a universal judgment is as much expected in these chapters as in Joel 1–2 (Eng.: 1:1 — 2:27). Just as Ezekiel 38–39 pictured a judgment on the whole world represented by Gog, Joel 4 (Eng.: 3) describes a universal judgment on "all nations" (כל-הגוים; Joel 4:2, 11 [Eng.: 3:2, 11]). The final wasting of Egypt and Edom, symbolic of all Israel's traditional enemies, described in Joel 4:19 (Eng.: 3:19) indicates the universality of the final judgment's target.[33]

In summary, both parts of Joel picture history ending with a final judgment that brings desolation and horror. In both sections (Joel 2:3; 4:19 [Eng.: 3:19]), Joel describes the judgment at history's end using the term שממה ("desolation"), the same noun employed in the picture of complete destruction in Jeremiah 4:27.[34]

Dualism

A dualism between the natural and supernatural worlds is expressed in Joel's vision of the invasion of a massive otherworldly force into the earthly realm. Although reminiscent of a mundane (inner-historical) locust crisis, the mythic-realistic images of Joel 2:1-11 transcend the usual realities of history and depict the kind of fantastic beings one finds in the Gilgamesh

---

31. Ahlström, *Temple Cult,* 76.

32. Prinsloo, *Theology,* 44.

33. Edom also represents all the nations in the proto-apocalyptic text Isa. 34:10 (cf. Mal. 1:3).

34. Joel 3:3 (Eng.: 2:30) also describes a completely destructive judgment. The picture of columns of "smoke" (עשן) here is reminiscent of the description in Isa. 34:10 of smoke going up forever after the cosmic end-time destruction.

epic.[35] These beings represent forces from another, nonearthly, plane of existence. Thus, the writer of Revelation 9:1-11 was able to interpret these images as monstrous spirits of hell:

> . . . he opened the shaft of the bottomless pit, and from the shaft rose smoke like the smoke of a great furnace, and the sun and the air were darkened with the smoke from the shaft [compare Joel 2:10]. Then from the smoke came locusts on the earth. . . . And in those days people will seek death but will not find it; they will long to die, but death will flee from them [compare Joel 2:6]. In appearance the locusts were like horses equipped for battle [compare Joel 2:4]. . . . They had scales like iron breastplates, and the noise of their wings was like the noise of many chariots with horses rushing into battle [compare Joel 2:5].

In both Joel 2:1-11 and Revelation 9:1-11 God guides the wretched forces of destruction against the earth (Joel 2:11; Rev. 9:1, 4-5). That these forces are under God's command is clear. Joel is drawing on Isaiah 13:4-6 where God musters an unwitting apocalyptic army (צבא מלחמה) for an attack as God's instruments of indignation.

As stated above, Joel's depiction of a coming transhistorical attack draws heavily on the current idea of the coming of a monstrous northern horde in the end times (Ezek. 38:4, 6, 9, 15, 22; 39:4, 11-12). Joel's designation of the horde as a עם רב ועצום ("a great and powerful people/army," Joel 2:2) reminds us of the "great army" (חיל רב) of Ezekiel 38:15 and the later reference in Daniel 11:25 to an "extremely large and mighty army" (חיל־גדול ועצום עד־מאד). Horses are a recurrent feature in apocalyptic-horde descriptions,[36] so the description of the apocalyptic enemy as horses in Joel 2:4 further reminds us of Gog, whose horses and horsemen are described in Ezekiel 38:4, 15. (Compare also the horses of the attacking nations in Zech. 12:4.) Finally, note how Joel takes up the apocalyptic expectation that the end-time army will be a dark power. Amos 5:20 and Zephaniah 1:15 had seen the Day of YHWH as dark and gloomy, and this idea is accepted by Ezekiel 38–39 and Joel 2:2 (compare Joel 3:4 [Eng.: 2:31]). Both Ezekiel 38:9, 16 and Joel 2:2 use this metaphor of dark obscurity (ענן) covering the land to describe the arrival of the apocalyptic enemy.[37]

---

35. See the discussion in Hugo Gressmann, *Der Messias* (Göttingen: Vandenhoeck & Ruprecht, 1929), 137–38.

36. For example, Franz Joseph Stendebach notes that mounted troops have a central role in the eschatological decisive battle (*Entscheidungskampf*) described in the Qumran War Scroll ("סוס," *TWAT* 5.791). Another example is the role of horses in the Apocalypse of John (e.g., Rev. 9:16-18).

37. See David Noel Freedman and B. E. Willoughby, "ענן," *TWAT* 6:272–73; and Wolff, *Joel*, 40.

The image of the horde as a dark power is developed as a moral dualism in Joel 4 (Eng.: 3). Here the conflict of Joel 2:1-11 is further elaborated as a cosmic struggle between the dualistically opposed forces of good and evil. Because Joel sees the cultic measures of 2:12-17 as successful, the depiction of future deliverance in Joel 3 and 4 (Eng.: 2:28 – 3:21) promises a change in God's alliance.[38] The apocalyptic enemy army is now treated as the forces in rebellion against God to be destroyed by the divine warrior. The description of the great wickedness of the attacking nations in Joel 4:13 (Eng.: 3:13) presents the forces as an embodiment of mass guilt.[39]

The next verse, Joel 4:14 (Eng.: 3:14), uses the key word המון ("tumultuous multitude," "multitudinous throng") to describe the enemy: "Multitudes, multitudes in the valley of decision!" It was seen in the previous discussion of the Gog horde that המון becomes important in proto-apocalyptic texts' descriptions of the end-time assault of the powers of chaos and hubris in rebellion against God.[40] Thus, Gog's evil army is described as a "tumultuous multitude" in Ezekiel 39:11, 15-16. Isaiah 13:4 also uses the term המון to picture the coming of the apocalyptic horde: "A sound of tumult on the mountains, Like that of many people! A sound of an uproar of kingdoms, Of nations gathering together!" Joel's use of the horde motif clearly borrows an image used in proto-apocalyptic texts to depict the collective powers massed together in the end times in opposition to God.

The book of Joel also contains a third type of dualism: a dualism involving the present age and the age to come. As a result of the onslaught of the northern army, creation is actually reversed according to Joel 2:10. Brevard S. Childs's view that רעש ("quake") is a catchword for the end-time return to chaos helps interpret this verse.[41] It describes the "shaking" (רעש) of the present creation bringing a return to *Urzeit* chaos that paves

---

38. The structure of the book of Joel is explained below.

39. Leslie C. Allen deftly observes, "It was only the enormity of their own *wickedness* that had brought them here to receive the annihilating judgment of God. So vital is the connection between the mass guilt of the nations and their massed presence that they can be run together poetically" (*The Books of Joel, Obadiah, Jonah and Micah*, NICOT [Grand Rapids, Mich.: Eerdmans, 1976], 118).

40. See A. Baumann, "המה" *TDOT* 3:416–17. The term המון in Ezekiel 38–39 already carries the connotation of chaos and hubris, which becomes further developed in full-blown apocalyptic texts. 1QM 15 describes the wicked enemy horde using this expression. In another example, 1QM 18 reads, "The hand of the God of Israel is raised against all the multitude."

41. Brevard S. Childs, "The Enemy from the North and the Chaos Tradition," *JBL* 78 (1959): 189–90.

the way for the advent of a new world.[42] Note also that Joel's use of רעש
is a good illustration of Childs's argument that in postexilic apocalyptic
eschatology, the "great-shaking" motif and the "enemy-from-the-north"
tradition fuse.[43] The coming of the northern apocalyptic army means the
return of primeval chaos, the final stage before the coming of the new age.
Thus, Joel's linguistic usages in chapter 2 make clear he is describing a
coming radical separation between the ages.

The motif of apocalyptic shaking appears again in Joel 4:16-17 (Eng.:
3:16-17). In these verses it is even clearer that the coming great shaking
will separate the old and new worlds. After the heavens and earth "quake"
(רעש), bringing a return to chaos, God announces God's dwelling in Zion,
and Jerusalem is finally established as holy. Compare the Isaiah Apocalypse,
where earth's foundations are shaken (Isa. 24:18) in preparation for
YHWH's reign on Zion (v. 23).

The radically and totally changed world, brought about by the Day of
YHWH (Joel 4:17 [Eng.: 3:17]), is elaborated in the following pericope,
Joel 4:18-21 (Eng.: 3:18-21).[44] In the present age, "sweet wine" (עסיס)
can be cut off (Joel 1:5), but in the millennial age the mountains will drip
with it (Joel 4:18 [Eng.: 3:18]) and the hills will flow with milk.[45] In this
age, the "streambeds" (אפיק) dry up (Joel 1:20), but in the millennial era

42. Recall that other proto-apocalyptic texts employ this "quaking" motif to
describe end-time chaos. Examples include Ezek. 38:20 and Isa. 13:13 (cf. Jer.
4:24). Further, the noun "earthquake" is used at Ezek. 38:19 and Zech. 14:4-5.
Later full-blown apocalyptic texts, such as 2 Esdras 6:11-17; *1 Enoch* 1:5-8; and
the *Assumption of Moses* 10:4, also describe earthquakes as part of the end-time
chaos ending the current era.

43. Childs, "Enemy," 197.

44. See Prinsloo, *Theology*, 118. Bergler can be critiqued for arguing that Joel
does not rigorously differentiate between a present and a future age (*Weltzeit*)
(*Schriftinterpret*, 347). Against Bergler, apocalyptic literature can use the categories
of the old age to describe the new one. See chapter 4, n. 13 above.

45. The rareness of this noun and the reversal depicted here suggest that this
pericope (Joel 4:18-21 [Eng.: 3:18-21]) is a product of the continuing Joel group.
Another important verbal link is that between Joel 4:21b (Eng.: 3:21b) and 4:17b
(Eng.: 3:17b). Note, however, that this section begins with the introductory
formula והיה ביום ההוא ("and it will come about in that day"), which was used in
Ezek. 38:18 and 39:11 to introduce later additions. Thus, this pericope may represent an eschatological supplement, added by the Joel group at a secondary stage in
the book's development. Joel 4:4-8 (Eng.: 3:4-8) may be another example of a
secondary addition to the book.

all will flow with water (Joel 4:18 [Eng.: 3:18]). Note especially that this section uses *Urzeit* paradisiacal language to describe the age to come. Thus, the river of Eden, known from Genesis 2:10-14, is seen in Joel 4:18 (Eng.: 3:18). As in other Zadokite millennial visions (Ezek. 47:1-12; Zech. 13:1; 14:8), a temple spring is the source of the river. Yehud will endure "forever" (לעולם) in this radically altered new world (Joel 4:20 [Eng.: 3:20]).

Secondary Features

Joel also exhibits several other features of proto-apocalyptic literature. Clearly, Joel shows an interest in determining the times (Joel 1:15; 2:1; 4:14 [Eng.: 3:14]).[46] Joel even starts to distinguish between different eras or ages (Joel 1:2; 2:2; 4:18-21 [Eng.: 3:18-21]). As shown above, in Joel God controls the bringing about of these different eras. With this view, Joel begins to develop a notion of apocalyptic determinism. As in Ezekiel 38–39, Joel 4 (Eng.: 3) says that God brings the nations against Jerusalem as pawns, predestined for judgment (Joel 4:2, 12 [Eng.: 3:2, 12]).

At points Joel employs ciphers or coded terms, an important feature of later full-blown apocalyptic texts. One example is the reference to the "northerner" (הצפוני) in Joel 2:20. Further, the "valley of Jehoshaphat" (עמק יהושפט), where the final judgment will take place (Joel 4:2, 12 [Eng.: 3:2, 12]), is probably not an actual name of a valley but a code word. As Leslie C. Allen states: "The change of name to *Verdict Valley* in v. 14 suggests that the present name is intended as a theological symbol rather than a topographical identification: 'the place where Yahweh is to judge.'"[47]

Finally, other secondary apocalyptic motifs occur in Joel 2:1-11; 3 (Eng.: 2:28-32); and 4 (Eng.: 3). Fire, an important end-time element in Joel 2:3, 5 and 3:3 (Eng.: 2:30), often appears in apocalyptic descriptions. Thus, the term אש ("fire") occurs in Ezekiel 38:19, 22; 39:6, 9, 10; Zechariah 12:6; and 13:9. Similarly, Malachi 3:19 (Eng.: 4:1) resembles Joel 2:3 in its use of the verb להט ("flame, set ablaze") to describe the judgments of the Day of YHWH. The focus on the idea of "blood" (דם) in Joel 3:3, 4 (Eng.: 2:30, 31) has parallels with other proto-apocalyptic texts. Isaiah 34:3; 63:6; and Ezekiel 38:22 associate large amounts of blood with apocalyptic judgment (compare Ezek. 39:18).[48] Note that Ezekiel

46. See Wolff, *Joel*, 14, 26, 64.

47. Allen, *Joel*, 109. See also Wolff, *Joel*, 76.

48. B. Kedar-Kopfstein writes, "In the End Time the blood of the Jews will be avenged by the blood of their enemies (Isa 49:26; Ezek 38:22, 39:17ff.)" ("דם," *TDOT* 3:250). Also see the references to blood in Joel 4:19, 21 (Eng.: 3:19, 21).

38:22 contains the apocalyptic association of fire and blood found in Joel 3:3 (Eng.: 2:30). All these secondary elements confirm the family resemblance of Joel to proto-apocalyptic literature.

The Place of the Apocalyptic Pericopes within Joel's Unified Structure

The apocalyptic texts being examined are integral parts of a book that stems from the priestly center of postexilic society. Joel and the school that transmitted and interpreted his words were located sociologically within the central-temple structures of Yehud. As noted in the preceding chapter, many scholars argue the postexilic period emphasized cult prophecy.[49] Joel was such a cult prophet and an important one.[50] Thus, the book presents

49. Already in 1914, Gustav Hölscher found a place in the temple for cult prophets (*Die Profeten* [Leipzig: J. C. Hinrichs, 1914], 143). Then, in 1923, Sigmund Mowinckel wrote a pioneering work on prophets within the Jerusalem cult, *Psalmenstudien III: Kultprophetie und prophetische Psalmen* (Oslo: Jacob Dybwad, 1923), 1–29. The phenomenon of cultic prophecy has also been treated by Aubrey R. Johnson, *The Cultic Prophet in Ancient Israel* (Cardiff: University of Wales Press, 1944); and *The Cultic Prophet and Israel's Psalmody* (Cardiff: University of Wales Press, 1979); Hans Joachim Kraus, *Worship in Israel*, trans. G. Buswell (Oxford: Basil Blackwell, 1966); and H. H. Rowley, *Worship in Ancient Israel* (London: SPCK, 1967), among others. Cultic prophecy was very important in the postexilic period. Robert R. Wilson notes the role of many prophets in the religious establishment after the exile (*Prophecy and Society in Ancient Israel* [Philadelphia: Fortress, 1980], 306). As seen in the discussion of Zechariah in the preceding chapter, the Hebrew Bible has preserved records of several important postexilic prophets associated with the central temple cult. For further discussion, see Thomas W. Overholt, *Channels of Prophecy: The Social Dynamics of Prophetic Activity* (Minneapolis: Fortress, 1989), 152.

50. Sigmund Mowinckel was more cautious about stating that Joel was a temple prophet than he was about figures such as Habakkuk and Nahum (*The Psalms in Israel's Worship*, trans. D. R. Ap-Thomas [Nashville: Abingdon, 1967], 2:93). He did admit that Joel shows the strong influence of cultic liturgy, however. In contrast, we must go further and agree with scholars such as Ivan Engnell, Richard Hentschke, and Johannes Lindblom that Joel was definitely a cult prophet. Kapelrud states, "The Book of Joel originated in the temple at Jerusalem which is clearly proved by 1:14, 2:1, 15, 17, 3:5 [Eng.: 2:32], 4:1, 6, 16, 17, 20, 21 [Eng.: 3:1, 6, 16, 17, 20, 21], a fact, which is also apparent elsewhere. Joel's entire attitude is characterized by the cult practices in the temple at Jerusalem" (*Joel Studies*, 11). Later, Kapelrud writes, "Joel in particular seems to have been closely associated

him acting as officiant in a national lament liturgy. Calls for national lament occur at Joel 1:5, 8, 11, 13, 14, 18; 2:15-17, and such calls usually come from someone of authority.[51] In Joel 1:13 and 2:17, Joel even dictates exact ritual instructions to the altar priests for implementing the national lament. He actually provides the priests with their prayer in Joel 2:17. The important role Joel plays in the cult is attested by his book's use of cultic language and liturgical patterns.[52] This latter area is discussed below.

Examination of the Joel text leaves little doubt that the apocalyptic material in Joel 2:1-11 and 3–4 (Eng.: 2:28 — 3:21) is from the same cultic prophet (and the cult-based circle with which he was associated) that authored the rest of the book. This can be demonstrated through an examination of the structure of the book and the interconnection of its sections through repetition of linguistic usages and idioms.[53]

The problem of the unity of Joel, and hence the issue of whether this cult prophet had a millennial worldview, hinges on the interpretation of the cry of alarm in 2:1-11. As will be clear from the discussion thus far, I disagree with scholars who contend that 2:1-11 merely describes a locust plague, the coming of an east-wind storm/sirocco, or the advance of a mundane army.[54] We have instead a vision of the coming of Ezekiel's

---

with the cult, and we should not hesitate in presuming that he was attached to the temple as a temple-prophet" (ibid., 177).

51. See Graham S. Ogden, "Joel 4 and Prophetic Responses to National Laments," *JSOT* 26 (1983): 97; and Prinsloo, *Theology,* 26.

52. See, e.g., R. Wilson, *Prophecy and Society,* 290.

53. A number of scholars have made related arguments about the substantial unity of Joel. Kapelrud defends Joel's unity via a cultic interpretation (*Joel Studies,* e.g., 176). Wolff's arguments for Joel's unity based on the book's symmetry are even more convincing (*Joel*). Other scholars who have read Joel as a unity include Wilhelm Rudolph, *Joel — Amos — Obadja — Jona,* KAT 13/2 (Gütersloh: Gütersloher Verlagshaus Gerd Mohn, 1971), 23–24, 88–92; Ahlström, *Temple Cult,* e.g., 137; Allen, *Joel;* Kathleen S. Nash, "The Palestinian Agricultural Year and the Book of Joel" (Ph.D. diss., Catholic University of America, 1989), 9; Graham S. Ogden and Richard R. Deutsch, *A Promise of Hope — A Call to Obedience: A Commentary on the Books of Joel and Malachi,* International Theological Commentary (Grand Rapids, Mich.: Eerdmans, 1987), 8; and Bergler, *Schriftinterpret,* 31.

54. In contrast to the majority opinion that Joel 2:1-11 continues the description of the mundane locust plague of Joel 1:4-7, K. Nash provides a fresh interpretation of this passage in terms of the seasonal weather patterns of Palestine. She argues that the language of this section corresponds to fears of a sirocco that the community would have been entertaining given their situation and the time of the agricultural year reflected in Joel 2. Nash argues that in Joel 2:1-11, "Joel de-

apocalyptic enemy from the north.[55] Although its language has been influenced by the description of a locust plague and by meteorological language in Joel 1, this pericope points forward to a crisis of the end time.

Whereas the desolation of Joel 1 has taken place in the past, Joel 2:1 states that the Day of YHWH is still "coming" (בא — Qal participle) although it is "imminent" (קרוב). Imperfect verb forms predominate in the ensuing verses, showing that the apocalyptic threat here described is still approaching.[56] Further, the future desolation of Joel 2:1-11 is said to be unique. Joel 2:2 states, "There has never been anything like it, nor will there be again after it, through the years of many generations."[57] This statement hardly applies to a mundane crisis.[58] In addition, the retrospective designation of the army as the "northerner" (הצפוני) in Joel 2:20 does not fit in with a description of a mundane locust or sirocco crisis. Locusts and siroccos come from the east out of the desert.[59] As argued above, Joel is

---

scribes the progress of a hot dusty sirocco windstorm in terms of the Lord leading his angelic army against Judah" ("Agricultural Year," 144, cf. also 11, 20, 139, 152, 156). Although Nash may be right that east-wind storm imagery is used here, such language is not an argument against Joel 2:1-11 being proto-apocalyptic literature. For example, Nash also sees Joel 4 (Eng.: 3), which she admits is eschatological, as employing sirocco language ("Agricultural Year," 142, 193). I argue that an apocalyptic worldview is also behind the use of this language in Joel 2. Much more is at issue here than simply an exaggerated and imaginative description of meteorological phenomena. Ogden's interpretation of Joel 2:1-11 is perhaps unique. This commentator sees here a picture of the invasion of 587 B.C.E. projected into the present (*Hope*, 27). There is little evidence to support this view.

55. As Wolff states, "While [Joel] 1:4-20 confronts an incipient economic catastrophe, hoping to avert it, 2:1-17 views in the light of this temporary crisis a coming, final catastrophe for Jerusalem, from which at first glance there seems no possible escape (2:3b, 11bβ)" (*Joel*, 6, cf. 42).

56. תלהט ("will blaze up"), v. 3; ירוצון ("they run"), v. 4; ירקדון ("they leap"), v. 5; יחילו ("they will writhe"), v. 6; ירצון ("they run"), יעלו ("they scale"), ילכון ("they march"), עבטון, ("they swerve" [?]), v. 7; ידחקון ("they crowd"), ילכון ("they march"), יפלו ("they burst"), יבצעו ("they break ranks"), v. 8; ישקו ("they will rush"), ירצון ("they run"), יעלו ("they climb"), יבאו ("they enter"), v. 9; יכילנו ("will be able to endure it"), v. 11.

57. See Wolff, *Joel*, 42, 45.

58. Kapelrud argues that if Joel's concern was merely with such a mundane crisis, his words would never have been handed down (*Joel Studies*, 52).

59. For the argument that Joel is using an apocalyptic technical term here, see Gressmann, *Der Messias*, 137. Wolff writes, "The rising apocalypticism, which is clearly recognizable in Joel, begins to make use of mythological terminology as

strongly driven by fear of Ezekiel's horde from the north here (Ezek. 38:6, 15; 39:2). In fact, many of the arguments in the preceding section show that Joel 2:1-11 refers not merely to the future but to the apocalyptic end of time.

Joel 2:1-11 combines apocalyptic motifs and ideas with locust, drought, and sirocco/east-wind imagery.[60] The best explanation for this phenomenon is that Joel saw in the present crises (described in Joel 1:2-12) a harbinger of the eschaton. Thus, already in Joel 1:15, as part of the lament in the temple over the present desolation, the connection is made to the approaching end-time threat.[61] It is not merely the eschaton in view here, it is the apocalyptic end. Joel 1:15 reverberates with the proto-apocalyptic description of Isaiah 13:6. Both texts read: כי קרוב יום יהוה \ כשד משדי יבוא \\ ("For near is the Day of YHWH, As destruction from the Almighty it comes").

When it is accepted that Joel 2:1-11 makes reference to an end-time desolation, the whole unified structure of Joel becomes clear. Indeed, the apocalyptic pericopes of Joel are integral to the book's literary symmetry. This symmetry has its midpoint at Joel 2:18, with the preceding texts describing a double desolation and the succeeding texts describing a double deliverance.[62] These doubled descriptions are best understood in light of Joel's

code words" (*Joel*, 62). See also Prinsloo, *Theology*, 74; and John D. W. Watts, *The Books of Joel, Obadiah, Jonah, Nahum, Habakkuk and Zephaniah*, CBC (Cambridge, England: Cambridge University Press, 1975), 33.

60. Note 65 below demonstrates how the language of Joel 2:1-11 is influenced by the present desolation. For the importance of east-wind storm language here, see the discussion of K. Nash's dissertation in n. 54 above.

61. The imperfect verb form, בוא, ("it will come"), makes clear that the Day is still in the future. Gressmann notes that already at 1:15 Joel indicates that the present locust plague is something uncanny (*unheimlich*), it is the early sign (*Vorbote*) for the nearing Day of YHWH (*Der Messias*, 134). See also Ernst Kutsch, "Heuschreckenplage und Tag Jahwes in Joel 1 und 2," *TZ* 18 (1962): 89–94; Alfons Deissler, *Zwölf Propheten* (Würzburg: Echter Verlag, 1981), 1:78; Rudolph, *Joel*, 57; and Kapelrud, *Joel Studies*, 52, 58, 71. An examination of sociological parallels to Joel lends support to this thesis. Other millennial groups have viewed present crises as harbingers or foretastes of the end times. The sociology of the apocalyptic texts of Joel will be elucidated below through reference to this comparative material.

62. Wolff writes, "When the book's entire message is taken into consideration, a decisive turning point—not only for the second chapter but for the book as a whole—becomes apparent at the junction between 2:17 and 2:18. Here there is an abrupt transition from the preceding cries of lament to the following oracles where divine response to the pleas is assured" (*Joel*, 7). Also see Bergler, *Schriftinterpret*, 31, 88, 341; and Ahlström, *Temple Cult*, 132.

harbinger belief. He believes that portents will presage doomsday, and that present salvation is just a foretaste of what is to come. This belief allows him to pair mundane and apocalyptic realities typologically so that each half of the book shifts from immediate, proleptic conditions to apocalyptic ones.

Form-critical and literary analyses make the literary feature of doubling in Joel clear: each half of the book has two parts, one deals with the present, one with the end times. A present, accomplished desolation is described in Joel 1:2-12 as part of a motivating introduction to a summons to communal lamentation. The vocabulary and motifs of this section reverberate strongly with Joel 2:18-27, an assurance oracle or promise (*Verheissung*) describing a present/immediate deliverance from this crisis.[63] The desolation described in Joel 2:1-11 (a cry of warning/alarm reporting a vision), however, finds its resolution/negation only in chapters 3 and 4 of Joel (Eng.: 2:28 – 3:21), which commentators agree contain promise oracles describing a future, end-time, deliverance.[64] This conclusion is clear from the linguistic reverberations and thematic reversals itemized in List 4.

List 4. Continuity of Joel 3–4 (Eng.: 2:28–3:21) and Joel 2:1-11

1. Joel 2:1, 11 ↔ 3:4 (Eng.: 2:31); 4:14 (Eng.: 3:14): The apocalyptic usage "the Day of YHWH" (יום יהוה) is an important element of con-

---

63. This has been observed by several scholars. For example, see Prinsloo, *Theology*, 71; and Redditt, "Peripheral Prophecy," 228. Ferdinand E. Deist cites the following correspondences to show how Joel 2:18-27 describes the liquidation of lack pronounced in Joel 1:2-20: 1:6, 10 ↔ 2:18; 1:10 ↔ 2:21 [also see 2:19, 24]; 1:12 ↔ 2:22; 1:16 ↔ 2:23; 1:19, 20 ↔ 2:22 [both pericopes mention the beasts of the field and the pastures of the wilderness]. See his "Parallels and Reinterpretation in the Book of Joel: A Theology of the Yom Yahweh?," in *Text and Context: Old Testament and Semitic Studies for F. C. Fensham*, ed. W. Claassen, JSOTSup 48 (Sheffield: JSOT Press, 1988), 63–64. Deist notes, however, that Joel 2:1-11 does not find its "liquidation" in Joel 2:18-27 (ibid., 67).

64. The parallel assurances of recognition in Joel 2:27 and 4:17 (Eng.: 3:17) help distinguish the two deliverance sections within Joel's symmetrical whole. On the one hand, the formula of Joel 2:27 serves to conclude the promise of deliverance from the effects of the drought and locust plague. On the other hand, the thought of Joel 2:27 is developed further in the remainder of Joel and is repeated at the end of Joel's speech in Joel 4:17 (Eng.: 3:17). Note that these assurances of recognition in Joel are reminiscent of Ezek. 39:22 and 28. Joel 3 (Eng.: 2:28-32) is marked as a new salvation oracle dealing with the future by the formula והיה אחרי־כן ("And it will come about after this") in v. 1 (Eng.: 2:28). The oracles of Joel 4 (Eng.: 3) are set off by the introductory formula בימים ההמה ובעת ההיא כי הנה ("For behold, in those days and at that time").

tinuity between the two sections. It should also be noted that throughout Joel, the Day of YHWH is described as "near" (קרוב): Joel 1:15; 2:1; 4:14 (Eng.: 3:14).

2. Joel 2:1 ↔ 4:17 (Eng.: 3:17): Both sections of Joel use Zion theology's motif of the cosmic mountain. God calls Zion, "my holy mountain" (הר קדשי).

3. Joel 2:2 (compare v. 10) ↔ 3:4 (Eng.: 2:31) (compare 4:15 [Eng.: 3:15]): In both parts of Joel, the Day of YHWH is characterized by "darkness" (חשך).

4. Joel 2:3, 5 ↔ 3:3 (Eng.: 2:30): "Fire" (אש) is a key element of the Day of YHWH in both parts of Joel.

5. Joel 2:3 ↔ 4:19 (Eng.: 3:19): The threat that Yehud would become a "desolate wilderness" (מדבר שממה) is reversed in the second part of Joel: this will now be the fate of the enemy nations. The same wording is used of the devastation in both parts of the book. It is the target of devastation that changes.

6. Joel 2:3 ↔ 3:5 (Eng.: 2:32): Within the course of the book, the threat that no one will escape the onslaught of the apocalyptic horde is reversed. The threat of Joel 2:3 is that the army will leave no פליטה ("escaped remnant"). However, the same term is used in the promise of Joel 3:5 (Eng.: 2:32) that there will be those who escape.

7. Joel 2:10 ↔ 4:16 (Eng.: 3:16): Both sections of Joel anticipate the great "shaking" (רעש) of the end times. Joel 4:16 (Eng.: 3:16) makes clear, however, that YHWH will be "a refuge for his people" when "the heavens and the earth tremble."

8. Joel 2:10 ↔ 4:15 (Eng.: 3:15) (compare 3:4 [Eng.: 2:31]): Both of these verses contain an identical colon describing the apocalyptic darkening of the sun and moon: שמש וירח קדרו.

9. Joel 2:10 ↔ 4:15 (Eng.: 3:15): Again, a colon is repeated in both sections of Joel: וכוכבים אספו נגהם ("and the stars lose their brightness").

10. Joel 2:11 ↔ 4:2, 9-12 (Eng.: 3:2, 9-12): The desolation-description of Joel 2 anticipates the coming of an apocalyptic army. The promise of future deliverance in Joel 4 (Eng.: 3) confirms that apocalyptic armies will come, but they are to be destroyed by God (Joel 4:2, 12 [Eng.: 3:2, 12]).

11. Joel 2:11 ↔ 4:16 (Eng.: 3:16): In both sections YHWH "utters his voice." However, whereas in Joel 2:11 God is leading the apocalyptic army, in Joel 4:16 (Eng.: 3:16) God utters God's voice to save Jerusalem (compare Ps. 46:6).

12. Joel 2:11 ↔ 3:4 (Eng.: 2:31): Both parts of Joel describe the Day of YHWH as both גדול ("great") and נורא ("awesome").

Discussion

The data of List 4 argue strongly against the view, popular since Duhm, that the cult-prophet Joel is responsible only for most of Joel 1–2 (Eng.: 1:1–2:27), while Joel 3–4 (Eng.: 2:28—3:21) is to be ascribed to an apocalyptic compiler. Although the language of Joel 2:1-11 is clearly inspired by the present desolation,[65] it already reflects the apocalyptic worldview behind Joel 3–4. Further, Joel 2:1-11; 3 (Eng.: 2:28-32); and 4 (Eng.: 3) are integral parts of Joel's literary presentation, which develops the theme of the Day of YHWH over the course of the book. Joel 2:1-11 presents the Day of YHWH as fearful—YHWH is leading an apocalyptic army of judgment against Yehud. Then, this threat is presented as averted through intercession discharged in the cult.[66] As a result, chapters 3 and 4 of Joel (Eng.: 2:28—3:21), with their clear reverberations and parallels to Joel 2:1-11, reverse the end-time threat.[67]

Several items in List 4 make clear the reversal from desolation to deliverance in Joel. As item 6 shows, future threat is changed into future deliver-

---

65. Joel 2:1-11 has important deliberate links with the preceding pericopes. Thus, as K. Nash admits, the locust infestation influenced the language of this pericope: "Joel saw in the army of locusts (גוי, 1:6; חילי, 2:25) and the drought of the preceding year the foreshadowing of the imminent יום יהוה ['Day of YHWH'], the LORD's army (חילו, 2:11) coming in the sirocco" ("Agricultural Year," 156). Deist shows how Joel 2:1-11 comments on and deepens the meaning of Joel 1:1-15: 2:2 ↔ 1:6; 2:2 ↔ 1:2-3; 2:3 ↔ 1:4; 2:3c ↔ 1:7; 2:4-10 ↔ 1:4; 2:11 ↔ 1:15 ("Parallels," 65). Also see Gressmann, *Der Messias,* 137; and Prinsloo, *Theology,* 40.

66. Within Joel's overall structure, the various *Gattungen* of Joel 1:13-20 and 2:12-17 call for and picture the needed cultic reactions and responses in the face of accomplished and threatened desolations. Joel 1:13-14 is a call to lament (*Aufruf*), Joel 1:15-18 contains cries of lament, Joel 1:19-20 is a prayer (*Gebet*), Joel 2:12-14 is a call to repentance, Joel 2:15-17a renews the summons/call to lament, and Joel 2:17b is another prayer of lament. It is unclear whether Joel actually proclaimed two separate exhortations corresponding to the present and future threats. In any case, in the present structure of the book these two pericopes function to separate the two distinct desolation descriptions, structuring the texts so as to help the reader distinguish the two descriptions, present from future.

67. In these chapters of promise of future deliverance, YHWH is pictured not at the head of the apocalyptic army (Joel 2:11), but dwelling in Zion (Joel 4:17 [Eng.: 3:17]), protecting Jerusalem against the enemy nations. Already at Joel 2:20 the attacking apocalyptic army is found guilty of hubris, and by Joel 4:11, 19-21 (Eng.: 3:11, 19-21) the army is identified with the enemy nations who have shed blood in Judah. As in Ezekiel 38–39, YHWH does summon and lead the armies against Jerusalem in Joel 4 (Eng.: 3), but this is for the purpose of their destruction.

ance. The future threat had been that nothing would escape the coming apocalyptic horde. Joel 3:1-5 (Eng.: 2:28-32) makes clear, however, that there will be "those who escape" (v. 5 [Eng.: 2:32]) on Mount Zion when the phenomena of items 8 and 12 come about. Commentating on Joel 3:3-4 (Eng.: 2:30-31), Wolff states:

> The phenomena are the same as those with which Jerusalem was threatened before the turning point (cf. 2:10); they are familiar from prophecies concerning the Day of Yahweh (cf. 3:4b [Eng.: 2:31b] with 2:11b!). The wonder of the response (2:18-19) to the entreaties (2:17) of those who were aroused (2:12-16) has led to a reversal of the direction of the Day of Yahweh.[68]

The reversal of apocalyptic judgment in the second part of Joel means it is redirected, not canceled. The data of items 7, 8, 9, and 11 show that Joel 4:14-17 (Eng.: 3:14-17) has an inverse correspondence to Joel 2:10-11. Both sections depict the arrival of the apocalyptic army accompanied by the darkening of the heavenly bodies. In the latter deliverance section, however, YHWH reverses the attack. God "utters his voice" from Jerusalem (Joel 4:16 [Eng.: 3:16]), instead of from the side of the attacking army (Joel 2:11). The reversal of item 5 shows that the apocalyptic devastation threatening Yehud has become the punishment of her enemies. Instead of their desolation, God's spirit will be poured out on Yehud's elect (Joel 3:1 [Eng.: 2:28]), now expected to survive the tribulations of the eschaton. This expectation of the endowment of the spirit resonates with the proto-apocalyptic descriptions in Ezekiel 39:29 and Zechariah 12:10.

I therefore concur with Duane A. Garrett's statement: "To argue that chaps. 1–2 (Eng.: 1:1 – 2:27) and chaps. 3–4 (Eng.: 2:28 – 3:21) speak from fundamentally different viewpoints (the former historical, the latter apocalyptic) misses the movement in chap. 2 toward an apocalyptic day of Yahweh."[69] One cannot remove eschatology from Joel 1–2 by attributing selected verses to a late editor. The book is too tightly arranged and unified for this. Joel 2:1-11 is already a proto-apocalyptic pericope, inextricably linked to the descriptions of the present locust and drought disasters, and to the apocalyptic chapters 3 and 4 of Joel (Eng.: 2:28 – 3:21). As Hugo Gressmann noted, you cannot make eschatology a late insertion into Joel without cutting out the heart of the book.[70]

The described unity of Joel is more than redactional. The references to the Day of YHWH in Joel 1 and 2 show no signs of being expansions.

---

68. Wolff, *Joel*, 68.
69. Duane A. Garrett, "The Structure of Joel," *JETS* 28 (1985): 290.
70. Gressmann, *Der Messias*, 136.

These references are in keeping with the other proto-apocalyptic family resemblances in Joel 2:1-11. And Joel 2:1-11 fits in well with the language and imagery of its context. This is not a case of disparate material of different origin and viewpoint being juxtaposed. Rather, the book is so intricately built up and structurally bound together that it must have been composed and configured by Joel or members of his group. Thus Wolff can state, "The basic construction of the four chapters derives from a single author."[71] Garrett is correct that the book is theologically unified by the Day-of-YHWH theme "typologically conceived of as coming about in several stages."[72]

Evidence of the Influence of Central Priests in Joel

Investigation thus far indicates that the cult prophet Joel wrote proto-apocalyptic literature, and that this millennial catalyst figure even held an influential position within the postexilic temple. This suggests that the text of Joel might fruitfully be investigated for the cultic terms and priestly language and theology found in Ezekiel and Zechariah.

In fact, the book's specific language and concerns indicate that the circle behind it consisted of members or associates of the central priesthood. Before presenting this evidence, however, a word of caution is in order. Similar caveats to those voiced in the discussion of the implications of Zechariah's idiom must be expressed. The problem of intertextuality, for example, is especially keen in Joel, who quotes extensively from collections of earlier prophetic material.[73] Since Joel draws on prophets of different sociological provenances, care must be taken in using his language to iden-

71. Wolff, *Joel*, 8. See the examples given by Wolff here.

72. Garrett, "Structure," 297; cf. Prinsloo, *Theology*, 112. In contrast to the position taken here, Brevard S. Childs states, "The issue has not been settled whether or not this [i.e., Joel's] literary unity derives from a single author or is a redactional creation. . . . I tend to think that the unity is redactional" (*Introduction to the Old Testament as Scripture* [Philadelphia: Fortress, 1979], 389). As in the discussion of Ezekiel 38–39, however, it is not crucial here to know whether the verbal and thematic interlocking within Joel is the product of the prophet himself or of his ongoing group. In either case, Joel's apocalyptic pericopes must be associated with a group supportive of the central cult.

73. Bergler sees in Joel a practice of citation that stretches evenly over the whole book (*Schriftinterpret*). See further the comments in K. Nash, "Agricultural Year," 14–15; R. Wilson, *Prophecy and Society*, 290; and Wolff, *Joel*, 10–11, 13. Ogden's "Appendix 2" lists Joel's major quotations (*Hope*, 56–57).

tify his support group or priesthood branch. As in the case of Zechariah, however, Joel's mixing of traditions does not prevent identification of the language and theology of the priests at the center of Yehudite society as predominant in his book.

One of Joel's great concerns is that the desolations he describes have interrupted temple worship.[74] He warns (Joel 1:9) that priestly ministry is disrupted because "grain offerings and libations" (מנחה ונסך) cannot be offered in the temple.[75] He voices similar anxiety in Joel 1:13, "The grain offering and the libation are withheld from the house of your God." Joel 1:16 then laments that gladness and joy have been cut off from the house of God (no doubt because the offering supplies have been cut off). As Ahlström notes, these terms, שמחה ("gladness") and גיל ("joy"), were very familiar in the Jerusalem cult.[76] Later in Joel 2:14, the grain offering and libation are again the focus of concern. This verse defines these offerings as

74. See Wolff, *Joel*, 31; Ahlström, *Temple Cult*, 29; and Prinsloo, *Theology*, 20.

75. This combination of offering terms in Joel (1:9, 13; 2:14) clearly represents a late, central-priestly usage. The usage is confined to P (Exod. 29:41; 30:9), especially what seem to be late parts of P (Num. 6:15, 17; 15:4-5, 6-7, 9-10, 24; 28:8, 9, 31; 29:6, 11, 16, 18, 19, 21, 22, 24, 25, 27, 28, 30, 31, 33, 34, 37, 38, 39), and to Zadokite texts in H (Lev 23:13, 18, 37) and Ezekiel (Ezek. 45:17). There are only two exceptions (2 Kings 16:13-15; Isa. 57:6), both of which are in polemical contexts dissimilar to that of Joel. Joel may be using this offering-term combination to refer to the daily offerings prescribed for the temple (Num. 28:3-8). Note, however, that the same two offerings are prescribed for the Feast of Booths (Num. 29:12-28; Lev. 23:33-44), the festival that may have provided the occasion for Joel's apocalyptic address to the congregation (see n. 79 below).

76. Ahlström, *Temple Cult*, 44; cf. Kapelrud, *Joel Studies*, 63–65; and Gary A. Anderson, *A Time to Mourn, A Time to Dance* (University Park: Pennsylvania State University Press, 1991), 19–26, 109–14. Note the use of גיל ("joy") to describe the rejoicing brought by agricultural bounty in Ps. 65:13. This psalm is a national hymn of rejoicing that would have been used on such occasions as the Feast of Booths (in situations opposite to that faced by Joel). Both the terms מחה ("gladness") and גיל ("joy") are used in the wedding procession on Zion pictured in Ps. 45:16. The two nouns are also used in Ps. 43:4, where Zion and the temple altar serve as the means to exceeding joy for the psalmist. This text, Psalm 43, actually one in structure with Psalm 42, seems to have particularly influenced Joel. In addition to making mutual reference to "gladness and joy," both Joel and the psalm refer to God's holy mountain (Ps. 43:3; Joel 2:1; 4:17 [Eng.: 3:17]); both see God as the people's stronghold (Ps. 43:2; Joel 4:16 [Eng.: 3:16]); and both pray that the nations should not say "Where is their God?" (Ps. 42:10; Joel 2:17). Note also that the verb ערג ("long for") occurs outside of Joel 1:20 only in Ps. 42:2.

a focus of Joel's hopes for blessing.[77] Clearly, Joel urges as a major emphasis replenishing the temple's supplies for the liturgy so cultic worship can again be conducted.

Even Joel's descriptions of the problems caused outside of the temple area by the drought and locusts employ the language of the Jerusalem temple. Joel 1:20, for example, strongly reflects the language of Psalm 42:2. As Arvid S. Kapelrud writes, "It cannot be merely incidental that two such rare expressions as תערג ['pant'] and אפיקי מים ['watercourses'] occur in both places."[78]

Joel's exhortations in view of the present and anticipated desolations make use of several cult terms and call for implementation of cult practices. Joel 1:14 and 2:15 call a "cultic assembly" (עצרה),[79] and both exhortation sections (Joel 1:13-20; 2:12-17) prescribe what this assembly is to do. Joel 1:13-14 describes cultic acts of contrition in detail. The exhortation in Joel 2:12-17, with its pronounced focus on the central cult, is even more interesting because it is placed within Joel's structure as the required response to the apocalyptic threat. Prinsloo calls attention to the cultic terminology used here: צום ("fasting"), בכי ("weeping"), מספד ("mourning"), v. 12; ברכה ("blessing"), מנחה ונסך ("a grain offering and a libation"), v. 14; קדשו־צום ("consecrate a fast"), קראו עצרה ("proclaim a solemn assembly"), v. 15; קדשו קהל ("sanctify the congregation"), v. 16; אולם ("temple porch"), מזבח ("altar"), and כהנים ("priests"), v. 17.[80] I shall argue below that behind this

---

77. Kapelrud writes, "It is characteristic of Joel's attitude, marked by the cult, that ברכה ['blessing'] above all implies that sacrificial offerings again can be regularly presented to Yahweh . . . ברכה ['blessing'] and מנחה ונסך ['grain offering and libation'] are to Joel only two sides of the same thing" (*Joel Studies*, 85).

78. Ibid., 70.

79. This usage recalls several late priestly texts that concern the Feast of Booths, an especially interesting fact if the action of Joel does take place at the time of this feast. Lev. 23:36 (H) indicates that the Feast of Booths includes a "holy convocation" (מקרא־קדש) that is called an "assembly" (עצרת). A parallel instruction occurs in Num. 29:35 (late P). 2 Chronicles 7:7-8 describes Solomon's holding of a "solemn assembly" (עצרת) as part of his Feast of Booths, and Neh. 8:18 describes the reinstating of this practice in the postexilic period. Perhaps Joel, upset that the required offerings for the Feast of Booths are unavailable, is urging here that a penitential assembly be substituted for the normal harvest festival. For this suggestion, see K. Nash, "Agricultural Year," 87, cf. 29, 84–85, 220, 224.

80. Prinsloo, *Theology,* 49. The phrase "sanctify the congregation" (v. 16) occurs only here in Joel, but similar usages are attested in priestly texts (Exod. 28:41; 29:1). The "temple porch" (v. 17) is referred to many times in Ezekiel 40–46, and

text is a communal/national lament ceremony convened by Joel during the
actual crises of drought and locust plague. Thus, the prayer in Joel 2:17 that
God's inheritance not be a "byword" (מָשָׁל) recalls the wording of vv. 13-15
of the communal lament in Psalm 44. These data confirm Joel's Jerusalemite
cultic-tradition roots.

Joel also uses language expected from a central-cult prophet in describing the immediate and future deliverance that result from his temple-based
program(s). In Joel 2:21, 23 the cult-associated roots שׂמח ("rejoice") and
גיל ("be glad") are repeated, reversing Joel 1:16. Also, the promise that the
people will praise YHWH in Joel 2:26 uses the verb הלל ("praise"), which
often expresses cultic adoration.[81] The language of the temple is also found
in the promises of the last part of Joel, the section of the book most often
described as apocalyptic. As Kapelrud states, Joel 4:1-21 (Eng.: 3:1-21)
is "thoroughly impressed by traditional cultic terms and thoughts."[82] For
example, the chapter emphasizes the coming salvation of elected Judah and
Jerusalem (vv. 1, 20) and reflects a firm concern, expressed in v. 17, that
the future Jerusalem be קדשׁ ("holy"). In this verse, Joel emphasizes the
same priestly holiness ideal seen in Ezekiel and Zechariah.

Joel's reliance on Zion theology is an important clue associating him
with the central priests and establishment of Jerusalem.[83] The book talks
constantly about "Zion" (צִיּוֹן: Joel 2:1, 15, 23; 3:5 [Eng.: 2:32]; 4:16, 17,
21 [Eng.: 3:16, 17, 21]) and Zion's election. Indeed, as in Zechariah 1:14
and 8:2, Joel 2:18 states that God will be "zealous" (קנא) for God's chosen
people and land. Further, as in Zechariah 8:3, Joel refers to Zion as "my
holy mountain" (הר קדשׁי; see List 4, item 2 above).[84] It is important to

---

the specific locale "between the porch and the altar" is also mentioned in Ezek.
8:16 (cf. 2 Chron. 8:12). The injunction for the priests to weep (v. 17; cf. 1:9, 13)
recalls Zech. 7:3, where the central priests are depicted as presiding over the issue
of cultic weeping.

81. Thus, Ahlström suggests this verse reflects a cultic setting (*Temple Cult,* 47).

82. Kapelrud, *Joel Studies,* 7.

83. Joel's adherence to Zion theology helps confirm that he functioned within
the central cult. Mowinckel was one of the first to show that prophets within the
temple cult regularly supported the ideology of the election and protection of Jerusalem as part of their social-maintenance functions. See his *Psalms,* 2:53–73. It is
clear from psalms such as 46 and 110 that the oracles of such cult prophets often
express this theology.

84. The idea of Zion as the holy mountain is taken up by Joel from the psalms
of the cult (e.g., Pss. 2:6 [a royal psalm]; 3:5; 43:3; 48:2 [a Song of Zion]; 99:9
[an enthronement psalm]) and from Judean prophetic tradition (e.g., Isa. 6:13;

observe that this theology of Zion as the elected holy mountain is expressed specifically in pericopes that are clearly proto-apocalyptic: Joel 2:1 and 4:17 (Eng.: 3:17).

The proto-apocalyptic pericopes of Joel 3 and 4 (Eng.: 2:28 — 3:21) are as strongly rooted in Zion theology as the rest of the book. Joel 3:5 (Eng.: 2:32) stresses Mount Zion as the locale of salvation where YHWH will provide for survivors of the end-time judgment.[85] In Joel 4 (Eng.: 3), Zion theology is especially evident in the motif of an inviolable city. The *Völkersturm* motif of Ezekiel 38–39 and Zechariah 12 and 14 is clear here.[86] The apocalyptic forces of chaos are gathered against Jerusalem (v. 2) accompanied by the great shaking (v. 16) associated with the northern threat. True to Zion theology, chapter 4 (Eng.: 3) then describes YHWH's protection of the elected mountain against the onslaught of these armies of chaos. Just as in Ezekiel 38:22, God enters into judgment (ונשפטתי) with the horde (v. 2) and destroys the enemy forces in the "valley of decision" before they can harm Zion (vv. 13-14). As v. 16 makes clear, there will be refuge in Zion at the time of this coming great shaking (see List 4, item 7 above). In the amazing turnabout discussed above (see List 4, item 11), Zion theology prevails over the threat of Joel 2:1-11. YHWH is protecting Jerusalem from within, not leading the horde as previously feared.

Joel 4:16 (Eng.: 3:16) most strongly introduces Zion theology into Joel's description of the final apocalyptic judgment. There are striking links in v. 16 with the theology of Psalm 46, which holds that God will be a refuge (v. 2) though the mountains quake (v. 4). Both the Joel and Psalm texts use the terms מחסה ("refuge") and רעש ("quake"). The term מחסה is also found in other psalms that express confidence in YHWH's protection (Pss. 14:6-7; 61:4; 62:8, 9; 71:7; 73:28; 91:2, 9; 94:22; 142:6). Its use in Psalm 94:22 is especially noteworthy because, like Joel 4:16 (Eng.: 3:16), this community lament expresses assurance of salvation in the face of national crisis.

Joel 4:16 (Eng.: 3:16) also advocates Zion theology in its assurance

---

11:9; 27:13; 56:7; 57:13; 65:11, 25; 66:20; Obadiah 16; Zeph. 3:11). It should be stressed that this usage is quite at home in Zadokite texts (e.g., Ezek. 20:40; 28:14; Zech. 8:3).

85. Prinsloo argues that Joel 3:5 (Eng.: 2:32) represents a classical use of the Zion tradition: "Zion and Jerusalem are pre-eminently the abode of Yahweh, citadels of security and stability. . . . In the midst of calamity and cosmic upheaval Yahweh is the one who offers his people security" (*Theology*, 87).

86. See the discussion of the "Later Reuse of the Gog Tradition" in chapter 4.

that YHWH is a מעוז ("stronghold") for the people of Israel. This usage is familiar from Isaiah's version of the Jerusalemite theology (Isa. 17:10; 27:5) and from the psalms (Pss. 27:1; 28:8; 31:3, 5; 37:39; 43:2; 52:9). Note that like Joel 4:16 (Eng.: 3:16), Isaiah 25:4 (within the Isaiah Apocalypse) affirms YHWH is both מחסה ("a refuge") and מעוז ("a stronghold").

The view of the new age in the eschatological salvation promise of Joel 4:18-21 (Eng.: 3:18-21) also betrays Zion theology. The vision of the temple spring in v. 18 was preserved in the temple's psalms (Pss. 36:8-9; 46:5; 65:10) and was an important theme in the future visions of the priests Ezekiel (Ezek. 47:1-12) and Zechariah (Zech. 14:8).[87] The final verse of the book of Joel (v. 21) states that YHWH dwells in Zion. This gives the Zion theology an emphatic final emphasis.[88] Joel has not just employed Zion language or traditions. Zion theology itself is at the base of Joel's apocalyptic expectations.

The language of Joel 4:17 and 21 (Eng.: 3:17 and 21) presents Zion theology in a manner particularly characteristic of central priests such as Ezekiel and Zechariah. These verses use an idiom that describes YHWH as שֹׁכֵן בְּצִיּוֹן ("dwelling/tenting in Zion"). As Hanson observes, it is in "hierocratic" writings that the Qal of the verb שכן ("tent") becomes the key term used to express the mode of YHWH's presence in Jerusalem.[89] This usage occurs in central-cult related texts such as some of the psalms (Pss. 68:17; 74:2; 135:21), and in Isaiah 8:18 where Zion is viewed as

---

87. See Ahlström, *Temple Cult*, 87; Paul Hanson, *The Dawn of Apocalyptic* (Philadelphia: Fortress, 1979), 377–78; Adam S. van der Woude, "Zion as Primeval Stone in Zechariah 3 and 4," in *Text and Context: Old Testament and Semitic Studies for F. C. Fensham*, ed. W. Claassen (Sheffield: JSOT Press, 1988), 244–45; and Carroll Stuhlmueller, C.P., *Rebuilding with Hope: A Commentary on the Books of Haggai and Zechariah,* International Theological Commentary (Grand Rapids, Mich.: Eerdmans, 1988), 150.

88. See Prinsloo, *Theology*, 117.

89. Hanson, *Dawn*, 249 n. 56; cf. Klaus Seybold, *Bilder zum Tempelbau: Die Visionen des Propheten Sacharja*, SB 70 (Stuttgart: Verlag Katholisches Bibelwerk, 1974), 85; and Wolff, *Joel*, 82. Note that the specifically hieratic idiom is the Qal verb used to describe the dwelling of YHWH himself. In contrast, the comparable idiom in Deuteronomistic writings uses שכן in the Piel stem to describe the dwelling of God's name: לְשַׁכֵּן שְׁמוֹ שָׁם ("to establish his name there," Deut. 12:11; 14:23; 16:2, 6, 11; 26:2; cf. Jer. 7:12). As Ahlström notes, Joel does not adopt the Deuteronomistic name-theology; Joel views YHWH himself as dwelling in the temple on the holy mountain (*Temple Cult*, 125).

the permanent dwelling for the divine presence.[90] Joel, however, probably draws on an even more specifically central tradition. In the exilic and post-exilic periods, the Ezekiel and Zechariah groups used the "tenting" language to describe God's future dwelling in the new temple in Zion (Ezek. 43:7,9; Zech. 2:14-15; 8:3).[91] Joel employs this latter technical usage, which helps to place him squarely within central-priestly circles.

The Sociology of the Millennial Group of Joel

Joel's millennial group clearly operated within the structures of the postexilic central cult. Contrary to the view of Plöger, Wolff, and others, the group was not peripheral, and there is no sign of opposition to the temple.[92] The book instead pictures Joel as an official of the central cult, and the terminology and forms in the book support this picture. Because central-priestly language and ideas appear as often in Joel's apocalyptic pericopes as they do elsewhere in the work, the proto-apocalyptic and liturgical characteristics of Joel relate as two dimensions of a single social setting.

It seems clear that the end-time language of Joel is the product of a group of the priests in control at Jerusalem. Thus, I must disagree with Hanson that no apocalyptic eschatology appears in the writings of the "hierocrats" after 515 B.C.E. Hanson's argument that any "apocalyptic thrust" that was part of the "hierocratic tradition" suddenly disappeared after the Second Temple was completed ignores the evidence of Joel.[93]

90. In a related usage, P employs שכן to describe God's dwelling among the Israelites in Exod. 25:8; 29:46; and Num. 5:3. Also note the use of the term משכן to denote God's "dwelling place" or "tabernacle" in P (e.g., Exod. 26:7, 12, 13; 36:14; 40:19; Num. 16:9; Lev. 17:4). P's use of the noun משכן is taken up in H (Lev. 26:11) and in Ezek. 37:27.

91. Hanson states, "This terminology is applied by Ezekiel in key passages which express the covenant conditions under which Yahweh will be present. . . . It is then adopted by Zechariah in the same sense to express the restoration hope of Yahweh's tenting in the midst of his People: 'I come and I tent in the midst of you' (Zech 2:14 [10]): 'I will return to Zion and will tent in the midst of Jerusalem' (Zech 8:3; see also 1 Chr 23:25)" (*Dawn*, 249 n. 56).

92. Redditt is certainly off the mark in arguing that Joel criticized the temple cult in the midst of catastrophe ("Peripheral Prophecy," 235–37).

93. Hanson states, "The proponents of the hierocratic tradition gained control of the post-exilic community in the last third of the sixth century, translated their visionary program into a rebuilt temple and a reconstituted Zadokite priesthood, and thereby were able to discard the visionary form of their program" (*Dawn*, 237, also see 231). As has been seen, elsewhere Hanson qualifies even the existence of a pre-515 "apocalyptic thrust," arguing that any such visionary

Because I am arguing that Joel interprets the Day of YHWH within a cultic context, some important caveats are in order. First, saying Joel is a cultic prophet (or better, a cultic millennial catalyst figure) does not deny him a spirit of innovation or an ability to criticize the cult.[94] Rather, analysis of Joel provokes a less restricted view of the nature of cultic prophets. Against H. H. Rowley's view, for example, the evidence of Joel shows cultic prophets could well be "challenging and forthright."[95] Although Joel intercedes and gives oracles within the cult, he gives a major warning of judgment and makes ethical demands (Joel 2:12-14) like other "canonical prophets."[96]

Second, Joel's cultic context does not restrict him to the categories of thought often associated with the terms *ritual* and *myth*. The worldview of Joel has roots in cultic myths, but the apocalyptic nature of the worldview means these myths have been eschatologized. Ahlström can thus be criticized for identifying Joel's theology as mythology and for coming close to seeing the Day of YHWH in Joel as merely YHWH's annual ritual battle against the powers of chaos.[97] As seen in chapter 2, the mythic-realistic

---

elements served "merely as carriers of a very pragmatic program" (*Dawn*, 232, cf. 288).

94. Issue is taken with those scholars, such as Plöger and Rowley, who see the utterances of cult prophets as mere accompaniments of ritual acts (Plöger, *Theocracy*, 99; Rowley, *Worship*, 170). Ezekiel was a central-cult prophet whose prophetic ministry went far beyond merely delivering set oracles within a prescribed liturgy.

95. Rowley, *Worship*, 175. The picture of cult prophecy in Joel confirms the need to critique Wellhausen's and Weber's view that prophecy was an anticultic protest movement. As Andrew D. H. Mayes writes, "The cult was much more central to all aspects of life and left more room for a prophetic type of spirituality than was formerly believed" (*The Old Testament in Sociological Perspective* [London: Marshall Pickering, 1989], 75). Cf. Peter L. Berger's statement, "Studies of Old Testament worship have shown that the cult itself left far more room for 'free-flowing spirituality' than the earlier interpreters thought" ("Charisma and Religious Innovation: The Social Location of Israelite Prophecy," *American Sociological Review* 28 [1963]: 944). Berger also writes, "Putting the prophet on an institutional payroll does not seem to have offered effective protection against his coming out with un-heard-of radicalisms" (ibid., 949).

96. Joel 2:12-14 makes clear that although repentance is to be expressed in cultic worship, it must be wholehearted. See Prinsloo's discussion of the use of the preposition ב ("with") here (*Theology*, 59).

97. Ahlström, *Temple Cult*, 71, 88. Elsewhere, Ahlström speaks of the "reality" of liturgy (ibid., 74).

crises of apocalypticism are understood as historically real. They interrupt history viewed in a linear, not cyclical, fashion.

Joel's Central-Cult Based Millennial Group Program

Many of the form-critical units of the book of Joel are associated with communal lamentation. Against Wolff, I find no reason to see these forms of Joel as detached from their original life-setting.[98] Rather, the book reflects an occasion where a lament liturgy was undertaken at a time of crisis.[99] Although Joel is now a structured literary work, the practical program for action taken by the Joel group at the time of the drought and locust crises can be extracted from the book. Joel's exhortation in the face of the end-time harbingers is to engage the central-cultic means for dealing with national threats. Psalms such as 74 and 80 picture similar national appeals for help at times of special need.[100] When viewed in this context, the book of Joel betrays an apocalyptic worldview in the central priests, who use cultic means and rituals to evoke recognition of the apocalyptic significance of the present crisis and attempt to find salvation in the midst of it.[101] The book of Joel assumes that cult intercession can avert apocalyptic disaster. The sociological evidence, discussed in chapter 3, allows for such use of the activities of a central cult by a millennial group in order to procure end-time salvation. Thus, the actions taken by the priesthood of the native god Oro in the Mamaia cult were similar to those found in Joel. The natives practiced traditional rituals within the central cult as their millennial group program.

The structure of the book makes clear that the group program of Joel

98. Wolff, *Joel*, 10. Wolff states that Joel had only a "meager interest" in the cultus (ibid., 84). Cf. Hanson's view that Joel "did not place primary trust in the cultic apparatus of the Jerusalem temple" (*People Called*, 314).

99. The book is not a cultic liturgy per se, but is based on a single, unique historical episode. See Allen, *Joel*, 31; and Ahlström, *Temple Cult*, 130–31.

100. See Johnson, *Israel's Psalmody*, 131–34, 150. In Joel, the central cult responds to the eschatological crisis as it would to a mundane one: the nation's religious leaders and the people appeal to YHWH through a national lament liturgy.

101. Thus, Gunther Wanke notes Joel's positive attitude to public worship: "The prophet desires to make the Jerusalem congregation newly aware of the eschatological message through the adoption and employment of cultic forms" ("Prophecy and Psalms in the Persian Period," in *The Cambridge History of Judaism*, ed. W. D. Davies and L. Finkelstein [Cambridge, England: Cambridge University Press, 1984], 1:177). Ahlström writes that Joel, like Haggai and Zechariah, viewed a right cult as the only foundation on which to build. "The cult prophet takes the cult seriously; for him a better world starts with a true cult that gives a true צדקה ['righteousness']" (Ahlström, *Temple Cult*, 61).

was based on the national-lament liturgical pattern of the central cult. Joel's structure, outlined above, places exhortations for cultic action after Joel's description of the present desolation and again after Joel's prediction of future, apocalyptic desolation.[102] These exhortations are viewed as successful, and oracles of salvation conclude the book. In the book's present form, this concluding section preserves the hopes of the Joel group for the imminent future. The group took hope because they had successfully carried out their cult-based response to the crises they experienced and were striving to continue to run a right cult.

When famines or plagues struck, Israel's authorities instituted a "fast" (צום) and proclaimed a festival for lamentation and repentance.[103] Thus, in Joel, in the face of the present desolation, the priests lament (Joel 1:13) and assemble the people in the temple for a fast (Joel 1:14). A recounting of the people's woes (Joel 1:15-18) follows, and Joel 1:19-20 even preserves an actual penitential prayer that might have been used in the temple. Kapelrud considers that the material in this section of Joel (1:13-20) reflects Joel's summonses and the lamentations he led from the temple on behalf of its authorities.[104] The reader knows of only a mundane crisis, pictured in Joel 1:2-12, at this point, although already the priests fear the threat of the eschaton at Joel 1:15.

As argued above, by the time the reader reaches Joel 2:12-17, it is clear that the present crisis brings with it a threat of apocalyptic doom. After these verses, however, the book presents only promises of present and future salvation. Given this structure, the exhortation to carry out a cultic program in Joel 2:12-17 is a major turning point in the book. The cultic injunctions here aim to transform apocalyptic doom into promise. Verses 12-14 of this section call for fasting and repentance. Next, vv. 15-17 give specific instructions for liturgical action. The command to convoke a solemn assembly at the temple is again repeated. Then the priests are ordered to "weep between the porch and the altar," and the language of their prayer (v. 17b) recalls that of traditional cultic laments.[105] The focus on cultic

---

102. Wolff argues that Joel's liturgical sections exhibit the typical, primary elements of a lament ceremony (*Joel*, 9). Ogden sees the book of Joel as a collection of authentic Joel lament liturgies of the postexilic cult (*Hope*, 7–14).

103. See Kraus, *Worship*, 225.

104. Kapelrud, *Joel Studies*, 4. Kapelrud states, "Joel's appeal to the priests to arrange for a penance for themselves and the people is sure to have been meant seriously. It has a strong cultic mark, because the cultic mode of expression was the one that was natural for the prophet" (ibid., 51).

105. Ahlström notes that Joel 2:17 reflects actual temple liturgy, giving rare detailed information on the priests' actions (*Temple Cult*, 53). The prayer that Israel

action and liturgy here strongly supports what has been said about Joel's millennial group program. If the book's present literary structure reflects the actions and priorities of the Joel group at the time of the drought and locust crises, then these cultic procedures constituted the group's practical program held necessary to assure deliverance through the presaged apocalyptic desolation.[106]

The structure of the book presents Joel 2:18-27; 3 (Eng.: 2:28-32) and 4 (Eng.: 3) as the part of the cultic lament ritual known as the oracle of salvation (*Priesterliches Heilsorakel*).[107] As Graham S. Ogden writes, "Obadiah and Joel 4 belong to the same category of prophetic literature — they both represent prophetic responses to the lament of the nation in its moment of crisis. These oracles thus form integral parts of the lament ritual, being the word of assurance to Israel that God has heard."[108] The book

---

not be a mockery of the nations is a frequent lament motif. See Gressmann, *Der Messias*, 135; and Ogden, *Hope*, 32.

106. Prinsloo finds that the terminology of Joel 2:15-16 "functions as practical cultic injunctions to people who have heeded the call to repentance" (*Theology*, 52). Blenkinsopp states that Joel assumes that "the averting of disaster could be achieved, if at all, only by the cultic act of the entire community." The threat can be turned aside "only by means of cultic acts performed in the Temple, in which the prophet played a leading role" (*History of Prophecy*, 253). Blenkinsopp relates Joel's cultic procedures only to mundane disasters. His statements would also hold true, however, if Joel's reaction was to an apocalyptic threat.

107. See Bergler, *Schriftinterpret*, 86; Kraus, *Worship*, 226; and Erhard S. Gerstenberger, *Psalms, Part I, with an Introduction to Cultic Poetry*, FOTL 14 (Grand Rapids, Mich.: Eerdmans, 1988), 253. The book of Joel can be compared to Psalm 60, a national lament that exhibits not only the intercessory but also the oracular speech behavior of the cultic prophet. See Kapelrud, *Joel Studies*, 90–91; and Johnson, *Israel's Psalmody*, 165. In vv. 6-8 of the psalm, a cult prophet gives a positive divine oracle in response to the preceding prayer for deliverance (Johnson, *Israel's Psalmody*, 169). In most other psalms the oracle of the priest/cultic prophet must be inferred and reconstructed on the basis of exclamations of confidence or changes in mood within the psalm. Indeed, Joachim Begrich first argued for the existence of the priestly oracle-of-salvation form mostly on the basis of its occurrence in Isaiah 40–55 ("Das priesterliche Heilsorakel," *ZAW* 52 [1934]: 81–92). Thus, in Psalm 20 for example, a priest's oracle seems to fit between v. 5 and v. 6, which inspires the following expression of confidence. See Claus Westermann, *Praise and Lament in the Psalms* (Atlanta: John Knox, 1981), 65, 70.

108. Ogden, "Joel 4," 103. The assurance-oracle section in Joel 3–4 (Eng.: 2:28 – 3:21) contains various logical units and forms. For example, the oracles of judgment against foreign nations here function as part of the divine assurance. See Ogden, *Hope*, 11.

of Joel has given the prophet's oracles a developed literary form and has structured them according to a definite pattern, but it still preserves the thrust of actual oracles of assurance Joel delivered during the crises he experienced.

Thus, the book of Joel reflects the course of the actual proceedings of a lament liturgy in the central cult, undertaken when apocalyptic doom threatened Yehud. The picture of the activity of a cult prophet in 2 Chronicles 20 helps clarify the *Sitz-im-Leben* here. As in Joel 1:14, Judah gathered to the temple to seek the help of YHWH in a time of national crisis (2 Chron. 20:4). According to 2 Chronicles 20:14, the Spirit of YHWH came upon a Levite who, in vv. 15-17, utters an oracle of salvation. A cultic functionary is seen taking the lead in predicting YHWH's victory. His oracle proved true: v. 28 pictures the victory celebration at the temple after YHWH defeats Israel's enemies.

The Relationship of Joel to the Zadokite Priesthood

Unfortunately, the book of Joel reveals nothing about Joel's lineage or background beyond his father's name, פתואל ("Pethuel"), which occurs only in Joel 1:1. Nevertheless, based on the above evidence, it is clear that Joel's views, station, and functions were within the central cult of his society. He was a temple professional with an important position, possibly even a priest.[109]

If he was a priest, given his role as temple officiant and his postexilic temple setting, he was probably of the Zadokite branch.[110] Joel's many important resonances with texts identified as Zadokite works in previous chapters support this inference. Chief among these texts is Ezekiel. Joel drew on Ezekiel's oracles of the Day of YHWH (for example, Ezekiel 7 and 30) and made specific use of Ezekiel's expectation of a coming assault by a northern army (Ezekiel 38–39).[111] As shown above, this Ezekiel

---

109. As Mowinckel observed, on some occasions priest and temple prophet were one and the same person (*Psalms,* 2:58). Joel is not distinguishing himself from the priests at Joel 1:13 and 2:17. Recall that Zechariah, a priest, also addressed priests as a group (Zech. 7:5).

110. Issue is taken with those writers, following Mowinckel, who assume Second Temple cultic prophets were restricted to the levitical group. Mowinckel argued that in the Second Temple, the cult prophets were demoted into the ranks of the Levites as singers (*Psalmenstudien III,* 17f.). See also Johnson, *Ancient Israel,* 72; and *Israel's Psalmody,* 174. As argued in the preceding chapter, Zechariah was both Zadokite priest and cult prophet. Joel may also have had both roles.

111. See pp. 172–180 above, and Zimmerli, *Ezekiel 2,* 321.

influence was an important reason why Joel saw a harbinger of the apocalyptic Day of YHWH in the locust and drought desolations.

Other idioms and language in Joel further suggest his special dependence on Ezekiel. For example, Joel 2:3 refers to "the garden of Eden" (גן־עדן), a usage found frequently in Ezekiel (Ezek. 28:13; 31:9, 16, 18; 36:35).[112] Joel's use of the noun מראה ("appearance") in an attempt to describe his vision recalls Ezekiel's idiom as well.[113] Joel's concern that God's people not again be a "reproach" (חרפה) among the nations (Joel 2:17, 19) was also stressed in Ezekiel (Ezek. 36:15; compare 22:4; 34:29). Israel had undergone its scattering among the nations (Joel 4:2 [Eng.: 3:2]; Ezek. 34:6; 36:19; 38:8; compare Zech. 2:2 [Eng.: 1:19]); now the nations should be punished for dissevering God's land (Joel 4:2 [Eng.: 3:2]; Ezek. 35:10; 36:1-5). As a final example, note that Joel 3:1 (Eng.: 2:28) adheres to the view of Ezekiel 39:28-29 that God will pour out God's Spirit on Israel in the end times, creating the ultimate union between the people and God.[114]

Although Joel was clearly a student of Ezekiel's prophecy, he cannot be identified as a specifically Ezekielian Zadokite. The language and style of Joel are not those of an epigone of Ezekiel, and Joel even differs from Ezekiel on some points. It is better to compare the Joel group to the Zecharian Zadokites. While employing Ezekielian language and motifs, Zechariah's followers formed a distinct group with alliances beyond the circle of Ezekiel's followers, who appear to have been somewhat intransigent.

Like Joel's group, the Zechariah circle drew on Ezekiel. Zechariah 12:10 reflects Ezekiel's motif of the pouring out of the Spirit just as Joel 3:1 (Eng.: 2:28) does. Ezekiel's motif of a temple spring (Ezek. 47:1) is also taken up by both Joel (Joel 4:18 [Eng.: 3:18]) and the Zechariah

---

112. Adalbert Merx argued from this that Joel was a student of Ezekiel (*Die Prophetie des Joel und ihre Ausleger* [Halle a. S.: Verlag der Buchhandlung des Waisenhauses, 1879], 65).

113. See Ezek. 1:5, 13, 14, 16, 26, 27, 28; 8:2, 4; 10:1, 9, 10; 11:24; 23:15, 16; 40:3; 41:21; 42:11; 43:3.

114. Thus, Zimmerli writes, "Here too Joel, which is related in its terminology to [Ezek] 39:29, will carry further the proclamation of salvation found in the book of Ezekiel (3:1ff)" (*Ezekiel 2*, 321). Also note Blenkinsopp's statement: "The closest parallels to this word about the re-creative powers of the divine Spirit [Joel 3:1-2 (Eng.: 2:28-29)] are to be found in the address of Ezekiel, or one of his disciples, to a defeated and dispirited people in exile (Ezek 39:29; 36:26; 37:1-14)" (*History of Prophecy*, 258). On Joel's acceptance of Ezekiel's linkage of prophecy and God's spirit (Ezek. 2:2; 8:3; 11:5; 37:1), see R. Wilson, *Prophecy and Society*, 261.

circle (Zech. 13:1; 14:8).[115] Because Zechariah and Joel both draw on Ezekiel but also adopt the views of other groups, one might hypothesize that their circles shared a closer discourse with each other than with Ezekiel's tradents. In support of the closer association of the Joel group with the followers of Zechariah than those of Ezekiel, one might note that the view of Jerusalem's holiness in Joel 4:17 (Eng.: 3:17) is closer to the conception of holiness of the Zechariah group (Zech. 2:5; 9:8; 14:20-21) than to the hard-line Zadokite view of Ezekiel 43:12.[116]

Despite the evidence suggesting that the Joel and Zechariah circles overlapped, differences of emphasis in their respective traditions mitigate against equating them. Thus, Joel differs from Zechariah in not mentioning a messiah.[117] Joel and Zechariah also differ in their statements about visions in the new age. Joel 3:1 (Eng.: 2:28) views visionary activity positively, while Zechariah 13:4 predicts that future prophets will be ashamed of their visions.[118]

Based on this discussion, the Joel group should be considered as one circle of Zadokite priests and their associates controlling the temple in Jerusalem. Although they were closer to the Zechariah group than to the Zadokite hard-liners who bore Ezekiel's prophecies, they cannot be identified with either. One can imagine the threat the drought and locust plague posed for these central priests. Because they were among those holding religious authority over society at that time, other groups within Yehud could have blamed them for the contemporary calamities.

Arena Class and Social Background

The wider social environment of the Joel group was the same as that of the Zechariah millennial group: a class A arena. The millennial group

---

115. On the basis of such evidence, Kapelrud concludes that "the Joel as well as the Zechariah traditions belong approximately to the same circles, associated with the temple in Jerusalem" (*Joel Studies*, 129).

116. Note here that Joel 4:17 (Eng.: 3:17) and Zech. 14:21 are also related in that both exclude those outside the cultus from the sacred city.

117. Joel 2:23 does not seem to reflect a messianic expectation as is sometimes alleged. Zechariah 14 does not mention a messiah either, however, and it is possible that some groups of Zadokites in the late Persian period did not stress this common secondary feature of apocalyptic worldviews.

118. Note, however, that comparison of Ezek. 39:29 and 13:1-23 indicates that both positions could have been held within one group. A group can attack what it views as unclean or idolatrous prophecy or ecstasy without condemning all such activity. See the discussion in Kapelrud, *Joel Studies*, 135.

of Joel held central power within an endogenous environment. As with the endogenous arena of the Zechariah group, the Persians did not oppose the Yehudites during Joel's time. Indeed, the Persian Empire provided for the community's peaceful existence. Wolff notes that in the arena of Joel, "as part of the smoothly functioning Persian Empire, the community is no longer troubled by external unrest."[119] One major difference between the social arenas of Joel and Zechariah must be emphasized, however. Whereas the Zechariah group was not generated or affected by a crisis, crises clearly helped motivate the worldview of Joel. The role of this factor in Joel's sociology must now be elaborated.

Significant new light is shed on the book of Joel by study of sociological parallels where millennialism is associated with plagues or crises. Many such sociological parallels are available for study. Thus, Norman Cohn lists the following cases where millennialism followed upon disaster:

> The plagues that preluded the First Crusade and the flagellant movements of 1260, 1348–9, 1391 and 1400; the famines that preluded the First and Second Crusades and the popular crusading movements of 1309–20, the flagellant movement of 1296, the movements around Eon and the pseudo-Baldwin; [and] the spectacular rise in prices that preluded the revolution at Münster.[120]

I argued in chapter 2 that one should look for positive motivations of millennial groups, rather than deprivation causes. In the case of the millennialism of Joel, this means rejecting a deprivation interpretation of the current desolations. The crises in Joel were not sufficiently prolonged for a

---

119. Wolff, *Joel*, 5. Similarly, Hanson places Joel after the reforms of Ezra and Nehemiah, which "had the effect of ushering in a period in which the Judean community dwelt securely under the local leadership of its Zadokite priests and the more distant sovereignty of the Persian crown" (*People Called*, 312).

120. Norman Cohn, *The Pursuit of the Millennium* (New York: Oxford University Press, 1970), 282. Cohn also notes that: "The greatest wave of millenarian excitement, one which swept through *the whole of society,* was precipitated by the most universal natural disaster of the Middle Ages, the Black Death" (ibid., emphasis added). Also see Cohn's "Medieval Millenarism: Its Bearing on the Comparative Study of Millenarian Movements," in *Millennial Dreams in Action: Essays in Comparative Study,* ed. S. Thrupp (The Hague: Mouton, 1962), 34; Yonina Talmon, "Millenarism" [sic], in *The International Encyclopedia of the Social Sciences* (New York: Macmillan Co. and Free Press, 1968), 10:354; Weston La Barre, "Materials for a History of Studies of Crisis Cults: A Bibliographic Essay," *Current Anthropology* 12 (1971): 15; and Wayne Suttles, "The Plateau Prophet Dance among the Coast Salish," *Southwestern Journal of Anthropology* 13 (1957): 392.

deprivation matrix to develop.[121] Even if more time had been involved, interpreting the drought and plague in Joel as causes of deprivation would not account for Joel 2:20 and its linking of Joel's crises to Ezekiel's end-time "northern army" (הצפוני).[122]

The language of Joel 2:20 implies that in Joel's case, crises touched off beliefs and fears in Joel's group for which its members were already predisposed. The current desolations pictured in Joel 1:2-12 were a positive motivating catalyst that acted on a group already expecting the eschaton on the basis of their studies of Ezekiel and Zechariah.[123] In other words, the crises were an eye-opener or portent: on the basis of the drought and plague, the eschaton was believed to have entered the group's field of vision.

The Savonarola movement in Florence, in which written and oral apocalyptic traditions formed an important basis for the rise of apocalyptic expectations during a crisis, provides an instructive sociological parallel.[124] As in the case of Joel, by Savonarola's time there was an important central deposit of eschatological tradition that expected Florentine leadership of the world in a coming age. The upheavals he experienced resonated with

---

121. For example, ten years of drought and famine and five years of plague preceded millennialism in some areas at the time of the First Crusade of 1095 (see Weston La Barre, *The Ghost Dance: Origins of Religion* [Garden City, N.Y.: Double-day, 1970], 255). Similarly, it was a prolonged drought, which had caused wide-spread famine, that led Solares' Argentinean millennial group to revolt against European rule (see Vittorio Lanternari, *The Religions of the Oppressed*, trans. L. Sergio [New York: Knopf, 1963], 182). Something other than the pent-up frustration that can be allowed in these two cases seems to be going on in Joel.

122. Cf. the discussion of Gressmann, *Der Messias*, 137.

123. See Wanke, "Prophecy and Psalms," 176. Lorenz Dürr argues that Ezekiel's picture of an end-time assault engendered Joel's reflex. In Joel, all it took was a locust swarm to fall over the land in order for fear of the great enemy from the north to strike people's hearts (*Die Stellung des Propheten Ezechiel in der Israelitisch-Jüdischen Apokalyptik*, Alttestamentliche Abhandlungen 9:1, ed. J. Nikel [Münster: Aschendorffschen Verlagsbuchhandlung, 1923], 99).

124. See the discussions of this movement in previous chapters and Donald Weinstein, "Millenarianism in a Civic Setting: The Savonarola Movement in Florence," in *Millennial Dreams in Action*, 194–203. Note that it is usually those of the upper strata of society who have the education and time to synthesize ideas from the writings and traditions of the past into new apocalyptic understandings (cf. the discussion in chapter 3, n. 107 above). Joel's status and his access to Jerusalem's priestly library put him in such a position (see n. 73 above).

Savonarola's study of these traditions. Like Joel, disposed by these upheavals, he drew heavily on the language and metaphors of previous apocalyptic writers in synthesizing a vision of the coming course of events.

Other cross-cultural comparisons help specify the role of the drought and plague in Joel. Such comparisons reveal that millennial groups often look for portents as harbingers of the end. Take the example of the nineteenth-century millennial cult among the Xhosa in South Africa noted in chapter 2. This cult held that two suns in the sky, a great darkness, and a violent gale would precede the end.[125] Similarly, the Ghost Dance movements expected catastrophes such as earthquakes, landslides, and storms before the coming of the new world.[126]

When such anticipated upheavals occur, groups can be shocked into expecting doomsday. For example, Cohn notes that in the flagellant movements of the thirteenth and fourteenth centuries, plagues boosted society's acceptance of their apocalyptic message.[127] Indeed, the first flagellant movements in Italy arose in the wake of a famine in 1258 and the outbreak of the plague in 1259. Cohn concludes that the famine and plague heralded the larger end-time crisis for the flagellants. "These afflictions were felt to be but a prelude to a final and overwhelming catastrophe."[128] By the same token, a crisis can inspire a millennial catalyst figure to announce that the end has arrived. This was the case with Konrad Schmid, the messiah of a fourteenth-century millennial group in central Germany. Cohn states, "It may well have been the particularly severe epidemic of 1368 which inspired Schmid to announce that the Last Judgement would be held and the Millennium begin in the following year."[129]

Joel's belief in end-time portents is clear from his use of the term מופת ("wonder/portent") in Joel 3:3 (Eng.: 2:30). As argued in detail above, as early as Joel 1:15 the drought and locust crises were seen as a portent of the Day of YHWH. Gressmann writes that just as screeching sea gulls forewarn of a nearing violent storm at sea, locusts announced to Joel the *Endkatastrophe*.[130] The apocalyptic texts that Joel studied expected crises

---

125. See Bryan R. Wilson, *Magic and the Millennium* (New York: Harper & Row, 1973), 239.

126. See Kenelm Burridge, *New Heaven, New Earth: A Study of Millenarian Activities* (New York: Schocken, 1969), 78; and Thomas W. Overholt, *Prophecy in Cross-Cultural Perspective: A Sourcebook for Biblical Researchers* (Atlanta: Scholars Press, 1986), 130.

127. Cohn, *Pursuit*, 144.

128. Ibid., 128.

129. Ibid., 144.

130. Gressmann, *Der Messias*, 135.

and chaos before the new age. When the severe crises came, they convinced Joel that his group was living in the last days.

It is not only the oppressed or those on the margins of society that can be shaken into millennialism by plagues and catastrophes.[131] As was the case with Joel's group, millennialism can also be catalyzed among the upper echelons of a society in this way. For example, consider the Spiritual Liberty millennial group that spread in northern France and Belgium in the sixteenth century. The outbreak of plague in Antwerp in 1530 drew in new members for this group from several strata of society, including upper-level figures. Cohn writes, "Wealthy merchants and even the jeweler of the French king Francis I were to be found amongst the followers who contributed funds."[132] In Mendieta's Spanish Franciscan millennialism, the catalyzing effect of plagues was on the Spanish colonizers, not the suffering natives. Millions of natives died from contagious diseases brought by the Spaniards.[133] But in the midst of these plagues it was the Spaniard Mendieta, a figure predisposed to interpret such crises as a harbinger of doomsday, who was filled with a view of apocalyptic doom.[134] Mendieta wrote, "Doubtless our God is filling up the throne-chairs in Heaven with Indians, so as soon to end the world."[135]

Any idea that apocalyptic expectations are an escape or a compensation for present frustrations is untenable in the millennial social arena being discussed. In this type of arena, desolation does not lead to fantasy's wishes but is a harbinger igniting latent fears.[136] The eschaton is not hoped for but feared as the catastrophic culmination of the experienced famines or

131. Contrast Cohn's generalizations in *Pursuit*, 58–60, 281–82.

132. Ibid., 170.

133. John L. Phelan notes that "particularly severe declines occurred during the great epidemics of 1576–1579 and 1595–1596" (*The Millennial Kingdom of the Franciscans in the New World*, 2d ed. [Berkeley and Los Angeles: University of California Press, 1970], 92).

134. Mendieta was working within a tradition that expected "the great time of troubles of the Apocalypse . . . to precede the establishment of the millennial kingdom on earth" (ibid., 104).

135. Quoted in ibid., 94. Phelan concludes, "The demographic crisis of the 1590's seemed fresh evidence to some of the mendicant chroniclers that the New World was in fact the End of the World" (ibid., 96, cf. 102).

136. Fear that the cosmic chaos of the eschaton might engulf one's group is not an unusual millennial belief. For example, at one point in Wodziwob's Ghost Dance of 1870, it was feared that the Native Americans would be destroyed along with the white man in the coming end-time cataclysm. See Lanternari, *Religions of the Oppressed*, 132.

plagues. A case in point is the thirteenth-century Italian millennial flagellant movements mentioned above. Cohn writes, "During the flagellant processions people behaved as though they feared that as punishment for their sins God was about to destroy them all by earthquake and by fire from on high."[137]

Certainly, the Day of YHWH was feared and lamented, not "wished for," in the millennialism behind the book of Joel. Joel's first reference to the Day of YHWH in Joel 1:15 responds to its nearness with the interjection "Alas!" (אההּ). Further, Joel fears that the Day would spell "devastation" (שׁד). It is understandable why Joel faced the Day of YHWH with the fear that it threatened decisive destruction. Even in Ezekiel 39:8, where the Day is shown as directed basically against Gog, Gog comes as an immense threat to Jerusalem. In later scenarios of the last battle, Jerusalem is more than merely threatened. In fact, Zechariah 14:1-3 directs the Day of YHWH against Israel first, and only then does the text make clear that the Day means destruction for the attacking nations.

Of course, the second part of Joel hopes that many Yehudites will escape apocalyptic destruction as a remnant (see item 6 in the list above). Even a group holding this hope, however, would not have wished to "endure" (כול) the refining and purifying trials of the end times (Joel 2:11; compare Mal. 3:23 [Eng.: 4:5]; Zech. 13:7-9). Thus, the data of Joel do not support the idea that apocalyptic worldviews are delusions or compensatory mechanisms arising in the face of lacks and frustrations. An expectation of immeasurably worse crises to come does not bring the emotional and psychological relief from present troubles postulated by deprivation theory.

A Sociology of Unification Rather than Alienation

Finally, the evidence of the book of Joel contradicts the view, now common among biblical scholars, that a sociology of hostile factions formed the social matrix of the emergence of proto-apocalyptic literature in the postexilic period.[138] Plöger, Wolff, and Hanson are among those who see an escha-

---

137. Cohn, *Pursuit,* 128. The groups interpreted famine and plague as meaning that God was angry with human obstinacy and had decided to kill everything on earth (ibid., 130).

138. To review, Plöger finds the origins of apocalypticism in factional conflict with those at the center of society. Hanson has also stressed a social arena where a group is oppressed by those in power as the background for the "dawn" of apocalyptic. Thus, e.g., Hanson writes, "It is understandable that the group which gains ascendancy increasingly emphasizes continuity with existing structures and the pragmatic application of traditional teachings to the affairs of community and cult, whereas the oppressed group appeals to a vision of divine

tological opposition party behind the writings of Joel. An alternative possibility, however, was outlined in chapter 3. At times, millennialism supports central morality and authority, and indeed rallies various factions around the central leadership. The millennial catalyst figure may even provide a focus of unity for previously hostile groups. Bryan Wilson states, "It requires supernatural sanction, of the type that the prophet embodies, to draw together otherwise dissociated or mutually hostile groups for common action."[139] Examples of this phenomenon include the millennial movement among the Lau Nuer, the Pueblo revolt of 1690, the Delaware Prophet movement, and the millennial movement surrounding Tenskwatawa. The sociology of Joel parallels this type of millennial activity.

There is little, if any, evidence of factional strife in the book of Joel. Joel has few harsh words for any group within the community. Even in Joel 2:12-14, the emphasis is not so much on repentance as on the need for a total turning to God for aid.[140] Of all of Yehud's groups, it is hardest to imagine that Joel attacked those in charge of the cultus. Plöger, Wolff, Hanson, and Redditt cannot be right.[141] There is no evidence of alienation from the temple establishment in Joel, quite the contrary. Joel relies on central-cultic functions as the primary means of dealing with the looming apocalyptic crisis.

Not only does Joel avoid alienating other groups, he warns the entire community of the present threat and includes everyone in his attempt to find God's salvation. Joel has no apocalyptic secret; he wants the whole community to know that the Day of YHWH is near. Thus, the entire populace is addressed at Joel 1:2, and Joel 1:14 calls for "all the inhabitants of the land" (כל ישבי הארץ) to be gathered to the temple. Joel's inclusiveness is also seen at Joel 2:16, where no group is deemed excusable from the assembly. Even the smallest infants and honeymoon couples are summoned.[142]

---

intervention which will supplant existing structures with a radically new order" (*Dawn*, 260).

139. B. Wilson, *Magic*, 224.

140. See Ogden, "Joel 4," 105; *Hope*, 11; and Wanke, "Prophecy and Psalms," 177. Wolff notes the absence of any reference to specific transgressions. Rather, the return is expressed with customary, central-cult rituals (*Joel*, 49).

141. Redditt argues that Joel found the cultus at a standstill in the midst of catastrophe (Joel 1:9) ("Peripheral Prophecy," 235). The context indicates, however, that it was the catastrophe itself that caused the lamentable standstill. If Joel had indeed thought that the priests and elders had abdicated leadership (Redditt, "Peripheral Prophecy," 236, 240), the book would contain indications of polemic.

142. Wolff states that vv. 15-17 "unequivocally summon all segments of the population and its leadership, without exception, to make lamentation and penance" (*Joel*, 5, cf. 51). Also see Prinsloo, *Theology*, 60.

Just as all were included in Joel's call for cultic response, all Yehudites are invited to experience salvation. Joel 3:1-5 (Eng.: 2:28-32) makes clear that the Spirit will be poured out on the entire community, "on all flesh" (עַל־כָּל־בָּשָׂר, v. 1 [Eng.: 2:28]).[143] Plöger and Redditt cannot be correct in arguing for a limitation of salvation to a peripheral sect here.[144] Verses 1-2 (Eng.: 2:28-29) include and validate all members of the community.[145] Verse 5 (Eng.: 2:32) states that "whoever calls" (כֹּל אֲשֶׁר־יִקְרָא) will be delivered.[146] The appearance of a remnant concept in this verse does not mean that the remnant must be equated with an underground conventicle or peripheral group. There is no *a priori* reason why a remnant cannot include those from all strata of a society including the center.

143. Redditt is incorrect to argue that in Joel 3:1-5 (Eng.: 2:28-32) "charisma replaces office," validating those whom he sees as the peripheral authors of the pericope ("Peripheral Prophecy," 232–33). As has been argued, the idea, traceable to Weber, that charisma is incompatible with the central-priestly office is no longer tenable. Cf. Mayes's conclusion: "The innovatory power of charisma does not necessarily imply social marginality" (*Old Testament,* 76; see Berger, "Charisma," 950). Redditt must be criticized for preserving Hanson's priest/prophet dichotomy, thus not allowing for such phenomena as charismatic priests. He states that the self-identity of the Joel group was "prophetic, not priestly" ("Peripheral Prophecy," 236).

144. As noted above, Plöger interprets Joel 3 (Eng.: 2:28-32) as meaning a hidden division of Israel is being prepared: "The sign of the outpouring of the spirit which characterizes eschatological Israel is also implicitly connected with separation and cleavage." Thus, the promise here applies only to "the Israel that has responded to the eschatological faith and considers the day of Yahweh as an eschatological entity" (*Theocracy,* 103). Plöger concludes that the section thus points to "a conventicle-type limitation" (*Theocracy,* 104). See also Redditt, "Peripheral Prophecy," 233.

145. See Wolff, *Joel,* 67. It is "extremely doubtful," Allen writes, "whether the passage really speaks of the limiting of God's ultimate blessing to a group" (*Joel,* 27). A similar inclusive but nationalistic view of apocalyptic salvation was held by colonizing millennial groups in the sixteenth-century "Age of Discovery." Phelan writes, "The idea that Spain would soon inaugurate the millennial kingdom on earth by uniting under one universal crown all the races of mankind was the prospect that dazzled explorers, statesmen, and ecclesiastics alike" (*Franciscans,* 107). As in the case of Joel 3 (Eng.: 2:28-32), however, this universalism was welded to particularism. Among other groups, the Turks and Old World Jews were not expected to convert.

146. The use of the idiom employed here in the psalms (Pss. 79:6; 80:18; 105:1; 116:4, 13, and 17) suggests the language of Joel 3:5 (Eng.: 2:32) means finding YHWH through the cult.

In summary, the evidence shows that the sociology behind Joel is a millennialism in which groups draw together, rather than clash. The locust and drought calamities indicated that something had gone terribly wrong for the exilic community, but its central priests did not blame other groups in this time of disaster. There is no evidence of polemic in Joel. Perhaps the act of blaming would have given another faction recognition, or implied that they had power in a way unacceptable to the Joel group. Alternatively, perhaps the common threat forced the various factions to put aside their differences.

Instead of blaming other groups for the crises, Joel used his role as millennial catalyst figure to rally everyone behind the Zadokites' program. Joel preempted disillusionment with the temple authorities with his message that the crises were not a reason for hopelessness and loss of confidence in the Jerusalem cult officials, but an omen of the imminent Day of YHWH. Since the Day could mean apocalyptic doom for Yehud, everyone must join the effort in the temple cult to find God's salvation. With this message, Joel unified his society and validated the authority of its establishment.[147] Joel's message thus functioned as a strong support for the Zadokites.

147. For this phenomenon within millennialism, see B. Wilson, *Magic,* 223–24.

7

Conclusion

The proto-apocalyptic biblical texts considered in chapters 4–6 are integral parts of literary works produced by central priests and exhibit definite central-priestly language and ideology. These texts are clearly proto-apocalyptic literature produced by the Zadokites at the center of exilic and postexilic Israelite society. Recognizing the actual nature of these texts, this study reinterpreted them by comparing power-holding millennial groups from other societies and cultures.

This study suggests that deprivation theory should be abandoned as an overarching principle of interpretation for apocalypticism.[1] This negative conclusion does *not* mean that apocalypticism lacks a characteristic sociology. Millennial groups exhibit clear identifying characteristics. It must be stressed, however, that these family resemblances occur among millennial groups, not among the social contexts for such groups. Thus, the sociological definition of apocalypticism should be limited to the group level, making it more accurate and precise. It is the social phenomenon of the millennial group that forms the *Sitz-im-Leben* for (proto-)apocalyptic literature.

1. In place of deprivation theory, the causation of millennialism should be understood in terms of predisposing factors and a process of apocalyptic catalysis. Millennial groups are catalyzed when a group's consciousness is expanded so that group members place themselves within a cosmic drama that is rapidly drawing to an end. This is often accomplished by reactualizing the group's mythic *Urzeit* archetypes within a linear view of history. Alternatively, catalysis is accomplished when apocalyptic beliefs already latent in a group's tradition undergo recrudescence due to factors such as crises viewed as end-time portents.

Millennial groups have a distinctive sociology, but also reflect the vary-ing influences of their members' social stratum and their society's place in relation to other peoples. Clarifying this shows that millennialism can oc-cur in a range of social matrices more varied and complex than usually allowed. In light of these facts, the deprivation hypothesis was replaced in this book with a more critical understanding of the variety of social, eco-nomic, and political conditions that millennial groups reflect. Although some social arenas harboring millennial groups involve marginalization, particular interest was taken in those milieus of millennialism that do not involve such conditions.

The typological variety of millennial groups suggests that apocalyptic literature is not limited to any one kind of tradition-stream. Rather, apoca-lypticism can arise in groups of different traditions whose leaders have varying roles in society. Thus, although some millennial groups are run by prophets, others are headed by priests.

Although millennialism sometimes involves a struggle between fac-tions, it may also create more unity and cooperation between various groups by providing an apocalyptic worldview as a common focus. In ad-dition, millennial groups, including those in power, may change with time. A group may routinize as its worldview becomes more mundane or radi-calize when its apocalyptic expectations become more fervent. Although overemphasized in discussions of the causation of millennialism, stressors and tensions may figure importantly in promoting radicalization of millen-nial groups.

As groups radicalize or routinize, changes in their social composition and alliances with other groups are possible. In some cases, members of a millennial group may form new alliances when they discover new com-monalities with other groups in their society. Sometimes group members even abandon central positions in society because of growing differences with their colleagues.

Developing better understandings of millennial groups established a basis for moving forward in interpreting Ezekiel 38–39, Zechariah, and Joel. In analyzing these texts, investigation proceeded from an examination of their proto-apocalyptic and central-priestly nature to a discussion of their social background. Exegesis controlled the use of comparative mate-rial. In each case, the proto-apocalyptic and central-priestly characteristics of the texts emerged as two dimensions of a single social setting. Several conclusions can be drawn.

Because Ezekiel 38–39 and Zechariah 1–8 come from the late exilic and early postexilic periods, modern scholarship's emphasis on an Israelite social background for the rise of Jewish apocalypticism is reaffirmed. The early appearance of proto-apocalyptic literature means it was not alien or decadent within biblical tradition. Although Persian and Hellenistic influences affected its development, Israelite groups are the source of Jewish apocalypticism, rather than Iran and Zoroastrianism. The discovery that some proto-apocalyptic literature arose among scholarly priests reinforces this conclusion about the native roots of apocalypticism.[2] These conservative groups studied their own traditions, not foreign ones.

Confirming the Israelite origins of apocalypticism, some biblical proto-apocalyptic literature was produced within the social center of exilic and postexilic Israelite society. Not all Israelite proto-apocalyptic texts stem from antiestablishment groups on the periphery of society. Although the "conventicle" interpretation may work for some texts, it can no longer be generalized to all.[3]

Members of the millennial groups examined were not only officials but also priests. Approaches tracing Israelite apocalypticism to the prophetic side of a supposed priest/prophet dichotomy should thus be held suspect. In fact, the complexity of postexilic society is such that the labels *prophet* and *priest* do not adequately define its groups. Thus, in the examination of the proto-apocalyptic texts, it was not deemed sufficient to stop at their designation as priestly. They were also assigned to specific phratries. All three texts were ascribed to the Zadokite priesthood.

Analysis of the group programs behind the proto-apocalyptic texts examined supports the conclusion that the groups that advocated them were composed of priestly officials. These programs upheld the established order of society. Thus, while the Ezekiel millennial group waited passively for God to destroy evil, its members planned a massive postbattle burial effort to cleanse the land for temple-cult rituals. Later, the millennial group program of Zechariah 1–8 included rebuilding the temple, reinstating the central cult, and enforcing society's central legal codes. Finally, at a time of national crisis, the Joel group turned to the ritual of the central cult for a millennial group program to avert apocalyptic doom.

Analysis of Zadokite millennial groups also reveals much about how they changed over time. Group radicalization was often accompanied not by abandonment of temple-establishment ideology, but by stronger

---

2. See Hartmut Gese, "Anfang und Ende der Apokalyptik, dargestellt am Sacharjabuch," *ZTK* 70 (1973): 40–41.

3. It has not been argued that all biblical proto-apocalyptic material was written by Zadokite priests or even that it was all produced from the center of society. The Hebrew Bible contains evidence of millennial groups that existed in several different social arenas.

expression of it. Radicalization of the Gog pericope was accompanied by an increasing focus on central-priestly issues (see Ezek. 39:11-16). Zechariah 14, which also represents a highly radicalized millennial stage, similarly exhibits more central-priestly concern than any other chapter in the Zechariah corpus.

Finally, inquiry into the social milieus of the groups examined yields definite results. These three Zadokite millennial groups fit best in arena classes A and C as summarized in the following chart:[4]

Chart 3. Placement of Zadokite Millennial Groups

	Endogenous Condition	Exogenous Condition	
		dominating/ colonizing	dominated/ colonized
	Class A	*Class B*	*Class C*
Group is Central in Own Society	Zechariah 1–8 Joel		Ezekiel 38–39
	Class D	*Class E*	*Class F*
Group is Peripheral in Own Society	The Zechariah group at the end of its career (?)		

The arena of the group that wrote Ezekiel 38–39 is closest to class C because of the group's continuing captivity in Babylon. This classification should be qualified, however, by noting the lack of evidence that Ezekiel and his priestly circle suffered or were persecuted in the exile. Also observe that the social arena of the Ezekiel millennial group changed over time. When the group returned to Yehud, its arena was no longer exogenous.

Although the Persians governed Yehud when the Zechariah millennial group was active, they exercised a rather distant sovereignty. Further, rather than causing the Yehudites unrest, the Persians supported Zechariah's restoration program. Thus, the millennial group behind Zechariah 1–8 can be assigned a class A arena. The continuing Zechariah group may have left this arena eventually, however. The anti-shepherd polemic of Zechariah 9–14 may indicate that the group ultimately separated from the civic estab-

---

4. For an explanation of this chart, see the discussion of Chart 2 in chapter 3.

lishment and those priests who cooperated with it. At the end of its career, the Zechariah group may thus have had a class D arena.

Although active at a later period, the Joel circle was part of the same priestly establishment of Persian-governed Yehud as the Zechariah group. Inasmuch as Persia continued to provide for the community's peaceful existence, this group's arena can also be considered class A. Although Joel and Zechariah 1–8 have the same arena class, the social background of Joel is different because it involved crises. A famine and plague heralded apocalyptic judgment for the Joel group.

Millennialism and the Zadokites in the Postexilic Period

Investigation of the individual Zadokite proto-apocalyptic texts provides for some broader observations about the postexilic Zadokites and instances of millennialism among them. There is insufficient evidence to outline the history of the Persian-period priestly leadership, but something of its ideas and programs are known and several instances where groups within it became millennial have been discovered.

The school of Ezekiel is a starting point for elucidating both the Zadokite priesthood and Zadokite millennialism. It was from the Zadokite priests in Jerusalem that this group's founder was deported — a fact confirmed by Ezekiel's resonances with H. Redactional analysis of Ezekiel shows this school's predictable hieratic interests. It was especially concerned with Israel's sacral worship and with cultic purity. Because millennialism appeared in the history of this school, it provides a paradigm of central-priestly apocalypticism. The Zadokite concerns of the Ezekiel group were not jettisoned but emphasized when this circle became a millennial group.

Since millennialism occurred within Ezekiel's group, an apocalyptic heritage within their own priestly tradition informed later Zadokites. When groups of Zadokites physically began restoration efforts, their driving vision contained strong elements of this legacy (see Zech. 1:14; 4:6; 6:8). Later, when crises threatened the temple community, the Zadokites' understanding of their situation again stemmed from this source (see Joel 1:15; 2:20).

Millennialism recurred among the Zadokites when the Zechariah group spurred on the reconstruction that culminated in a rebuilt temple in 515 B.C.E. The apocalyptic vision behind the group's temple-rebuilding efforts was heavily influenced by both prophetic and apocalyptic material in Ezekiel. Tensions between Ezekiel and Zechariah, however, suggest these two books preserve differing Zadokite reconstruction programs. Ezekiel 42–43 emphasizes the themes of separation and gradation of holiness, whereas Zechariah 1–8 envisions YHWH permeating Jerusalem. Further, a strong distinction between Zadokites and other priestly groups is present in Ezekiel 40–48 but not in Zechariah 1–8. Finally, Zechariah differs from Ezekiel in emphasizing a high priest.

Such tensions suggest the existence of Zadokite subgroups: the Zadokite priesthood must be considered heterogeneous. Ironically, though Ezekiel's Zadokite lineage is easiest to document, Ezekiel's tradents should probably be considered merely a conservative offshoot of the Zadokite phratry.

The book of Joel attests to still another millennial outburst among the Zadokites, this time from a period after the temple was rebuilt. Like Zechariah, Joel clearly treasured Ezekiel's prophecy. Indeed, Ezekiel's writings helped predispose Joel's group for millennialism. Nevertheless, Joel's circle probably represents yet a third Zadokite subgroup beside that of Ezekiel and Zechariah. Unlike Ezekiel, Joel retains repentance as feasible (Joel 2:12-14) and does not stress gradations of holiness for the future Jerusalem (Joel 4:17 [Eng.: 3:17]). Unlike Zechariah, Joel does not emphasize a messiah and views visionary activity as acceptable in the coming age. Thus, although the Joel group probably overlapped with the tradents of Ezekiel and Zechariah, it was socially distinct.

Although Zadokite millennialism was heterogeneous, it is appropriate to summarize here some of the elements of continuity in the different Zadokite proto-apocalyptic texts. Ezekiel's influence was significant in the reappearance of motifs and themes in these texts. For example, Zechariah 12:10 and Joel 3:1 (Eng.: 2:28) both share Ezekiel's motif of the end-time pouring out of God's spirit (Ezek. 39:29). Two other shared motifs may now be described, both of which have a double background in Ezekiel and in the liturgy of a major cultic festival.

All the Zadokite representatives studied emphasize an expectation of an end-time assault on Jerusalem, combining it with the enemy-from-the-north tradition. Ezekiel 38–39 employs the cult's mythical image of the attack of the many nations on Jerusalem (Pss. 2:1-5; 46; 48; and 75 [compare Ps. 65:7]) to depict the judgment at the end of time. Ezekiel's familiarity with the motifs of the temple cult made it natural for him to use this idea of a massive attack against Zion to describe the decisive cosmic event of the end times. Because subsequent Zadokite groups treasured Ezekiel's writings, this motif was mediated into their proto-apocalyptic literature. Thus, in Zechariah 12:1-9, Jerusalem is attacked by the nations of the earth but is defended by the divine warrior. Zechariah 14 again describes how all the nations battle against Jerusalem until defeated by God and the "holy ones." Then, Joel 2:1-11 interprets a locust crisis as a harbinger of the advance of the end-time horde. Joel 4 (Eng.: 3) specifies this threat as the attack of the nations on Jerusalem that Ezekiel and Zechariah envisioned.

A second motif shared by the apocalyptic visions of both Joel and Zechariah is that of agricultural success. Postexilic texts such as Haggai 1:10; Zechariah 10:1; and Joel 1:2-20 all indicate that meteorological and agricultural problems concerned the Yehudites. Since fertility was a problem for the postexilic community, the apocalyptic expectations of their authorities naturally stressed agricultural abundance. Fertility of the land, rain, and bounty are described in Zechariah 8:12 and 14:6-11, 16. The picture of millennial prosperity in Joel 4:18 (Eng.: 3:18) similarly focuses on abundant water and fertility. While the new age promises rain for Israel, her enemies will be blasted by desert conditions (Zech. 14:17; Joel 4:19 [Eng.: 3:19]).

The hope for a perennial temple-stream to irrigate the land is a corollary of this Zadokite agricultural focus. The river of paradise, already associated with the temple mount by the cult's psalms, was promised for the new age by Ezekiel 47:1-12. Zechariah 14:8 (compare Zech. 13:1) and Joel 4:18 (Eng.: 3:18) continue this promise in their visions of the millennial era. According to these visions, Edenlike waters will lead to marvelous fertility for Israel in the eschaton.

Both of the above described motifs relate to the same cultic festival, the Feast of Booths. As discussed, the motif of the nations' attack on Jerusalem and their rout and destruction has often been understood as a cultic myth of the YHWH-enthronement component of this feast. Concerned with fruitful harvests, its liturgy also stressed rain as God's gift (Deut. 16:15; Ps. 65:9-13). Because the Feast of Booths was associated with a vision of YHWH's enthronement and universal reign resulting in Israel's fertility, it is a logical background of the apocalyptic expressions of the Zadokite millennial groups.

This suggested shared view of the importance of the Feast of Booths in Zadokite millennialism is supported by the evidence of Zechariah and Joel. Zechariah 14:16-19 most explicitly references the feast (חג הסכות, v. 16). This text may well draw on the Holiness Code's stress on the feast (Lev. 23:34-43) and on the use of motifs associated with it in Ezekiel 38–39. However, the Zechariah group's own execution of the festival in the postexilic central cult probably influenced them most directly.

Joel not only similarly draws on the motifs of the Feast of Booths but also probably delivered his oracles at the time when this harvest festival should have been taking place. Thus, Joel is upset that the required offerings for the feast (מנחה ונסך, "grain offerings and libations") are unavailable. Also, Joel 1:14 and 2:15 use the term "cultic assembly" (עצרה), which recalls several hieratic texts concerning the feast (Lev. 23:36; Num. 29:35; 2 Chron. 7:7-8). This evidence supports Kathleen S. Nash's view that Joel urged substituting a penitential assembly for the Feast of Booths the year the drought and locusts struck.[5]

Sociological Implications for the Postexilic Period

The conclusions drawn in this book bear significantly on the problem of the relationship of eschatology to the cult in the Persian period. The common notion that the temple cult harbored only a nonfuturistic, realized eschatology appears doubtful. A more critical view of the postexilic cult is needed allowing it sufficient elasticity to have encompassed linear conceptions of time and eschatological perspectives. The temple's cult was even elastic enough to encompass millennialism.[6]

The findings of this book also confirm the importance of scribalism in the postexilic period, especially among priestly circles. Yehudite priestly texts strongly reflect learned activity and systematic study. Zadokite millennialism may have been one factor promoting this phenomenon. Cross-culturally, groups expecting the eschaton try to learn signs signaling the end times and rituals assuring them a place in the new age. A mood of eschatological expectation after the exile similarly led Yehudite millennial groups to turn to their received writings for guidance in these matters. Thus, Zechariah and especially Joel made heavy use of the postexilic heritage of prophetic texts.

Finally, it now appears too simple to characterize the postexilic period as a time rife with factional conflict. The postexilic proto-apocalyptic texts do not all presuppose a matrix of polarization of groups or class strata. Thus, the group behind Zechariah 1–8 used a more pastoral and hortatory approach rather than an indicting and condemning one in dealing with covenant infidelity. Their millennialism did not alienate other groups but rallied various factions around rebuilding the temple cult.

The book of Joel similarly shows no evidence of factional strife or alienation of any groups from the temple establishment. Joel includes the whole community in his summons to lamentation in the temple. Then, when Joel delivers oracles of salvation, the promises are for "all flesh" and "whoever calls." Thus, the sociology behind Joel is a millennialism that is neither caused by alienation nor divides the community. Rather, Joel's message unified his society.

5. See the discussion of Nash's view in chapter 6, n. 79.

6. Hugo Gressmann was thus correct to emphasize the importance of the *Heilspropheten* in the postexilic cult (*Der Messias* [Göttingen: Vandenhoeck & Ruprecht, 1929], 134).

The Place of the Exile in the Rise of Apocalypticism

One final question — a major one — remains. If the deprivations of the loss of nationhood and of the exile are not the key to the rise of Israelite millennialism, why do the biblical proto-apocalyptic texts stem from the postexilic period? Some tentative suggestions can be offered.

First, the presupposition of this question itself is now open to question. Not all proto-apocalyptic texts are intrusions into their contexts from a later, postexilic period. This assumption is often based on the idea that eschatologizing and apocalyptic redaction result from dissonance in a group's worldview when its prophecy fails or is devalued by a hostile group.[7] But this idea is not true of all apocalyptic texts within prophetic books. Some apocalyptic texts were created as part of the original processes that produced such books. Thus, Ezekiel 38–39 was not an incongruent postexilic intrusion into Ezekiel. It arose as part of the original compilation of the book by Ezekiel or his early Zadokite circle. In light of this insight, the proto-apocalyptic texts of other books, such as Isaiah, should be reinvestigated to see if they all presuppose the postexilic period. Similarly, reassessment should be made of the genre of texts (such as Jeremiah 4?) that scholars have hesitated to label proto-apocalyptic because their dates are too early to reflect postexilic factional conflict.

Second, positive motivating factors in the exilic and postexilic periods can be identified that provide a more critical understanding of the rise of apocalypticism than viewing the exile as a deprivation setting. More is involved than new foreign influence on Israelite religion at this time, though this had some effect. The exile involved important additional factors that predisposed some Israelite groups for millennialism. For example, the mere perception of the ending of an era can motivate the rise of millennial groups. Thus, as the year 2000 approaches, there is a greater interest in apocalypticism in our own culture.[8] Similarly, Israel's exile marked the end of an era and raised expectations of coming radical change in the world.

---

7. Robert P. Carroll is a major expositor of this view. Carroll writes, "With its roots in prophecy, apocalyptic became the resolution of the dissonance caused by the lack of fulfillment of prophecy in the early post-exilic period" (*When Prophecy Failed* [New York: Seabury, 1979], 205).

8. Yonina Talmon notes that millennialism abounded in the transition between the end of the Middle Ages and the beginning of modern times ("Millenarism" [sic], *The International Encyclopedia of the Social Sciences* [New York: Macmillan and Free Press, 1968], 10:355). Hillel Schwartz describes how notions of major change can still be a factor catalyzing millennialism today. Thus, Schwartz writes, "The historical myth persists because it seems to many that the year 2,000 will be truly millennial" ("Millenarianism, An Overview," in *The Encyclopedia of Religion*, ed. Mircea Eliade [New York: Macmillan, 1987], 9:530).

The new era brought about by the exile was accompanied by much change for people to absorb, and groups can be predisposed for millennialism by changes in their world. Thus, European revolutions and signs of a general apostasy in England helped pave the way for Irvingite millennialism. In Joel's case, the drought and locust plagues were perceived as so extraordinary that they facilitated a group worldview change. By the same token, the exile must have been a foundation-shaking change. This change in the exiles' world was accompanied by changes in their beliefs and ways of thinking. For example, at this time many people realized their conception of God was too small: YHWH must be more than just a national God working within history. In other words, older worldviews did not account for people's new world-scale consciousness. As a result, they were predisposed for acceptance of a new universe of meaning.

At the same time, like Joel's crises, the exile was a major portent presaging the eschaton. As in Joel, crises can be viewed as harbingers of greater future changes and crises. For some groups, the exile thus appeared as an early sign of a coming worldwide judgment by God, and the restoration looked like a preparation for God's eschatological salvation. In this way, the postexilic period was a time when some groups were predisposed for the rise of millennialism. This period was also a time when the influence of many of the eschatological writings of Israel's earlier prophets made themselves felt in important ways.[9] As in the case of Joel, in the postexilic period even a locust plague could shake groups mining apocalyptic portents out of earlier texts into millennialism.

Stepping back and taking a larger view of the exilic and postexilic periods does not change the assessment of deprivation theory developed in studying Ezekiel 38–39, Zechariah 1–8, and Joel. In both the general and specific cases, there are clear positive factors motivating a worldview change to apocalypticism. A search for deprivations that caused millennialism in these cases is unnecessary.

Avenues for Future Research

The approach taken in this book has further implications for the general study of the apocalyptic texts of the ancient Near Eastern and Mediterranean world. Its constructive paradigms for analysis of millennial groups could

9. See Ezek. 38:17; Zech. 1:4-5; and the references to Joel's practice of citation listed in chapter 6, n. 73 above. As Willem S. Prinsloo observes, eschatological promises of YHWH's judgment of the nations and blessing of Israel must have become highly significant in postexilic times (*The Theology of the Book of Joel* [New York: Walter de Gruyter, 1985], 105, 112).

help clarify the sociology of some of these texts. For example, the sociology of the Akkadian apocalypses should be reexamined in the light of suggestions that some of these texts were written by power-holding groups.[10] The sociology of some Jewish apocalypses might also profitably be reevaluated. The "crisis" behind the *Testament of Abraham,* as an example, may be merely the inevitability of death,[11] and the circles behind *Jubilees* and the *Testament of Moses* were probably not antiestablishment groups.[12]

I have concentrated on Zadokite millennialism, and future examination of the subsequent history of this phenomenon is needed. Such study should of course include continued examination of the Qumran community, which was apparently founded by Zadokites.[13] Evidence such as the Qumran text 4Q Miqṣat Maʿaseh Ha-Torah suggests that these Qumran Zadokites were involved in an inner-establishment dispute. Having withdrawn from the temple's ritual, they were in dialogue with those remaining within Jerusalem's priestly administration over such disputed matters as sacrificial law and ritual purity.[14]

Finally, continued study of how millennial groups change over time would be fruitful. For example, further work is needed on the factors giving rise to apocalyptic pessimism. Future research should question whether changes in group composition and orientation similar to that of the Zechariah group are behind pessimistic literary additions to other apocalyptic works such as Daniel and Revelation.

10. See William Hallo, "Akkadian Apocalypses," *IEJ* 16 (1966): 231–42; and Robert R. Wilson, *Prophecy and Society in Ancient Israel* (Philadelphia: Fortress, 1980), 123.

11. See John J. Collins, *Daniel with an Introduction to Apocalyptic Literature,* FOTL 20 (Grand Rapids, Mich.: Eerdmans, 1984), 22.

12. See George W. E. Nickelsburg, "Social Aspects of Palestinian Jewish Apocalypticism," *Apocalypticism in the Mediterranean World and the Near East,* ed. D. Hellholm (Tübingen: J. C. B. Mohr, 1983), 648.

13. Some Qumran sources refer to the community, or its leaders, as the "Sons of Zadok" (see especially the Damascus Document 3:20 – 4:4). See George W. E. Nickelsburg, *Jewish Literature Between the Bible and the Mishnah* (Philadelphia: Fortress, 1981), 133–34; Jerome Murphy-O'Connor, O.P., "The Judean Desert," in *Early Judaism and its Modern Interpreters,* ed. R. Kraft and G. Nickelsburg (Philadelphia: Fortress; and Atlanta: Scholars Press, 1986), 139–41; and Geza Vermes, *The Dead Sea Scrolls in English* (New York: Penguin, 1962), 63.

14. For now, see Philip R. Davies, "The Social World of Apocalyptic Writings," in *The World of Ancient Israel,* ed. R. E. Clements (Cambridge, England: Cambridge University Press, 1989), 258; and Lawrence H. Schiffman, "The New Halakhic Letter (4QMMT) and the Origins of the Dead Sea Sect," *BA* 53 (1990): 64–73.

Bibliography

Aberle, David F. "A Note on Relative Deprivation Theory as Applied to Millenarian and Other Cult Movements." In *Millennial Dreams in Action: Essays in Comparative Study,* ed. S. Thrupp, 209–14. The Hague: Mouton, 1962.

———. "The Prophet Dance and Reactions to White Contact." *Southwestern Journal of Anthropology* 15 (1959): 74–83.

Ackroyd, Peter R. "Apocalyptic in Its Social Setting." *Int* 30 (1976): 412–15.

———. "Archaeology, Politics and Religion: The Persian Period." *Iliff Review* 39/2 (1982): 5–24.

———. *Exile and Restoration.* OTL. Philadelphia: Westminster, 1968.

———. "Two Old Testament Historical Problems of the Early Persian Period." *JNES* 17 (1958): 13–27.

Adas, Michael. *Prophets of Rebellion: Millenarian Protest Movements against the European Colonial Order.* Chapel Hill: University of North Carolina Press, 1979.

Ahlström, Gosta W. *Joel and the Temple Cult of Jerusalem.* Leiden: Brill, 1971.

Ahroni, Reuben. "The Gog Prophecy and the Book of Ezekiel." HAR 1 (1977): 1–27.

Allan, Graham. "A Theory of Millennialism: The Irvingite Movement as an Illustration." *British Journal of Sociology* 25 (1974): 296–311.

Allen, Leslie C. *The Books of Joel, Obadiah, Jonah and Micah.* NICOT. Grand Rapids, Mich.: Eerdmans, 1976.

Amsler, Samuel. *Aggée, Zacharie, Malachie.* CAT 11c. Paris: Delachaux & Niestlé, 1981.

———. "Zacharie et l'origine de l'apocalyptique." VTSup 22, pp. 227–31. Congress Volume: Uppsala, 1971. Leiden: Brill, 1972.

Anderson, Bernhard W. *Understanding the Old Testament.* Englewood Cliffs, N.J.: Prentice-Hall, 1986.

Anderson, Gary A. *A Time to Mourn, A Time to Dance.* University Park: Pennsylvania State University Press, 1991.

Astour, Michael C. "Ezekiel's Prophecy of Gog and the Cuthean Legend of Naram-Sin." *JBL* 95 (1976): 567–79.

Avigad, Nahman. *Bullae and Seals from a Post-Exilic Judean Archive.* Qedem 4. Jerusalem: Hebrew University Institute of Archaeology, 1976.

Baldwin, Joyce G. *Haggai, Zechariah, Malachi.* London: Tyndale, 1972.

Barber, Bernard. "Acculturation and Messianic Movements." *American Sociological Review* 6 (1941): 663–69.

Barr, James. "Jewish Apocalyptic in Recent Scholarly Study." *BJRL* 58 (1975): 9–35.

Barth, Hermann, and Odil Hannes Steck. *Exegese des Alten Testaments: Leitfaden der Methodik.* Neukirchen-Vluyn: Neukirchener Verlag, 1971.

Begrich, Joachim. "Das priesterliche Heilsorakel." *ZAW* 52 (1934): 81–92.

Bercovitch, Sacvan. *The Puritan Origins of the American Self.* New Haven: Yale University Press, 1975.

Berger, Peter L. "Charisma and Religious Innovation: The Social Location of Israelite Prophecy." *American Sociological Review* 28 (1963): 940–50.

Bergler, Siegfried. *Joel als Schriftinterpret.* Beiträge zur Erforschung des Alten Testaments und des Antiken Judentums 16. Frankfurt am Main: Verlag Peter Lang, 1988.

Bewer, Julius A. *A Critical and Exegetical Commentary on Obadiah and Joel.* ICC. New York: Scribner's, 1911.

Blenkinsopp, Joseph. *Ezekiel.* Interpretation. Louisville: John Knox, 1990.

———. *A History of Prophecy in Israel.* Philadelphia: Westminster, 1983.

Block, Daniel I. "Gog and the Pouring Out of the Spirit." *VT* 37 (1987): 257–70.

Boardman, Eugene P. "Millenary Aspects of the Taiping Rebellion (1851–64)." In *Millennial Dreams in Action: Essays in Comparative Study,* ed. S. Thrupp, 70–79. The Hague: Mouton, 1962.

Bright, John. *A History of Israel.* 3d ed. Philadelphia: Westminster, 1981.

Brownlee, William H. "'Son of Man Set Your Face,' Ezekiel the Refugee Prophet." *HUCA* 54 (1983): 83–110.

Bruce, F. F. (Frederick Fyvie). "The Earliest Old Testament Interpretation." In *The Witness of Tradition. OTS* 17, pp. 37–52. Leiden: E. J. Brill, 1972.

Burden, J. J. "Esegiël, Priester en Profeet." *Theologia Evangelica* 18/1 (1985): 14–21.

Burridge, Kenelm. *New Heaven, New Earth: A Study of Millenarian Activities.* New York: Schocken, 1969.

———. "Reflections on Prophecy and Prophetic Groups." *Semeia* 21 (1981): 99–102.

Burrows, Millar. *The Literary Relations of Ezekiel.* Philadelphia: Jewish Publication Society, 1925.

Carley, Keith W. *The Book of the Prophet Ezekiel.* CBC. Cambridge, England: Cambridge University Press, 1974.

———. *Ezekiel among the Prophets.* SBT, 2d Series, 31. Naperville, Ill.: Allenson, 1974.

Carroll, Robert P. "Twilight of Prophecy or Dawn of Apocalyptic?" *JSOT* 14 (1979): 3–35.

———. *When Prophecy Failed.* New York: Seabury, 1979.

Chapman, G. Clark, Jr. "Falling in Rapture Before the Bomb." *The Reformed Journal* 37/6 (June 1987): 11–14.

Charles, R. H. (Robert Henry). *The Apocrypha and Pseudepigrapha of the Old Testament.* Oxford: Clarendon, 1913.

Charlesworth, James H., ed. *The Old Testament Pseudepigrapha.* Vol. 1, *Apocalyptic Literature and Testaments.* Garden City, N.Y.: Doubleday, 1983.

Chesneaux, Jean (contributor). "Current Anthropology Book Review: The Religions of the Oppressed: A Study of Modern Messianic Cults by Vittorio Lanternari." *Current Anthropology* 6 (1965): 447–65.

Childs, Brevard S. "The Enemy from the North and the Chaos Tradition." *JBL* 78 (1959): 187–98.

———. *Introduction to the Old Testament as Scripture.* Philadelphia: Fortress, 1979.

Clements, Ronald Ernest, ed. *The World of Ancient Israel: Sociological, Anthropological and Political Perspectives.* Cambridge, England: Cambridge University Press, 1989.

Clines, David J. *Ezra, Nehemiah, Esther.* NCBC. Grand Rapids, Mich.: Eerdmans, 1984.

Cody, Aelred. *Ezekiel with an Excursus on Old Testament Priesthood.* Wilmington, Del.: Glazier, 1984.

Coggins, Richard J. *Haggai, Zechariah, Malachi.* Old Testament Guides. Sheffield: JSOT Press, 1987.

Cohn, Norman. "Medieval Millenarism: Its Bearing on the Comparative

Study of Millenarian Movements." In *Millennial Dreams in Action: Essays in Comparative Study*, ed. S. Thrupp, 31–43. The Hague: Mouton, 1962.

———. *The Pursuit of the Millennium*. New York: Oxford University Press, 1970.

Collins, John J. *The Apocalyptic Imagination: An Introduction to the Jewish Matrix of Christianity*. New York: Crossroad, 1984.

———. *Daniel with an Introduction to Apocalyptic Literature*. FOTL 20. Grand Rapids, Mich.: Eerdmans, 1984.

———. "Introduction: Towards the Morphology of a Genre." *Apocalypse: The Morphology of a Genre. Semeia* 14 (1979): 1–20.

———. "The Jewish Apocalypses." *Semeia* 14 (1979): 21–59.

Collum, Danny. "Armageddon Theology as a Threat to Peace." *Faith and Mission* 4/1 (1986): 55–64.

Coogan, Michael. "Life in the Diaspora: Jews at Nippur in the Fifth Century B.C." *BA* 37/1 (1974): 6–12.

Cross, Frank Moore. *Canaanite Myth and Hebrew Epic*. Cambridge, Mass.: Harvard University Press, 1973.

Daniels, Ted. *Millennialism: An International Bibliography*. New York: Garland, 1992.

Davies, Philip R. "The Social World of Apocalyptic Writings." In *The World of Ancient Israel*, ed. R. E. Clements, 251–71. Cambridge, England: Cambridge University Press, 1989.

Day, Peggy L. *An Adversary in Heaven: śāṭān in the Hebrew Bible*. HSM 43. Atlanta: Scholars Press, 1988.

Deissler, Alfons. *Zwölf Propheten*. Würzburg: Echter Verlag, 1981.

Deist, Ferdinand E. "Parallels and Reinterpretation in the Book of Joel: A Theology of the Yom Yahweh?" In *Text and Context: Old Testament and Semitic Studies for F. C. Fensham*, ed. W. Claassen, 63–79. JSOTSup 48. Sheffield: JSOT Press, 1988.

———. "Prior to the Dawn of Apocalyptic." In *The Exilic Period: Aspects of Apocalypticism*, 13–38. OTWSA 25/26 (1982/1983).

Dentan, Robert C. "The Book of Zechariah, Chapters 9–14, Introduction and Exegesis." *IB* 6:1089–1114.

Duhm, Bernhard. "Anmerkungen zu den Zwölf Propheten: X. Buch Joel." *ZAW* 31 (1911): 184–88.

Dumbrell, W. J. "Kingship and Temple in the Post-Exilic Period." *The Reformed Theological Review* 37 (1978): 33–42.

———. "Some Observations on the Political Origins of Israel's Eschatology." *The Reformed Theological Review* 36 (1977): 33–41.

Dürr, Lorenz. *Die Stellung des Propheten Ezechiel in der Israelitisch-Jüdischen Apokalyptik*. Alttestamentliche Abhandlungen 9:1, ed. J. Nikel. Münster: Aschendorffschen Verlagsbuchhandlung, 1923.

Eliade, Mircea. "'Cargo Cults' and Cosmic Regeneration." In *Millennial Dreams in Action: Essays in Comparative Study*, ed. S. Thrupp, 139–43. The Hague: Mouton, 1962.

Eliot, John. "Letter from Rev. John Eliot, 1664." In *The New England Historical and Genealogical Register*, 9:131–33. Boston: Drake, 1855.

Elliger, Karl. *Das Buch der zwölf Kleinen Propheten*. ATD 25/2. Göttingen: Vandenhoeck & Ruprecht, 1959.

Erling, B. "Ezekiel 38–39 and the Origins of Jewish Apocalyptic." In *Ex Orbe Religionum Studia Geo Widengren*, 1:104–14. Leiden: E. J. Brill, 1972.

Ewald, Heinrich. *Die Propheten des alten Bundes*. Göttingen: Vandenhoeck & Ruprecht, 1841.

Faith, Karlene. "One Love — One Heart — One Destiny: A Report on the Ras Tafarian Movement in Jamaica." In *Cargo Cults and Millenarian Movements*, ed. G. Trompf, 295–341. Berlin: Mouton de Gruyter, 1990.

Festinger, Leon, Henry W. Riecken, and Stanley Schachter. *When Prophecy Fails: A Social and Psychological Study of a Modern Group That Predicted the Destruction of the World*. New York: Harper & Row, 1964 (1st ed.: 1956).

Fine, Lawrence. "Medieval Jewish Apocalyptic Literature." In *The Encyclopedia of Religion*, ed. M. Eliade, 1:342–44. New York: Macmillan, 1987.

Firth, Raymond W. *Elements of Social Organization*. New York: Philosophical Library, 1951.

Frost, Stanley B. "Apocalyptic and History." In *The Bible in Modern Scholarship*, ed. J. P. Hyatt, 98–113. Nashville: Abingdon, 1965.

Frye, Richard N. "Qumran and Iran: The State of Studies." In *Christianity, Judaism and Other Greco-Roman Cults*. Morton Smith *Festschrift*, ed. Jacob Neusner, 3:167–73. Leiden: E. J. Brill, 1975.

Garrett, Duane A. "The Structure of Joel." *JETS* 28 (1985): 289–97.

Gerstenberger, Erhard S. *Psalms, Part 1, with an Introduction to Cultic Poetry*. FOTL 14. Grand Rapids, Mich.: Eerdmans, 1988.

Gese, Hartmut. "Anfang und Ende der Apokalyptik, dargestellt am Sacharjabuch." *ZTK* 70 (1973): 20–49.

Gibson, John C. L. *Canaanite Myths and Legends*. Edinburgh: T. & T. Clark, 1978.

Glock, Charles Y. "The Role of Deprivation in the Origin and Evolution of Religious Groups." In *Religion and Social Conflict,* ed. R. Lee and M. W. Marty, 24–36. New York: Oxford University Press, 1964.

Glock, Charles Y., and Rodney Stark. *Religion and Society in Tension.* Chicago: Rand McNally, 1965.

Gottwald, Norman K. *The Hebrew Bible: A Socio-Literary Introduction.* Philadelphia: Fortress, 1985.

———. "Problems and Promises in the Comparative Analysis of Religious Phenomena." *Semeia* 21 (1981): 103–12.

Greenberg, Moshe. "The Design and Themes of Ezekiel's Program of Restoration." *Int* 38 (1984): 181–208.

Gressmann, Hugo. *Der Messias.* Göttingen: Vandenhoeck & Ruprecht, 1929.

———. *Der Ursprung der israelitisch-jüdischen Eschatologie.* Göttingen: Vandenhoeck & Ruprecht, 1905.

Guiart, Jean. "The Millenarian Aspect of Conversion to Christianity in the South Pacific." In *Millennial Dreams in Action: Essays in Comparative Study,* ed. S. Thrupp, 122–38. The Hague: Mouton, 1962.

Gunkel, Hermann. *Schöpfung und Chaos in Urzeit und Endzeit.* Göttingen: Vandenhoeck & Ruprecht, 1895.

Hallo, William. "Akkadian Apocalypses." *IEJ* 16 (1966): 231–42.

Halpern, Baruch. "The Ritual Background of Zechariah's Temple Song." *CBQ* 40 (1978): 167–90.

Hals, Ronald M. *Ezekiel.* FOTL 19. Grand Rapids, Mich.: Eerdmans, 1989.

Hamerton-Kelly, Robert G. "The Temple and the Origins of Jewish Apocalyptic." *VT* 20 (1970): 1–15.

Hammershaimb, Erling. "The Change in Prophecy during the Exile." In *Some Aspects of Old Testament Prophecy from Isaiah to Malachi,* 91–112. Copenhagen: Rosenkilde og Bagger, 1966.

Hanson, Paul D. "Apocalypse, Genre." In *IDBSup,* 27–28.

———. "Apocalypticism." In *IDBSup,* 28–34.

———. *The Dawn of Apocalyptic.* Philadelphia: Fortress, 1979.

———. "In Defiance of Death: Zechariah's Symbolic Universe." In *Love and Death in the Ancient Near East.* Marvin Pope *Festschrift,* ed. J. Marks and R. Good, 173–79. Guilford, Conn.: Four Quarters, 1987.

———. "Malachi." In *Harper's Bible Commentary,* ed. J. Mays, 753–56. San Francisco: Harper & Row, 1988.

———. *Old Testament Apocalyptic.* Nashville: Abingdon, 1987.

———. *The People Called: The Growth of Community in the Bible.* San Francisco: Harper & Row, 1986.

———. "Prolegomena to the Study of Jewish Apocalyptic." In *Magnalia Dei: The Mighty Acts of God*, ed. F. M. Cross, W. Lemke, and P. D. Miller, Jr., 389–413. Garden City, N.Y.: Doubleday, 1976.

———. *Visionaries and their Apocalypses*. Philadelphia: Fortress, 1983.

———. "Zechariah, Book of." In *IDBSup*, 982–83.

Harrelson, Walter. "The Celebration of the Feast of Booths According to Zech xiv 16-21." In *Religions in Antiquity*. Goodenough *Festschrift*, ed. J. Neusner, 88–96. Leiden: Brill, 1968.

Harrison, Roland Kenneth. *Introduction to the Old Testament*. Grand Rapids, Mich.: Eerdmans, 1969.

Hilgenfeld, Adolf. *Die jüdische Apokalyptik in ihrer geschichtlichen Entwicklung*. Jena: F. Mauke, 1857.

Hill, Michael. *A Sociology of Religion*. New York: Basic Books, 1973.

Hine, Virginia H. "The Deprivation and Disorganization Theories of Social Movements." In *Religious Movements in Contemporary America*, ed. I. Zaretsky and M. Leone, 646–61. Princeton, N.J.: Princeton University Press, 1974.

Hoffmann, Hans Werner. "Form — Funktion — Intention." *ZAW* 82 (1970): 341–46.

Hoffmann, Yair. "The Day of the Lord as a Concept and a Term in the Prophetic Literature." *ZAW* 93 (1981): 37–50.

Hölscher, Gustav. "Die Entstehung des Buches Daniel." *TSK* 92 (1919): 113–38.

———. *Die Profeten*. Leipzig: J. C. Hinrichs, 1914.

Hossfeld, Frank L. *Untersuchungen zu Komposition und Theologie des Ezechielbuches*. FB 20. Würzburg: Echter, 1977.

Howie, Carl G. "Gog and Magog." In *IDB*, 2:436–37.

Hurvitz, Avi. *A Linguistic Study of the Relationship Between the Priestly Source and the Book of Ezekiel*. Paris: Gabalda, 1982.

Irwin, William A. *The Problem of Ezekiel*. Chicago: University of Chicago Press, 1943.

Jeremias, Christian. *Die Nachtgesichte des Sacharja*. Göttingen: Vandenhoeck & Ruprecht, 1977.

Johnson, Aubrey R. *The Cultic Prophet in Ancient Israel*. Cardiff: University of Wales Press, 1944.

———. *The Cultic Prophet and Israel's Psalmody*. Cardiff: University of Wales Press, 1979.

Kähler, Martin. *The So-Called Historical Jesus and the Historic, Biblical Christ*. Trans. C. Braaten. Philadelphia: Fortress, 1988 (1st German ed., 1892).

Kaminsky, Howard. "The Free Spirit in the Hussite Revolution." In

Millennial Dreams in Action: Essays in Comparative Study, ed. S. Thrupp, 166–86. The Hague: Mouton, 1962.

Kapelrud, Arvid S. *Joel Studies.* Uppsala: Lundequistska Bokhandeln, 1948.

Käsemann, Ernst. "The Beginnings of Christian Theology." In *New Testament Questions of Today,* 82–107. Trans. W. J. Montague. Philadelphia: Fortress, 1969.

Kaufmann, Yehezkel. *The Religion of Israel.* Trans. M. Greenberg. Chicago: University of Chicago Press, 1960.

Klein, Ralph W. *Ezekiel: The Prophet and His Message.* Columbia: University of South Carolina Press, 1988.

———. *Israel in Exile.* OBT. Philadelphia: Fortress, 1979.

Koch, Klaus. *The Growth of the Biblical Tradition: The Form-Critical Method.* Trans. S. M. Cupitt. New York: Macmillan, 1969.

———. *The Rediscovery of Apocalyptic.* Naperville, Ill.: Allenson, 1972.

Kraus, Hans Joachim. *Worship in Israel.* Trans. G. Buswell. Oxford: Basil Blackwell, 1966.

Kuhrt, Amélie. "The Cyrus Cylinder and Achaemenid Imperial Policy." *JSOT* 25 (1983): 83–97.

Kutsch, Ernst. "Heuschreckenplage und Tag Jahwes in Joel 1 und 2." *TZ* 18 (1962): 89–94.

La Barre, Weston. *The Ghost Dance: Origins of Religion.* Garden City, N.Y.: Doubleday, 1970.

———. "Materials for a History of Studies of Crisis Cults: A Bibliographic Essay." *Current Anthropology* 12 (1971): 3–44.

Lamarche, Paul. *Zacharie IX–XIV: Structure littéraire et messianisme.* Paris: J. Gabalda, 1961.

Landau, Yehezkel. "The President and the Prophets." *Sojourners* 13/6 (June-July 1984): 24–25.

Lang, Bernhard, ed. *Anthropological Approaches to the Old Testament.* Philadelphia: Fortress, 1985.

Lanternari, Vittorio. "Nativistic and Socio-religious Movements: A Reconsideration." *Comparative Studies in Society and History* 16 (1974): 483–503.

———. *The Religions of the Oppressed.* Trans. L. Sergio. New York: Knopf, 1963.

Lasswell, Harold D. "Collective Autism as a Consequence of Culture Contact: Notes on Religious Training and the Peyote Cult at Taos." *Zeitschrift für Sozialforschung* 4 (1935): 232–47.

Lawrence, Peter. "The Fugitive Years: Cosmic Space and Time in Melanesian Cargoism and Mediaeval European Chiliasm." In *Millennialism and Charisma,* ed. R. Wallis, 285–315. Belfast, Northern Ireland: Queen's University, 1982.

Levenson, Jon D. *Theology of the Program of Restoration of Ezekiel 40–48.* Missoula, Mont.: Scholars Press, 1976.

Lewis, I. M. (Ioan Myrddin). *Ecstatic Religion.* New York: Routledge, 1971.

———. "Spirit Possession and Deprivation Cults." *Man* n.s. 1 (1966): 307–29.

Lindblom, Johannes. *Prophecy in Ancient Israel.* Philadelphia: Fortress, 1962.

Linton, Ralph. "Nativistic Movements." *American Anthropologist* 45 (1943): 230–40.

Lofland, John. *Doomsday Cult.* Englewood Cliffs, N.J.: Prentice-Hall, 1966.

Long, Burke O. "Perils General and Particular." *Semeia* 21 (1981): 125–28.

Long, Charles H. "Cargo Cults as Cultural Historical Phenomena." *JAAR* 42 (1974): 403–14.

Lücke, Friedrich. *Versuch einer vollständigen Einleitung in die Offenbarung Johannis und in die Gesammte apokalyptische Literatur.* Bonn: E. Weber, 1852.

Lust, Johan. "The Final Text and Textual Criticism. Ez 39,28." In *Ezekiel and His Book: Textual and Literary Criticism and Their Interrelation,* ed. J. Lust, 48–54. Leuven, Belgium: Leuven University Press, 1986.

———. "The Order of the Final Events in Revelation and in Ezekiel." In *L'Apocalypse johannique et l'Apocalyptique dans le Nouveau Testament,* 179–83. Leuven: Leuven University Press, 1980.

MacRae, George W., S. J. "The Meaning and Evolution of the Feast of Tabernacles." *CBQ* 22 (1960): 251–76.

Mannheim, Karl. *Ideology and Utopia: An Introduction to the Sociology of Knowledge.* Trans. L. Wirth and E. Shils. New York: Harcourt, Brace and Co., 1936 (1st German ed., 1929).

Mason, Rex. *The Books of Haggai, Zechariah and Malachi.* CBC. Cambridge, England: Cambridge University Press, 1977.

———. "The Relation of Zech 9–14 to Proto-Zechariah." *ZAW* 88 (1976): 227–39.

———. "Some Echoes of the Preaching in the Second Temple? Tradition Elements in Zechariah 1–8." *ZAW* 96 (1984): 221–35.

Mastin, Brian A. "A Note on Zechariah 6:13." *VT* 26 (1976): 113–15.

Mauch, Theodore M. "Zechariah." In *IDB,* 4:941–43.

Mayes, Andrew D. H. *The Old Testament in Sociological Perspective.* London: Marshall Pickering, 1989.

———. "Sociology and the Old Testament." In *The World of Ancient Israel: Sociological, Anthropological and Political Perspectives,* 39–63. Cambridge, England: Cambridge University Press, 1989.

McBride, S. Dean, Jr. "Biblical Literature in its Historical Context: The Old Testament." In *Harper's Bible Commentary,* ed. J. Mays, 14–26. San Francisco: Harper and Row, 1988.

McEvenue, Sean E. "The Political Structure in Judah from Cyrus to Nehemiah." *CBQ* 43 (1981): 353–64.

Meeks, Wayne A. *The First Urban Christians: The Social World of the Apostle Paul.* New Haven: Yale University Press, 1983.

Merx, Adalbert. *Die Prophetie des Joel und ihre Ausleger.* Halle a.S.: Verlag der Buchhandlung des Waisenhauses, 1879.

Meyer, Lester V. "An Allegory Concerning the Monarchy: Zech 11:4-17; 13:7-9." In *Scripture in History and Theology: Essays in Honor of J. Coert Rylaarsdam,* ed. A. Merrill and T. Overholt, 225–40. Pittsburgh: Pickwick, 1977.

Meyers, Carol, and Eric Meyers. *Haggai, Zechariah 1–8.* AB 25B. Garden City, N.Y.: Doubleday, 1987.

Meyers, Eric. "The Shelomith Seal and Aspects of the Judean Restoration: Some Additional Reconsiderations." ErIsr 17 (1985): 33–38.

Milgrom, Jacob. *Leviticus 1–16.* AB 3. Garden City, N.Y.: Doubleday, 1991.

Millar, William R. *Isaiah 24–27 and the Origin of Apocalyptic.* Missoula, Mont.: Scholars Press, 1976.

Miller, J. Maxwell, and John H. Hayes. *A History of Ancient Israel and Judah.* Philadelphia: Westminster, 1986.

Miller, Patrick D., Jr. *The Divine Warrior in Early Israel.* Cambridge, Mass.: Harvard University Press, 1973.

Mitchell, Hinckley. *Haggai, Zechariah, Malachi and Jonah.* ICC. New York: Scribner's, 1912.

Mooney, James. *The Ghost-Dance Religion and the Sioux Outbreak of 1890.* Lincoln: University of Nebraska Press, 1991.

Mowinckel, Sigmund. *He That Cometh.* Nashville: Abingdon, 1954.

———. *Psalmenstudien III: Kultprophetie und prophetische Psalmen.* Oslo: Jacob Dybwad, 1923.

———. *The Psalms in Israel's Worship.* Trans. D. R. Ap-Thomas. Nashville: Abingdon, 1967.

Müller, Hans P. "Mantische Weisheit und Apokalyptik." VTSup 22, 268–93. Congress Volume: Uppsala, 1971. Leiden: Brill, 1972.

Murphy-O'Connor, Jerome, O. P. "The Judean Desert." In *Early Judaism and its Modern Interpreters,* ed. R. Kraft and G. Nickelsburg, 119–56. Philadelphia: Fortress, and Atlanta: Scholars Press, 1986.

Nash, Kathleen S. "The Palestinian Agricultural Year and the Book of Joel." Ph.D. diss., Catholic University of America, Washington, D. C., 1989.

Nash, Philleo. "The Place of Religious Revivalism in the Formation of the Intercultural Community on Klamath Reservation." In *Social Anthropology of North American Tribes,* ed. F. Eggan, 377–442. Chicago: University of Chicago Press, 1937.

Neil, William. "Zechariah, Book of." In *IDB,* 4:943–47.

Nicholson, Ernest W. "Apocalyptic." In *Tradition and Interpretation,* ed. G. W. Anderson, 189–213. Oxford: Clarendon, 1979.

Nickelsburg, George W. E. *Jewish Literature Between the Bible and the Mishnah.* Philadelphia: Fortress, 1981.

———. "Social Aspects of Palestinian Jewish Apocalypticism." In *Apocalypticism in the Mediterranean World and the Near East,* ed. D. Hellholm, 641–54. Tübingen: J. C. B. Mohr, 1983.

Nobile, Marco. "Beziehung zwischen Ez 32, 17–32 und der Gog-Perikope (Ez 38–39) im Lichte der Endredaktion." In *Ezekiel and His Book: Textual and Literary Criticism and their Interrelation,* ed. J. Lust, 255–59. Leuven, Belgium: Leuven University Press, 1986.

North, Francis S. "Aaron's Rise in Prestige." *ZAW* 66 (1954): 191–99.

North, Robert. "Prophecy to Apocalyptic via Zechariah." VTSup 22, 47–71. Congress Volume: Uppsala, 1971. Leiden: Brill, 1972.

O'Brien, Julie. *Priest and Levite in Malachi.* SBLDS 121. Atlanta: Scholars Press, 1990.

Ogden, Graham S. "Joel 4 and Prophetic Responses to National Laments." *JSOT* 26 (1983): 97–106.

Ogden, Graham S., and Richard R. Deutsch. *A Promise of Hope — A Call to Obedience: A Commentary on the Books of Joel and Malachi.* International Theological Commentary. Grand Rapids, Mich.: Eerdmans, 1987.

Olson, Theodore. *Millennialism, Utopianism, and Progress.* Toronto: University of Toronto Press, 1982.

Orlinsky, Harry M. "Whither Biblical Research?" *JBL* 90 (1971): 1–14.

Overholt, Thomas W. *Channels of Prophecy: The Social Dynamics of Prophetic Activity.* Minneapolis: Fortress, 1989.

———. "Model, Meaning, and Necessity." *Semeia* 21 (1981): 129–32.

———. *Prophecy in Cross-Cultural Perspective: A Sourcebook for Biblical Researchers.* Atlanta: Scholars Press, 1986.

Pedersen, Joh[anne]s. *Israel: Its Life and Culture.* 4 vols. London: Oxford University Press, 1940.

Penniman, T. K. (Thomas Kenneth). *A Hundred Years of Anthropology.* London: Duckworth, 1935.

Petersen, David L. *Haggai and Zechariah 1–8.* OTL. London: SCM, 1984.

———. *The Roles of Israel's Prophets.* JSOTSup 17. Sheffield: JSOT Press, 1981.

———. "Zechariah." In *Harper's Bible Commentary,* ed. J. Mays, 747–52. San Francisco: Harper and Row, 1988.

———. "Zechariah's Visions: A Theological Perspective." *VT* 34 (1984): 195–206.

Petitjean, Albert. *Les Oracles du proto-Zacharie: un programme de restauration pour la communauté juive après l'exil.* Paris: J. Gabalda, 1969.

Phelan, John L. *The Millennial Kingdom of the Franciscans in the New World.* 2d ed. Berkeley and Los Angeles: University of California Press, 1970.

Pierce, Ronald W. "Literary Connectors and a Haggai/Zechariah/Malachi Corpus." *JETS* 27 (1984): 277–89.

———. "A Thematic Development of the Haggai/Zechariah/Malachi Corpus." *JETS* 27 (1984): 401–11.

Plöger, Otto. *Theocracy and Eschatology.* Trans. S. Rudman. Richmond, Va.: John Knox, 1968.

Plumstead, A. W. (Arthur William). *The Wall and the Garden.* Minneapolis: University of Minnesota Press, 1968.

Pope, Marvin. "Notes on the Rephaim Texts from Ugarit." In *Essays on the Ancient Near East in Memory of Jacob Joel Finkelstein.* Memoirs of the Connecticut Academy of Arts and Sciences 19, ed. M. Ellis, 163–82. Hamden, Conn.: Archon, 1977.

Portnoy, Stephen L., and David L. Petersen. "Biblical Texts and Statistical Analysis: Zechariah and Beyond." *JBL* 103 (1984): 11–21.

Prinsloo, Willem S. *The Theology of the Book of Joel.* New York: Walter de Gruyter, 1985.

Pritchard, James B., ed. *Ancient Near Eastern Texts Relating to the Old Testament.* 3d ed. Princeton, N.J.: Princeton University Press, 1969.

Rad, Gerhard von. *Old Testament Theology.* Trans. D. Stalker. New York: Harper and Row, 1965.

———. *Wisdom in Israel.* Trans. J. Martin. New York: Abingdon, 1973.

Radday, Yehuda T., and Moshe A. Pollatscheck. "Vocabulary Richness in Post-Exilic Prophetic Books." *ZAW* 92 (1980): 333–46.

Redditt, Paul L. "The Book of Joel and Peripheral Prophecy." *CBQ* 48 (1986): 225–40.

———. "Israel's Shepherds: Hope and Pessimism in Zechariah 9–14." *CBQ* 51 (1989): 631–42.

Ribeiro, René. "Brazilian Messianic Movements." In *Millennial Dreams in Action: Essays in Comparative Study,* ed. S. Thrupp, 55–69. The Hague: Mouton, 1962.

Robinson, Theodore H., and Friedrich Horst. *Die Zwölf Kleinen Propheten.* HAT 1/14. Tübingen: J. C. B. Mohr, 1938.

Rogerson, John William. *Anthropology and the Old Testament.* Sheffield: JSOT Press, 1984.

Rowland, Christopher. "The Visions of God in Apocalyptic Literature." *Journal for the Study of Judaism* 10 (1979): 137–54.

Rowley, H. H. (Harold Henry). *The Relevance of Apocalyptic*. London: Lutterworth, 1944.

———. "Ritual and the Hebrew Prophets." *JSS* 1 (1956): 338–60.

———. *Worship in Ancient Israel*. London: SPCK, 1967.

Rudolph, Wilhelm. *Haggai — Sacharja 1–8 — Sacharja 9–14 — Maleachi*. KAT 13/4. Gütersloh: Gütersloher Verlagshaus Gerd Mohn, 1976.

———. *Joel — Amos — Obadja — Jona*. KAT 13/2. Gütersloh: Gütersloher Verlagshaus Gerd Mohn, 1971.

Russell, D. S. (David Syme). *Apocalyptic: Ancient and Modern*. Philadelphia: Fortress, 1978.

———. *The Method and Message of Jewish Apocalyptic*. Philadelphia: Westminster, 1964.

Sæbø, Magne. "Vom Grossreich zum Weltreich: Erwägungen zu Pss. lxxii 8, lxxxix 26, Sach. ix 10b." *VT* 28 (1978): 83–91.

Sandeen, Ernest R. "Millennialism." In *The New Encyclopaedia Britannica*, 12:200–203. 15th ed. Macropaedia. Chicago: Benton, 1974.

Schiffman, Lawrence H. "The New Halakhic Letter (4QMMT) and the Origins of the Dead Sea Sect." *BA* 53 (1990): 64–73.

Schmithals, Walter. *The Apocalyptic Movement: Introduction and Interpretation*. Trans. John E. Steely. Nashville: Abingdon, 1975.

Scholem, Gershom. *Sabbatai Ṣevi: The Mystical Messiah 1626–1676*. Princeton, N.J.: Princeton University Press, 1973.

Schwartz, Gary. *Sect Ideologies and Social Status*. Chicago: University of Chicago Press, 1970.

Schwartz, Hillel. "The End of the Beginning: Millenarian Studies, 1969–1975." *RelSRev* 2/3 (1976): 1–14.

———. "Millenarianism, An Overview." *The Encyclopedia of Religion*, ed. Mircea Eliade, 9:521–32. New York: Macmillan, 1987.

Schweitzer, Albert. *The Quest of the Historical Jesus*. New York: Macmillan, 1957 (1st German ed., 1906).

Sellin, Ernst. *Studien zur Entstehungsgeschichte der jüdischen Gemeinde nach dem babylonischen Exil*. Leipzig: A. Deichert, 1901.

———. *Das Zwölfprophetenbuch*. KAT 12/1. Leipzig: A. Deichert, 1922.

Seybold, Klaus. *Bilder zum Tempelbau: Die Visionen des Propheten Sacharja*. SB 70. Stuttgart: Verlag Katholisches Bibelwerk, 1974.

Shaked, Shaul. "Qumran and Iran: Further Considerations." *Israel Oriental Studies* 2 (1972): 433–46.

Shaw, P. E. (Plato Ernest). *The Catholic Apostolic Church Sometimes Called Irvingite: A Historical Study*. Morningside Heights, N.Y.: King's Crown, 1946.

Shepperson, George. "The Comparative Study of Millenarian Movements." In *Millennial Dreams in Action: Essays in Comparative Study,* ed. S. Thrupp, 44–52. The Hague: Mouton, 1962.

———. (contributor). "Current Anthropology Book Review: The Religions of the Oppressed: A Study of Modern Messianic Cults by Vittorio Lanternari." *Current Anthropology* 6 (1965): 447–65.

———. "Nyasaland and the Millennium." In *Millennial Dreams in Action: Essays in Comparative Study,* ed. S. Thrupp, 144–59. The Hague: Mouton, 1962.

Sierksma, F. (contributor). "Current Anthropology Book Review: The Religions of the Oppressed: A Study of Modern Messianic Cults by Vittorio Lanternari." *Current Anthropology* 6 (1965): 447–65.

Simpson, George. "The Ras Tafari Movement in Jamaica in its Millennial Aspect." In *Millennial Dreams in Action: Essays in Comparative Study,* ed. S. Thrupp, 160–65. The Hague: Mouton, 1962.

Sinclair, Lawrence A. "Redaction of Zechariah 1–8." *BR* 20 (1975): 36–47.

Smend, Rudolf. "Anmerkungen zu Jes. 24–27." *ZAW* 4 (1884): 161–224.

Smith, Morton. *Palestinian Parties and Politics That Shaped the Old Testament.* London: SCM, 1971.

Soggin, J. Alberto. *Introduction to the Old Testament.* OTL. Trans. J. Bowden. Philadelphia: Westminster, 1976.

Spier, Leslie, Wayne Suttles, and Melville J. Herskovits. "Comment on Aberle's Thesis of Deprivation." *Southwestern Journal of Anthropology* 15 (1959): 84–88.

Stendebach, Franz Joseph. *Prophetie und Tempel: Die Bücher Haggai — Sacharja — Maleachi — Joel.* Stuttgart: Verlag Katholisches Bibelwerk, 1977.

Stone, Michael E. "Lists of Revealed Things in the Apocalyptic Literature." In *Magnalia Dei: The Mighty Acts of God,* ed. F. M. Cross, W. Lemke, and P. D. Miller, Jr., 414–52. Garden City, N.Y.: Doubleday, 1976.

Stuhlmueller, Carroll, C. P. *Rebuilding with Hope: A Commentary on the Books of Haggai and Zechariah.* International Theological Commentary. Grand Rapids, Mich.: Eerdmans, 1988.

Suttles, Wayne. *Coast Salish Essays.* Seattle: University of Washington Press, 1987.

———. "The Plateau Prophet Dance among the Coast Salish." *Southwestern Journal of Anthropology* 13 (1957): 352–96.

Talmon, Yonina. "Millenarism" [sic]. In *The International Encyclopedia of the Social Sciences,* 10:349–62. New York: Macmillan Company and Free Press, 1968.

Taylor, John B. *Ezekiel: An Introduction and Commentary.* Leicester, England: Tyndale, 1969.

Thomas, D. Winton. "The Book of Zechariah, Chapters 1–8, Introduction and Exegesis." In *IB,* 6:1053–1088.

Thrupp, Sylvia L. "Millennial Dreams in Action: A Report on the Conference Discussion." In *Millennial Dreams in Action: Essays in Comparative Study,* ed. S. Thrupp, 11–27. The Hague: Mouton, 1962.

Towner, W. Sibley. "Daniel." In *Harper's Bible Commentary,* ed. J. L. Mayes, 695–706. San Francisco: Harper & Row, 1988.

Troeltsch, Ernst. *The Social Teaching of the Christian Churches.* 2 vols. Trans. O. Wyon. New York: Harper Torchbooks, 1960 (1st German ed., 1911).

Trompf, Gary W., ed. *Cargo Cults and Millenarian Movements: Transoceanic Comparisons of New Religious Movements.* Berlin: Mouton de Gruyter, 1990.

Tucker, Gene M. *Form Criticism of the Old Testament.* Old Testament Guides to Biblical Scholarship. Philadelphia: Fortress, 1971.

van der Kroef, Justus. "Messianic Movements in the Celebes, Sumatra, and Borneo." In *Millennial Dreams in Action: Essays in Comparative Study,* ed. S. Thrupp, 80–121. The Hague: Mouton, 1962.

van der Woude, Adam S. "Serubbabel und die messianischen Erwartungen des Propheten Sacharja." *ZAW* 100 Suppl. (1988): 138–56.

———. "Zion as Primeval Stone in Zechariah 3 and 4." In *Text and Context: Old Testament and Semitic Studies for F. C. Fensham,* ed. W. Claassen, 237–48. Sheffield: JSOT Press, 1988.

Vaux, Roland de. *Ancient Israel.* New York: McGraw-Hill, 1961.

Vawter, Bruce, C.M. "Apocalyptic: Its Relation to Prophecy." *CBQ* 22 (1960): 33–46.

Vermes, Geza. *The Dead Sea Scrolls in English.* 2d ed. New York: Penguin, 1962.

Vielhauer, Philipp. "Apocalypses and Related Subjects, Introduction." In *New Testament Apocrypha,* ed. E. Hennecke and W. Schneemelcher, 2:579–607. London: Lutterworth, 1965.

Voget, Fred W. "The American Indian in Transition: Reformation and Accommodation." *American Anthropologist* 58 (1956): 249–63.

Wallace, Anthony F. C. "Revitalization Movements." *American Anthropologist* 58 (1956): 264–81.

Wallis, Roy, ed. *Millennialism and Charisma.* Belfast, Northern Ireland: Queen's University, 1982.

Wanke, Gunther. "Prophecy and Psalms in the Persian Period." In *The Cambridge History of Judaism,* ed. W. D. Davies and L. Finkelstein, 1:162–88. Cambridge, England: Cambridge University Press, 1984.

Waterman, Leroy. "The Camouflaged Purge of Three Messianic Conspirators." *JNES* 13 (1954): 73–78.

Watts, John D. W. *The Books of Joel, Obadiah, Jonah, Nahum, Habakkuk and Zephaniah.* CBC. Cambridge, England: Cambridge University Press, 1975.

Weber, Max. *The Sociology of Religion.* Trans. E. Fischoff. Boston: Beacon, 1963 (1st German ed., 1922).

Weinstein, Donald. "Millenarianism in a Civic Setting: The Savonarola Movement in Florence." In *Millennial Dreams in Action: Essays in Comparative Study,* ed. S. Thrupp, 187–203. The Hague: Mouton, 1962.

———. *Savonarola and Florence: Prophecy and Patriotism in the Renaissance.* New Jersey: Princeton University Press, 1970.

Weiss, Johannes. *Jesus' Proclamation of the Kingdom of God.* Philadelphia: Fortress, 1971 (1st German ed., 1892).

Wellhausen, Julius. *Die Kleinen Propheten übersetzt und erklärt.* 3d ed. Berlin: Georg Reimer, 1898.

———. *Prolegomena to the History of Ancient Israel.* Gloucester, Mass.: Peter Smith, 1973 (1st German ed., 1878).

———. "Zechariah, Book of." In *Encyclopaedia Biblica,* ed. T. Cheyne, 4:5390–95. New York: Macmillan, 1903.

Werblowsky, R. J. Zwi. "Messiah and Messianic Movements." In *The New Encyclopaedia Britannica,* 11:1017–22. 15th ed. Macropaedia. Chicago: Benton, 1974.

Westermann, Claus. *Praise and Lament in the Psalms.* Atlanta: John Knox, 1981.

Wevers, John W. *Ezekiel.* NCBC. Greenwood, S.C.: Attic Press, 1969.

Widengren, Geo. "The Persian Period." In *Israelite and Judaean History,* ed. John H. Hayes and J. Maxwell Miller, 489–538. Philadelphia: Westminster, 1977.

Wilder, Amos N. "The Rhetoric of Ancient and Modern Apocalyptic." *Int* 25 (1971): 436–53.

Williams, F. E. "The Vailala Madness in Retrospect." In *Essays Presented to C. G. Seligmann,* ed. E. E. Evans-Pritchard, et al., 369–79. London: K. Paul, Trench, Trubner, 1934.

Wilson, Bryan R. *Magic and the Millennium.* New York: Harper & Row, 1973.

Wilson, Robert R. "Ezekiel." In *Harper's Bible Commentary,* ed. J. Mays, 652–94. San Francisco: Harper and Row, 1988.

———. "From Prophecy to Apocalyptic: Reflections on the Shape of Israelite Religion." *Semeia* 21 (1981): 79–95.

———. "The Problems of Describing and Defining Apocalyptic Discourse." *Semeia* 21 (1981): 133–36.

———. *Prophecy and Society in Ancient Israel.* Philadelphia: Fortress, 1980.

————. *Sociological Approaches to the Old Testament.* Old Testament Guides to Biblical Scholarship, ed. G. Tucker. Philadelphia: Fortress, 1984.

Winston, David. "The Iranian Component in the Bible, Apocrypha, and Qumran: A Review of the Evidence." *HR* 5 (1966): 183–216.

Wittgenstein, Ludwig. *Philosophical Investigations.* 3d ed. Trans. G. Anscombe. New York: Macmillan, 1958.

Wolff, Hans Walter. *A Commentary on the Books of the Prophets Joel and Amos.* Hermeneia. Philadelphia: Fortress, 1977.

Worsley, Peter. *The Trumpet Shall Sound: A Study of "Cargo" Cults in Melanesia.* 2d ed. New York: Schocken, 1968.

Zimmerli, Walther. *Ezechiel.* Neukirchen-Vluyn: Neukirchener, 1969.

————. *Ezekiel 1.* Hermeneia. Trans. R. E. Clements. Philadelphia: Fortress, 1979.

————. *Ezekiel 2.* Hermeneia. Trans. J. D. Martin. Philadelphia: Fortress, 1983.

————. "The Message of the Prophet Ezekiel." *Int* 23 (1969): 131–57.

Index of Authors

Index of Biblical References (selected)